Law Office Technology and Administration
Custom Edition

Aspen Custom Publishing Series

Law Office Technology and Administration
Custom Edition

Curated by

Paralegal Studies and Legal Studies Programs
Ivy Tech Community College

Selected pages from

Contemporary Law Office Management 2E,
by Lori Tripoli

Law Office Technology
by George E. Guay, III

Wolters Kluwer Legal & Regulatory US serves customers worldwide with CCH, Aspen Publishers, and Kluwer Law International products. (www.WKLegaledu.com)

To contact Customer Service, e-mail customer.service@wolterskluwer.com, call 1-800-234-1660, fax 1-800-901-9075, or mail correspondence to:

Wolters Kluwer
Attn: Order Department
PO Box 990
Frederick, MD 21705

Printed in the United States of America.

1 2 3 4 5 6 7 8 9 0

978-1-4548-8055-4

CONTENTS

Acknowledgments   *xv*

CHAPTER 1

CLIENTS   1

| Lori Tripoli, *Contemporary Law Office Management*, 2E |

A. The Attorney-Client Relationship   2
B. Types of Clients   3
    1. Corporate   3
    2. Association   4
    3. Individual   4
    4. Government   5
C. Choosing Clients Well   5
        Florida Bar v. Barrett   7
D. Managing Client Relationships   10
E. Retaining Clients   11
        Ruby v. Abington Memorial Hospital   12
F. Client Satisfaction   19
G. Terminating Representation   19

CHAPTER 2

HUMAN RESOURCES   27

| Lori Tripoli, *Contemporary Law Office Management*, 2E |

A. Firm Mission Statement and History   27
B. Employment Law   29
    1. Types of Employment   29
        a. Employment at Will   29
        b. Contract Employees   29
    2. Federal Statutes   29
        a. Equal Employment Opportunity Act   29
            Hishon v. King & Spalding   30
        b. Fair Labor Standards Act   33
        c. Americans with Disabilities Act   33
            *Settlement Agreement Between The United States of America
            and Joseph David Camacho, Esquire, Albuquerque, New
            Mexico Under the Americans with Disabilities*   33
        d. Family and Medical Leave Act   36

		e.	Age Discrimination in Employment Act	37
		f.	Equal Pay Act	40
		g.	Consolidated Omnibus Budget Reconciliation Act of 1985	40
		h.	Patient Protection and Affordable Care Act (Obamacare)	41
	3.	State Law		41
C.	Recruiting and Hiring Process			42
	1.	Interviewing Candidates		42
	2.	Reference and Background Checks		43
D.	Workplace Policies and Procedures			44
E.	Employee Handbook			44
	1.	Elements of a Handbook		44
	2.	Orientation and Training		46
F.	Performance Evaluation			46
G.	Compensation and Benefits			47
H.	Employee Relations			47
I.	Supervisory Techniques			48
J.	Disciplinary Action			48
K.	Termination			48
	1.	Voluntary		48
	2.	Involuntary		49
L.	Employee Retention			49
M.	Diversity in Law Firms			50
	1.	Minorities		50
	2.	Women		51
N.	Workplace Morale			52
	1.	Law Firm Stresses		53
	2.	Balancing Work and Personal Time		53

CHAPTER 3

THE PHYSICAL LAW OFFICE   **59**

Lori Tripoli, *Contemporary Law Office Management*, 2E

A.	Facility Management		60
B.	Workplace Safety		61
C.	Disaster Preparedness		63
D.	Equipment and Supplies		64
E.	Telecommunication Systems		65
F.	Parking Spaces		66
G.	Office Design and Decor		67
	1.	Firm Image	68
	2.	Firm Politics: Varying Office Size Based on Rank Versus Same-Size Offices	68
	3.	Ergonomics	69
	4.	Efficiency	69
	5.	Professional Designers	69
H.	Office Space Planning When Making a Move		70
	1.	Location	70
	2.	Cost	71

		3.	Lease Options	71
		4.	Growth Projections	71
		5.	Accessibility	72
		6.	Public and Work Areas	72
			a. Reception	73
			b. Attorney Areas	73
			c. Staff Areas	73
			d. Conference Rooms	74
		7.	Security	74
		8.	Amenities	74
		9.	Image	75
		10.	Parking	75
		11.	Mechanical Systems	75

CHAPTER 4

MONEY MANAGEMENT   81

Lori Tripoli, *Contemporary Law Office Management*, 2E

A.	Financing a Law Practice	81
B.	Budgets	82
C.	Timekeeping	84
	1. Tracking Time	85
	2. Billable-Hour Requirements	86
	3. Timekeeping Systems	86
D.	Client Billing	86
	1. What Exactly Is a Client Charged For?	87
	2. Contents of a Bill	87
	3. Billing Systems	87
E.	Fee Agreements	89
	1. Hourly Rates	89
	2. Task-Based Billing	90
	3. Incentive Billing	90
	4. Contingent Fees	90
	Campbell v. Bozeman Investors of Duluth	90
	5. Flat Fees	95
	6. Prepaid Legal Services	95
	7. Retainers	95
	8. Court-Awarded Fees	96
	9. Statutory Fees	96
	10. Referral Fees	96
F.	Fee Collection	97
	1. Overseeing the Process	97
	2. Delinquent Bills	97
G.	Client Trust Funds	98
H.	Escrow Funds	98
I.	Accounting	98
J.	Safeguards	99

CHAPTER 5

FILE MANAGEMENT   105

Lori Tripoli, *Contemporary Law Office Management*, 2E

A.	Opening a New File	106
	Abubakar v. County of Solano	107
B.	Contents of Client Files	114
C.	File Management Systems	115
	1. Filing Conventions	115
	2. Storage and Tracking	117
	3. Paperless Files	118
	4. File Ownership	119
	5. Proper Disposal of Files	120
	Disciplinary Counsel v. Shaver	120

CHAPTER 6

DOCKET MANAGEMENT   127

Lori Tripoli, *Contemporary Law Office Management*, 2E

A.	Calendaring	127
	Daniels v. Sacks	128
B.	Docket Control	134
	1. Deadlines	134
	2. Reminders	137
	Pincay v. Andrews	141
C.	Case Management	144

CHAPTER 7

KNOWLEDGE AND RECORDS MANAGEMENT   151

Lori Tripoli, *Contemporary Law Office Management*, 2E

A.	What Is Records Management?	152
	1. Records Retention	153
	2. Indexing and Records Retrieval	155
	3. Record Destruction	156
	4. Lawyer and Staff Training	157
B.	Records Management Systems	158
C.	The Importance of Knowledge Management	159
D.	Ethical Issues	160
	1. Security	160
	2. When Lawyers Leave Law Firms	161
	Gibbs v. Breed, Abbott & Morgan	162
E.	Special-Interest Area: E-mail	167

CHAPTER 8

OFFICE PRODUCTIVITY SOFTWARE 175

George E. Guay, III, *Law Office Technology*

A.	Common Features of Software	175
	1. Bars and Ribbons and Pulldowns	175
	2. Suites	176
B.	Microsoft Office Suite	176
	1. Word 2007	176
	a. Office Button	176
	b. Tabs	178
	2. Excel	220
	a. Features	220
	b. Tabs	223
	3. PowerPoint	242
	a. Home Tab	243
	b. Insert Tab	249
	c. Design Tab	251
	d. Animations Tab	252
	e. Slide Show Tab	254
	f. Review Tab	256
	g. View Tab	256
C.	OpenOffice.Org	257
	1. Writer	258
	2. Base	263
	3. Calc	263
	4. Math	264
	5. Impress	264
	6. Draw	265
D.	Google Docs	265
	1. Software in the Cloud	265
	2. Features	266
	a. Access	266
	b. The First Screen	266
	c. Search	267
	d. Link	267
	e. Toolbar and Tabs	268
E.	Conclusion	268
F.	Terms	268
G.	Hypotheticals	269

CHAPTER 9

PRACTICE-SPECIFIC SOFTWARE	273

George E. Guay, III, *Law Office Technology*

A.	Bankruptcy	273
	1. In General	274
	a. Terms	274
	b. Type of Petition	274
	c. Software	274
	d. Electronic Filing	275
	2. Content	275
	a. Familiar Tabs	275
	b. Pages Tab	275
B.	Software for Managing a Corporation	286
	1. What is a Corporation?	286
	2. Software	287
	a. Type	287
	b. Features	287
	3. Essential Corporate Documents	293
C.	Divorce—Financials	297
	1. Introduction	297
	2. Software	297
	a. Type	297
	b. Features	297
	3. Critical Information	299
	a. Case Information	299
	b. Assets and Liabilities	300
	c. Tax Information	303
D.	Real Estate	307
	1. Real Estate Concepts	307
	a. Overview	307
	b. Property	307
	2. Software	308
	a. Easy HUD Real Estate Software	308
	b. Features	309
E.	Trusts	322
	1. Introduction	322
	2. Software	322
	3. Features	323
	a. Buttons	323
	b. Tabs	323
F.	Wills	328
	1. The Nature of a Will	328
	2. Software	329
	3. Estate Planning	329
	a. Gathering Data	330
	b. Children	330

	4.	Useful Documents	331
		a. Power of Attorney	332
		b. Durable Power of Attorney	332
		c. Medical Power of Attorney	334
		d. Living Will	335
G.	Conclusion		335
H.	Terms		336
I.	Hypotheticals		338

CHAPTER 10

PRACTICE MANAGEMENT AND CASE MANAGEMENT SOFTWARE 347

George E. Guay, III, *Law Office Technology*

A.	Critical Software Concepts		347
	1.	The Database	347
	2.	Practice Management Software Versus Case Management Software	348
B.	The Nature of Practice Management Software		348
	1.	Front Office and Back Office	348
		a. Front Office Functions	349
		b. Back Office Operations	356
	2.	Types of Practice Management Software	359
		a. AbacusLaw	359
		b. Amicus Attorney	361
		c. Needles	364
		d. Tabs3	366
		e. Lexis-Nexis Practice Management Software	370
		f. Clio	375
		g. ProLaw	376
C.	Case Management Software		377
	1.	Rules of Discovery	378
	2.	Types of Discovery	378
	3.	Exemptions from Discovery	378
	4.	Depositions	379
		a. Nature of the Process	379
		b. Software	379
		c. Examples of Software	381
	5.	Electronically Stored Information	382
		a. Avoiding a Manual Review of Requested Information	382
		b. Processing Data	382
		c. E-Mail	383
		d. Litigation Holds	383
		e. Metadata	383
	6.	Defensible Discovery Strategy	384
		a. Preparing a Defensible Discovery Strategy	384
		b. Inadvertent Disclosure and "Clawback"	384
		c. The Electronic Data Reference Model	384

7. Reviewing ESI   386
8. ESI Review Software   386
    a. ICONECT nXT   386
    b. Intella   386
    c. Lexis-Nexis ediscovery Solutions   388
    d. Masterfile   390
    e. Case Logistix   392
9. Examples of ESI Review Services   393
    a. Categorix   394
    b. Daegis ediscovery   394
D. Conclusion   396
E. Terms   396
F. Hypotheticals   397

CHAPTER 11

TELECOMMUNICATIONS AND DATA MANAGEMENT   399

George E. Guay, III, *Law Office Technology*

A. Telecommunications   399
    1. Networks   399
        a. Intranet   400
        b. Internet   403
        c. Security   405
        d. Voice Over Internet Protocol (VOIP)   406
        e. Videoconferencing   406
    2. E-Mail   407
        a. Risks   407
        b. Confidentiality   408
    3. Smartphones   409
        a. Operating Systems (OS)   409
        b. Applications (Apps)   409
        c. Common Features   410
        d. Battery Life   411
        e. Cellular Wireless Standards: 3G and 4G   411
        f. Firewalls   411
B. Data Management   411
    1. Passwords   411
    2. Retention   412
    3. VOIP and Voice Mail   412
    4. Disposal of Equipment   412
C. Conclusion   413
D. References   413
E. Terms   413

CHAPTER 12

TECHNOLOGY AND THE LAW FIRM OF THE FUTURE   417

Lori Tripoli, *Contemporary Law Office Management*, 2E

A. How Technology Has Changed the Practice of Law and Law
    Office Management   418
    1. Consolidation   419
    2. Outsourcing and Offshoring   419
    3. Virtual Law Practices   421
    4. Social Networking   421
    5. Unbundling Legal Services   424
B. Market and Generational Shifts   424
    1. Price and Performance   425
    2. Working with Millennials   426
C. Typical Technology Used by Law Firms   427
D. Safeguarding Information   429
        Lawyer Disciplinary Board v. Markins   429
    1. The Internet and the Cloud   434
    2. Intranets and Extranets   435
    3. Disaster Recovery Plan   435
E. The Future of the Legal Industry   436

Index   *443*

ACKNOWLEDGMENTS

Figures 4.27, 4.32, 4.43; ProLaw, Case Logistix, and LiveNote copyright © 2016 Thomson Reuters. All rights reserved. Reprinted by permission.

CHAPTER

1

Clients

CHAPTER OUTCOMES

By the end of this chapter, a student will be able to:

- Evaluate ethical quandaries arising in attorney-client relationships
- Formulate processes and approaches to manage the attorney-client relationship
- Identify client types
- Develop proposals for obtaining legal work appropriately
- Explain the significance of a firm's client base to its overall success in the marketplace

Law students and others in the legal field sometimes make judgments about clients and their suitability. Some say, "Oh, I would never represent a rapist" or "I could never work for the tobacco industry." Others maintain that someone accused of rape is the one who most needs a good lawyer so that he can be assured a fair trial. A lawyer who refuses to work for the tobacco industry might have a hard time determining where the tobacco industry ends. If a tobacco company has merged with a food company, can she represent the food company?

Some people like to put "good client" and "bad client" hats on an entire industry or set of clients without realizing that not all "good" clients are always good and not all "bad" clients are completely bad. As in every other area of the law, there tend to be shades of gray. Upstanding clients sometimes make inappropriate choices. Clients who have scuffled with the law in the past might have been subject to government overreaching or to police brutality. It all depends.

The attorney-client, or even law-firm-client relationship, is hardly a passive one. Lawyers and those supporting them must help gain and then retain clients. Providing good service and a satisfying outcome are only a part of the equation. How do you manage the negative outcome? How do you determine whether the client might need assistance from the firm in other areas? How can you make sure the client speaks positively about the firm to others?

Just as lawyers, paralegals, law office managers, and the entire legal team must be proactive in managing their relationships with clients, clients, too, are not necessarily passive in their approach to the lawyers who are helping them with the problem. Clients tend to want the maximum amount of value for the money they are paying. They want results, they want to be informed, and they don't want to feel like an inefficient operation is padding their legal bills.

Learning how to keep clients satisfied, and learning how to identify opportunities to gain more clients or more work—and then how to actually bring new clients and work aboard—are vital skills for those working in today's legal industry.

A.   THE ATTORNEY-CLIENT RELATIONSHIP

A lawyer or a law firm will not be in business very long without clients. Great attention must be paid to client relationships by everyone in a firm, from the managing partner down through the receptionist. It should go without saying that all clients ought to be treated with courtesy and respect. Some lawyers go to great lengths to foster good client relations. Firms might buy their clients season tickets to sports events, or they might sponsor "spa days" for female lawyers and female clients to bond.

Naturally, the attorney-client relationship ultimately depends on the quality of the work performed by the lawyer for the client. Lawyers are ethically bound to provide competent service to their clients. Consider *Model Rules of Professional Conduct* Rule 1.1, available on the **American Bar Association's** Web site. Lawyers also must act with diligence and promptness in representing clients. Consider **Model Rule 1.3.**

Beyond being a moral obligation, providing this level of client service simply makes good business sense. After all, a lawyer wants nothing more than to generate recommendations and referrals and future business from the client.

Lawyers must keep their clients informed! **Model Rule 1.4 requires prompt communication between lawyers and their clients.**

As straightforward as these ethical requirements seem to be, lawyers still sometimes have difficulty meeting their obligations. The following disciplinary actions were taken by the Attorney Grievance Commission in Maryland:

- An attorney was disbarred "for failing to communicate with his clients, failing to comply with his clients' requests for information, failing to provide the legal services, and failing to return any portion of the unearned fee."[1]
- Another lawyer was disbarred "for failing to act with reasonable diligence and competence, failing to communicate with his clients, failing to return the clients' files upon request, failing to expedite litigation, and misrepresenting to his clients the status of their cases."[2]
- One lawyer was suspended for 60 days "for failing to appear at trial and failing to adequately communicate with his client. Upon termination of representation, Respondent entered into a settlement and release of claims agreement with the client without advising the client to seek independent counsel."[3]

---

1. Attorney Grievance Commission of Maryland, *37th Ann. Rep., July 1, 2011 thru June 30, 2012,* at 2, *available at* http://www.courts.state.md.us/attygrievance/annualreport.html.
2. *Id.*
3. *Id.* at 4.

B.   TYPES OF CLIENTS

Some law practices are highly dependent on having individuals as clients. Family law practices, for instance, are geared toward the individual client (typically, a person seeking a divorce). Other law practices have a mix of clients, both individuals and businesses. In developing their business, lawyers need to think about their mix of clients. Do they prefer to work for just a few steady corporate clients? Or is their business dependent on many one-time clients seeking their help? Lawyers should also give some consideration to the effect the loss of a client might have on their practice. The loss of a single client to a divorce lawyer with thousands of them might not have much of an impact; the loss of a corporate client who provides one-third of the firm's income every year could, however, be devastating.

As law firms grow, the level of service they provide to big clients as opposed to small clients needs to be considered. Lawyers tend to like clients with **deep pockets**—those that can easily afford steep legal fees. Lawyers are also drawn to **bread-and-butter clients**—those whose legal work might not be the most exciting but who generate a steady stream of business for the firm.

In running a business, lawyers must decide how they want to service their clients. Are all clients treated equally? Should they be? If a Fortune 500 corporate client is throwing $10 million worth of legal fees to the firm every year, shouldn't it command better service than a one-time client who is paying the firm $10,000 to handle her divorce? It is said that each client likes to think that it is the only client of the firm. That, no doubt, is probably true. But the reality is that a firm typically depends on a number of clients to survive. Shouldn't clients be tiered? Should some receive platinum-quality service, some receive gold service, and others receive silver service? Should a client who is paying a lawyer $100 per hour expect the same quality of service as one paying $600 per hour?

While depending on clients to generate fees, lawyers must nevertheless resist the temptation to "churn" client cases. **Churning** is the inappropriate practice of running up hourly legal fees with excessive discovery requests and other matters to create additional legal work, thus generating more fees.

In addition to **external clients** (outside entities that hire the firm to perform legal work), associates, paralegals, and others in a firm have **internal clients**—partners and other workers in the firm who give them assignments so that they can meet their billable-hour requirements. A lawyer in a firm may typically assign work to any number of associates or paralegals. A good associate or paralegal will make sure that she or he is at the top of the list of a lawyer who is doling out plum assignments.

1.   Corporate

A corporation is an artificial being created by law—in essence, a fictional person with legal rights and responsibilities. Lawyers working for corporations must remember that the corporation is the client, not the people who represent the corporation, such as the chief executive officer, the general counsel, or other actors. Some in-house lawyers resent efforts by their outside law firms to drum up business by pressuring the corporation's executives to hire them. These

deep pockets: Abundant financial resources.

bread-and-butter client: A steady client that generates a consistent stream of business for a firm.

churning: The inappropriate practice of running up hourly legal fees with excessive discovery requests and other matters to create additional legal work, thus generating more fees.

external client: Outside entities that hire the firm to perform legal work.

internal client: Partners and others in a law firm who dole out assignments to lawyers, paralegals, and others in the law firm's staff.

lawyers prefer that all legal matters be managed through the corporation's legal department.[4]

The *Model Rules of Professional Conduct,* in recognition of the difficulties associated with representing an organization, address some of the problems that might arise in the course of representing a business. Consider Model Rule 1.13, available on the American Bar Association's Web site.

Corporations vary in the ways they handle their relationships with outside counsel. Some companies have quite large in-house legal staffs and farm out only more mundane legal work. Others maintain a fairly small in-house team and outsource the bulk of the legal work. Either way, outside law firms tend to be subject to a fair amount of oversight by the in-house client, who is likely to negotiate fees, scrutinize bills, and question overall strategy.[5]

In addition to overseeing work done by outside counsel more closely, some corporate clients control legal budgets by, for instance, making law firms submit competitive bids for new work or consolidating the number of outside law firms they use, a practice referred to as **convergence.**

convergence: A corporation's practice of consolidating the number of outside law firms it uses.

Many companies work with relatively few law firms—between two and ten.[6] Culling the number of outside firms used can be cost-effective for the corporation, as its outside lawyers become very familiar with the workings of the business and can be persuaded to offer discounts for a high volume of legal work and to hold seminars and other training for in-house counsel.

One way that law firms can strengthen their ties to their corporate clients is through **secondment,** the practice of lending associates to a corporate client so the associates can gain an improved understanding of that client's business. Typically, the law firm continues to pay the associates' salaries, although the client might pay for some expenses.[7]

secondment: The practice of lending associates to a corporate client so the associates gain an improved understanding of that client's business.

2. *Association*

Associations, like any other business, have legal needs that must be met. Contracts, employment, tax, real estate, insurance, litigation, and intellectual property are some areas in which associations might require legal advice. Some law firms have specific trade and professional associations practices dedicated to serving associations and nonprofit organizations.

3. *Individual*

Individuals can need a lawyer's help for any number of reasons. They need wills prepared, they might need a prenuptial agreement to be drafted, they may be

---

4. *See, e.g.,* Debra Cassens Weiss, *How Law Firms End Up on IBM GC's Do-Not-Hire-List,* A.B.A. J. (Apr. 4, 2013), *available at* http://www.abajournal.com/news/article/ibms_general_counsel_explains_how_law_firms_get_on_his_do-not-hire_list.

5. *See, e.g.,* Ashley Post, 61% of GCs Unsatisfied with Law Firm Rates, Inside Counsel (July 16, 2013), available at http://www.insidecounsel.com/2013/07/16/61-of-gcs-unsatisfied-with-law-firm-rates?goback=.gde_117520_member_258523640.

6. *See, e.g.,* Megan Leonhardt, *Companies Use More Law Firms to Lower Costs,* Law360 (Oct. 17, 2012), *available at* http://www.law360.com/articles/387326/companies-use-more-law-firms-to-lower-costs.

7. Leigh Jones, *Firms Lend Associates to Clients,* Nat'l L.J. (Dec. 4, 2007), *available at* http://www.law.com/jsp/ihc/PubArticleIHC.jsp?id=1196676275514.

involved in a personal injury lawsuit. **Private clients** are individuals with a high net worth. Some law firms have private-client departments that focus on the special needs of these extremely wealthy individuals. This type of practice tends to involve tax and commercial work and other measures taken to protect assets. As wealthy individuals diversify their holdings, their legal needs tend to cross jurisdictions. Private-client practices are becoming increasingly global in nature.

private client: An individual client who has a high net worth.

4. Government

In 2010, government employment accounted for 18 percent of all attorney jobs.[8] "At the Federal level, attorneys investigate cases for the U.S. Department of Justice and other agencies. Government lawyers also help develop programs, draft and interpret laws and legislation, establish enforcement procedures, and argue civil and criminal cases on behalf of the government."[9] State and local governments hire lawyers as well. Many work in the criminal justice system.

The government also sometimes hires outside lawyers to help on cases. For instance, famed litigator David Boies, who went on to represent Vice President Al Gore in the controversy over which presidential candidate won the year 2000 election (*Bush v. Gore*, 531 U.S. 98 (2000)), was special trial counsel for the U.S. Department of Justice in its antitrust litigation against Microsoft. Boies had successfully defended IBM in an earlier antitrust matter pursued by the federal government.[10] The federal government saw how well a lawyer in the private sector could do; the next time around, the government had him on its side—at a bargain rate of $33.33 per hour.[11]

C. CHOOSING CLIENTS WELL

A law firm is a business. Lawyers have services to sell, and lawyers need buyers, or clients. The question is, Does the client choose the lawyer, or does the lawyer choose the client?

Clients find out about prospective lawyers in any number of ways: by hearing word-of-mouth referrals, by doing research online or elsewhere, by seeing lawyers give speeches at industry conferences (referred to by many lawyers as "dog-and-pony shows"), and by inviting the lawyer to make a presentation to the client. Lawyers put on these presentations, referred to in the industry as "beauty pageants," for prospective corporate clients. A company might invite several law firms to make presentations on different days and then select the single firm it found most desirable.

---

8. Bureau of Labor Statistics, U.S. Department of Labor, *Occupational Outlook Handbook, 2012-13 Edition, Lawyers, available at* http://www.bls.gov/ooh/legal/lawyers.htm (last updated Aug. 4, 2013).

9. U.S. Department of Labor, Bureau of Labor Statistics, *Occupational Outlook Handbook, 2010—11 Edition: Lawyers, available at* http://www.bls.gov/oco/ocos053.htm (last updated Dec. 17, 2009).

10. Jared Sandberg, *Microsoft's Tormentor*, Newsweek (Mar. 1, 1999, n.p.), *available at* http://libsys.uah.edu:3206/ehost/detail?vid=14&hid=103&sid=7c4f83bc-2bf3-4d66-899c-d996aaedb652%40sessionmgr102.

11. *Id.*

A wise lawyer does not leave client selection to chance. A lawyer has to make a decision: Will just any client do? Can the client pay its bills? Is the client difficult? Is the client likely to generate more work for the lawyer or for the firm? If a lawyer had a choice between two clients, one who always paid his bills on time, had plenty of legal work to throw to the firm, and was pleasant to deal with, and another client whose account had to be in collection before he would pay a bill, who constantly harangued and lied to his lawyer, and who needed help on only a single matter, which client do you think the lawyer would rather accept?

Just as a client does not need to hire the first lawyer she interviews, a lawyer does not need to accept business from the first prospective client who walks through the firm's front door.

Client intelligence is the practice of gathering and analyzing information about clients or prospective clients:

> CI [competitive intelligence] can help a law firm figure out which other law firms have been representing a company that it is interested in targeting as a client. . . . If the company has worked with only one counsel for a number of years, the law firm may decide not to go after that company as a potential client. If the law firm discovers that the target corporation has worked with one law firm in the past but recently brought on another one, it might conclude that the company is looking for new counsel and that there is an opportunity that it should pursue. Another possibility is that the company "churns through law firms" and is therefore not a good prospective client at all.[12]

Today, law firms are aggressive in seeking business from good clients. Corporate clients aren't blindly loyal; they, like any other business or individual, are looking for a good deal. A law firm that is aware that a corporation might be shopping its legal work around will make an effort to win that business. Some large law firms even bring along project managers when pitching a prospective corporate client for more business.[13] Through **legal project management**, the work to be done can be clearly defined, the appropriate team selected, and the work to be done clearly planned and budgeted, undertaken, and supervised.

legal project management: The application of project management principles to legal matters to enhance value for clients while maintaining profitability for the law firm providing service to the client.

runner: Someone hired to solicit personal injury cases on

Of course, drumming up business must be done within the constraints of pertinent ethical rules. Soliciting clients inappropriately, such as by "chasing ambulances," is not acceptable. In 1978, the U.S. Supreme Court held that states or state bar associations "constitutionally may discipline a lawyer for soliciting clients in person, for pecuniary gain, under circumstances likely to pose dangers that the State has a right to prevent."[14] In short, lawyers are not permitted to "chase ambulances" or to hire **runners** to solicit clients.

---

12. Steven A. Meyerowitz, *Features: Eye on the Competition: What Are Rival Firms Doing? Are Clients Turning to Other Counsel? It's Not So Hard to Find Out—and It May Be Crucial to Your Professional Future to Do So,* 26 Pa. Law. 30, 30 (Jan./Feb. 2004).

13. For more information on legal project management, see, e.g., Alan Cohen, *The Eureka Moment—The Implementation of Legal Project Management,* LegalWeek.com (Sept. 14, 2012), *available at* http://www.legalweek.com/legal-week/feature/2204722/the-eureka-moment-the-implementation-of-legal-project-management; Association of Corporate Counsel, *ACC Value Challenge: Guide to Project Management* (2011), *available at* http://www.acc.com/valuechallenge.

14. *Ohralik v. Ohio State Bar Assn.,* 436 U.S. 447, 449 (1978).

FLORIDA BAR V. BARRETT
897 So.2d 1269 (Fla. 2005)

behalf of a
lawyer.

DISPOSITION: DAVID A. BARRETT IS HEREBY DISBARRED FROM THE PRACTICE OF LAW IN THE
STATE OF FLORIDA.

JUDGES: PARIENTE, C.J., AND WELLS, ANSTEAD, LEWIS, QUINCE, CANTERO, AND BELL,
J.J., CONCUR.
OPINION

Per curiam.

We have for review a referee's report regarding alleged ethical breaches by
attorney David A. Barrett. We have jurisdiction. *See* Fla. Const. art. V, § 15. We
approve the referee's findings of fact and recommendations as to guilt. For the
reasons explained below, we decline to approve the recommended sanction of a
one-year suspension and instead disbar Barrett.

I. FACTS

The Florida Bar filed a complaint against respondent David A. Barrett, alleging numerous counts of misconduct involving two unethical schemes to solicit
clients. After a multiple-day hearing, the referee issued a report making the following findings and recommendations.

Barrett was the senior partner and managing partner in the Tallahassee law
firm of Barrett, Hoffman, and Hall, P.A. In approximately January 1993, Barrett
hired Chad Everett Cooper, an ordained minister, as a "paralegal." Although
Cooper had previously worked for a law firm in Quincy, Florida, Cooper's primary duty at Barrett's law firm was to bring in new clients. As Cooper testified,
Barrett told him to "do whatever you need to do to bring in some business" and
"go out and . . . get some clients." Cooper was paid a salary averaging $20,000
and, in addition to his salary, yearly "bonuses" which generally exceeded his
yearly salary. In fact, Cooper testified that Barrett offered him $100,000 if he
brought in a large case.

To help Cooper bring in more personal injury clients to the law firm, Barrett
devised a plan so that Cooper could access the emergency areas of a hospital and
thus be able to solicit patients and their families. In order to gain such access,
Barrett paid for Cooper to attend a hospital chaplain's course offered by Tallahassee Memorial Hospital.

In approximately March of 1994, Molly Glass's son was critically injured when
he was struck by an automobile while on his bicycle. While her son was being
treated in the intensive care unit at Tallahassee Memorial Hospital, Cooper met
the Glass family. Cooper, who dressed in "clothing that resembled a pastor,"
identified himself to the family as a chaplain and offered to pray with them.
Thereafter, Cooper gave a family member of Molly Glass the business card of
attorney Eric Hoffman, one of the partners in Barrett's law firm, and suggested
that the family call the firm. Neither Barrett nor Cooper knew Molly Glass prior
to Cooper's solicitation at the hospital. After her son died, Molly Glass retained
Barrett's law firm in a wrongful death action. A settlement was negotiated, and
she was pleased with the result until May of 1999, when she read a newspaper
article about improper solicitation of clients and realized that Cooper's actions

in the hospital constituted inappropriate solicitation. The referee specifically found that Cooper was Barrett's agent at the time that Cooper solicited Molly Glass and that Barrett ordered the conduct and ratified it by paying Cooper a salary and bonuses.

In April 1994, Cooper referred his friend, Terry Charleston, to Barrett's law firm. Charleston was an automobile accident victim whose injuries left him a quadriplegic. After the case was settled for over $3 million, Cooper was paid a bonus that year of $47,500.[1] Barrett attempted to justify the extremely large bonus, contending that the bonus was based on personal services, pastoral services, and companionship that Cooper provided to Charleston. The referee rejected this explanation, finding that Barrett lied about the reason for the bonus. Instead, the referee found that Barrett gave Cooper the bonus for bringing in the case, and thus Barrett engaged in an illegal fee-splitting plan.

On September 19, 1997, Barrett, who had the ultimate authority for hiring and firing in his law firm, fired Cooper. . . . However, even after Cooper was fired, his relationship with Barrett did not end.

While Cooper obtained accident reports and solicited patients for a chiropractor, he also continued to solicit clients for Barrett. After the patients were seen by the chiropractor, the accident reports were forwarded to Barrett's law partner, Hoffman. Cooper was paid $200 for each client who was brought into the law firm. The referee specifically found that Barrett knew about this scheme and that he ratified the conduct of Hoffman and Cooper. Barrett micromanaged the office, especially the finances, and personally signed the checks to Cooper in the amount of $200 per client for soliciting eight clients. Moreover, Barrett inquired as to whether there was insurance coverage before authorizing the firm's checks written to Cooper for soliciting clients. In addition to Molly Glass, the referee found that Barrett improperly solicited twenty-one other clients in violation of the *Rules of Professional Conduct.*

Finally, in May 1996, Barrett sent Cooper to Miami and Chicago in order to solicit clients as a result of the Value Jet airplane crash in the Everglades. Although Barrett denied any knowledge about this, his own business records show that $974.24 was paid for Cooper's travel expenses. The referee found that Barrett's testimony regarding this matter was not credible. While neither solicitation resulted in clients for Barrett's firm, the referee concluded these were inappropriate solicitation attempts directed by Barrett.

Based on the above factual findings, the referee found that Barrett was guilty of violating the following sections of the *Rules Regulating the Florida Bar:* 4-5.1(c)(1) (responsibilities of a partner); 4-5.3(b)(3)(A) (responsibilities regarding nonlawyer assistants); 4-5.4(a)(4) (sharing fees with nonlawyers); 4-7.4(a) (solicitation); 4-8.4(a) (violating or attempting to violate the rules of professional conduct); 4-8.4(c) (engaging in conduct involving deceit); and 4-8.4(d) (engaging in conduct in connection with the practice of law that is prejudicial to the administration of justice). In turning to the recommended discipline, the referee found the following aggravating circumstances applied in this case: (1) Barrett had a dishonest or selfish motive; (2) he exhibited a pattern of misconduct; (3) he was guilty of multiple offenses; (4) he submitted false statements during the disciplinary process by lying to the referee; (5) the victim was in a vulnerable

---

1. Since Cooper knew Charleston before referring him to the law firm, the only issue raised to the referee was whether Barrett had engaged in an improper fee-splitting plan with a nonlawyer.

condition; and (6) Barrett had substantial experience in the practice of law. As to mitigation, the referee found that four mitigating circumstances applied here: (1) Barrett did not have a prior disciplinary record; (2) he made full and free disclosure to the disciplinary board or had a cooperative attitude toward the proceedings; (3) character witnesses testified to Barrett's good character and reputation; and (4) Barrett exhibited remorse as to the effect of his conduct upon his family, friends, and clients. After considering the foregoing aggravating and mitigating factors, the referee recommended that Barrett be suspended from the practice of law for one year and be ordered to pay the Bar's costs.

The Florida Bar appeals to this Court, contending that we should increase the discipline to disbarment. Respondent cross-appeals and challenges whether (1) the referee made independent findings of fact; (2) the referee improperly denied several preliminary motions; (3) there is sufficient proof to support the referee's findings of fact; and (4) the sentence is excessive in light of our previous Bar discipline decisions.

II. ANALYSIS

DISCIPLINE

Both parties appeal the recommended discipline of a one-year suspension. Barrett argues that a twenty-day suspension is appropriate based on previous solicitation cases. The Bar argues that the appropriate discipline for such egregious ethical misconduct is disbarment. We agree with the Bar.

Barrett used deception to gain access to hospital patients by paying for Cooper to complete a hospital chaplain's course and sending him under the guise of providing spiritual comfort to people in their most needy time, when at the time Cooper was an attorney's employee being paid to obtain clients. Barrett then changed his scheme when "it was getting pretty hot," instead relying on Cooper to obtain clients while he worked for a chiropractor. His schemes resulted in twenty-two improperly solicited clients. Additionally, Barrett also engaged in an illegal fee-splitting plan with Cooper. Moreover, this is not a situation where Barrett failed to realize his actions were wrong; he engaged in the conduct intentionally and then fired Cooper when he became concerned about the possibility of being caught. As this Court has held, when an attorney "affirmatively engages in conduct he or she knows to be improper, more severe discipline is warranted." *Florida Bar v. Wolfe*, 759 So.2d 639, 645 (Fla. 2000). Finally, the instant case had substantial aggravating circumstances, including that (1) Barrett engaged in this type of improper solicitations based on a selfish motive to obtain clients; (2) the improper solicitations were a part of organized schemes that lasted for years; (3) multiple offenses occurred, including two different schemes which led to at least twenty-two improper solicitations; (4) Barrett lied to the referee during the proceedings; (5) one of the victims was especially vulnerable and in fact retained Barrett's law firm only because she was angry that somebody else had tried to take advantage of her during a time in which she was clearly preoccupied with her son's critical injuries; and (6) Barrett had substantial experience in the practice of law. While the referee did find that mitigating circumstances applied, these pale by comparison to the aggravating circumstances in this case. Any discipline less than disbarment is far too lenient based on the amount and type of misconduct which occurred here and would not fulfill the three purposes of lawyer discipline.

In sum, members of The Florida Bar are ethically prohibited from the solicitation of clients in the manner engaged in by Barrett. The Court expects that its rules will be respected and followed. This type of violation brings dishonor and disgrace not only upon the attorney who has broken the rules but upon the entire legal profession, a burden that all attorneys must bear since it affects all of our reputations. Moreover, such violations harm people who are already in a vulnerable condition, which is one of the very reasons these types of solicitations are barred. Therefore, this Court will strictly enforce the rules that prohibit these improper solicitations and impose severe sanctions on those who commit violations of them.

III. Conclusion

We approve the referee's findings of fact and recommendations as to guilt, but we decline to approve the recommended discipline of a one-year suspension and instead disbar respondent. Accordingly, David A. Barrett is hereby disbarred from the practice of law in the State of Florida. The disbarment will be effective thirty days from the date this opinion is filed so that Barrett can close out his practice and protect the interests of existing clients. If Barrett notifies this Court in writing that he is no longer practicing and does not need the thirty days to protect existing clients, this Court will enter an order making the disbarment effective immediately. Barrett shall accept no new business after this opinion is filed.

It is so ordered.

The *Model Rules of Professional Conduct* limit the circumstances under which a lawyer may solicit prospective clients. Consider Model Rule 7.3.

D. MANAGING CLIENT RELATIONSHIPS

client team: A group of lawyers, paralegals, and others within a firm who work together for a given client.

Law is a service industry. Law firms emphasize client service and business development far more than they once did. Law firms might even form **client teams,** groups of lawyers, paralegals, and others within a firm who work for a given client. A group meets regularly to assess a client's needs.

cross-selling: Marketing other practice groups within a firm to a client.

Lawyers within a firm often seek **cross-selling** opportunities so that the client may retain the firm for other legal needs the firm might be able to service. For instance, a practice group doing environmental work for a corporate client might also try to market the firm's real estate practice to the client.

intranet: A computer network that allows users within the firm to access information and to communicate with one another internally.

Client relationship management software can track client contacts and document a lawyer's contact with prospective clients. Such software can also track lawyer expertise, so if a client is looking for someone who happens to understand the pesticide registration process at the U.S. Environmental Protection Agency, a lawyer can do a search on the firm's **intranet** and find out who that lawyer is. Client relationship management software can also specify whether the firm represents a given company, and, if so, who the external contact is, who the internal contact is, and what types of legal matters are handled.

Some examples of client relationship management software are:

- ContactEase from Cole Valley Software (http://www.colevalley.com)
- InterAction by LexisNexis (http://www.interaction.com)

- Office Accelerator from Baseline Data Systems (http://www.baselineconnect.com)
- ProLaw by Thomson Reuters (http://www.elite.com)

Such software can only document the real-world relationship that is occurring. Having good relationships with clients involves doing good work for them, being responsive to them, and anticipating their needs and responding appropriately to those needs. Personality, of course, is involved, too: a lawyer needs to get along well with clients. As the practice of law becomes more global, lawyers also need to understand cultural differences—and even alert their clients to them:

> These practices extend well beyond table manners. They extend deep into the workplace and can affect everything from where individuals are or should be seated, to how business will function after a deal is concluded. "There are tremendous cultural differences in the way people negotiate that are critical," . . . " Frenchmen and Englishmen will want to sit at different distances from other parties at a negotiating table" . . . . [15]

E.   RETAINING CLIENTS

Clients will be wooed by others, so lawyers, as well as secretaries, paralegals, and other staff, must pay attention to client retention and to client service:

> Getting and keeping clients within the exceedingly competitive legal industry mandates a self-motivated and highly dedicated effort. Clients want to be solicited, courted, accommodated, and satisfied. To be successful, lawyers must go to the client, not wait for the client to come to them. Creating a sense of urgency and a passion for finding clients will result in new clients; waiting for the telephone to ring will not.[16]

Client retention also is an issue when a lawyer moves to another firm or when two firms merge. Optimally, a firm wants to keep all of its clients when it merges with another firm. Model Rule 1.6, which addresses the confidentiality of a client's information, now allows a lawyer to reveal certain information if a law firm merger or change of employment is contemplated so long as attorney-client privilege would not be compromised and the client would not be harmed. Clients should be informed as soon as possible of a firm's merger.

---

15. Lori Tripoli, *Disney-Style Debacles Prove Need for Client Sensitivity Training*, Of Counsel, Jan. 5, 1998, at 7, 8.

16. Julie A. Eichorn, *Feature: Looking Behind the Glass: 10 Critical Strategies to Developing New Client Business*, 69 Tex. B.J. 1064, 1065 (2006).

RUBY V. ABINGTON MEMORIAL HOSPITAL

50 A.3d 128 (Pa. Super. Ct. 2012)

BEFORE: GANTMAN, SHOGAN AND LAZARUS, JJ.

OPINION BY SHOGAN, J.:

Appellant, Young, Ricchiuti, Caldwell & Heller, LLC ("YRCH"), appeals from the trial court's May 26, 2011 order denying YRCH's Petition for Determination of Attorneys' Fees and ordering that an earlier attorneys' fee award be apportioned such that Appellee, The Beasley Firm, LLC ("Beasley"), receives 75% of the fees and YRCH receives the remaining 25%. We affirm.

The trial court set forth the factual and procedural history of this matter as follows:

> Mr. Keith Erbstein, Esquire worked at the Beasley Firm, LLC., a Philadelphia-based personal injury law firm, for approximately 35 years. During the course of his employment with the Beasley Firm (hereinafter: Beasley or the Beasley Firm), Mr. Erbstein signed two separate employment contracts. The Undersigned ultimately found the two aforementioned contracts controlled the determination of the Petition for Determination of Attorneys' Fees.
>
> This Court is convinced that Mr. Erbstein was a highly intelligent, skilled and knowledgeable attorney at the time that he signed the employment contracts material hereto. The record reveals that in 1996 Mr. Erbstein signed an "Employment Agreement" with Beasley, wherein Mr. Erbstein specifically agreed to immediately reimburse the Beasley Firm any outstanding case costs and pay 75% of any fees recovered thereon should he leave the firm for any reason. (*See,* 1996 Employment Agreement, ¶ 8.) Thereafter, in 2004, Mr. Erbstein signed the "Operating Agreement," a second employment contract, with Beasley, wherein Mr. Erbstein once again confirmed his willingness to comport with the Firm's employment terms.
>
> To elucidate matters for the Appellate Court, the record confirms that Mr. Erbstein committed himself to the terms of the 2004 Operating Agreement in August 2004.[1] The Undersigned found that Mr. Erbstein agreed to the following material terms. First, "Withdrawal Require[d] by Firm" in § 9.2 of the 2004 Operating Agreement holds:
>
> > Subject to the provisions of Section 9.4 ['Obligations to Withdrawn Member'] below, **the Management Committee may at any time require a Member to withdraw from the Firm at any specified date by giving not less than three (3) months' prior written notice to such Member** [. . .]
>
> Second, the record reflects that Mr. Erbstein also agreed to § 9.5 governing the future handling of 'Client Files' and holds:
>
> > (i) **As to all client files which a withdrawing Member may take, pursuant to the written direction to the Firm by the respective Client,** the withdrawing Member shall, prior to withdrawal from the Firm, bill each such file; accurately account for time dedicated to a client file; provide an accounting to the Firm for all files, fees owed thereon and unreimbursed expenditures due and owing, up through the date of withdrawal; and all such fees and

---

1. The exact date on the copy of the contract provided to the court is not clear. Arguably it could be interpreted as either August 21, 2004 or August 31, 2004; therefore, the Undersigned was not more specific for fear of being incorrect as to the precise date.

unreimbursed expenditures shall be payable to and **remain the sole property** of the Firm. (emphasis added).

    [. . .]

(iii) Other provisions of this Agreement notwithstanding, **with reference to all 'contingency fee' cases succeeded to by the withdrawing Member pursuant to the terms of this Agreement, unless otherwise established by the Managing Member, the withdrawing Member shall account to the Firm for all fee arrangements on all such files in accordance with the provisions of Exhibit 'C'** [which is 'Form-Employment Agreement' confirming the aforementioned split fee agreement] hereto[2] (emphasis added).

Thereafter, in October 2004, Mr. Erbstein brought the above-captioned negligence case into the Beasley Firm. The Plaintiffs in the Ruby matter signed a contingency fee agreement with the Beasley Firm and Mr. Erbstein. The record indicates that the action was instituted shortly thereafter. The case continued through the normal uneventful litigation course while Mr. Erbstein was at Beasley.

Unfortunately, for reasons not disclosed to this Court, on November 17, 2005, Mr. Erbstein was notified in writing that he was going to be released from the Beasley Firm on February 17, 2006, three (3) months notice, in accordance with § 9.2 of the 2004 Operating Agreement. Thereafter, Mr. Erbstein obtained employment with the law firm of Young, Ricchiuti, Caldwell & Heller, LLC (hereinafter: YRCH). Mr. Erbstein worked his last day at Beasley on January 26, 2006.

On January 28, 2006, Mr. Erbstein notified the Rubys about his change in employment. In line with the terms of the employment agreements, Mr. Erbstein gave the Rubys the choice to continue their relationship with Beasley or to follow him to his new practice. The Rubys opted to have their case litigated by Mr. Erbstein as opposed to the Beasley Firm. As such, at the direction of Mr. Erbstein, the Rubys severed their relationship with the Beasley Firm and signed an almost identical contingency fee agreement with YRCH. Importantly, the record reveals that Mr. Erbstein maintained control of the file until sometime in the summer of 2008, when he contracted a severe illness. (*See,* YRCH Memorandum of Law in Support of Petition for Attorneys' Fees filed 3.11.11). Thereafter, other members of the YRCH Firm handled the case and brought it to its ultimate resolution in January 2011. (*See,* YRCH Memorandum of Law in Support of Petition for Attorneys' Fees filed 3.11.11). Subsequent to the settlement, a dispute arose regarding the distribution of the $643,333.32 in attorneys' fees between YRCH and Beasley. The matter was transferred from Montgomery County Orphans Court to the Undersigned for resolution. The Undersigned entertained several memorandums of law and oral argument on the dispute. Thereafter, this Court entered its May 20, 2011 Order determining that the Appellant, the law firm YRCH is only entitled to 25% of the attorneys' fees and the Appellee, the Beasley Firm, shall receive 75% of the fee, pursuant to the contract(s) which Mr. Erbstein signed while working at the Beasley Firm.

Trial Court Opinion, 10/13/11, at 1-4 (emphasis in original).

YRCH presents the following issues for this Court's consideration:

---

2. Section 6 of the Employment Agreement (Exhibit "C") states **"[i]n the event that you leave this office for any reason and a client or clients choose(s) to continue with your representation, you will receive 25% of the net fee on any case you take with you regardless of its age, or the time spent on the file before or after you leave the office. You will immediately reimburse the office for all costs then expended on the file before the file(s) leave(s) this office."** (emphasis added)

1. Can a law firm enforce an agreement with its members against another law firm not party to that agreement?
2. Can a law firm that discharges one of its members successfully assert a claim for work performed on his contingency fee cases so far in excess of *quantum meruit* that both his ability to practice law and his clients' rights to choose counsel are compromised?

YRCH's Brief at 2.

The trial court's determination in this case is based on its interpretation of the 1996 Employment Agreement and 2004 Operating Agreement. . . . .

In support of its first issue on appeal, YRCH argues that because it was not a party to the contracts establishing Beasley's claim, specifically the Operating Agreement and the Employment Agreement providing for Beasley's 75% share of fees recovered on Erbstein's cases, it is not legally bound by that contract. YRCH's Brief at 9-10. In support of the proposition that "a contract cannot legally bind persons not party thereto," YRCH relies on this Court's opinion in *In the Matter of the Estate of Barilla*, 369 Pa.Super. 213, 535 A.2d 125 (1987).

In *In the Matter of the Estate of Barilla*, this Court was asked to determine whether third parties to an antenuptial agreement could breach the terms of the agreement by acts which prevented the appellant's performance. *In the Matter of the Estate of Barilla*, 535 A.2d at 128-129. Such is not the case before us presently. Indeed, YRCH would have us ignore the reality of the circumstances giving rise to Beasley's claim. YRCH claims that Beasley is not entitled to the attorneys' fees contemplated in its agreement with Erbstein on the belief that YRCH may not be bound to a contract to which it is not a party. While this presents an interesting issue, it does not accurately characterize the relative importance of the employment contract or the parties' relationship to the same. The question is not whether YRCH is **bound** by the employment agreement, but whether, and to what degree, may YRCH take a share of the attorneys' fees subject to the employment agreement.

We observe, and discuss more fully below, that the trial court properly employed rules concerning contract interpretation to conclude that Beasley was entitled to its contractual share of the attorneys' fees. However, in order to reach the next analytical step to conclude that YRCH take its share of those fees subject to the terms of the employment contract, we must refer to concepts and ramifications contemplated in the Uniform Partnership Act. 15 Pa.C.S.A. §§8301-8365. Moreover, while the courts of this Commonwealth have had no occasion to address the precise issue presently before us, we do find significant similarity, in fact and legal analysis, in cases emanating from California's appellate courts. We agree with the sound reasoning of the California Court of Appeals and adopt the same, insofar as it applied identical statutory provisions of the Uniform Partnership Act to facts similar or identical to our own.

The California Court of Appeals in *Rosenfeld, Meyer & Susman v. Cohen*, 146 Cal.App.3d 200, 194 Cal.Rptr. 180 (1983), *overruled on other ground, Applied Equipment Corp. v. Litton Saudi Arabia Ltd.*, 7 Cal.4th 503, 28 Cal.Rptr.2d 475, 869 P.2d 454 (1994), was asked to determine whether departing partners breached their fiduciary duty to their former law firm when they continued representation of the firm's client following departure. *Cohen*, 146 Cal.App.3d at 216, 194 Cal.Rptr. 180. Importantly, the Court was also asked whether the firm was entitled to a share of the fees from the "unfinished business" performed by departing partners. *Id.* As in the case before us, the departing partners left the firm and contacted the firm's client, which in turn discharged the firm and retained the departing partners to continue representation of the client until the subsequent resolution of the lawsuit. The Court began its analysis by noting the following:

> The concept of unfinished business arises from the rule of law that upon the dissolution of a partnership, the partnership is not terminated but continues to exist for the limited purpose of winding up its affairs and completing all unfinished business.[4] Thus, on May 1, 1974, the day following the dissolution of RM & S, there existed three entities: C & R (comprised of [departing partners]), a new RM & S (comprised of the partners of [the former partnership] remaining on Apr. 30, 1974), and the dissolved RM & S which had not yet been wound up. Until the dissolved partnership was wound up, the partners of the dissolved RM & S continued to owe fiduciary duties to each other, especially with respect to unfinished business.

Id. (emphasis added). The Court then moved on to opine as to the consequences attending the client's discharge of the old firm and retention of the departing partners:

> Given the facts of this case, though [the client] had a right to terminate the contract with RM & S and hire C & R, C & R could not avoid what was tantamount to a conflict of interest—i.e., the fiduciary duty it owed to RM & S.
>
> > [The client's] purported discharge of RM & S is irrelevant to the issue of C & R's breach of their fiduciary duty to the remaining partners of RM & S. [ ]A partner's fiduciary duty to complete unfinished business on behalf of the dissolved partnership arises on the date of dissolution and governs each partner's future conduct regarding this business. [ ]Since the [client's] action remained exactly the same case before and after RM & S's dissolution, C & R's liability for failing to complete the [client's] case for the dissolved RM & S and for entering into a contract personally to profit from the unfinished business of the dissolved RM & S survived execution of the C & R [client] agreement and [client's] discharge of RM & S.

Id. at 219, 194 Cal.Rptr. 180 (internal headnotes omitted).

In *Jewel v. Boxer,* 156 Cal.App.3d 171, 203 Cal.Rptr. 13 (1984), as in the case at bar, departing law partners contacted clients whose cases had been handled by the old firm. *Jewel,* 156 Cal.App.3d at 175, 203 Cal.Rptr. 13. At issue before the Court of Appeals was the proper allocation of attorneys' fees received from those

---

4. The Uniform Partnership Act provides: "**The dissolution of a partnership is the change in the relation of the partners caused by any partner ceasing to be associated in the carrying on as distinguished from the winding up of the business.**" (Corp.Code, § 15029.) "On dissolution the partnership is not terminated, but continues until the winding up of partnership affairs is completed." (Corp.Code, § 15030.) "Except so far as may be necessary to wind up partnership affairs or to complete transactions begun but not then finished, dissolution terminates all authority of any partner to act for the partnership, [¶] (1) With respect to the partners, [¶] (a) When the dissolution is not by the act, bankruptcy or death of a partner . . . ." (Corp.Code, § 15033.)

cases originating with the old firm but transferred to and resolved by the new partnership. *Id.* The appellants argued that "the substitutions of attorneys transformed the old firm's unfinished business into new firm business and removed that business from the purview of the Uniform Partnership Act," thereby limiting the old firm's recovery to *quantum meruit* damages based on services rendered by the old firm. *Id.* at 176, 203 Cal.Rptr. 13. The Court of Appeals disagreed and concluded that recovery should be based on the partners' respective interest in the old firm. Of particular relevance to the matter before us, the Court of Appeals offered the following discussion:

> [W]e must look to the circumstances existing on the date of dissolution of a partnership, not events occurring thereafter, to determine whether business is unfinished business of the dissolved partnership. Thus, in *Rosenfeld* a client's retention of a new firm consisting of two former partners of the dissolved firm that previously handled the client's case did not transform the case into new partnership business: **'It is clear that a partner completing unfinished business cannot cut off the rights of the other partners in the dissolved partnership by the tactic of entering into a 'new' contract to complete such business.'** Accordingly, the substitutions of attorneys here did not alter the character of the cases as unfinished business of the old firm. To hold otherwise would permit a former partner of a dissolved partnership to breach the fiduciary duty not to take any action with respect to unfinished partnership business for personal gain.

Id. at 177-179, 203 Cal.Rptr. 13 (internal citations omitted and emphasis added).

It is critical to note that *Jewel,* unlike the present case, did not involve a written agreement with respect to the allocation of attorneys' fees. Therefore, the Court of Appeals analyzed the Uniform Partnership Act as the default rule to be applied in the absence of a written agreement between the parties. Notwithstanding that distinction, the Court of Appeals acknowledged the role the Uniform Partnership Act played in the absence of a written agreement between the parties:

> [F]ormer partners are obligated to ensure that a disproportionate burden of completing unfinished business does not fall on one former partner or one group of former partners, unless the former partners agree otherwise. It is unlikely that the partners, in discharging their mutual fiduciary duties, will be able to achieve a distribution of the burdens of completing unfinished business that corresponds precisely to their respective interests in the partnership. **But partners are free to include in a written partnership agreement provisions for completion of unfinished business that ensure a degree of exactness and certainty unattainable by rules of general application.** If there is any disproportionate burden of completing unfinished business here, it results from the parties' failure to have entered into a partnership agreement which could have assured such a result would not occur. The former partners must bear the consequences of their failure to provide for dissolution in a partnership agreement.

Jewel, 156 Cal.App.3d at 179-180, 203 Cal.Rptr. 13 (emphasis added). Therefore, the rules promulgated in the Uniform Partnership Act provide the foundation on which parties, by way of a written partnership agreement, may expand the parameters of their relationship.

Unlike the parties in *Jewel,* Beasley and Erbstein did enter into an agreement that accounted for the distribution of attorney fees following Erbstein's departure which were attributable to cases originating with Beasley. Specifically, Erbstein agreed that, "[i]n the event [Erbstein] leave [s] this office for any reason and a client or clients choose(s) to continue with your representation, you will receive 25% of the net fee on any case you take with you regardless of its age or time spent on the file before or after you leave the office." Beasley's Response in Opposition to the Petition for Determination of Attorney's Fees of Young Ricchiuti Caldwell & Heller, LLC, 2/11/11, at Exhibit A ¶ 8. This distinction notwithstanding, we must look to the circumstances at the time Erbstein left Beasley to determine whether the Rubys' case constituted unfinished business. As there is no dispute that the Rubys' case was in the midst of litigation at the time of Erbstein's departure, there can be no doubt that it indeed constituted unfinished business. Consequently, Erbstein, and in turn YRCH, "cannot cut off the rights of the other partners in the dissolved partnership by the tactic of entering into a 'new' contract to complete such business." *Jewel,* 156 Cal.App.3d at 178, 203 Cal.Rptr. 13 (quoting *Cohen,* 146 Cal.App.3d at 219, 194 Cal.Rptr. 180). Accordingly, while YRCH is not bound by the contract between Erbstein and Beasley, it may only take its share of attorneys' fees subject to the terms of the employment agreement. Having determined that YRCH may take Erbstein's share of the attorneys' fees subject to the terms of the employment agreement, we turn to YRCH's claim regarding the enforceability of those terms.

In support of its second issue, YRCH claims and devotes considerable analysis to the notion that Beasley's claim for attorneys' fees, as provided for in the employment contract with Erbstein, is tantamount to a restrictive covenant designed to eliminate competition *vis-à-vis* Erbstein. YRCH's Brief at 10-14. YRCH concludes that insofar as the agreement contains a restrictive covenant on Erbstein's legal practice, it is unenforceable. Further, it makes a passing remark that the elimination of competition had the "added bonus of a financial gain far beyond the *quantum meruit* value of its services." *Id.* at 11. YRCH also claims that the fee-splitting arrangement between Erbstein and Beasley somehow impacts a client's right to choose his or her counsel. *Id.* at 10. All of YRCH's claims are without merit.

At the outset, we observe that YRCH does little more than make the bald proposition that the provision in the employment agreement splitting attorneys' fees is a restrictive covenant. Relying on case law inapplicable to the facts before us, YRCH then analyzes whether this provision is enforceable, concluding that it is not enforceable. YRCH's Brief at 11-14. However, YRCH fails to direct this Court to any authority suggesting that fee-splitting arrangements constitute a restrictive covenant.

Ordinarily, a restrictive covenant forbids or curtails a party's ability to work. *See Hess v. Gebhard & Co. Inc.,* 570 Pa. 148, 808 A.2d 912 (2002) ("Restrictive covenants, of which non-disclosure and non-competition covenants are the most frequently utilized, are commonly relied upon by employers to shield their protectible [sic] business interests."). By its terms, a restrictive covenant is simply a promise not to engage in some conduct otherwise permitted but for the presence of the covenant. YRCH proffers no evidence suggesting that either YRCH or Erbstein could not obtain its own clientele, successfully engage in the practice of law, or was either geographically or temporally limited in their practice because Beasley receives a share of a recovery in the cases it formerly held. YRCH purports that somehow Erbstein was restricted because he could not continue representation of the Rubys without compensating Beasley. We are not persuaded by YRCH's argument that one's ability to procure clients is constrained by some ancillary obligation having no bearing on clients retained after the dismissal of the obliged attorney.

YRCH also cursorily argues that Beasley's share of attorneys' fees eliminated competition and had the "added bonus of a financial gain far beyond the *quantum meruit* value of its services." YRCH's Brief at 11. To the extent that YRCH claims Beasley's award exceeded the amount it would have under a *quantum meruit* theory, we agree with the trial court wherein it states:

> This was not a *quantum meruit* type of situation. Beasley never attempted to say it was entitled to a portion of the over $600,000 fee because of work its attorneys did. Rather, Beasley has always only asserted that it was entitled to the fees in accordance with the Erbstein-Beasley employment contracts.

. . .

Trial Court Opinion, 10/13/11, at 9, 10—11.

In Pennsylvania, the quasi-contractual doctrine of unjust enrichment (*quantum meruit*) does not apply when a written agreement or express contract exists between the parties. *Lackner v. Glosser*, 892 A.2d 21, 34 (Pa.Super.2006) (citing *Mitchell v. Moore*, 729 A.2d 1200, 1203 (Pa.Super.1999)). As the trial court noted, there is a written agreement in controversy in this matter, namely the employment agreements between Beasley and Erbstein. Accordingly, a *quantum meruit* theory has no place in determining the rights of the parties in this action. Therefore, YRCH's arguments with respect to this theory of recovery fail.

Finally, to the extent that YRCH argues that the employment agreement somehow negatively impacts a client's right to choose his or her attorney, we disagree. Again, we look to the sound reasoning articulated by the California Court of Appeals in *Jewel*, where the appellant proffered a similar argument:

> [T]he right of a client to the attorney of one's choice and the rights and duties as between partners with respect to income from unfinished business are distinct and do not offend one another. Once the client's fee is paid to an attorney, it is of no concern to the client how that fee is allocated among the attorney and his or her former partners.

Jewel, 156 Cal.App.3d at 178, 203 Cal.Rptr. 13. We agree.

After review of the record, we glean nothing which would suggest that the change in representation had any impact whatsoever on the Rubys' choice of counsel or their recovery following settlement. Once their claim was resolved and attorneys' fees calculated, it was of no concern to the Rubys how that fee was allocated between Beasley and YRCH. Therefore, we are not persuaded that consideration of a client's right to choose counsel has any bearing on the facts and issues in this matter. Accordingly, we conclude YRCH's argument is without merit.

Order affirmed.

F. CLIENT SATISFACTION

In an effort to retain clients, some firms solicit feedback. This can be done informally in a face-to-face communication simply by having a servicing partner take a client out to lunch.

Some firms have begun conducting formal client satisfaction surveys in an effort to measure client satisfaction. Getting people to tell the truth in such surveys can be challenging, especially if the lawyer who worked on a matter is the same one who is conducting the survey. Even dissatisfied clients are sometimes reticent to tell their lawyers to their faces about unhappiness with the service received. A survey returned simply with superlatives doesn't add much value. As a result, some firms have hired outside third parties to conduct client satisfaction surveys.

One way to increase the return rate of written surveys is to include them with a client's bill. Because some people are disinclined to put criticism in writing, however, a client satisfaction interview may be more productive. Before the interview or the survey is conducted, careful thought should be put into how questions are worded. To get people talking, pose open-ended questions rather than ones that are likely to generate a yes or no answer.

Large corporate clients may have more formal measures in place to assess their own satisfaction with their outside counsel. Thanks to technological advances, they can compare and contrast the rates that their outside firms charge. They can dive deeper into those charges by assessing how much is paid per hour for associate work at outside law firms, how much time and money is spent on attorney travel, and how much money is spent paying law firms by the hour as opposed to by the project or according to some other means. Clients might use this data to drive down their legal fees through negotiations with firms that are exceeding certain performance metrics.[17]

Even as some clients might be looking more toward data-driven cost decisions, their lawyers, and the clients themselves, might wonder whether all aspects of a legal team's performance can be measured. A large corporate client faced with a daunting legal problem might opt for the big-name, expensive, high-profile attorney. Yes, another firm might have been able to handle the matter less expensively. But if the company loses the case, isn't its own general counsel going to be under fire for going with the cheaper lawyer?

G. TERMINATING REPRESENTATION

Lawyers are obligated to maintain client confidentiality. A relationship of trust needs to develop between lawyer and client, and a certain measure of candor is necessary for the lawyer to fully represent a client. The law of evidence recognizes this need for confidential communications between lawyers and clients; typically, such confidences are said to be privileged communications not subject to disclosure. This is referred to as the attorney-client privilege.

---

17. *See, e.g.*, Sharon D. Nelson & John W. Simek, *Big Data: Big Pain or Big Gain for Lawyers?*, 39 Law Practice Magazine n.p. (July/Aug. 2013), *available at* http://www.americanbar.org/publications/law_practice_magazine/2013/july-august/hot-buttons.html.

Suppose, though, that a client charged with battering his wife tells his lawyer that he is going to kill her. Is the lawyer obligated to keep that information a secret?

Tarasoff v. Regents of the University of California, 551 P.2d 334 (Cal. 1976), held that therapists have a duty to warn if a client presents a serious danger. In 1969, Prosenjit Poddar killed Tatiana Tarasoff. Her parents, who brought a lawsuit against Poddar's therapists, maintained that Poddar had told his psychologist of his intent to kill Tarasoff. Poddar was briefly detained by campus police, but was released. The defendants asserted that they owed no duty of reasonable care to Tatiana Tarasoff. The Supreme Court of California held:

> that defendant therapists cannot escape liability merely because Tatiana herself was not their patient. When a therapist determines, or pursuant to the standards of his profession should determine, that his patient presents a serious danger of violence to another, he incurs an obligation to use reasonable care to protect the intended victim against such danger. The discharge of this duty may require the therapist to take one or more of various steps, depending upon the nature of the case. Thus it may call for him to warn the intended victim or others likely to apprise the victim of the danger, to notify the police, or to take whatever other steps are reasonably necessary under the circumstances.[18]

Should the duty to warn extend to lawyers as well? "Prior to 2002, the Rules allowed, but did not require, disclosure of confidential information regarding the representation of a client when the lawyer reasonably believed such a disclosure would prevent the client from committing a crime resulting in death or substantial bodily injury."[19]

In 2002, the *Model Rules of Professional Conduct* were modified to specify that a lawyer may reveal information to prevent death or significant harm. Consider Model Rule 1.6.

Ethically, lawyers are not permitted to help clients break the law, but they are allowed to discuss with clients the consequences of violating the law pursuant to Model Rule 1.2(d). If a client insists on breaking the law, a lawyer is obligated to stop representing that client, according to Model Rule 1.16.

There are plenty of other reasons to fire a client. Some see it as a good business measure to get rid of the three lowest-paying clients every year and to replace them with higher-paying clients. Clients who aren't paying their bills are ripe for termination. Clients who are difficult are good candidates as well.[20]

disengagement letter:
A letter from a lawyer terminating her representation of a client.

When terminating representation, a lawyer is obligated, under Model Rule 1.16, to return the client's file to the client or forward it to the client's new counsel. A lawyer should send the client a **disengagement letter** explaining that the lawyer is terminating the case. A lawyer cannot ethically drop a client in the middle of litigation without exigent circumstances; in that case, a lawyer might be required to seek a court's permission to withdraw from the case and could be ordered to continue serving that client.

---

18. *Tarasoff v. Regents of the University of California*, 551 P.2d 334, 339 (Cal. 1976).

19. Joshua James Sears, *The 2003 Symposium Edition: Modern Methods in Legal Ethics: Theoretical and Practical Approaches: Comment: Blood on Our Hands: The Failure of Rule 1.6 to Protect Third Parties from Violent Clients, and the Movement Toward a Common-Law Solution*, 39 Idaho L. Rev. 451, 452—53 (2003).

20. *See, e.g.*, Mary L. C. Daniel, *Fire Your Clients. Or Your Staff. Or Yourself*, GPSolo, July/Aug. 2006, at 44, 45.

Even after ending a relationship with a client, the lawyer still has an obligation not to take on a new client in the same or a similar matter whose interests are adverse to those of the original client under Model Rule 1.9.

CHECKLIST

- Law firms depend on successful client relationships.
- Lawyers are obligated to provide competent service and to act with diligence in representing clients.
- Ethically, lawyers are required to communicate promptly with clients.
- There are four main types of clients: corporations, associations, individuals, and governments.
- A lawyer representing a corporation represents a business entity, not the individuals who make up that corporation.
- Lawyers should be proactive in seeking new clients. They can use client intelligence to target ideal clients.
- To be more efficient and to aid their clients, some law firms are implementing legal project management principles to plan, budget, and oversee the work that they will undertake for a client.
- Client solicitation must occur within the bounds of ethical rules. Ambulance chasing is impermissible.
- Client relationships should be closely managed so that a client's needs can be identified and met.
- Client satisfaction can be assessed with surveys, interviews, or informal client contacts.
- Although lawyers are obligated to keep client confidences, lawyers may reveal information to prevent reasonably certain death or substantial bodily harm.
- Lawyers may not help clients violate the law.
- A lawyer is obligated to withdraw from a case if a client insists on breaking the law.
- A lawyer may also fire a client for other reasons.
- A lawyer cannot drop a client in the middle of a lawsuit except in exceptional circumstances; a court's permission may be required.
- Even after ending a relationship with a client, a lawyer still has ethical obligations to that client.
- When a law firm is merging with another firm, clients should be informed as soon as possible of the change.

VOCABULARY

bread-and-butter client (2)
churning (2)
client team (10)
convergence (3)

cross-selling (10)
deep pockets (2)
disengagement letter (20)
external client (2)
internal client (2)
intranet (10)
legal project management (6)
private client (4)
runner (6)
secondment (3)

CAREER PREPARATION TIPS

As you contemplate your own future role in the legal industry, think about how you may help your firm—or yourself—obtain clients. Even if your formal entrance into the legal field is years away, what steps might you take now to develop the ability to get and retain clients? Are there fields that you might volunteer in to learn how a business works or to gain contacts already working in the area? For instance, if you plan to work for the real estate practice of a law firm, might you volunteer at a housing organization now? If you tend toward social reticence, are there social groups that you could join to develop speaking skills and the ability to make idle chitchat that could further your career? How might you improve your people skills?

IF YOU WANT TO LEARN MORE

The American Bar Association's Center for Professional Responsibility offers a lot of material on ethical issues. The *Model Rules of Professional Conduct* and commentary are accessible at this site. http://www.americanbar.org/groups/professional_responsibility.html

The Association of Corporate Counsel is a bar association for in-house counsel with 30,000 members in more than 75 countries. http://www.acc.com/

Bloomberg, the company founded by New York City Mayor Michael Bloomberg, chronicles business news. http://www.bloomberg.com

Fast Company covers business practices and trends and reports on innovative practices by companies. http://www.fastcompany.com

Forbes covers financial markets, business, technology, corporate governance, and other areas. http://www.forbes.com

Martindale offers a searchable directory of lawyers. Searches can be conducted by name, by state, and by other search terms. In-house counsel, government lawyers, and corporate legal departments can also be located. www.martindale.com

---

READING COMPREHENSION

1. What ethical obligations does a lawyer have to his or her current clients?
2. What are some of the reasons lawyers can face discipline for providing poor client service?
3. How does legal representation of a corporation differ from representation of an individual?
4. Why should a lawyer research prospective clients?
5. What are permissible ways for a lawyer to pursue prospective clients?
6. How does legal project management aid clients?
7. In what circumstances may a lawyer disclose confidential information provided by a client?
8. What are some examples of inappropriate solicitations of potential clients?
9. When should a lawyer fire a client?
10. Can a lawyer represent a fired client's opponent in a lawsuit?

DISCUSSION STARTERS

1. Running up a client's legal bill by doing excessive work on the case can be very tempting to lawyers who must generate income to pay their own bills. Consider the following:

    > Virtually all the economics of law practice—including those of the large firms who charge $250_600 per hour for their services—cut against ethical behavior. If a client has a deep pocket and is able to pay the lawyers' fees many lawyers **churn** the case in order to enhance earnings. If the clients can not afford the fees as the case progresses they risk receiving only "partial" representation in which lawyers may do just enough work to justify having used up the available money. When funds are depleted the lawyers then figure out how to dispose of the problem or claim, or provide bargain basement service in the sense of "you get what you pay for."[21]

    What ethical rules are violated by the practice of churning? How can churning be proven? How can lawyers avoid the temptation to churn cases?

2. In 2013, e-mails about cost overruns from lawyers within a major law firm became part of the court record in a billing-dispute lawsuit. One of the e-mails read that a lawyer within the firm "had random people working full time on random research projects in standard . . . 'churn that bill, baby!' mode. That bill shall know no limits." Another lawyer

---

21. David Barnhizer, *Profession Deleted: Using Market and Liability Forces to Regulate the Very Ordinary Business of Law Practice for Profit*, 17 Geo. J. Legal Ethics 203, 223 (2004).

wrote in regarding the matter, "I hear we are already 200k over our estimate—that's Team DLA Piper!" Exhibit 5 to Supporting Affidavit of Larry Hutcher, *DLA Piper LLP (US) v. Victor*, No. 650374/2012 (N.Y. Sup. Ct. filed Mar. 21, 2013). Much negative publicity followed, and the firm issued a statement maintaining that the e-mails simply represented "an unfortunate attempt at humor" and that the client was not overbilled. *DLA Piper Calls E-Mails Cited in Lawsuit an 'Offensive' Attempt at Humor*, N.Y. Times DealBook (Mar. 26, 2013), http://dealbook. nytimes.com/2013/03/26/dla-piper-warns-employees-against-offen- sive-humor-in-e-mails/

If you worked at the firm where this happened, how might you have addressed the negative publicity? Given the existence of these e- mails, did the firm's leadership make a cost-effective decision to pur- sue litigation seeking legal fees from the particular client at issue in this matter? If you became aware that a law firm's lawyers had written e-mails such as this, would you still retain the firm? What precautions might you take to ensure bills were not inappropriately padded?

3. Read *Florida Bar v. Barrett*. Were Barrett's clients dissatisfied with the service they received? Was Barrett effective at representing his clients? Was the punishment Barrett received too harsh? Look up your state's rules on solicitation of clients.

4. Research legal project management. Are there any negative impacts of implementing legal project management at a law firm? Why might any- one be opposed to legal project management at his or her firm? Might a client be opposed to legal project management? How can any resist- ance, by a law firm or by a client, be overcome?

5. Read *Ruby v. Abington Memorial Hospital*. What did you learn about part- nership agreements from this case? Why was the lawyer at the center of this case dismissed from his previous firm? What impact do you think this litigation had on the client that was involved? Would this litigation impact client opinions about either law firm involved?

6. Draft a sample letter to a client informing her that your law firm is merging with another. What information should be included in such a letter? Of what rights should the client be informed? Should a letter be written in a way intended to keep the client as a client?

7. Draft a sample letter to a client informing her that the lawyer working on her case is moving to another law firm. What information should be included in such a letter? How should this letter differ from the one involving a law firm merger?

8. Look up some sample client satisfaction surveys, and research recent law review articles on these surveys. What questions should be asked on such a survey? How might those questions be posed to generate a highly informative answer?

9. Suppose you work for a nonprofit organization dedicated to providing food to poor people in your state. The nonprofit is seeking outside counsel. What qualifications would you look for in a law firm? What size firm might be an ideal match for the nonprofit?

CASE STUDIES

1. Select one large corporation in your area and conduct some competitive intelligence on it. What types of legal problems might the company face? Who is the company's general counsel? What law school did that general counsel attend? Who currently represents the corporation?

2. Your law firm is considering pitching both Walmart and Sears for legal work. What sort of legal representation might these two companies need? Who are their current counsel? What might be the advantage of working for one corporation rather than the other?

3. Look up a case where a lawyer sued a client for nonpayment of the client's bill. Were there any early indicators that the lawyer-client relationship would sour? Why didn't the client pay the bill? What was the outcome of the case?

4. Your client tells your firm that she will call the firm from her car while she is driving to her next appointment. Suppose that talking on a cell phone without a separate headset while driving is illegal in your state. Is your firm obligated to terminate its representation of the client?

5. Look up your state's rules on returning client files to the client when representation is terminated. You might also need to research case law and ethical opinions to determine the answers to the following questions: Must a lawyer's notes be provided to the client? Must copies of all e-mails be provided to the client? Should managerial documents (for instance, giving an assignment related to the file to an associate and specifying the number of hours to be spent on the task) be included?

CHAPTER
2

Human Resources

CHAPTER OUTCOMES

By the end of this chapter, a student will be able to:

- Explain the importance of a law firm's mission statement
- Prepare a law firm history
- Contrast different types of employment within a firm
- Discuss applicable employment statutes within the context of the legal workplace
- Identify appropriate recruiting, hiring, and termination practices
- Assemble an employee handbook

To function effectively as a business, a law firm needs to be staffed by lawyers and nonlegal personnel who, in turn, need to be paid regularly and promptly. Benefits packages must be developed and maintained, schedules coordinating holiday and summertime absences must be developed, and applicable state and federal laws regulating the workplace must be followed.

The responsibilities for these tasks fall to someone charged with human resources management. In large law firms, an entire department might have these duties. In a small one, a law office manager might do these jobs as part of his day-to-day responsibilities. Details about recruiting and hiring staff fall to the human resources group, as do responsibilities for training personnel. A forward-thinking human resources staff is also concerned with employee retention and workplace morale.

At the very least, a successful human resources team must stay abreast of developments in employment law. As this chapter will demonstrate, failure to follow appropriate employment statutes can be very expensive.

A. FIRM MISSION STATEMENT AND HISTORY

Leaders at law firms typically agree on a **mission statement**, a short description of the law firm explaining the type of work it undertakes and perhaps describing the firm's overall philosophy. A mission statement might be drafted by a

mission statement: A short description of the law firm explaining the type of work it undertakes and perhaps describing the firm's overall philosophy.

law office manager and then tweaked by upper-level lawyers at the firm. The mission statement should identify the core values of the firm. The mission statement educates people about the firm's capabilities as well as its perspective and approach to the law. By reviewing a mission statement, both clients and prospective hires can learn where the law firm stands on certain issues—whether they are quality-of-life matters, particulars about billable hours and client service, the types of cases the firm focuses on, or the firm's understanding of a lawyer's role.

In drafting—and agreeing on—a mission statement, lawyers, unfortunately, sometimes end up writing a series of platitudes that could essentially describe any number of firms. For instance, a firm might describe itself in a mission statement as a "full-service firm where client service is paramount." Many firms, even ones that do not have enough staff to be truly full service and able to handle any legal problem, describe themselves in such a general way.

Ideally, a mission statement should be a straightforward explanation of who the law firm is, why it exists, and what it can do for clients. Distinguishing characteristics—key elements that separate the firm from its competition—should be included in the statement. Specific practice areas might be identified along with general categories of clients, such as businesses, Fortune 500 corporations, individuals, insurance companies, or criminal defendants.

The mission statement helps lawyers, staff, and clients understand the purpose and the approach of the law firm. The statement can be very useful to the firm itself as a basic guideline for making important business decisions. For instance, if the firm brands itself as a full-service one, then its long-range hiring plans might include expansion to points around the globe. The mission statement can be useful to prospective hires in educating them about the firm. By reviewing the mission statement, a job candidate can inform herself about the prospective law firm and decide whether the firm's approach and outlook are appealing.

firm history: An explanation of a firm's purpose.

In addition to crafting mission statements, some firms commission book-length histories. Some law firms in the United States have now been in existence for more than a century. A **firm history** can provide insight into how the firm, as an institution, has made its decisions and tell what has worked in the past and, possibly, what has not worked so well. Recitations of big wins and successful strategies create a bit of an institutional memory, which may fade with time and turnover. Lawyers who are aware of their firm's historical perspective have a better understanding of the organization they work for, why it functions as it does, and how and why it has historically succeeded.

A firm history might discuss the founders of the firm, why the firm was originally formed, and how and why the firm expanded into different areas of law over the years. Both a mission statement and a firm history can be helpful recruiting and retention tools, giving prospective and current employees some understanding of what a firm is about, why it came into being, and how they are part of a team and of a tradition.

B.   EMPLOYMENT LAW

Both federal and state laws govern employment conditions in workplaces. To function well, a law firm's human resources staff should be familiar with the intricacies of these laws and with their applicability to a given firm. Some laws apply only to businesses that have a threshold number of employees.

1.   *Types of Employment*

a.   Employment at Will

Typically, law firm staff, as well as associates, are **employees at will.** In other words, they do not have a contract with the firm specifying a period of employment. Rather, they work "at will." This means that either the employer or the employee can end the arrangement at any time.

employment at will: A work relationship that has no contract and can be terminated at any time by either the employer or the employee.

b.   Contract Employees

To avoid the costs associated with recruiting new associates and grooming them for eventual partnership positions, law firms are increasingly turning to contract attorneys to help them with mundane, routine work. **Contract employees** might be hired to perform a certain job or to work for the firm for a certain period of time. When the job is finished or the time period ends, so does the contract attorney's employment with the firm. These positions typically offer no promotion potential. They can be attractive to lawyers who are unwilling to work the number of billable hours required of associates who are on the partnership track. The downside is that these positions are less prestigious and typically the work is not especially intellectually stimulating.

Some law firms are also hiring paralegals as contract employees to do work on a provisional basis, either for a certain time period or until a specified project is concluded. Again, the advantage to law firms is that they do not need to maintain a high level of staffing during slower periods.

contract employee: Someone hired on a temporary basis and typically with no benefits.

2.   *Federal Statutes*

Although employment at a firm may be on an at-will basis (meaning, essentially, that employment can end at any time), employers are nevertheless bound to follow laws that are applicable to them. A discussion of some pertinent federal employment laws follows.

a.   Equal Employment Opportunity Act

Title VII of the Civil Rights Act of 1964 prohibits employment discrimination based on race, color, religion, sex, or national origin. The law, which applies to employers with 15 or more employees, makes it unlawful to "fail or refuse to hire or to discharge any individual, or otherwise to discriminate against any individual with respect to his compensation, terms, conditions, or privileges of employment, because of such individual's race, color, religion, sex, or national origin."[1]

The law was amended in 1978 to bar discrimination on the basis of pregnancy.

sexual harassment: Inappropriate advances, requests for sexual favors, or verbal or physical conduct of a sexual nature.

Court decisions have interpreted Title VII to bar sexual harassment in the workplace. **Sexual harassment** is defined as follows:

> Unwelcome sexual advances, requests for sexual favors, and other verbal or physical conduct of a sexual nature constitute sexual harassment when (1) submission to such conduct is made either explicitly or implicitly a term or condition of an individual's employment, (2) submission to or rejection of such conduct by an individual is used as the basis for employment decisions affecting such individual, or (3) such conduct has the purpose or effect of unreasonably interfering with an individual's work performance or creating an intimidating, hostile, or offensive working environment.[2]

Title VII also created the Equal Employment Opportunity Commission, a five-member commission charged with implementing and enforcing the statute and investigating complaints against employers. The commission is empowered to pursue violators in court.

The law has been strengthened by providing for compensatory and punitive damages for victims of intentional discrimination. Discrimination lawsuits may now be presented to juries rather than simply heard by judges.

HISHON V. KING & SPALDING
467 U.S. 69 (1984)

PRIOR HISTORY: **CERTIORARI TO THE UNITED STATES COURT OF APPEALS FOR THE ELEVENTH CIRCUIT.**

JUDGES: BURGER, C.J., DELIVERED THE OPINION FOR A UNANIMOUS COURT. POWELL, J., FILED A CONCURRING OPINION.

OPINION

Chief Justice BURGER delivered the opinion of the Court.

[1A] We granted certiorari to determine whether the District Court properly dismissed a Title VII complaint alleging that a law partnership discriminated against petitioner, a woman lawyer employed as an associate, when it failed to invite her to become a partner.

I

A

In 1972 petitioner Elizabeth Anderson Hishon accepted a position as an associate with respondent, a large Atlanta law firm established as a general partnership. When this suit was filed in 1980, the firm had more than 50 partners and

---

1. 42 U.S.C. § 2000e-2(a)(1).
2. 29 C.F.R. § 1604.11(a) (2013).

employed approximately 50 attorneys as associates. Up to that time, no woman had ever served as a partner at the firm.

Petitioner alleges that the prospect of partnership was an important factor in her initial decision to accept employment with respondent. She alleges that respondent used the possibility of ultimate partnership as a recruiting device to induce petitioner and other young lawyers to become associates at the firm. According to the complaint, respondent represented that advancement to partnership after five or six years was "a matter of course" for associates "who [received] satisfactory evaluations" and that associates were promoted to partnership "on a fair and equal basis." Petitioner alleges that she relied on these representations when she accepted employment with respondent. The complaint further alleges that respondent's promise to consider her on a "fair and equal basis" created a binding employment contract.

In May 1978 the partnership considered and rejected Hishon for admission to the partnership; one year later, the partners again declined to invite her to become a partner. Once an associate is passed over for partnership at respondent's firm, the associate is notified to begin seeking employment elsewhere. Petitioner's employment as an associate terminated on December 31, 1979.

B

Hishon filed a charge with the Equal Employment Opportunity Commission on November 19, 1979, claiming that respondent had discriminated against her on the basis of her sex in violation of Title VII of the Civil Rights Act of 1964, . . . 42 U.S.C. § 2000e *et seq.* Ten days later the Commission issued a notice of right to sue, and on February 27, 1980, Hishon brought this action in the United States District Court for the Northern District of Georgia. She sought declaratory and injunctive relief, backpay, and compensatory damages "in lieu of reinstatement and promotion to partnership." This, of course, negates any claim for specific performance of the contract alleged.

The District Court dismissed the complaint on the ground that Title VII was inapplicable to the selection of partners by a partnership. . . . A divided panel of the United States Court of Appeals for the Eleventh Circuit affirmed. We granted certiorari, . . . and we reverse.

II

At this stage of the litigation, we must accept petitioner's allegations as true. A court may dismiss a complaint only if it is clear that no relief could be granted under any set of facts that could be proved consistent with the allegations. . . . The issue before us is whether petitioner's allegations state a claim under Title VII, the relevant portion of which provides as follows:

"(a) *It shall be an unlawful employment practice for an employer*
"(1) to fail or refuse to hire or to discharge any individual, or otherwise to *discriminate against any individual with respect to his* compensation, *terms, conditions, or privileges of employment, because of such individual's* race, color, religion, *sex*, or national origin." 42 U.S.C. § 2000e-2(a) (emphasis added).

Petitioner alleges that respondent is an "employer" to whom Title VII is addressed.[3] She then asserts that consideration for partnership was one of the "terms, conditions, or privileges of employment" as an associate with respondent. . . . If this is correct, respondent could not base an adverse partnership decision on "race, color, religion, sex, or national origin."

Once a contractual relationship of employment is established, the provisions of Title VII attach and govern certain aspects of that relationship. In the context of Title VII, the contract of employment may be written or oral, formal or informal; an informal contract of employment may arise by the simple act of handing a job applicant a shovel and providing a workplace. The contractual relationship of employment triggers the provision of Title VII governing "terms, conditions, or privileges of employment." Title VII in turn forbids discrimination on the basis of "race, color, religion, sex, or national origin."

Because the underlying employment relationship is contractual, it follows that the "terms, conditions, or privileges of employment" clearly include benefits that are part of an employment contract. Here, petitioner in essence alleges that respondent made a contract to consider her for partnership. Indeed, this promise was allegedly a key contractual provision which induced her to accept employment. If the evidence at trial establishes that the parties contracted to have petitioner considered for partnership, that promise clearly was a term, condition, or privilege of her employment. Title VII would then bind respondent to consider petitioner for partnership as the statute provides, *i.e.*, without regard to petitioner's sex. The contract she alleges would lead to the same result.

. . .

B

Respondent contends that advancement to partnership may never qualify as a term, condition, or privilege of employment for purposes of Title VII. First, respondent asserts that elevation to partnership entails a change in status from an "employee" to an "employer." However, even if respondent is correct that a partnership invitation is not itself an offer of employment, Title VII would nonetheless apply and preclude discrimination on the basis of sex. The benefit a plaintiff is denied need not *be* employment to fall within Title VII's protection; it need only be a term, condition, or privilege *of* employment. It is also of no consequence that employment as an associate necessarily ends when an associate becomes a partner. A benefit need not accrue before a person's employment is completed to be a term, condition, or privilege of that employment relationship. Pension benefits, for example, qualify as terms, conditions, or privileges of employment even though they are received only after employment terminates. . . . Accordingly, nothing in the change in status that advancement to partnership might entail means that partnership consideration falls outside the terms of the statute. . . .

We conclude that petitioner's complaint states a claim cognizable under Title VII. Petitioner therefore is entitled to her day in court to prove her allegations. The judgment of the Court of Appeals is reversed, and the case is remanded for further proceedings consistent with this opinion.

---

3. The statute defines an "employer" as a "person engaged in an industry affecting commerce who has fifteen or more employees for each working day in each of twenty or more calendar weeks in the current or preceding calendar year," § 2000e(b), and a "person" is explicitly defined to include "partnerships," § 2000e(a). The complaint alleges that respondent's partnership satisfies these requirements. App. 6.

It is so ordered.

b. Fair Labor Standards Act

Overtime pay requirements, as well as minimum wage requirements, are governed by the Fair Labor Standards Act.[3] Periodically, the minimum wage is raised. "Time and a half," or 1.5 times an employee's regular pay rate, must be paid for overtime work, which is hours worked in excess of 40 per week. Some exemptions from these requirements are provided for administrative, professional, executive, outside sales, and certain computer employees.

The U.S. Department of Labor is empowered to pursue backpay from employers who have underpaid employees in violation of the statute. Both civil and criminal actions might be brought. Employees may also bring suit. Employers can be liable for backpay and for an equal amount as liquidated damages. Violators of the statute are subject to fines as well as imprisonment.

c. Americans with Disabilities Act

The Americans with Disabilities Act of 1990[4] bars discrimination against people with disabilities who are otherwise qualified to perform a job. Employers are required to make reasonable accommodation for employees so long as that accommodation does not cause undue hardship.

The statute, as amended, now applies to employers with 15 or more employees (Originally, only employers with 25 or more employees were subject to its requirements.)

The law also prohibits discrimination against people with disabilities by people or businesses who run a place of "public accommodation."

"Disabilities" are not defined very specifically in the statute. A disability is deemed to be "(A) a physical or mental impairment that substantially limits one or more of the major life activities of such individual; (B) a record of such an impairment; or (C) being regarded as having such an impairment . . . . "[5]

Both individuals as well as the federal government may bring suit against employers for violations of the statute.

SETTLEMENT AGREEMENT BETWEEN THE UNITED STATES OF AMERICA AND JOSEPH DAVID CAMACHO, ESQUIRE, ALBUQUERQUE, NEW MEXICO UNDER THE AMERICANS WITH DISABILITIES

Act DJ #202-49-37

BACKGROUND

1. This matter was initiated by a complaint filed under title III of the Americans with Disabilities Act ("ADA"), 42 U.S.C. §§ 12181 *et seq.*, with the United

---

3. 29 U.S.C. §§ 201-219.
4. 42 U.S.C. §§ 12101 *et seq.*
5. 42 U.S.C. § 12102(2).

States Department of Justice ("Department") against Joseph David Camacho, Attorney At Law, Albuquerque, New Mexico.

2. The complaint was filed by the National Association of the Deaf Law and
Advocacy Center on behalf of Carolyn Tanaka, alleging that Mr. Camacho
refused to secure a qualified sign language interpreter when necessary to
ensure effective communication with her.

3. The NAD Law and Advocacy Center made the following allegations: Ms.
Tanaka is deaf and uses sign language for communication. Ms. Tanaka
retained Mr. Camacho as legal counsel in *Tanaka v. University of New Mexico
Hospital, et al.,* C. No: 04cv00645 in the United States District Court for the
District of New Mexico. In that lawsuit, Ms. Tanaka alleged that the University of New Mexico Hospital failed to provide a qualified interpreter on
numerous occasions during the admission of her son, K.T., then age six, to
the hospital from April 30, 2002, through May 3, 2002. During the course of
his representation of Ms. Tanaka, Mr. Camacho also failed to provide qualified interpreter services despite Ms. Tanaka's repeated requests. Instead,
Mr. Camacho asked that Ms. Tanaka's then-nine-year-old son, K.T., "interpret" at appointments between Ms. Tanaka and Mr. Camacho. Ms. Tanaka
refused to have her son act as an "interpreter" in these complicated legal
matters. On or around September 2004, Mr. Camacho sent Ms. Tanaka
Interrogatories and Request for Production of Documents for her to answer
in connection with her complaint against the University of New Mexico Hospital. Ms. Tanaka had great difficulty understanding the Interrogatories and
Request for Production of Documents. Ms. Tanaka again requested a qualified interpreter so that she could effectively communicate with Mr. Camacho regarding how to answer the discovery requests. Mr. Camacho again
refused to provide a qualified interpreter in order to communicate effectively with and assist Ms. Tanaka in answering the Interrogatories and
Request for Production of Documents. On October 28, 2004, Mr. Camacho
sent Ms. Tanaka a letter stating in part, "It is my understanding that you
refuse to cooperate unless I provide you with an interpreter, which will cost
me approximately eighty dollars an hour. I have never had to pay to con-
verse with my own client. It would be different if you did not have anyone to
translate for you. However, you have a very intelligent son who can do it for
you. It appears that we are not able to work together. I believe that you
should find another attorney as I am going to withdraw from this case." First,
he contends that he represented her effectively and competently, and gave
her the same quality of service that he provides to any other non-disabled client. On November 9, 2004, Mr. Camacho made a motion to withdraw as Ms.
Tanaka's attorney, stating an "irreconcilable conflict." On December 20,
2004, Mr. Camacho's motion to withdraw was granted. The case against the
Hospital was dismissed "due to her failure to respond to discovery."

4. Mr. Camacho disputes portions of Ms. Tanaka's allegations. He has submitted a statement to the Department contending that he was able to communicate effectively with Ms. Tanaka by means of written notes, e-mail, telephone
relays and through the interpretation of Ms. Tanaka's nine-year-old son. He
also points out that he hired an interpreter for the hearing on his withdrawal
from Ms. Tanaka's case. To demonstrate that he communicated effectively
with Ms. Tanaka, Mr. Camacho has submitted to the Department a list of
pleadings that he prepared on Ms. Tanaka's behalf. He contends that he

represented her effectively and competently, and gave her the same quality of service that he provides to any non-disabled client. Mr. Camacho maintains that he withdrew from the case because Ms. Tanaka stopped returning his phone calls and e-mail messages in connection with the discovery requests referred to above.

5. The Attorney General is authorized to enforce title III of the ADA. 42 U.S.C. § 12188(a)(2). In addition, the Attorney General may commence a civil action to enforce title III in any situation where the Attorney General believes a pattern or practice of discrimination exists or a matter of general public importance is raised. 42 U.S.C. § 12188(b)(1)(B).

6. Title III specifically defines discrimination as, among other things:

> the failure to take such steps as may be necessary to ensure that no individual with a disability is excluded, denied services, segregated or otherwise treated differently than other individuals *because of the absence of auxiliary aids or services,* unless the entity can demonstrate that taking such steps would fundamentally alter the nature of the good, service, facility, privilege, advantage, or accommodation being offered or would result in an undue burden.

42 U.S.C. § 12182(b)(2)(A) (emphasis added); see 28 C.F.R. § 36.303. The ADA defines "auxiliary aids" to include, among other things, "qualified interpreters or other effective methods of making aurally delivered materials available to individuals with hearing impairments . . . . " 42 U.S.C. § 12102(1). A public accommodation is required to furnish appropriate auxiliary aids and services where necessary to ensure effective communication with individuals with hearing impairments. 28 C.F.R. § 36.303. The preamble to the regulation lists communications involving legal matters as an example of a type of communication that can be "sufficiently lengthy or complex to require an interpreter for effective communication." 28 C.F.R. pt. 36, App. B at 703 (2005).

7. The title III regulation defines "qualified interpreter" as "an interpreter who is able to interpret effectively, accurately and impartially both receptively and expressively, using any necessary specialized vocabulary." 28 C.F.R. § 36.104. The preamble to the definition of "qualified interpreter" explains:

> Public comment also revealed that public accommodations have at times asked persons who are deaf to provide family members or friends to interpret. In certain circumstances, notwithstanding that the family member or friend is able to interpret or is a certified interpreter, the family member or friend may not be qualified to render the necessary interpretation because of factors such as emotional or personal involvement or considerations of confidentiality that may adversely affect the ability to interpret "effectively, accurately, and impartially."

28 C.F.R. pt. 36, App. B at 684-685 (2005) (internal quotes in original).

PARTIES

8. The Parties to this Settlement Agreement ("Agreement") are the United States of America ("United States") and Joseph David Camacho, Esq.

9. Joseph David Camacho is an attorney in private practice, providing legal services, and therefore, a public accommodation under Title III of the ADA. 42 U.S.C. § 12181(7)(F); 28 C.F.R. § 36.104.

FINDINGS

10. The United States has investigated the allegations that Mr. Camacho failed to provide Ms. Tanaka with effective communication and finds the allegations meritorious.
11. To resolve this matter without further litigation, Mr. Camacho is willing to agree to the terms of this settlement agreement. In exchange, the United States agrees to terminate its investigation of this matter, without resorting to litigation, except as provided in paragraph 18.
12. In order to avoid litigation of the issues discussed herein, and in consideration of the mutual promises and covenants contained in this Agreement, the Parties hereby agree to the following:

REMEDIAL ACTION

13. Consistent with the ADA, Mr. Camacho will not discriminate against any individual on the basis of disability in the full and equal enjoyment of the goods, services, facilities, privileges, advantages, or accommodations of his private practice by refusing or failing to secure qualified interpreters when necessary to ensure effective communication with clients who are deaf and use sign language.
14. Mr. Camacho will adopt, maintain, and enforce the policy attached hereto, and by reference incorporated herein, as Exhibit 1 to this Agreement on effective communication with individuals with disabilities. Within ten (10) days of the effective date of this Agreement, Mr. Camacho will post of the policy in a conspicuous area of his law office where members of the public can readily read the policy. . . .

MONETARY RELIEF FOR COMPLAINANT

15. The ADA authorizes the United States Attorney General to seek a court award of compensatory damages on behalf of individuals aggrieved as the result of violations of the ADA. 42 U.S.C. § 12188(b)(2)(B); 28 C.F.R. § 36.504(a)(2). Within thirty (30) days of the effective date of this Agreement, Mr. Camacho agrees to pay Carolyn Tanaka $1,000.00 in damages. . . .

EXHIBIT 1 POLICY ON EFFECTIVE COMMUNICATION WITH INDIVIDUALS WITH DISABILITIES

To ensure effective communication with clients and companions who are deaf or hard of hearing, we provide appropriate auxiliary aids and services free of charge, such as: sign language and oral interpreters, note takers, written materials, assistive listening devices and systems, and real-time transcription services.

d.   Family and Medical Leave Act

Under the Family and Medical Leave Act,[6] employees are allowed 12 weeks of unpaid leave due to health conditions, birth, adoption of a child,

---

6. 29 U.S.C. §§ 2601 *et seq.*

or care for a family member who is ill. The statute applies to employers with 50 or more employees. Eligible employees are those who worked 1,250 hours during the preceding year and who have been employed by the employer from whom leave is requested for at least one year. The employee, upon returning to work, must be given her prior job or an equivalent one. The employer must maintain group health plan benefits for the employee during the absence period on the same terms as if the employee had been in the office.

Employees may file suit against their employers for violations of the statute. They can receive both monetary damages and equitable relief (such as reinstatement to their previous jobs). The Department of Labor may also pursue employers for violations of the law.

e.   Age Discrimination in Employment Act

The Age Discrimination in Employment Act of 1967, as amended,[7] bans discrimination against people age 40 and older. It is unlawful for employers

1.   to fail or refuse to hire or to discharge any individual or otherwise discriminate against any individual with respect to his compensation, terms, conditions, or privileges of employment, because of such individual's age;
2.   to limit, segregate, or classify his employees in any way which would deprive or tend to deprive any individual of employment opportunities or otherwise adversely affect his status as an employee, because of such individual's age; or
3.   to reduce the wage rate of any employee in order to comply with this chapter.[8]

Although voluntary early retirement plans are permissible under the law, employee benefit plans may not "require or permit the involuntary retirement"[9] of employees because of their age. Mandatory retirement for employees who are executives or in high policy-making positions are permissible so long as these employees are entitled to retirement benefits.[10] Law firms sometimes have compulsory retirement ages for partners. These firms typically argue that the partners are not "employees" subject to age discrimination in employment laws.

Still, law firms can run into trouble when, in an effort to increase per-partner profits, they start getting rid of long-time practitioners who might be underperforming. Consider the following experience:

It wasn't Mrs. O'Leary's cow who set things off in Chicago this time.
Rather, it seems that the leadership of a local institution called Sidley & Austin [now known as Sidley Austin] has been kicking over the lanterns lately, presumably infusing much-needed new energy into the 134-year-old law firm. Guided by executive committee chairman Thomas Cole and management

---

7. 29 U.S.C. §§ 621 *et seq.*
8. 29 U.S.C. § 623(a).
9. 29 U.S.C. § 623(f)(2)(A).
10. 29 U.S.C. § 631(c)(1).

committee chairman Charles Douglas, the firm has big plans—for expanding abroad, for pushing its technology and e-commerce practice at home, and, most jarring for this collegial old organization, for pruning a few dead branches in the partnership.

. . .

Sidley's demotion . . . of some two dozen partners to senior counsel or counsel positions caused something of a gossip firestorm.

Sidley "was always very genteel," observes one local lawyer. "No one ever got fired. That was just the Sidley way. Culturally, this just turns everything on its head."

"The decision was driven by greed," maintains one consultant familiar with the doings. "At an October [1999] partnership meeting, the *AmLaw 100* was circulated. It showed that Sidley has good revenues, but profits per partner are much lower than at other firms."

. . .

So even the Sidleys of the world must nudge some people toward the door in any kind of economic weather. Some partners know they're not going to make it; they've been given the subtle hints, but they're going to hang on until the guards come and put their pens and folders into a box for them. They know what's expected, but they also know the minimum they need to do or pretend to do in order to survive—for awhile.

. . .

Sidley & Austin was founded five years before Chicago burned. It's seen a lot worse than the current brushfire and will likely be standing strong after a few of its more ruthless competitors have torn themselves in half.[11]

The U.S. Equal Employment Opportunity Commission filed suit "alleging that Sidley Austin Brown & Wood, the giant Chicago-based international law firm, violated the Age Discrimination in Employment Act (ADEA) when it selected 'partners' for expulsion from the firm on account of their age or forced them to retire."[12]

A lengthy inquiry took place. The commission informed Sidley of its investigation in July 2000 and filed suit against the firm in 2005:

The EEOC case is a "class" age discrimination case brought, first, with respect to 31 former Sidley & Austin partners who were involuntarily downgraded and expelled from the partnership in October of 1999 on account of their age, and, second, with respect to other partners who were involuntarily retired from Sidley & Austin since 1978 on account of their age pursuant to a mandatory retirement policy. The ADEA prohibits employers with 20 or more employees from making employment decisions, including decisions regarding the termination of employment, on the basis of age (over 40). The ADEA also prohibits such employers from utilizing policies or rules which require employees to retire when they reach a particular age (over 40).[13]

Two years later, the firm settled the suit for $27.5 million (see Figure 2-1).

---

11. Lori Tripoli, *New Leaders at Sidley Pursue New Profits, but Not at Any Cost*, Of Counsel, Jan. 3, 2000, at 1, 9-12.

12. Press Release, U.S. EEOC, EEOC Charges Sidley & Austin with Age Discrimination (Jan. 13, 2005), *available at* http://www.eeoc.gov/press/1-13-05.html.

13. *Id.*

Figure 2.1
Press Release 10-5-07

$27.5 Million Consent Decree Resolves EEOC Age Bias Suit Against Sidley Austin

Law Firm Partners Brought Within Protection of Federal Law Against Employment Discrimination

CHICAGO—The international law firm of Sidley Austin LLP will pay $27.5 million to 32 former partners who the U.S. Equal Employment Opportunity Commission alleged were forced out of the partnership because of their age, under a consent decree approved by a federal judge. (EEOC v. Sidley Austin LLP, N.D. Illinois No. 05 C 0208.)

The EEOC brought the suit in 2005 under the federal Age Discrimination in Employment Act (ADEA). A major issue in the case was whether partners in the law firm were protected as employees under the ADEA. The decree was signed by Federal District Judge James B. Zagel of the Northern District of Illinois yesterday afternoon, October 4, 2007, and entered on the court's docket this morning. The decree provides that "Sidley agrees that each person for whom EEOC has sought relief in this matter was an employee with the meaning of the ADEA."

The consent decree also includes an injunction that bars the law firm from "terminating, expelling, retiring, reducing the compensation of or otherwise adversely changing the partnership status of a partner because of age" or "maintaining any formal or informal policy or practice requiring retirement as a partner or requiring permission to continue as a partner once the partner has reached a certain age."

Ronald S. Cooper, General Counsel of the EEOC, said, "This case has been closely followed by the legal community as well as by professional services providers generally. It shows that EEOC will not shrink from pursuing meritorious claims of employment discrimination wherever they are found. Neither the relative status of the protected group members nor the resources and sophistication of the employer were dispositive here."

Cooper added, "The demographic changes in America assure that we will see more opportunities for age discrimination to occur. Therefore, it is increasingly important that all employers understand the impact of the Age Discrimination in Employment Act on their operations and that we re-emphasize its important protections for older workers."

The $27.5 million will be paid by Sidley Austin to 32 former partners of the firm for whom the EEOC sought relief because they either were expelled from the partnership in connection with an October 1999 reorganization or retired under the firm's age-based retirement policy.

The amounts of the individual payments to the former partners were submitted under seal and approved by the court. The average of all the payments to partners under the decree will be $859,375. The highest payment to any former partner will be $1,835,510, and the lowest payment $122,169. The median payment (the value in the middle of all payments) is $875,572.

During the term of the decree, which expires Dec. 31, 2009, Abner Mikva, retired Federal Court of Appeals Judge and former Member of Congress and White House Counsel, will deal with any complaints received from Sidley partners and report to the EEOC.

The EEOC litigation team has been headed by John Hendrickson, Regional Attorney for the Chicago District, and includes Supervisory Trial Attorney Gregory Gochanour and Trial Attorneys Deborah Hamilton, Laurie Elkin, and Justin Mulaire. Proceedings in the U.S. Court of Appeals for the Seventh Circuit were handled by Carolyn Wheeler and Jennifer Goldstein of the EEOC Office of General Counsel's Appellate Services.

Hendrickson said, "The EEOC v. Sidley Austin litigation has always been a high priority for both our agency and the law firm, and the litigation has reflected that—tough, determined, professional. The litigation has yielded a number of important legal decisions, ensuring the protection of professionals from discriminatory employment actions and ratifying the authority of EEOC to investigate and obtain relief for victims of age discrimination on its own initiative."

Hendrickson added, "The public has benefited because the EEOC and Sidley were able to sit down and talk with each other and craft a workable resolution in a complex lawsuit. That doesn't always happen. Not all employers are resolved to deal with tough issues and to get on with business. Sidley was so resolved, and today's decree reflects its determination to get this case behind it and to address a situation which the EEOC believed required its attention."

George Galland, Jr. of the Chicago law firm of Miner Barnhill & Galland acted as a mediator in the case and facilitated the parties' negotiations.

The EEOC enforces federal laws prohibiting discrimination in employment. Further information about the Commission is available on its web site at www.eeoc.gov.

Source: **Press Release, U.S. Equal Employment Opportunity Commission (Oct. 5, 2007), http://www.eeoc.gov/press/10-5-07.html**

f.   Equal Pay Act

The Equal Pay Act of 1963, as amended, bars pay discrimination based on sex:

> No employer having employees subject to any provisions of this section shall discriminate, within any establishment in which such employees are employed, between employees on the basis of sex by paying wages to employees in such establishment at a rate less than the rate at which he pays wages to employees of the opposite sex in such establishment for equal work on jobs the performance of which requires equal skill, effort, and responsibility, and which are performed under similar working conditions, except where such payment is made pursuant to (i) a seniority system; (ii) a merit system; (iii) a system which measures earnings by quantity or quality of production; or (iv) a differential based on any other factor other than sex: *Provided,* That an employer who is paying a wage rate differential in violation of this subsection shall not, in order to comply with the provisions of this subsection, reduce the wage rate of any employee.[14]

g.   Consolidated Omnibus Budget Reconciliation Act of 1985

The Consolidated Omnibus Budget Reconciliation Act of 1985, or COBRA, allows employees who leave their jobs to continue their health

---

14. 29 U.S.C § 206(d)(1).

insurance coverage for themselves, their spouses, and their children for 18 months (and, in some cases, longer if the employee became disabled) through the employer's group health plan by paying for it. The spouse and children have the right to elect to continue coverage on their own. In certain situations (such as divorce), the spouse and dependent children can keep the coverage for periods up to 36 months. New employees and their covered beneficiaries must be notified of their right to continuation benefits under COBRA.[15]

The law applies to employers with 20 or more employees.[16]

h. Patient Protection and Affordable Care Act (Obamacare)

In 2010, President Barack Obama signed into law the Patient Protection and Affordable Care Act,[17] which requires employers to provide health insurance coverage and requires individuals to maintain minimum levels of health insurance coverage or be subject to a penalty. Assessments of $2,000 per full-time employee will be made against employers with more than 50 employees if they do not offer health care coverage. Individuals must maintain health insurance, and, if they do not, will be required to pay a yearly financial penalty or 2.5 percent of household income (with some exceptions).[18] Small businesses and individuals can seek coverage through health insurance exchanges the new law created. The effective dates for various elements of the law are staggered over several years.

After the Supreme Court upheld the constitutionality of the individual mandate requiring individuals to obtain health insurance coverage as a tax within the taxation powers of Congress,[19] the Obama administration announced that it was postponing until 2015 the requirement that employers offer health insurance to their employees or face fines.[20]

3. State Law

States sometimes have more stringent versions of employee-protection statutes. Both federal laws and applicable state laws should be taken into consideration when developing a law office's procedures.

---

15. §§ 1 *et seq.*, 100 Stat. 82; 29 C.F.R. pt. 2590.

16. U.S. Department of Labor, Employee Benefits Security Administration, *Fact Sheet: Consolidated Omnibus Budget Reconciliation Act (COBRA)*, http://www.dol.gov/ebsa/newsroom/fscobra.html (last visited Aug. 16, 2013).

17. Pub. L. No. 111-148, 124 Stat. 119 (2010), amended by Health Care and Education Reconciliation Act of 2010, Pub.L. No. 111-152, 124 Stat. 1029 (2010).

18. Henry J. Kaiser Family Foundation, *Focus on Health Reform: Summary of Coverage Provisions in the Affordable Care Act, available at* http://www.kff.org (last updated July 17, 2012).

19. *National Federation of Independent Business v. Sebelius,* 132 S.Ct. 2566 (2012).

20. Peter Grier, *Obamacare 101: Why Major Part of Health Law Is Delayed, and Who's Affected,* CSMonitor.com (July 3, 2013), *available at* http://www.csmonitor.com/USA/DC-Decoder/2013/0703/Obamacare-101-Why-major-part-of-health-law-is-delayed-and-who-s-affected-video. For more information about the Patient Protection and Affordable Care Act and its implementation, see U.S. Department of Labor Employee Benefits Security Administration, Affordable Care Act, *available at* http://www.dol.gov/ebsa/healthreform/ (last visited Aug. 16, 2013).

C. RECRUITING AND HIRING PROCESS

Typically, recruiting and hiring at law firms occur on two separate tracks: one for attorneys and a different one for support personnel. Although law office management staff may assist in hiring attorneys, most of these recruiting efforts fall to attorneys at a firm, who typically visit law schools in the fall of each year to interview prospective hires for summer associate or first-year associate positions. Lawyers within the firm also recruit more senior attorneys. Large law firms have a lawyer hiring committee or a lawyer recruiting committee. Law office management personnel likely assist in organizing the process, scheduling interviews, and coordinating the necessary paperwork. Some firms have dedicated recruitment coordinators to handle this function.

Law office management staff is likely to have a more direct role in the hiring of support staff, although, again, the supervising attorney typically has approval authority for any potential hire.

headhunter: A recruiter.

Some firms are using innovative ways to recruit—for example, by developing podcasts or by posting Web videos featuring interviews with associates about working at the firm. Others use traditional recruiting tools and might rely on advertising available positions and using outside recruiting firms, or **headhunters,** to assist in finding potential hires. After all, not only is a firm considering a candidate; the candidate is also assessing the firm. Potential hires often have numerous job offers; a law firm, as in other areas, must compete for the best candidates.

1. Interviewing Candidates

During an interview, a law office manager or appropriate human resources staff person should provide the interviewee with information about the firm, about the job, and about the firm's expectations of the candidate chosen to do that job. A job candidate should be a good match for the firm. Ideally, a candidate's goals, work ethics, capabilities, experience, and accomplishments will mesh with the law firm's objectives in hiring for a given position.

An interview can sometimes seem like a casual conversation between two people new to each other, but the interviewer must take care not to pose inappropriate or illegal questions. Asking whether a candidate is a U.S. citizen, or if the candidate is pregnant or married, is not permissible. Prior to conducting an interview, the interviewer should consider the questions to be posed and draft them in ways that remain within the confines of the law. A manual on current employment law might be consulted.

Likewise, job candidates must prepare for the possibility that an inappropriate or illegal question will be asked during a job interview. The candidate should practice ahead of time how he will deal with such a question. Certainly, declining to answer is one option, as is exclaiming, "That's illegal and I could sue!" The likelihood that an interview would proceed well after such an utterance, is, however, not very high. That's not to say that a candidate should answer illegal questions; rather, the candidate might respond somewhat evasively. For example, in response to "Are you pregnant?" a candidate might answer, "Let's hope not!"

That does not really tell the interviewer whether the candidate is or is not pregnant and, at the same time, is responsive to the question.

2. *Reference and Background Checks*

Firms typically ask prospective hires for references. For fear of litigation, though, some references, and even some former employers, may be reluctant to give out more than very basic information. Law firms sometimes ask prospective hires to sign a waiver or release authorizing a reference or former employer to speak freely about the candidate without fear of reprisal in the form of a lawsuit.

Firms should confirm prior employment and verify educational background and degrees obtained. Doing so is especially important given that, on at least one occasion, someone posing as a lawyer has misled a law firm:

> Manhattan District Attorney Robert M. Morgenthau announced today the indictment of a 32-year-old man for pretending to be a lawyer and stealing at least $284,350.50 from the law firm where he had been employed.
>
> The defendant, Brian Valery, began working as a paralegal at the law firm of Anderson Kill & Olick, P.C. . . . in their New York office . . . on December 2, 1996. He earned a salary of $21,000 per year at that time. Within a five-year period, he was promoted to the position of Law Clerk, earning $70,000 per year.
>
> The investigation revealed that in the fall of 1998, Valery told his employers that he was enrolled at Fordham University School of Law in the evening division and they adjusted his work schedule to accommodate night classes for the next four years. In May 2002, Valery told the firm that he had graduated from Fordham Law School and he was promoted to the legal staff at Anderson Kill & Olick and started practicing as an attorney in the areas of General Litigation, Insurance Recovery, and Corporate and Commercial Litigation. His salary was increased to $115,000 per year.
>
> Soon after his purported graduation from law school, Valery took time off from work for the purpose of studying for the New York State bar examination. Subsequently, the defendant told his employers that he had failed the bar in both July 2002 and February 2003, but that he had passed the July 2003 exam and was admitted to the New York State bar in October 2004. Valery continued to practice as an attorney at Anderson Kill & Olick until October 2006. At that time, the firm discovered that Valery had not attended Fordham Law School, had never taken the New York State bar examination, and was not admitted to practice law. As a result, Anderson Kill & Olick fired him. His annual salary at that time was $155,000.
>
> Valery is charged with Grand Larceny for stealing the differential between the salaries he received while working in the position of attorney and the top paralegal salaries during that same period, plus $74,500 in bonuses.
>
> . . .
>
> Valery is being charged with Grand Larceny in the Second Degree, a class C felony, which is punishable by up to 15 years in prison, and Practicing and Appearing as an Attorney-at-Law Without Being Admitted and Registered, a class A misdemeanor, which is punishable by up to one year in prison. . . . The defendant was arraigned today in New York State Supreme Court, Part 60.[21]

---

21. News Release, New York County District Attorney's Office (June 5, 2007), on *file with author.*

Failure to verify education attained and to confirm that the candidate passed the bar exam was a costly mistake for this firm. The firm ended up offering to reimburse its clients for the lawyer fees they paid for the employee's services.[22]

The employee who posed as a lawyer eventually pleaded guilty to second-degree larceny and admitted to stealing more than $200,000 from his firm by "claiming" a lawyer's salary.[23] He was sentenced to five years' probation and had to perform 100 hours of community service and pay restitution of $225,000.[24]

D.   WORKPLACE POLICIES AND PROCEDURES

A law firm should develop policies and procedures for dealing with all aspects of law firm operations, from scheduling vacation time to covering phones while the receptionist is at lunch to closing the office due to inclement weather, and so on.

Such policies and procedures rarely need to be developed from scratch. Many resources are available offering sample policies, which law firms can then modify to suit their own particular needs.

E.   EMPLOYEE HANDBOOK

Ideally, a law firm should have an employee manual, or handbook, that serves as an introduction to a law firm and addresses standard operating procedures for office conduct. These handbooks can be provided to all new hires. All employees should have them so that they can be easily referred to. The handbook might address the firm's operations, basic office procedures, standards of decorum (such as a dress code), and firm programs and benefits offered.

1.   Elements of a Handbook

The depth, breadth, and length of a handbook will vary depending on the size of the firm and on the level of interest from firm managers in crafting uniform procedures across all of the firm's offices. Although managing attorneys at a very large firm might be tempted to create a phone book-length directory covering many possible workplace functions and scenarios, the reader should be kept in mind. The more burdensome an employee manual becomes to a user, the less likely an employee is actually to use it.

---

22. Alison Leigh Cowan, *Case of the Paralegal Who Played a Lawyer Raises Many Questions*, N.Y. Times (Jan. 22, 2007), *available at* http://www.nytimes.com/2007/01/22/nyregion/22lawyer.html?pagewanted=1&_r=1.

23. Associated Press, *Manhattan: Fake Lawyer Pleads Guilty*, N.Y. Times (Oct. 11, 2007), http://www.nytimes.com/2007/10/11/nyregion/11mbrfs-lfake.html?scp=1&sq=%22Brian+Valery%22&st=nyt.

24. Laura Italiano, *Bogus Att'y Takes a Trip*, N.Y. Post (Jan. 31, 2008), http://www.nypost.com/p/news/regional/item_amUYyNTZ5jHRRQBAyBeH3M.

To make the use of an employee handbook easier, firms develop electronic versions of handbooks. Employees can search for key terms electronically to find pertinent information quickly.

A handbook can contain any amount of information. Essentially, the material in a handbook covers the responsibilities an employee owes to the firm. The handbook might include the firm's mission statement and a short history of the firm, an explanation of how the firm is organized, a discussion of the types of clients the firm represents, and an overview of how the firm operates. Sometimes this material is referred to as a firm résumé.

The firm's organization should be covered in some detail in a handbook. Key people at the firm should be identified, as should departments, department chairs, committees (such as management committee, associates committee, etc.), committee chairs, and so forth. The handbook might include the entire roster of the firm, organized by practice group, department, and support function, such as human resources.

The handbook should provide contact information for managers as well as for other services, such as the mail room, whom to contact if an employee is sick, whom to call about getting a new client number, whom to call for computer problems, how to handle snow days, how to make vacation requests, and so forth. Other elements of a handbook may include the following:

- policy statements on e-mail and appropriate office use of the Internet
- policies and procedures for recruitment and promotion
- job descriptions for support personnel (e.g., legal secretaries, receptionists, paralegals)
- rules of conduct
- a policy statement on lawyers or others serving on corporate boards of directors and on investing in clients' businesses
- a description of official office hours
- procedures for handling clients and others who visit the firm (for instance, some firms do not allow clients into lawyers' offices but limit them to conference rooms)
- procedures for reserving conference rooms
- a policy statement on protecting confidentiality
- telephone procedures and a script for answering phone calls, the procedure for delivering telephones messages, and so forth
- procedures for reporting and addressing sexual harassment
- policies on various matters, such as dress code, holidays, use of office equipment, and timekeeping
- legal notices on equal opportunity employment
- an explanation of disciplinary procedures
- a description of health and retirement plans
- an explanation of training opportunities
- information about facilities, where conference rooms are located, how to book them, where the library is, where administrative offices are, where reception is, etc.
- a discussion of security and emergency procedures
- reimbursement procedures (petty cash, travel, etc.)

Of course, a law firm's manual should also include certain legal niceties such as an explanation that the handbook can be modified. It's probably a good idea to include a disclaimer indicating that the handbook does not create an employment contract. Some courts have held that an employee manual can be considered a contract unless the manual includes a disclaimer clearly indicating that no contract is created.

Employees should be required to sign an acknowledgment that they have received and read the handbook. The contents of the handbook might be reviewed during a new employee's inaugural activities.

2. *Orientation and Training*

Orientation can ease a new hire's stress. Entering a new environment, meeting new colleagues, and adapting to a new office's way of business can be anxiety-producing. Providing a welcome introduction to a particular firm not only puts the new employee at ease but also helps others in the firm accept the new hire.

Lawyers, in particular, are known for not engaging in a lot of on-the-job "hand holding." In other words, historically, they've tended to throw work to a new staff person and expect him or her to pitch in and learn the job by doing it. Nowadays many firms have made great strides in providing more formal orientation and training both for their new lawyers and for new staff people.

Ideally, a new hire should be provided with a job description enumerating his duties and should have a sit-down meeting both with his supervisor and with appropriate human resources staff people, who can make sure that all appropriate paperwork is completed and workplace notices and handbooks are provided to the new employee.

It should be remembered that new staff at a firm may have only limited knowledge about the firm and its functions or even about the job they are to perform. Assigning someone to show the new person around—to introduce her to the appropriate people at the firm, to show her where to park, to explain when she can go to lunch, to explain where the library is, and how the firm kitchen operates (does the person who takes the last cup of coffee make the next pot?), and so forth—can really make a new hire feel welcome.

Training should not be a one-time, introductory event but should reoccur at various times during an employee's tenure at the firm, such as when new technology is introduced or as part of career- or performance-enhancing initiatives. Some law firms have periodic seminars for associates as well as for the support staff who work with them so that everyone will have a better understanding about how a type of case or work will ideally be conducted and what the role of each individual assigned to the matter is.

F. PERFORMANCE EVALUATION

Some firms hire new employees on a trial basis for, say, an initial three-month period. At the end of the trial, the performance of the employee will be assessed, and a decision will be made about hiring the employee on a permanent basis. If, at the end of the three-month period, the employee's performance is deemed to be unsatisfactory, the individual and the firm will part ways. Such an arrangement helps a law firm rid itself of poor performers without undue hassle.

Even after initial trial periods, staff performances should be reviewed annually, as should the performance of lawyers at the firm. A firm might have a very formal process in which every lawyer a staffer works with completes a questionnaire assessing the employee's performance on a given project. These assessments are then compiled and presented to the employee by a human resources person and a supervising attorney. If the employee's performance requires improvement, an action plan may be developed and certain milestones identified.

G.   COMPENSATION AND BENEFITS

An employee's salary and a description of benefits typically are included in an offer letter from the firm. Such a letter usually specifies that employment is at will. In other words, an employee can be fired without cause at any time. The letter might also indicate that a new hire is being hired initially for a trial period of, say, 90 days. During the probationary period, the new hire's performance will be assessed, and a decision whether to extend employment will be made.

When an applicant accepts the offer, additional details about benefits, payment schedules, and the like are provided to the new employee.

H.   EMPLOYEE RELATIONS

At law firms of all sizes, some effort should be made to foster good relations between lawyers and nonlegal staff. Traditionally, there has been some tension between legal and nonlegal personnel, as lawyers tend to accrue greater benefits, both financial and otherwise, than nonlegal staff do. This difference can be very evident in some firms on simmering Friday afternoons when the lawyers gather in a conference room for cocktails, but secretaries and administrative support are excluded from the party.

Some friction occurs at all levels of the firm's hierarchy, from management committee members to partners to associates to paralegals to everyone else. After all, why shouldn't the managing partner of a major law firm command the best parking space in the lot? Every workplace has a pecking order. One group may believe that another group unfairly receives certain **perquisites,** but the group that receives them typically believes it is entitled to them and others are not. For example, lawyers at some law firms have become very contentious in dividing up of office space. Who should have the large corner offices with the best views? The firm's best rainmakers? Department chairs? Should space be assigned according to the number of years a lawyer has been in the profession? According to the number of years a lawyer has been with the firm? In some other way?

perquisite, or "perk": A benefit or special privilege bestowed on an employee in addition to salary.

Wise law firm management will be focused on fostering teamwork rather than letting perceived slights fester.

I. SUPERVISORY TECHNIQUES

Law firms can take measures to foster better relations among team members at a firm. Giving nonlegal staff a say in some policy decisions can make those staffers feel more affiliated with, and more loyal to, a firm.

When training new lawyers, some firms also include the support staff those new lawyers will be working with. Everyone is made to feel a part of the team. Other firms encourage "low-level" staff members to expand their list of duties. For instance, a receptionist who is going to school at night to earn her accounting degree might be given some number-crunching assignments to handle between answering phone calls. Similarly, a legal secretary might be consulted for input on a firm's new filing system, since she is likely to use it frequently. Firm activities that include lawyers as well as staff people also help build a team.

J. DISCIPLINARY ACTION

Unfortunately, some employees might turn out to be "bad actors"—people who are not dedicated to their jobs, who do not respect the clients or their coworkers, or who engage in inappropriate behavior.

Performance problems should be raised during annual, semiannual, or even periodic reviews. It's possible that an employee is experiencing a difficulty that, when known, could be resolved with some modifications to the employee's workload or with the addition of some training.

During a review, a plan of action might be discussed for improving the employee's performance, and a schedule might be worked out, with the implications of failure to improve made clear to the employee.

If performance problems stem from other sorts of behaviors, such as apparent abuse of sick leave, or inappropriate conduct, such as sexual harassment, a higher level of supervisory and human resources personnel might become involved in the matter. Disciplinary action, such as a warning placed in an employee's file or a reassignment, might be discussed. In certain instances, a firm might also consult an outside employment law lawyer to be certain it is conforming with the most recent legal requirements in dealing with problem employees or complaints by other employees about a problem employee.

K. TERMINATION

1. Voluntary

It is customary for employees who are leaving a firm voluntarily to provide two weeks' notice of their departure. The procedure for giving notice might be mentioned in the employee handbook. Employees who are retiring may provide even more advance notice about their plans to retire.

Although an employee might be tempted to be less than cordial when leaving a firm, he or she should remember that potential future employers might be calling the firm to confirm employment and to seek references. If at all possible, an employee who leaves the firm voluntarily should maintain good relations with the firm.

2.   *Involuntary*

Unfortunately, sometimes circumstances require that a firm and an employee who is not measuring up part ways. Depending on the situation, a staff person's employment may be terminated immediately, or he or she may be given notice that her position is ending and that after a certain date she will no longer be employed by the firm.

L.   EMPLOYEE RETENTION

Turnover at law firms can be strikingly high. Some estimates are that law firms lose 20 percent of associates in a year.[25] Replacing those lawyers is an expensive endeavor.

Much attrition is attributable to billable-hours requirements for lawyers. In the early 1960s, if a lawyer billed 1,300 hours annually, he was considered to be working a full-time job.[26] Nowadays, billable hours exceed 2,000 hours. Over the past few decades, loyalty to one's firm has diminished, a situation not helped by the tendency of law firms to lay off lawyers as well as staff people during economic downturns. Leaders at firms are realizing that, in addition to high salaries, lawyers are interested in benefits, and some firms are boosting their benefits packages in an effort to retain lawyers. For example, one firm increased its parental leave policy, allowing 18 weeks, rather than 12 weeks, for birth mothers who are primary caregivers and for adoptive parents. Biological fathers and other primary caregivers can take 10 weeks off, up from 8. Associates can also work a reduced number of hours for six months upon their return and will not have the same billable-hours requirements as a full-time lawyer.[27]

attrition: A reduction in the number of people in a group, such as law firm employees.

Some firms are considering alternatives to billable hours and are designing alternative work schedules. Lawyers may be required to work in the office during certain core hours but then may telecommute for the remainder of the time. Other firms are focusing on perquisites such as on-site cafeterias and child care. Paid sabbaticals are another way to allow someone to take time away from the firm to explore other alternatives without severing the relationship entirely.

---

25. Deena Shanker, *Why Are Lawyers Such Terrible Managers?*, CNN Money (Jan. 11, 2013), *available at* http://management.fortune.cnn.com/tag/turnover/.

26. *See* Denise Howell, *On Life Support: Was the Formula for a Good Work/Life Balance Figured Out in the 1970s?*, Am. Law., Apr. 1, 2008, *available at* http://www.law.com/jsp/tal/PubArticleTAL.jsp?hubtype=Inside&id=1207065967602.

27. Kellie Schmitt, *Latham Ramps Up Parental Benefits; Will Other Firms Follow?*, Recorder (San Francisco), Dec. 14, 2007, *available at* http://www.law.com/jsp/article.jsp?id=1197597876583.

Retention rates have also suffered as law firms have consolidated. Partners and associates may leap to other firms several times within a career. Compensation schemes for partners can also be detrimental to attorney retention. If partners become dissatisfied with the money that they are earning, they may be inclined to look for more profitable places to work.[28]

In times of economic downturn, layoffs[29]—of both lawyers and staff can occur. For those who remain, the workplace can become more tense—which, in turn, may yield even more staff turnover.

M.   DIVERSITY IN LAW FIRMS

Often criticized as white-male bastions,[30] law firms today are more diverse than they once were, though not yet ideal. In some measure, the shift toward law firms being more reflective of society as a whole is attributable to clients—some are assessing a law firm's diversity as well as the firm's level of expertise, depth, and cost. This shift is attributable to "A Call to Action," an initiative begun in 2005 by one general counsel of a corporation to encourage other corporations to look for diversity in the law firms those corporations retained. Signatories to A Call to Action pledged to consider diversity of lawyers at the law firms their corporations might hire.[31]

1.   Minorities

The percentage of minority lawyers at large law firms has increased slowly, moving from 9.7 percent in 2000 and peaking at 13.9 percent in 2008. That percentage then dipped during the recession, only reaching 13.9 percent again in 2013.[32] Despite increased percentages of both women and minorities in law school classes, progress in the private sector has been slow in coming.

Although 33.3 percent of lawyers are female, as of 2012, only 19.9 percent are partners, and only 15 percent are equity partners. Just 4 percent of large law firm

---

28. *See* Noam Scheiber, The Last Days of Big Law, 244(12) New Republic 24-33 (Aug. 5, 2013).

29. *See, e.g.*, Peter Lattman, Mass Layoffs at a Top-Flight Law Firm, DealBook (June 24, 2013), *available at* http://dealbook.nytimes.com/2013/06/24/big-law-firm-to-cut-lawyers-and-some-partner-pay/?_r=0; Andrew Strickler, *Jones Day Lays Off 65 IT Workers*, Law360 (June 21, 2013), *available at* http://www.law360.com/articles/452281/jones-day-lays-off-65-it-workers; Andrew Ramonas & Matthew Huisman, *As Profits Sink, Patton Boggs Lays Off 65*, AmLaw Daily (Mar. 3, 2013), *available at* http://www.americanlawyer.com/PubArticleFriendlyALD.jsp?id=1202590750045.

30. *E.g.*, Don J. DeBenedictis, *Survey: New Grads Changing Bar: Minority, Female Lawyers Increasing, but Their Pay Is Below That of White Males*, 77 A.B.A. J. 34 (Nov. 1991); Martha Craig Daughtrey, *Commentary: Going Against the Grain: Personal Reflections on the Emergence of Women in the Legal Profession*, 67 Mont. L. Rev. 159, 160 (2006); Alex M. Johnson, Jr., *Why I Am Not a Lawyer: A Contextual Reply*, 8 Nexus 13 (2003).

31. *Call to Action: Diversity in the Legal Profession, Commitment Statement*, *available at* http://apps.americanbar.org/women/leadershipacademy/2010/handouts/calltoaction.pdf (last visited Aug. 16, 2013).

32. Brian Zabcik, *2013 Diversity Scorecard: Firms Regain Lost Ground*, American Lawyer (June 6, 2013), *available at* http://www.americanlawyer.com/PubArticleTAL.jsp?id=1202600856240&2013_Diversity_Scorecard_Firms_Regain_Lost_Ground&slreturn=20130503092008.

managing partners were women. Interestingly, 45 percent of associates in private practice in 2012 were women, and 46.3 percent of summer associates were female.[33]

The presence of minority lawyers in law firms is not reflective of enrollment of minorities in law schools. Minorities have made up some 20 percent of students at law schools since the 1998-1999 academic year. In the 2012-2013 school year, minorities made up 25.8 percent of enrollment. Back in 1971-1972, they accounted for just 6.1 percent of enrollment.[34]

2.   *Women*

Gender diversity at law firms could also be improved. Women are sometimes challenged to continue working at top law firms given the time commitment required. Typically, women graduate from law school and, theoretically, work their way up the associate ranks toward partnership during their peak childbearing years. After a few years of putting in long hours at a law firm, many women opt out:

> There are two conflicting challenges to a female attorney's work-life balance. The first is the idea that successful attorneys with high numbers of billable hours cannot raise children if they are never home with them. The second is the perception that a good mother cannot rise to partnership if her priority is her home. In either case, she will lose. For some women, these roles demand a large amount of time, spreading them too thin to feel successful at either. The life of a professional woman is demanding; she must deal with the extreme pressures of work, only to come home to a "second shift" of caring for children and doing housework—activities in which most men fail to take their proportionate share.[35]

Law firms have made increasing efforts to accommodate the needs of their family-oriented attorneys. Some have offered part-time schedules and telecommuting options. At large law firms, a little over 6 percent of attorneys worked on a part-time basis in 2012. Of those, though, 70 percent were female.[36] These figures are low even though 98 percent of the law firms allowed part-time work in 2012.[37]

---

33. A.B.A. Commission on Women in the Profession, *A Current Glance at Women in the Law* (Feb. 2013), *available at* http://www.americanbar.org/content/dam/aba/marketing/women/current_glance_statistics_feb2013.authcheckdam.pdf.

34. American Bar Association Section of Legal Education & Admissions to the Bar, *First Year J.D. and Total J.D. Minority Enrollment for 1971-2012*, http://www.americanbar.org/content/dam/aba/administrative/legal_education_and_admissions_to_the_bar/statistics/jd_enrollment_1yr_total_minority.authcheckdam.pdf (last visited Aug. 16, 2013).

35. Lea E. Delossantos, *COMMENT: A Tangled Situation of Gender Discrimination: In the Face of an Ineffective Antidiscrimination Rule and Challenges for Women in Law Firms—What Is the Next Step to Promote Gender Diversity in the Legal Profession?* 44 Cal. W. L. Rev. 295, 303-304 (2007).

36. Press Release, NALP, *Rate of Part-Time Work Among Lawyers Unchanged in 2012 Most Working Part-time Continue to Be Women* (Feb. 21, 2013), *available at* http://www.nalp.org/part-time_feb2013?s=part%2Dtime%20lawyers.

37. *Id.*

Although making up about 50 percent of law school classes for decades,[38] women are far from making up 50 percent of the leadership at law firms. Women at law firms hit what some describe as a "maternal wall," a barrier to success:

> In the legal workplace, the effect of the maternal wall becomes readily apparent when female attorneys become pregnant: it is the change in assignments once the pregnancy is announced; it is the constant questions, rumors, and innuendos about whether she will return after her maternity leave; it is the receipt of a nominal or non-existent bonus during the year she has her baby. When she returns from maternity leave, the maternal wall is the non-challenging assignments she gets because everyone assumes her heart and head will be with her baby and not at work; it is the bonuses or promotions she does not get because she does not bill the same hours as her male colleagues, who also may be new fathers but who have wives to stay at home; it is the opportunities she does not get because they involve travel, and it is assumed she will not travel; it is being treated like half of an attorney if she tries to work a reduced-hour schedule. Sometimes, it is the decision to put off motherhood until her career is well-established; and finally, it is the heartbreak when she realizes that she may have waited too long.[39]

N.　WORKPLACE MORALE

Lawyer retention continues to be a problem for law firms, particularly large firms that have hired associates from top law schools. The practice of law at a top law firm can be repetitive and unexciting—not at all as television shows or films depict the workday of an attorney:

> One cluster of problems involves the substance of legal practice and the gap between expectations and realities. Individuals often choose law as a career with little knowledge of what lawyers actually do. Law in prime time media offers some combination of wealth, power, drama, or heroic opportunities. Law in real time is something else, particularly for those at the bottom of the pecking order. The sheer drudgery of many legal matters, particularly in large firms, exacts a heavy price. It is not surprising that recent graduates from the most prestigious schools, although working in the most prestigious firms, express the greatest dissatisfaction with their careers; they expected more from their credentials.
>
> Commentators identify further problems with the substance of legal work. Delgado and Stefancic fault formalism, the law's excessive focus on precedent and authority. Critics also emphasize the adversarial, zero-sum, and uncivil aspects of practice, as well as the pressure without control that characterizes much of associate life. When lawyers function largely as scriveners, or as scapegoats for acrimony not of their own making, they are bound to feel disaffected.[40]

---

38. *See, e.g.*, American Bar Association Section of Legal Education & Admissions to the Bar, *Legal Education Statistics, First Year and Total J.D. Enrollment by Gender 1947-2011*, http://www.americanbar.org/content/dam/aba/administrative/legal_education_and_admissions_to_the_bar/statistics/jd_enrollment_1yr_total_gender.authcheckdam.pdf (last visited Aug. 16, 2013).

39. Nicole Buonocore Porter, *Re-Defining Superwoman: An Essay on Overcoming the "Maternal Wall" in the Legal Workplace*, 13 Duke J. Gender L. & Pol'y 55, 56 (2006).

40. Deborah L. Rhode, *Symposium: Perspectives on Lawyer Happiness: Foreword: Personal Satisfaction in Professional Practice*, 58 Syracuse L. Rev. 217, 223-24 (2008).

Law firms can make efforts to increase lawyer satisfaction. They might make efforts to provide more challenging assignments and try to improve the firm's culture.

1. Law Firm Stresses

Putting in a lot of hours, working as an adversary, and constantly picking apart an opponent's arguments all take their toll. Lawyers might turn to drugs or alcohol as a way to alleviate workplace stress. Some suffer silently. By some estimates, 19 percent of lawyers experience depression at some point, while only 6.7 percent of the general population does. An estimated 20 percent of lawyers—twice that of the general population—abuse alcohol.[41]

Some states have created lawyer assistance programs to help lawyers who have substance abuse problems. Indicators of substance abuse by attorneys include the following:

Early Stage

- **Professional:** client neglect, unreturned phone calls, late for depositions, cancelled appointments, numerous "sick" days.
- **Legal:** 1st DUI, open container, disorderly conduct.
- **Ethical:** late for hearings, "technical" trust violations (reconciliations, ledger cards), "last minute" filings, failure to diligently prosecute/defend.

Late Stage

- **Professional:** failure to come to the office and/or appear for hearings, intoxicated in court, unprofessional appearance/hygiene, inappropriate mood (depressed, angry, withdrawn), abandonment of practice.
- **Legal:** 2nd DUI, controlled substance charge, domestic violence.
- **Ethical:** substantive trust violations (misappropriation), statute of limitations violations, dishonesty to tribunal.[42]

2. Balancing Work and Personal Time

Ultimately, the individual lawyer is responsible for achieving a balance between work and personal time that satisfies, or at least is tolerable to, him or her. Law firms have made efforts to ease lawyers' pain, but the reality of big-firm practice still demands dedication and a concomitant time commitment. Lawyers who do not want to dedicate 80 hours a week to their careers have sought out alternative

---

41. *See, e.g.,* Cassens Weiss, *Lawyer Depression Comes Out of the Closet,* A.B.A. J. L. News Now (Dec. 13, 2007), http://www.abajournal.com/news/lawyer_depression_comes_out_of_the_closet; Tyger Latham, *The Depressed Lawyer,* Psychology Today (May 2, 2011), http://www.in.gov/judiciary/ijlap/substance-abuse/signs-symptoms.html.

42. Indiana Judges and Lawyers Assistance Program, *Signs and Symptoms in Attorneys, available at* http://www.in.gov/judiciary/ijlap/2357.htm (last visited on Aug. 16, 2013).

paths—moving to smaller law firms, going on part-time status, working in-house, telecommuting. Some lawyers actually do put their careers on hold for a while as they pursue other interests, and then they return to the profession, or even to their original law firm, years later.

CHECKLIST

- The human resources management team at a law firm is charged with handling all phases of employment at a firm, from hiring to performance appraisal through termination and retirement.
- A law firm's mission statement specifies the type of work a firm does, explains the firm's philosophy and core values, and educates prospective clients about the firm's capabilities and its approach to the law.
- Associates as well as staff at law firms are typically hired as employees at will. Some firms hire temporary, or contract, employees to work for the firm for specified periods of time or to handle specific projects.
- The Equal Employment Opportunity Act prohibits employment discrimination based on race, color, religion, sex, or national origin.
- The Fair Labor Standards Act establishes a minimum wage and overtime pay requirements.
- The Americans with Disabilities Act bars discrimination against people with disabilities who are capable of performing a job. Employers are required to make reasonable accommodation for employees so long as that accommodation does not cause undue hardship.
- The Family and Medical Leave Act provides that employees may take 12 weeks of unpaid leave due to health conditions, birth, adoption of a child, or care for a family member who is ill.
- The Age Discrimination in Employment Act of 1967 bans discrimination against people aged 40 and older.
- The Equal Pay Act bars discrimination based on sex.
- The Consolidated Omnibus Budget Reconciliation Act of 1985, or COBRA, allows employees who leave their jobs to continue their health insurance coverage for themselves, their spouses, and their children for 18 months (and, in some cases, longer if the employee became disabled) through the employer's group health plan by paying for it.
- The Patient Protection and Affordable Care Act, known as Obamacare, requires employers to provide health insurance coverage and individuals to maintain minimum levels of insurance or they face a penalty.
- Typically, recruiting and hiring at law firms occur on two separate tracks: one for attorneys and a different one for support personnel.
- A law firm should have an employee manual, or handbook, that serves as an introduction to a law firm and addresses standard operating procedures for office conduct.
- Turnover at law firms is expensive for the firms. Firms are taking steps to reduce their attrition rates and to improve workplace morale.
- Firms are paying greater attention to diversity and are making efforts to hire more women and minorities.
- Many states have created lawyer assistance programs to help lawyers who have substance abuse problems.

VOCABULARY

attrition (49)
contract employee (28)
employment at will (28)
firm history (27)
headhunter (42)
mission statement (27)
perquisite, or "perk" (47)
sexual harassment (30)

CAREER PREPARATION TIPS

Remember when undertaking a job hunt that you are selecting an employer as much as an employer is selecting you. Research law firm mission statements and firm histories, search for any case law or record of employment violations, and look at the media coverage of firms or other organizations for which you would like to work. Consider how you might modify mission statements or otherwise add value to a firm with respect to its human resources obligations. Assess whether you might be interested in being involved with human resources and talent management. How might you enhance a firm's culture?

IF YOU WANT TO LEARN MORE

The Center for WorkLife Law is a nonprofit organization focusing on research and advocacy in the area of worklife law. The PAR Research Institute, formerly known as the Project for Attorney Retention, studies retention and develops best practices and is now part of the Center for WorkLife Law. http://www.worklifelaw.org

Information about equal employment opportunity law is available from the Equal Employment Opportunity Commission. http://www.eeoc.gov

Information on the Americans with Disabilities Act, proposed regulations, enforcement actions, legal briefs, settlement agreements, and the like is Act home page. http://www.ADA.gov

The Fair Labor Standards Act is addressed on the site of the U.S. Department of Labor. http://www.dol.gov/compliance/laws/comp-flsa.htm

The Web site Lawyers with Depression, started by a practicing lawyer who suffered from depression, is dedicated to lawyers who are similarly afflicted. http://www.lawyerswithdepression.com/

Materials helpful for human resources management and other aspects of law office management are available from the Legal Management Resource Center, which is hosted by the Association of Legal Administrators. Some materials are accessible by nonmembers. http://www.alanet.org/research/

Minority Corporate Counsel Association. http://mcca.com/

Information about the Family and Medical Leave Act is available from the U.S. Department of Labor. http://www.dol.gov/whd/fmla/

READING COMPREHENSION

1. How does a firm's mission statement differ from a firm's history?
2. What are the negative aspects to working for a law firm as a contract employee?
3. How have law firms tried to evade liability for workplace discrimination?
4. Can a lawyer decline to represent a prospective client because the prospective client has a disability?
5. Must a firm hold a job open for an employee who takes time off pursuant to the Family and Medical Leave Act?
6. Why is it important to conduct a background check of a prospective employee?
7. For what purposes is an employee handbook used?
8. What steps are some law firms taking to encourage employee retention?
9. What challenges do women and minorities still face at law firms?

DISCUSSION STARTERS

1. Read *Hishon v. King & Spalding*. How did the defendant law firm attempt to evade its responsibilities under the Equal Employment Opportunity Act? Consider the circumstances in which an individual associate was pursuing a high-powered law firm. Do you think that was an intimidating situation to be in? Do you think the outcome of the case was fair?
2. Review the settlement agreement between Joseph David Camacho and the United States. How did Camacho violate the Americans with Disabilities Act? Do you think the punishment was fair or overly broad? What impact to you think this matter had on Camacho's law practice?
3. Read the U.S. Equal Employment Opportunity Commission's announcement concerning its settlement of an age discrimination suit with the law firm Sidley Austin. What misbehavior was the law firm accused of? How did the firm attempt to evade its responsibilities under the Age Discrimination in Employment Act? Do you think the settlement was fair?

4. Consider the information presented in the chapter on the percentages of women and minorities in law firms. Given the increasing numbers of women and minorities attending law school, why aren't more of them becoming partners and associates in law firms? What do you suppose women and minority law school graduates do if they are unable to obtain a job at a major law firm?

5. Suppose you are a young lawyer at a major law firm. Would you be willing to accept a lower salary in exchange for a reduction in billable-hours requirements? Would the amount of your education loans have an impact on your decision?

CASE STUDIES

1. Locate a law firm's mission statement online and review and critique it. What message does the statement convey? What are the statement's weak points? How might the message be strengthened? Is the statement too general?

2. Choose one element of a law firm staff manual to study. Research variations for drafting the element, and compare and contrast them. For instance, one element in a law firm manual might address casual Fridays.

3. Look at several law firm histories and compare and contrast them. You might consider accessing these sites:
   - http://www.drinkerbiddle.com/about-us
   - http://www.saul.com/about-history.html
   - http://www.cgsh.com/about/firmtimeline/
   - http://www.arnoldporter.com/about_the_firm_who_we_are_history.cfm
   - http://www.youtube.com/watch?v=QFEWV64RISU

   In undertaking your analysis, address each of the following. What common elements does each firm history have? Which history is more compelling? How do you think the firms want the reader to respond to the history? What does the history tell prospective employees and prospective clients about the firm's character and track record? What might have been omitted from the firm's history? Research negative episodes in the firm's past. Were those covered in the firm history? How long is the firm's history? Is the length appropriate, or should it be shorter or longer? Why?

4. Suppose you are a candidate in a job interview, and the interviewer asks an inappropriate question, such as "How will you handle child care?" How might you respond? Would your response differ depending on the amount of interest you have in being offered the job for which you are interviewing?

5. How would you react to receiving a poor performance evaluation?

6. Suppose you are a human resources manager at a law firm who has been asked to deal with a mail-room clerk who is chronically late and frequently absent from work. How would you address the problem?

CHAPTER

3

The Physical Law Office

CHAPTER OUTCOMES

By the end of this chapter, a student will be able to:

- Recognize facility management issues that arise with respect to law firms and propose solutions
- Develop workplace safety hazards for law offices and devise means to minimize those hazards
- Discuss how law firms are incorporating principles of sustainability in facility operations
- Evaluate a firm's selections of equipment and supplies and office design and decor
- Plan a law office's move

As bland as some law offices appear to be, a fair amount of thought may actually have gone into the presentation of the space. Walk into the reception area of a large law firm, and you might be met with a decor that signals cold, clean efficiency. Walk into a street-level firm that focuses on immigration law in a poor area, and you might see what looks like a storefront, with big windows and welcoming signs in English and in other languages—making a foreigner's experience of asking for legal help in a non-native land a bit less intimidating. A law office, with its space alone, conveys an image. Is this a luxurious, high-end firm where every client's whim will be accommodated? Is this a family law practice, with a lot of clients traipsing in to see their lawyers and bringing their kids along? The right planning can enhance a client's experience—and satisfaction—as well as make a lawyer's workday more pleasant.

Signals about firm culture can be gleaned from a firm's space. Is the managing partner in an office on the top floor, or can the firm's leaders be found "in the trenches" near lower-level partners and associates? Are paralegals relegated to dark, cramped spaces in lower floors, or are their offices or workstations near the lawyers they interact with frequently? Is the art on the walls staid and old, or is it contemporary and brightly colored? Are the walls white or paneled? Many elements of a firm's appearance can signal information about a firm's approach to the law, to its clients, and to its personnel. And, of course, a well-planned workspace can boost efficiency.

A.   FACILITY MANAGEMENT

**facility man-
agement:**
Coordination of
a business's
workspace,
involving over-
sight of build-
ings as well as
services.

A law firm might be a tenant in a building, own its own building, or even own a portion of a building. No matter what the arrangement, someone needs to assume the responsibility for **facility management.** If the space is leased, a landlord or its management company typically makes sure that the windows are cleaned periodically, that the boiler in the building is functioning, and that public hallways and the lobby are maintained. Responsibility for general cleaning of the firm's offices may vary—again, the landlord's cleaning team might dust, vacuum, and empty trash cans. Alternatively, the firm might be responsible for hiring its own cleaning crew. If that is the case, someone needs to make those arrangements, schedule cleaning, and be sure that the cleaning crew is paid. These tasks might fall to a law office manager.

The responsibilities for different sorts of facility management tasks might be given to various people. An overhead light bulb might blow out, a pipe might burst, carpeting might have become stained and need to be cleaned. How is each of these scenarios handled both within the firm itself and with respect to the landlord or managing agent? If an associate spills a cup of coffee on the carpeting in her office, whom should she contact to get it cleaned? A point person within the firm may be designated to handle facilities issues. That person, in turn, might carry on any necessary correspondence with building management or with the firm's hired cleaning crews or other vendors servicing the firm, such as plumbers, fish-tank maintenance crews, or florists. If the refrigerator in the firm kitchen breaks, who fixes it? Who is responsible for making the call to get someone to fix it? Who is responsible for paying the repairperson? All of these matters must be addressed.

sustainability:
The conditions
in which
humans and
nature can exist
in harmony so
that social, eco-
nomic, and
environmental
needs of cur-
rent and future
generations can
be met.

Environmental concerns are also addressed in facility management and elsewhere within law firms. Law firms might decrease the impact of their businesses on the environment by taking measures to reduce the amount of energy used in their offices, by recycling paper and other materials, and by taking other steps to preserve and protect resources. In so doing, law firms may realize significant financial savings while being better "corporate citizens." The U.S. Environmental Protection Agency explains that **sustainability** is "the conditions under which humans and nature can exist in productive harmony, that permit fulfilling the social, economic and other requirements of present and future generations."[1]

The Council of American Bar Association Section of Environment, Energy and Resources has approved a Sustainability Framework for Law Organizations that demonstrates how sustainability relates to the legal industry. The framework includes a model policy and implementation guidelines. Efforts to become more sustainable typically begin by conducting a benchmark survey indicating how many resources are used and where. Then a plan for reducing the amount of resources used can be developed and implemented.[2] Some firms are also

---

1. U.S. Environmental Protection Agency, *Sustainability: Basic Information,* http://www.epa.gov/sustainability/basicinfo.htm (last visited Aug. 18, 2013).
2. For additional information on how a law firm can become more sustainable, *see, e.g.,* U.S. Environmental Protection Agency, *ABA/EPA Law Firm Climate Challenge,* http://www.epa.gov/greenpower/initiatives/aba_challenge.htm (last updated Oct. 16, 2012).

developing sustainability policies, reporting on their efforts, creating committees on sustainability, and hiring chief sustainability officers or other staff to manage sustainability efforts.[3]

Law firms undertake sustainable efforts for many reasons. They can demonstrate that they are concerned about the planet, improve workplace morale, and save money.[4] Corporate clients increasingly are inquiring about their lawyers' sustainability efforts. Becoming more sustainable can be a way for law firms to be more competitive.

B. WORKPLACE SAFETY

Despite being staffed with fine legal minds, law firms are, unfortunately, not crime-free zones. An employee might still be involved in an ugly divorce and an embittered, about-to-be-former spouse might stalk the person, an office worker could commit a petty theft and lift wallets from lawyers' purses, a disgruntled former client might hack into the firm's Web site, or a random act of violence might occur. Crime can happen anywhere, at firms of all shapes and sizes, in high-end buildings and low-rent ones.

Consider these events that have happened in law firms:

- In July 2013, a former client of the Upton Law Firm, a small firm in Covington, Louisiana, began shooting a gun in the firm's parking lot, then broke through its security system while its law firm manager was inside, and fired more shots in the office before killing himself there.[5]
- A temporary worker in the Atlanta, Georgia, office of Paul Hastings shot and killed a secretary at the firm before killing himself outside the building. Apparently, the two had been romantically involved at one point.[6]
- A partner at Boggs, Boggs & Bates in Clayton, Missouri, was shot and killed and found by the office cleaning people. Another lawyer in the building told a reporter that security was nonexistent in the building.[7]
- A 26-year-old Florida lawyer who had recently been elected to the board of governors of his state bar association's young lawyers division and who was

---

3. *See, e.g.,* Lori Tripoli, *Sustainability: What Law Firms Have at Stake,* Of Counsel 19-22 (May 2012); William R. Blackburn, *Sustainability: How Values-Driven Law Firms Are Surviving Tough Times and Prospering Over the Long Term,* Law Practice Today (Sept. 2010), *available at* http://apps.americanbar.org/lpm/lpt/articles/pdf/ftr09103.pdf; ABA, *The ABA-EPA Law Office Climate Challenge,* http://www.americanbar.org/groups/environment_energy_resources/projects_awards/aba_epa_law_office_climate_challenge.html (last visited Aug. 18, 2013).

4. *See, e.g.,* William R. Blackburn, *SEER Sustainability Framework for Law Organizations* (Dec. 10, 2010), *available at* http://www.americanbar.org.

5. Heather Nolan, *One Dead After Bizarre Shooting at Covington Law Firm,* Times-Picayune (July 30, 2013), *available at* http://www.nola.com/crime/indexssf/2013/07/police_investigating_bizarre_s.html; Martha Neil, *Ex-Client Committed Suicide After Breaking into Law Firm and Firing Dozens of Rounds, Say Police,* ABA J. (July 30, 2013), *available at* http://www.abajournal.com/news/article/ex-client_presumed_dead_after_breaking_into_la_law_firm_and_shooting_every/.

6. *Murder-Suicide at Paul Hastings in Atlanta,* Above the Law (blog), (Apr. 28, 2008).

7. Allison Retka, *'Prince of a Guy' Shot Dead in Clayton Law Office,* Daily Rec. (St. Louis), Dec. 21, 2006, n.p.

expecting his first child with his wife, was shot and killed in his office by his father-in-law.[8]

- In July 1993, an unhappy former client of Pettit & Martin in San Francisco went on a rampage at the firm's offices and shot 14 people, killing eight of them, before killing himself.[9]

Although no office is really impenetrable, law firms can take measures to better insulate themselves from the likelihood of violence and other crimes. They can engage in better employee screening and "harden" their office building to make it more secure from attacks on power lines, on the Internet, or from human outsiders. Security measures can be developed, implemented, and enforced. For instance, a firm might require all visitors, even deliverypersons, to sign in. Those who have business with someone at the firm might be escorted to the appropriate meeting place so that they cannot wander freely around the offices. Staff may be taught about workplace violence issues. For example, a firm might train employees how to recognize the warning signs of violence and what to do if violence erupts at the law firm.[10]

The possibility of someone engaging in inappropriate behavior in an office can be decreased if visiting clients are required to be escorted by a firm employee. A firm should establish whether messengers may deliver documents to someone personally in the office or whether they must leave their material with the firm's receptionist. A firm might also install a "panic button" that would alert either the police or senior firm officials to an immediate problem. A code phrase might be established for the firm's receptionist to use in case of trouble that would not be apparent to an evildoer. Procedures for locking office doors should be established. Will the doors be locked at 5:00 P.M. every day? Who will be responsible for locking them? Who is entitled to have a key to the office for weekend access? Those keys should be tracked. If an employee leaves the firm, the key must be turned in.

Procedures should be developed for handling emergencies. Important telephone numbers should be posted at several places in an office, along with the firm's address and location. People typically know to dial 911 in an emergency. But must a 9 be dialed first to get to an outside line? If an office building has guards at the front desk, is their number posted so that security could be summoned before police arrive? Knowing one's own workplace address might seem obvious, but workers under duress typically are not able to focus on details such as addresses. They might come to work via subway and never really notice the exact street name or number. If an office building is in an office park, a worker might not be able to accurately describe which building the firm is in.

The procedures manual should address various scenarios, such as what to do if someone has a heart attack in the office or suffers an injury on the job. Where are first-aid materials located? Who is responsible for notifying the person's family or significant others? Where can that information be found? A firm should also develop fire evacuation plans as well as plans for responding to natural

---

8. *Meador Murdered at Work: 30-Year-Old Lawyer Was Just Elected to YLD Board*, Fla. B. News, Feb. 2005, at 10.

9. *See, e.g.*, Benjamin Sells, *Our Fears Ignite When Tragedy Strikes So Close to Home*, Ill. Legal Times, July 1994, at 29; Jill Chanen, *After San Francisco, Law Firms Take Aim at Office Security*, Chi. Law., Aug. 1993, at 78.

10. *See, e.g.*, Jill E. Jachera & Joseph A. Piesco Jr., *Violence in the Workplace*, Metropolitan Corp. Couns., Northeast Ed., Nov. 2001, at 24.

calamities such as floods, earthquakes, or hurricanes. Procedures for something as seemingly minor as a power failure should also be established. Who is responsible for calling in the problem to the appropriate utility? Must an account number be accessed? Where is that information stored? Should all computers be turned off if a power failure occurs? Should other precautionary steps be taken? These sorts of matters should be thought about ahead of time—procedures should be developed and distributed, and everyone at the firm should be educated about them.

C.   DISASTER PREPAREDNESS

Responses to large-scale catastrophes should also factor into a law firm's planning. As unlikely as these sorts of events are, they do happen—and their consequences can be far-reaching for businesses. The 9/11 terrorist attacks on the World Trade Center in New York City in 2001 dislocated some law firms and inspired leadership at others to take **disaster preparedness plans** seriously.[11]

All sorts of calamities—floods, fires, terrorist attacks—may occur. Think of the bombing of the Alfred P. Murrah Federal Building in Oklahoma City in 1995, the delivery of anthrax-contaminated letters to government and private offices in 2001, the blackout on much of the East Coast of the United States in 2003, the impact of Hurricane Katrina on New Orleans and Mississippi in 2005, and the damage brought by Hurricane Sandy to the East Coast of the United States in 2012. In such cases, landline phone systems might not work, cell phones may be jammed, e-mail messages may not be delivered through servers, and employees might not know where or to whom they are supposed to report. While it is impossible to envision every sort of worst-case scenario, a plan should be developed for employees to follow in emergency situations. Should they all be required to report within a certain time? To whom should they report if the office is no longer accessible? How will employees who do not report be contacted? Via phone? Via their own personal e-mail accounts? Who will be responsible for contacting these people? Where are updated contact lists kept and maintained?

> **disaster preparedness plan:** A set of procedures devised for responding to emergency situations.

Technological aids can help law firms in times of crisis. Electronic alert systems can be set up in advance and instant notifications sent out.[12]

In addition, a disaster preparedness plan should include data backup, procurement and maintenance of appropriate insurance, and a means for keeping employee contact information up to date. People must be able to contact one another. Along those lines, more than one person at a firm should know where its assets are and should maintain account numbers, inventories, and records of service providers and service contracts. Perhaps most important, the firm should not merely draft a disaster response plan—it should also actually conduct disaster exercises in which employees practice implementing that plan.

---

11. Brenna G. Nava, *Comment, Hurricane Katrina: The Duties and Responsibilities of an Attorney in the Wake of a Natural Disaster*, 37 St. Mary's L.J. 1153, 1161-62 (2006) (citations omitted).

12. *See, e.g.*, Geoffrey N. Smith, *Thinking the Unthinkable*, Law Firm Inc., Nov. 2007 (quoting Steven Spiess, executive director, Cravath, Swaine & Moore).

business continuity plan: A set of procedures and information for continuing to provide services in the face of a disruptive event.

A **business continuity plan** should establish a hierarchy of people responsible for handling the firm's business in the event of a disaster. Who will phone key clients to reassure them? Where are their names and contact information? Who is responsible for contacting insurers? Where are copies of appropriate policies? Files should be backed up and stored in remote locations or in the cloud. After 9/11, some New York City law firms had to call their adversaries to try to re-create their files.[13] Although a spirit of cooperation tends to exist after a terrorist attack, better preparation can prevent the scampering that some firms had to do when disaster did indeed strike. A business continuity plan will help a firm determine damage to its personnel, building, and technology, and will provide a roadmap of steps to take to get the business operational again following a disaster.[14]

It should also be remembered that disasters have a psychological impact on people. Employees, stunned by events and, perhaps, by grief at the loss of coworkers and friends, probably will not be functioning as well as they normally do. Disasters are life-changing. It's only to be expected that the trauma of such an occurrence will trickle down to the workplace. A firm might consider bringing in grief counselors or providing employees with other options should the stress of events have too great an impact on their work.

D. EQUIPMENT AND SUPPLIES

Lawyers need certain basic materials to work with: paper, pens, computers, printers, copiers. They also need access to a law library and to online databases of the law, such as Lexis or Westlaw. Someone needs to order those supplies, arrange for access to fee-based databases, and purchase and maintain the equipment. A law office manager might be responsible for reordering supplies, planning for future needs, making sure that equipment is maintained, overseeing service contracts and warranties, and making sure that new hires get the machines they need, such as a desktop computer, a laptop, an iPhone, or other smartphone that has Internet access and e-mail capability, and a tablet computer.

Large law firms may have information technology (IT) departments to handle technological issues for the entire firm. These firms are in positions to develop their own software when it is needed or to have it specially developed by someone else. IT specialists within a firm might vet products and make recommendations to a law firm committee that has purchasing authority. Because a large firm makes significant purchases, vendors might bid for the firm's business. Other firms might look to outside consultants when making IT decisions. It is important to let the people who will actually be using an application give it a try to make sure they like it. Firms might try to obtain an evaluation copy of a software program prior to making a major purchase:

> There's usually a big difference between what people say things can do and what
> they actually can do. . . . It's not that those software vendors are used car salesmen

---

13. *See, e.g.,* Constance L. Hays, *Trying to Reweave Threads of Tattered Offices,* N.Y. Times, Sept. 23, 2001, at Money and Business 7.

14. ABA Special Committee on Disaster Response and Preparedness, Surviving Disaster: A Lawyer's Guide to Disaster Planning (2011), available at http://www.americanbar.org/groups/committees/disaster.html.

trying to unload lemons. "They just don't necessarily know the intricacies of your environment and how you've customized other applications[.]"[15]

No matter the size of the firm, data storage, accessibility, and backup must be addressed. Decision makers also must be sure that lawyers and staff know how to use office equipment and software. Lawyers tend to resist taking time out for training sessions, while administrative staff tend to be better trained on applications. If the lawyers at a firm are not going to take the time to learn how to use all of the fancy add-ons in a computer program, why pay to procure them?

Lawyers must be able to communicate with their clients. A client who cannot open attachments because her lawyer is using an older version of a software program is quickly going to become an unhappy client. A firm's aptitude with technology can actually affect firm retention and recruiting. Lawyers want and need the support of technology to do their jobs well; a law office lagging in this area will not be so attractive to them. Moreover, the comments to Model Rule 1.1 addressing competence specify that a lawyer should keep current about applicable technology used in law practice along with its benefits and risks.[16]

In the past, law firms largely drove the decision about which technology to use. Would the firm use computers or Mac-based applications? Would the word processing program be WordPerfect or Microsoft Word? Now, more and more, clients are driving that decision.

Lawyers must remember to plan for the future and anticipate their upcoming technological needs. At this point, typewriters are essentially obsolete, and, with the improvement in scanning capability from document to computer, fax machines are not often needed anymore either.

With advances in technology, there is always talk about shifting to a paper-free office. Despite advances in digital storage and scanning abilities, law offices still require significant amounts of paper, although they may use less paper than in earlier decades as lawyers rely less on printouts and review more documents and correspondence on-screen. Client files may be more accessible—and more portable—on a computer than in a thick accordion file. Lawyers rely less on paper products such as books and magazines, as they have moved to a digital medium.[17]

Even so, hard copies of many documents must still be kept and maintained. Among its supplies, a law firm needs a fair number of filing cabinets as well as a means of tracking files and providing long-term storage for them.

E. TELECOMMUNICATION SYSTEMS

Much of a lawyer's business is conducted via telephone, whether land-based or wireless. Similarly, lawyers do a lot of work via the Internet, transmitting documents and sending e-mail messages to clients, courts, opposing counsel, and

---

15. Lori Tripoli, *Don't Get Caught with a 1.0 in a 5.0 World*, Of Counsel, May 2007, at 10, 12 (quoting Mark Wilson, senior manager of applications development and project management at Dickstein Shapiro in Washington, D.C.).

16. Model Rules of Prof'l Conduct R. 1.1 cmt (2013).

17. Paper cut, 26(37) Lawyer 30 (Sept. 24, 2012).

**telecommuni-
cation system:**
Means of trans-
mitting signals
for the purpose
of communicat-
ing via tele-
phone, com-
puter, radio,
television, and
other devices.

others. Clients might expect a response to an e-mail message within hours, not days. A lawyer's need for e-mail access can be nearly constant. Security of these **telecommunication systems** must be maintained so that data transmitted or accessed from a remote location are safe. Telecommunication systems may need to be expanded as the firm and its needs grow.

Very basic questions about a firm's telephone service must be addressed. How are calls handled that are received at the firm's main telephone number? How easily are those phone calls forwarded to appropriate extensions or to lawyers in remote offices? What happens during busy times? Are calls automatically directed to voice mail? If a call is placed on hold, does music play? If so, what is the source of that music? Are radio stations clients of the firm? Should their stations be played? What arrangements must be made for a conference call to be conducted, recorded, and transcribed? Does caller ID work even if a call is first received at the firm's main phone number and then forwarded to a lawyer? Does each phone time calls to help lawyers track their billable hours? How quickly can employees learn the phone system?

**Voice over
Internet Proto-
col (VoIP):** A
means of trans-
mitting voice
communica-
tions over the
Internet.

Lawyers and appropriate personnel at firms must keep up with technological advances, such as the use of **Voice over Internet Protocol** (VoIP), which can reduce costs. Advances in telephone capabilities allow each lawyer to have a single phone number that forwards calls seamlessly and makes communications from clients easier. Wireless capacity, both for cell phone calls and for transmission of data, must also be considered, budgeted for, and securely protected.

When a firm procures a new telecommunication system, a strategy for converting to the new system must be developed. For instance, a firm might roll out its new telecommunication system in one office at a time, starting with smaller ones, to see how it goes and work out glitches before the large home office makes the transition. Sometimes, despite a firm's best intentions and significant investment, major malfunctions occur.[18]

F.   PARKING SPACES

Parking would seem to be a simple matter. If there's a lot, park in it; if not, park wherever you can. Yet all sorts of issues can arise if a law firm has a designated parking area. Who will get the best spots? Will they be reserved for senior partners? For an "employee of the year"? Or should parking simply be first come, first served? Should spaces closest to the office be designated for clients?

Will free parking be provided for lawyers only, or for lawyers and staff? Will clients be reimbursed for their parking costs or have their parking tickets stamped? All clients or only major clients? And who will decide?

A firm might choose to use parking as a sustainability incentive for its personnel. For instance, bike racks might be set up close to the firm's front doors, and

---

18. *See, e.g.,* Matt Hamblen, *Detroit Law Firm Fends off 'Nasty' VoIP Problems,* Computerworld (Aug. 9, 2006), http://www.computerworld.com/action/article.do?command=viewArticleBasic&articleId=9002298.

the closest parking spaces might be reserved for people who carpool or for those who drive an environmentally friendly car, such as a Toyota Prius.

Parking can also be linked to security. If someone is leaving the firm after dark, should an escort to the parking lot be provided? If so, who is that escort? A security guard from the firm's building? Is escort service provided as part of the firm's lease? If not, will additional fees be charged for escort service? Will escort service be available to everyone, or only to clients or lawyers?

G. OFFICE DESIGN AND DECOR

A law firm's physical appearance makes a statement about the firm's mission, its attitude, and even its level of success. Old, aristocratic, staid law firms might still choose dark, wood-paneled interiors and artwork featuring centuries-old paintings of forebears or ships. Firms doing business with a lot of dot-com, cutting-edge, new-generation companies might choose a bright interior with design elements conveying a message of high energy and creativity. A firm with battered wooden desks and dust bunnies in the corners or one with a decor not updated since the 1970s also sends a message about how it is performing—and the message might not be such a good one.

Ideally, a firm's space should be efficient as well as effective in both conveying the image the firm seeks and pleasing clients. Balancing all three with budgetary needs can be challenging. If a firm's decor appears too luxurious, it may actually be off-putting even to high-end clients who might believe their legal bills are going to fund the firm's interior designer. An interior that features contemporary, progressive art may offend big-business clients who have a more conservative view of the world.

Both a firm's exterior and public spaces must be considered, as should individual lawyer offices and staff work areas. A firm might develop basic or very detailed guidelines for lawyers and others about decorating their workspaces. The firm's lease might limit some of the changes that can be made, such as to window treatments and wall colors. Firms might have standard-issue furniture for everyone or allow partners to choose from a few different models—or grant them free rein entirely in selecting office furniture. Some lawyers choose to incorporate elements of the practice in decorating their spaces. For instance, one prominent divorce lawyer collects antique marriage certificates, which she has framed and mounted on her office walls. Whether clients are permitted to visit a lawyer's office may influence how it is decorated. Lawyers tend to spend a lot of time in their offices and may opt to create a workspace that is pleasing to them personally.

For staff, a firm should consider the extent to which decoration of personal workspace will be permitted. Again, whether clients ever view the space should be a consideration. Some offices hold "decorate your carrel" contests—with sometimes outrageous results. Guidelines, ideally, should be drafted and included in the firm's handbook.

1. *Firm Image*

Color, furniture style, wall coverings—all convey subtle messages about a law firm. Are the drapes clean or dusty? Is the firm's reception area bright and full of light, or does it darkly convey an air of solemnity? Is the overall effect of a firm's decor one of lavishness or of stark efficiency? Will clients be impressed, or will they think they are paying their lawyers too much money?

Not only are clients affected and influenced by a firm's appearance, but so are the people who work there. In making decorating decisions, a firm should consider its demographics. Older lawyers might prefer a more hierarchical approach to offices, with large ones designated for more senior partners. The younger generation might be satisfied with good electronics—up-to-the-minute computers with speakers and in-office wireless Internet access so they can use their laptops anywhere.

The appearance of the firm's offices can also affect recruiting. Do paralegals work in high-walled, gray cubicles in windowless interior space, or do they have a more open workspace or even an office? Must junior associates share an office? Are more senior support staff granted personal office space? The work environment may be a vital factor in a prospective hire's willingness to come on board.

2. *Firm Politics: Varying Office Size Based on Rank Versus Same-Size Offices*

Traditionally, large offices in law firms were designated for senior-ranking partners. Both office size and location (such as in the corner of a building and on a high floor) conveyed one's place in the firm's hierarchy. Windowless, interior offices were designated for paralegals or other firm staff; offices that have windows were reserved for lawyers, with office size increasing as the lawyer's status within the firm rose.

More recently, though, office space has been shrinking. When one Philadelphia- based boutique firm relocated, partner offices were downsized from 20 feet by 15 feet at the firm's former space to 15 feet by 15 feet in the new one. Everyone was issued a standard set of furniture, except for some partners who brought their own.[19]

Determining who gets the prime real estate in a law office can cause political intrigue. A firm might base such decisions on pecking order (with firm leadership getting the prime choices), on tenure with the firm, on the number of years since graduating from law school, or on any number of factors. Sometimes jockeying for a prime office can seem like playing musical chairs. Having a system in place for determining how office spaces are assigned, though, can minimize the amount of politics and grousing about who gets what and when.

As for the furnishings in the offices, the law firm itself might choose the furniture for associates and for staff. At one time, when a lawyer was elevated to partner, he or she was given a stipend of $12,000 or more to decorate the office. As budgets have tightened, some firms stopped doing that, and some even require that uniform furniture be used or that selections be made from several

---

19. Lori Tripoli, *Trading Spaces*, Law Firm Inc., Jan./Feb. 2006.

predetermined options.[20] Nowadays freshly minted partners might be a bit reticent to spend a lot of money on their new offices, since they know they'll be switching offices within their firm as their careers proceed, or they might even switch firms at some point in the future.

3. Ergonomics

The term *ergonomics* refers to how well people interact with the objects that they use. **Ergonomics** is defined as "an applied science concerned with the characteristics of people that need to be considered in designing things that they use in order that people and things will interact most effectively and safely—called also *human engineering, human factors engineering*[.]"[21]

Lawyering might seem like a relatively hazard-free position, but job-related injuries can still occur. If your computer screen is not set at a proper level, your neck might hurt at the end of the day, or your back might ache from sitting in an improperly positioned chair. Repetitive stress injuries, such as carpal tunnel syndrome, can occur in workers who use computer keyboards.

In addition to providing well-designed office furniture and equipment, law firms (and any other business, for that matter) should make sure that computers and related equipment are properly positioned. Workers should be trained to maintain appropriate posture. Ergonomics experts can be hired to assist in office design and setup and to teach personnel how to properly use equipment to minimize the risk of repetitive stress injury. Productivity can increase in an ergonomically designed office.

ergonomics: The study of the relationship between people and their working environment geared toward maximizing productivity while ensuring health and safety of workers by providing appropriately designed tools for work-related tasks.

4. Efficiency

Workspaces and, indeed, entire law offices should be designed to maximize worker efficiency. To the extent a budget allows, sufficient electrical outlets, telephone extensions, Internet connections, printers, and other equipment should be provided so that workers, whether staff or attorneys, do not waste time on unbillable activities.

At the same time, a firm, both for economic reasons and to be economically responsible, may want to incorporate sustainable design elements into the workplace. Natural lighting might be used to reduce electricity bills, office lights might be turned off at night, and temperature levels might be lowered during nighttime hours in the winter and raised in the summer. Energy-efficient light bulbs might be procured and other efforts taken to reduce waste and to recycle otherwise discarded items.

5. Professional Designers

Architects, interior designers, and other consultants who focus on office space or even specialize in the design of law offices can be retained to provide advice

---

20. *Id.*

21. Medline Plus Medical Dictionary, entry for ergonomics, http://www2.merriam-webster.com/cgi-bin/mwmednlm (last visited Aug. 18, 2013).

on how a firm can develop the most impressive, yet functional, workspace given its budgetary constraints. It may seem that all that's needed are a few desks, chairs, phones, and computers, but to be in business, far more attention to work-space is needed to create an appealing environment that is attractive to both workers and clients. Getting advice from experts can prevent a firm from making costly mistakes. So, for example, a decorator might be able to inform an other-wise oblivious firm that gray is not the ideal color for carpeting. Yes, it's neutral, inoffensive, and likely to hide dirt, but it's also associated with boredom, sadness, and grief. Intense colors, though possibly unappealing to some, can improve workers' creativity, energy levels, and productivity.

feng shui: A Chinese term meaning "wind and water" — an ancient Chinese practice of har-monizing the environment and balancing its energy pat-terns to achieve health, happi-ness, and prosperity.

Other consultants, such as feng shui experts, can also help law firms optimize their workspace. Practitioners of **feng shui** believe that the placement of objects affects the energy flow within a space.[22] Feng shui principles are incorporated into many buildings in Asian countries but are a more recent consideration in Western ones.

H.   OFFICE SPACE PLANNING WHEN MAKING A MOVE

A law firm might need to move into new space for any number of reasons. A firm might have outgrown its current location, firm finances might have improved or worsened, or a lease might simply be terminating. A firm might relocate to a new building entirely, or it may be able to add space to its current location by, for example, leasing additional floors in a building. Depending on the flexibility of the firm's space, a firm experiencing growth might be able to renovate—move walls and rearrange other aspects of the office—to accommodate either more or fewer lawyers.

Should a firm opt to move, a checklist identifying all of the tasks that must be considered and undertaken should be developed and followed.

1.   *Location*

Real estate agents like to say that location is everything, and in many ways it is. But a location that might be optimal for one law firm may be far less than ideal for another. Much depends on the size of the firm, the types of law it practices, and the residential and transportation needs of its lawyers and employees. Are lawyers in the firm in court a lot, or do they not really litigate but instead focus on transactions-based work? If the lawyers do make frequent court appearances, should the firm be near the county courthouse or a federal courthouse? Should the firm be near a government agency it frequently interacts with?

How to attract and keep clients should be considered as alternative locations are evaluated. What sorts of clients will be visiting the firm? Will they be primarily corporate clients who are used to certain amenities, such as nearby parking and

---

22. *See, e.g.,* David Leffler, *Going Solo: How to Feng Shui Your Law Office,* GP Solo (July/Aug. 2012), *available at* https://www.americanbar.org/newsletter/publications/gp_solo_magazine_home/gp_solo_magazine_index/solo_lawyer_office_feng_shui_clean_organize.html.

guest space so that they can temporarily use desks, telephones, and computers to remain in contact with their own offices? Or are many of the firm's clients individuals involved in family law issues, such as divorce and custody agreements? These clients might be more interested in a law firm that has a children's play area or that is less intimidating than one catering to a corporate clientele.

Attracting and keeping employees are also important. Staff, too, might be keenly interested in the availability of public transportation, in nearby places to eat lunch or to grab a cappuccino, and in the overall atmosphere of the building and the firm's space.

2.   Cost

The cost of relocating the firm from an old space to a new one must be considered. Although the rent on a new space might be significantly lower than the rent at the firm's current location, once the costs of packing everything up, having it moved, preparing the new space for the firm, and changing the firm's stationery, signage, Web site, and advertising materials are factored in, staying put might actually be the better choice.

Typically, commercial space is rented by the square foot. Rates per square foot vary depending on the area in which a building is located, whether it's in an urban or more remote area, and on the quality of the building itself. Top-tier buildings (typically referred to as Class A buildings) with luxurious lobbies, doormen, security, and other amenities command the highest prices. Lower-tier buildings, with fewer amenities, rent at lower rates.

3.   Lease Options

When renting commercial office space, a law firm might be obligated to sign a lease committing it to the space for a number of years. Depending on the terms of the lease, the firm might be obligated to pay for all expenses associated with the space, such as maintenance and upkeep, utilities, and other costs.

Of course, a firm does not have to rent space at all. It could consider buying space on its own. It does not have to purchase an entire building; it might instead buy a commercial condominium or commercial cooperative.

Real estate costs can be a significant component of a firm's annual budget. Given client interest in reducing legal costs and advances in technology, firms tend to be using smaller spaces than they once did. Interior spaces once dedicated to administrative staff are increasingly being used for junior lawyers.[23]

4.   Growth Projections

Before committing to a particular space for a period of years, a law firm should consider its plans for expansion or, in a worst-case scenario, for contraction if, for instance, a practice group should leave. Will the firm be obligated to pay rent

---

23. Jennifer Smith, *Law Firms Say Good-Bye Office, Hello Cubicle, Wall Street J.* (July 15, 2012), available at *http://online.wsj.com/article/SB10001424052702303612804577528940291670100.html.*

for empty office space? If the firm is unable to recruit more lawyers immediately, can it sublet the space? If the firm is interested in expanding, can it get an option to rent the floor immediately above or below it when leases for those spaces expire?

The physical space a firm is interested in obtaining should be assessed for its flexibility in being modified. Would adding additional lawyers, or even entire practice groups, be relatively easy? Space that can be easily modified might be preferable if a firm is anticipating significant growth. Can interior walls be easily modified, or adjacent office space easily rented?

Consideration should also be given to a firm's additional equipment needs as it expands. A space's electrical wiring should be inspected to determine whether it could handle anticipated spikes in energy needs. If the wiring is not adequate, can it be relatively easily and inexpensively upgraded?

Of course, a firm might be planning to add personnel but still might not need a whole lot of extra space if, for instance, those personnel might be telecommuting or spending significant chunks of time outside the office.

5. Accessibility

How, exactly, the space will be used by the people who work there should be assessed. Will conference rooms frequently be used for depositions and negotiations with opposing counsel and their clients? Are the people visiting the firm likely to be combatants (e.g., a divorcing husband and wife)? Should there be separate reception areas? Will conference rooms frequently be commandeered by litigators who need a "war room" to prepare for major trials? Who will be coming to the firm, and how often? Are high-profile people clients of the firm? If so, alternative entrances might be considered so that these clients can avoid recognition and limit press coverage.

Access for people with disabilities must also be addressed. Depending on the size of the firm and other factors, handicapped-accessible entrances might be required, and handicapped-accessible bathrooms may need to be installed.

6. Public and Work Areas

Some areas of the firm will be accessible to clients, messengers, delivery persons, and others doing business with the firm, while other portions of the firm, such as staff break rooms, are unlikely to be seen by anyone other than employees. Those staff-only areas may be decorated in a more functional, efficient way than public areas through which clients are likely to pass.

In addition, of course, if the firm is in a building that houses other businesses, public areas of the building itself—such as the entrance, lobby, elevators, and hallways—will make an impression. Moreover, there may be varying levels of security depending on the location of the building. Firm security might require all visitors to sign in upon entering the building. These public spaces can convey all sorts of messages to visitors. Is the lobby plush and spacious? Are people loitering outside the front of the building and smoking cigarettes? Are the elevators fast-moving, or are they old and rickety? Are hallways wide, clean, and well lit, or are they narrow and poorly maintained?

a.   Reception

In its reception area, a firm makes an initial impression on everyone who walks through the firm's doors. A receptionist should greet every visitor immediately. Busy firms may have more than one receptionist stationed at the entrance. Depending on the firm, visitors might be offered coffee or other beverages.

Although firms sometimes like to have their receptionists answer telephones and handle mail as well as assist visitors to the firm, the receptionist's work area should be designed to maintain appropriate confidentiality of any materials the receptionist is working on.

Attention should be paid to security as well. The firm should develop a policy concerning when doors into the reception area will be locked and unlocked and should establish who will be responsible for locking the doors at appropriate times. At the very least, a receptionist should have a telephone with emergency numbers either programmed into it or easily accessible. Additional security measures might include a silent alarm that the receptionist can activate should he or she experience any difficulty with a visitor. Additionally, access to other firm areas might be barred until someone arrives to escort a visitor to an appropriate area. The receptionist, too, might have the ability to remotely lock or unlock doors to the interior of the law firm.

b.   Attorney Areas

Before designing its space, a law firm should determine who will have access to the lawyers' offices and the firm's conference rooms. Some firms require that all meetings take place in conference rooms, so those areas are carefully maintained and well decorated, while lawyer and staff offices might not be quite so sumptuous. If lawyers are likely to meet with clients in their offices, then more money may be allotted to fixing up those spaces to make a positive impression.

c.   Staff Areas

Paralegal workspaces, secretary stations, the firm's mail room, file rooms, copy and fax centers, and a staff lounge are areas that are unlikely to be visited by clients. Of these, secretary stations are probably the most visible, so they should be appealing and well maintained. If there's likely to be a lot of client traffic, the workspace should be designed to protect the privacy and security of client documents that might be worked on, and the secretary should take precautions to make sure that such materials are not unattended and open to view should she step away from her workspace.

A staff lounge or kitchen might contain cabinets, a sink, coffee makers and hot water heaters (for tea and other hot beverages), a microwave oven, a toaster, a refrigerator, table and chairs, and possibly a television. A dishwasher may also be included. Large law firms may feature a cafeteria.[24]

---

24. *See, e.g.,* Lydia DePillis, *Cafeteria Society,* Washington City Paper (Feb. 15, 2012), *available at* http://www.washingtoncitypaper.com/blogs/housingcomplex/2012/02/15/cafeteria-society/; Elie Mystal, *'Cravatheteria' Rebounds—And Other Firm Cafeterias Clean Up Their Acts as Well, Above the Law* (Aug. 20, 2012), *available at* http://abovethelaw.com/2012/08/cravatheteria-rebounds-and-

A delivery room for mail and privately delivered parcels might be set up in an area easily accessible to postal carriers and other delivery people but somewhat remote from lawyers and other personnel. Procedures for identifying and handling suspicious packages should be established. Lawyers often work on high-profile cases that can generate all sorts of responses from members of the general public. Similarly, clients or the opposing side in a case can sometimes take inappropriate actions. Precautions should be taken when handling materials delivered to the firm.

d. Conference Rooms

Large law firms might have a dozen or more conference rooms at each branch. These rooms might be of varying sizes and used for varying purposes. Some firms have reservation systems to book conference rooms. Small firms can often get by with a less formal approach. Litigators tend to take over conference rooms for months at a time as final preparations for trial are made. They tend to use these rooms on a round-the-clock basis and keep many vital documents in these rooms when they are in use.

Conference rooms are generally equipped with long, large tables and luxurious chairs. They typically have conference call capabilities and might feature screens for PowerPoint and video presentations. Conference rooms might also have a wet bar area, because drinks and food are often served during conferences. Small conference rooms may not have such amenities.

7. Security

The firm's people and the documents the firm houses must be kept safe. Files should be kept in fireproof safes, and important documents, such as wills, should be kept in a firm safe. Access to files should be limited, and files should be tracked when they are removed from cabinets. Backup files should also be maintained, and digital versions should be backed up, too, so that they are recoverable in the case of a system crash of some sort.

8. Amenities

Lawyers and staff members tend to spend a lot of time in the office. They often work late and on weekends. Given the amount of time people spend in the office, some firms provide amenities. A kitchen is a basic one, but a firm might also have a gym on the premises so that lawyers can exercise during work hours without having to leave the office. Lawyers have been known to pull all-nighters at the office, so bathrooms with showers might be provided as well.

Large firms may also offer on-site or nearby daycare and designate nursing rooms for new mothers.

---

other-firm-cafeterias-clean-up-their-acts-as-well/; Julie Triedman, *Dishing the Dirt on Where the Am Law 200 Dines*, Am Law Daily (Mar. 7, 2012), *available at* http://amlawdaily.typepad.com/amlawdaily/2012/03/nyc-health-department-on-law-firm-cafeterias.html.

Libraries are continually evolving as more material is placed in digital format and available on the Internet. Libraries have increasingly been scaled down as more and more resources are available digitally and can be accessed on computers, tablets, and smartphones.[25] Libraries, depending on the firm, might serve different functions. At large law firms, they might have several full-time librarians and staff people. Libraries at small firms might also be used as conference rooms, or they might house paralegal staff.

9.   Image

From the quality of the building a firm is housed in to the quality of its interior decor, a firm is making an overall presentation. Some consideration should be given to the neighbors of the firm. Are nearby businesses other, similar firms that are likely to compete with the firm? Or might there be opportunity for referral of overflow work? Are businesses that the firm might like as clients situated nearby?

The firm's clientele should be similarly assessed before any decision about a new firm location is made. If, for instance, one of the firm's clients is Verizon, should the firm be in a high-rise building that is home to other telecommunication companies? If the firm represents conservative religious groups, should it share a building with quite liberal companies? Similar questions should be asked when the firm buys supplies. If Hewlett-Packard is a client, should the firm be buying Xerox printers? If Staples is a client, should the firm use legal pads and pens from OfficeMax?

10.   Parking

Lawyers at a small firm might like nothing more than to practice in a converted old Victorian building that's in the center of the business district. But if clients visit the office frequently, they need a place to park unless the firm is in a city like New York, where many people take taxis or use public transportation to get from point to point. Other areas are more car-centric. Does that charming Victorian even have a driveway? Is there only 30-minute metered parking in front of the building, or are longer periods allowed? Where is the closest public parking lot? How much does parking there cost?

Such a charming Victorian space may still be perfect for a practice that doesn't see a lot of client traffic. Is most work with clients done over the phone or via e-mail? Do the lawyers typically visit clients at their businesses? Is public transportation easily accessible? If so, then lawyers might have more freedom in choosing an unconventional space for their office.

11.   Mechanical Systems

Although lawyers don't need to become experts in building maintenance to become a tenant in one, they should nevertheless give some thought to a

---

25. *See, e.g.,* Lucy Rieger, *The NEW Normal Library Space,* AALL Spectrum 24-27 (Dec. 2011).

building's heating and cooling system and its ventilation. Some buildings have mold problems. Indoor air quality is important to workers. As energy prices rise, utility bills are increasingly important to everyone.

green building: A structure that uses resources efficiently and is environmentally friendly.

An office space with programmable thermostats and the ability to heat or cool specific zones at different times can save on energy bills. A firm seeking out a new space might inquire about the energy efficiency of a building. More buildings are incorporating environmentally friendly and energy-efficient features. Natural building materials might be used, solar panels may provide some energy for the building, and natural light might be more available than in older, less **green buildings**.

CHECKLIST

- A law office, with its space alone, conveys an image.
- Law firms increasingly are making their operations and facilities more sustainable.
- Signals about firm culture can be gleaned from a firm's space.
- A law firm might be a tenant in a building, own its own building, or even own a portion of a building. No matter what the arrangement, someone needs to take care of maintenance of the facility.
- Workplace safety is a topic of concern for law firms. Law firms can take measures to better insulate themselves from the likelihood of violence and other crimes. They can engage in better employee screening and "harden" their office building to make it more secure from attacks on power lines, on the Internet, or from human outsiders. Security measures can be developed, implemented, and enforced.
- Firms should develop a disaster preparedness plan and should practice evacuating the firm in case of a calamity. Such a plan should include arrangements for lawyers and staff to contact one another if there is an evacuation. In addition, the plan should address data backup, procurement and maintenance of appropriate insurance, and a means for keeping employee contact information up to date.
- A business continuity plan should establish a hierarchy of people responsible for handling firm business in the event of a disaster.
- No matter the size of the firm, data storage, accessibility, and backup must be addressed. Decision makers also must ascertain that lawyers and staff know how to use office equipment and software. Lawyers must remember to plan for the future and anticipate their upcoming technological needs.
- Not only are clients affected and influenced by a firm's appearance, but so are the people who work there. In making decorating decisions, a firm should consider its demographics.
- Recently, office space and firm libraries have been shrinking.
- In addition to providing well-designed office furniture and equipment, law firms (and any other business, for that matter) should make sure that computers and related equipment are properly positioned for employees.
- Law firms planning a move should create and follow a checklist.

- When a law firm is making a decision about a new space, location, cost, lease options, growth projections, accessibility, public and private work areas, security, amenities, firm image, parking, and mechanical systems should all be considered.

VOCABULARY

business continuity plan (63)
disaster preparedness plan (63)
ergonomics (68)
facility management (59)
feng shui (69)
green building (75)
sustainability (59)
telecommunication system (65)
Voice over Internet Protocol (VoIP) (65)

CAREER PREPARATION TIPS

In trying to assess the financial viability of prospective employers, you might research information about their office space and how much money they are spending on it. The physical locations of law firms, and the years they have committed to specific locations, can give an indication of the firm's long-range plans for the location and for its expansion plans. A viable place to begin researching information about law firms' physical locations is in real estate trade publications and in the real estate sections of newspapers.

In planning your own career, you might consider where you want to work. Do you want to work in the location where you currently reside, in another specific city, or wherever you get a desirable job? Research law firms in areas where you would like to work. If granted an interview at a firm, consider asking questions about physical space and sustainability. You might also ask for a tour of the firm and of your potential workspace.

IF YOU WANT TO LEARN MORE

American Red Cross. http://www.redcross.org
   Centers for Disease Control and Prevention. http://www.bt.cdc.gov/planning/
   Department of Homeland Security. http://www.dhs.gov

Federal Emergency Management Agency. http://www.fema.gov

Human Factors and Ergonomics Society. http://www.hfes.org

Law Technology News. http://www.lawtechnews.com

Disorders that can result from job environments and conditions and suggestions for ways to avoid work-related injuries are addressed at the Medline Plus Web site. http://www.nlm.nih.gov/medlineplus/ergonomics.html

Learn about the Occupational Safety and Health Administration's approach to preventing musculoskeletal disorders in the workplace. https://www.osha.gov/SLTC/ergonomics/

Access a checklist developed by the Alabama State Bar for setting up a new law office. http://www.alabar.org/pmap/articles/011110-Checklist.pdf

U.S. Green Building Council. http://www.usgbc.org

The ABA Section of Environment, Energy and Resources Law Firm Sustainability Framework provides a model policy and implementation guidelines to help law offices become more sustainable. http://www.americanbar.org/groups/environment_energy_resources/projects_awards/model_law.html

The Law Firm Sustainability Network promotes sustainability in the legal industry. http://www.lfsnetwork.org

READING COMPREHENSION

1. What information about a law firm's culture can be gleaned from an assessment of its physical interior?
2. What is sustainability, and why are some law firms taking measures to become more sustainable?
3. What sorts of security threats do law firms face, and how can firms minimize or prevent those threats?
4. What elements should be included in a disaster preparedness plan?
5. How can a firm's information technology capabilities affect firm retention?
6. How might a law firm's decor vary depending on the types of clients the firm services?
7. What are disadvantages to leasing office space rather than owning the space?
8. How can office space and other amenities be used to provide incentives to lawyers and staff?
9. Why might a firm be interested in being in an environmentally friendly building?

DISCUSSION STARTERS

1. Research a recent disaster that affected a business in your area. What precautionary steps might the business have taken to minimize the damage? What could other businesses learn from this experience?
2. How might the business continuity plan of a small firm differ from that of a large firm?
3. Find a recent court decision in your state involving a repetitive stress injury in an office environment. Who brought the suit? Against whom? Who won? How could the employer in the case have created a better work environment?
4. Research commercial office space rental rates in your area. What is the cost of rental space? How do rates for high-end space compare with those at the low end? Which amenities would you be willing to forgo?
5. A real estate firm issued a press release indicating that a major law firm had renewed a lease for 26 floors of an office building for 20 years. The size of the space and the cost of its rental was included in the press release, which also included a quotation from the law firm's chief operating officer. Why would a law firm consent to such details about its business being publicized? Are there any negative repercussions to information about a firm's real estate transactions concerning its own business being reported in the media?
6. Consider the tasks involved in setting up a new law office. Which would best be handled by an attorney, which by a law office manager, which by a paralegal, and which by a secretary?

CASE STUDIES

1. Suppose a partner in a two-lawyer firm dies unexpectedly. What actions need to be taken by the other lawyer at the firm and by the firm's paralegal and secretary?
2. A 60-lawyer office currently located in an urban area is considering relocating to the suburbs, where rents are considerably lower. How should the firm go about determining whether to undertake such a move?
3. Suppose you are a supervising attorney at a law firm where six paralegals sit in a central bay area in carrels. An older paralegal whose workstation was next to a window is retiring. Who should get the retiring paralegal's space, and how should the decision be made?
4. You are on your law firm's art committee. Your firm is a 50-lawyer firm in a major city that focuses on business litigation. Art needs to be placed in the firm's reception areas on several floors and in three large conference rooms. What type of art, and by which artists, would you recommend that the firm purchase? How much do you recommend paying for the art?

5. You have just been elevated from associate to partner at the branch office of a 500-lawyer firm with offices in 12 cities. You have an $8,000 stipend to buy furniture and decorate your office. Provide an itemized list identifying the materials you would purchase and their prices.

6. Locate the sustainability policies of several law firms and compare and contrast them. What elements do these policies have in common? How do they differ? What aspects of the policies relate to the physical law office? What elements relate to procurement? Might any prospective clients be opposed to these policies? Do the policies seem sufficiently proactive given the number of attorneys and staff at the firm? What sorts of clients does the firm have? How might they have impacted the development of the firm's sustainability policy?

   Some sources to consider:

   http://www.pepperlaw.com/About_Sustainability_Policy.aspx
   http://www.porterwright.com/sustainability_policy/
   http://www.hogefenton.com/about-us/sustainability
   http://www.lowestein.com/?p=3524
   http://www.millermartin.com/our-firm/sustainability
   http://www.hatlawfirm.com/about/sustainability

   Also consider whether the firms that have posted their sustainability policies have also reported on the results of their sustainability efforts.

7. Locate the sustainability reports of several law firms and critique them. In what areas might law firms make more efforts to achieve sustainability? Are the firms proceeding quickly enough? Are the reports very specific, or are they somewhat vague and general? How might the reports be improved?

8. Review the ABA Special Committee on Disaster Response and Preparedness guide, *Surviving Disaster: A Lawyer's Guide to Disaster Planning* (available at http://www.americanbar.org) and compare the elements described in the guide to a law firm's response to a recent disaster. From what you have been able to learn, did the firm follow the measures in the guide? How might the firm have responded differently to the disaster?

CHAPTER

4

Money Management

CHAPTER OUTCOMES

By the end of this chapter, a student will be able to:

- Discuss money management needs of law firms
- Interpret different types of budgets
- Distinguish between billable and unbillable time
- Track time for recordkeeping and billing purposes
- Compare and contrast fee arrangements
- Explain fee collection
- Prepare a client bill
- Compare client trust accounts to law firm funds and escrow funds
- Propose safeguards to protect client and law firm funds

In good times and in bad, a law firm's finances must be well managed. Lawyers and other timekeepers in a firm must track their productivity, clients must be sent bills and then pay them, and someone within the firm needs to follow up if a client is remiss in making a payment. The firm's revenues must be managed, and operating expenses must be paid. After all, someone needs to make sure that the firm's own bills—for rent, utilities, supplies, and the like—are paid, and, of course, the firm needs to make payroll. To remain in business, a firm must remain profitable. Firms also must take precautions to prevent employees from embezzling money.

In 2012, DLA Piper generated $2.44 billion in revenue. In all, 20 large law firms grossed more than $1 billion each in revenue in 2012[1]—so there is a lot of money to be overseen.

A. FINANCING A LAW PRACTICE

The primary way a law firm makes money is by providing legal services to clients who pay for them. While lawyers are happily representing clients, they're also

---

1. Paul M. Barrett, *'American Lawyer' Revenue List Shows New No. 1 Firm: DLA* Piper, Bloomberg Businessweek (Apr. 26, 2013), *available at* http://www.businessweek.com/articles/2013-04-26/american-lawyer-revenue-list-shows-new-no-dot-1-firm-dla-piper.

incurring overhead costs associated with running their business. Rent on the law firm's office space must be paid, technology systems must be purchased, utility bills come due, insurance premiums must be paid, and the payroll for support staff and associates must be met.

Although every law firm's financial resources must be managed, lawyers aren't always adept at managing them. Historically, law school education focused on teaching students to "think like a lawyer"—not how to run their business once they become one. Firms might hire an in-house accountant or outsource some of this work to external accountants or to financial advisors. It's imperative that someone at the firm manage its resources well—otherwise, a firm risks disaster. Consider the example of Dewey & LeBoeuf, a major law firm that sought bankruptcy protection. Founded in 1909 in New York City, the firm that eventually became Dewey & LeBoeuf at one time had more than 1,400 lawyers,[2] in excess of 300 partners, and more than $600 million in annual gross revenue before collapsing in 2012 and filing for bankruptcy.[3] A law firm is a business that must be financially sound. When a law firm is experiencing a degree of difficulty that requires it to seek bankruptcy protection, employees, clients, and creditors may be shortchanged. Partners may be involved in litigation concerning the firm and may have to pay to settle these suits.[4]

B.   BUDGETS

budget: An estimate of a firm's revenues and expenses.

A **budget**, which estimates the firm's revenues and expenses, is a helpful tool for attorneys in managing their business. For large firms, creating the upcoming year's budget can be a time-consuming process as they estimate the revenue each partner, associate, and billing staff (law clerks, paralegals, and so on) is likely to generate. These figures might be based on the results of prior years or on additional research and interviews of the income generators, or some mix of each. For instance, a changing economy or the loss—or addition—of a major client can have a significant impact on a firm's projected revenues.

The amount of income a firm is likely to generate is calculated by multiplying the number of hours each timekeeper will bill by the hourly rate charged. So, if Lawyer A charges $400 per hour and is expected to bill 2,000 hours, then the amount of income that lawyer will generate is $800,000.

Of course, in the real world, firms set billable-hour expectations, but lawyers and others don't always meet them. A lawyer might get sick, a paralegal might go on parental leave, a partner's primary client might leave the firm, or a billing partner might write off some hours of a junior associate because the inexperienced lawyer was inefficient in completing a project and billing the client for more would not really be fair. To anticipate such events in budget preparation, a

---

2. *In re Dewey & LeBoeuf, LLP*, 478 B.R. 627, 632 (Bankr. S.D.N.Y. 2012).

3. Brian Baxter, *Dewey Filing Delineates Firm's Financial Affairs, Potential Merger Partners*, Am Law Daily (July 27, 2012), *available at* http://americanlawyer.com.

4. *See, e.g., In re Dewey & LeBoeuf, LLP*, 478 B.R. 627, 632 (Bankr. S.D.N.Y. 2012); *Entegra Power Group LLC v. Dewey & LeBoeuf, LLP (In re Dewey & LeBoeuf)*, No. 12-12321 (MG), 2013 WL 3327755 (Bankr. S.D.N.Y. July 2, 2013).

firm might use a **time-to-billing percentage,** adjusting downward the amount that will actually be billed to clients. So, if the firm requirements for all timekeepers amount to 100,000 hours to be billed, the firm, to anticipate more realistic revenue, might use a time-to-billing percentage of 95 percent, anticipating that bills for only 95,000 hours will be sent to clients. In an income budget, the amount of revenue the firm projects will be further reduced by the firm's **realization rate**, the percentage a firm actually receives from clients as opposed to the amount billed. So, if a firm bills for 95,000 hours at a rate of $100 per hour, or $9,500,000, but receives only $8,500,000 from clients, the firm's realization rate is 89 percent.

Clients might not pay their bills, they might argue their bills down, or they might even declare bankruptcy. In these situations, the law firm itself will not receive 100 percent of the amount it billed. The firm, for instance, might realize only 80 percent of the amount it bills clients—meaning the firm has an 80 percent realization rate.

By putting together an **income budget** that projects all sources of income, a firm can estimate its gross income, or revenues received before the payment of any expenses. Of course, just as each source of income is an entry in a budget, so, too, must all expenses be identified. The **net profit** or loss of a firm is revenues minus expenses. Expenses include costs associated with the following items:

- salaries
- malpractice insurance
- rent
- utilities
- professional accounting services
- copying costs
- employee benefits, such as health insurance, paid by the firm
- taxes
- housekeeping
- travel that is not billed to clients
- legal books and periodicals
- access to legal databases such as Lexis and Westlaw
- bar association dues
- office supplies
- equipment, such as computers, office furniture, and copiers
- software
- marketing

One of the ways to manage a firm's finances is to establish an **operating budget**, which indicates projected revenues as well as projected expenses. Periodically, the projected figures in a budget should be compared to the actual ones so that the firm's leaders can assess how the firm is doing. **Variance reporting** is a comparison of the numbers actually achieved with the estimated amounts.

The actual results should be tallied so the firm can do a better job of predicting its operating budget entries and controlling its finances. If a firm is experiencing a shortfall in revenues during a given month, for example, it may then take efforts to either increase revenues or decrease expenses. Figure 4-1 displays a sample operating budget.

Firms must also manage their cash flow, which is cash receipts minus cash payments over a period of time. After bills are sent out, money does not start

time-to-billing percentage: The amount of time billed divided by the amount of time recorded.

realization rate: The percentage a firm actually receives from clients as opposed to the amount billed.

income budget: A projection of all sources of income.

net profit: Revenues minus expenses.

operating budget: A projection of both revenues and expenses.

variance reporting: A comparison of the projected expenses and income with the amounts actually achieved.

Figure 4.1
Sample Law Firm Budget

BUDGET

Year: 20xx

Income:	Budgeted	Actual
Fee income	$	$ . . . .
Other income	$	$ . . . .
Total Income:	**$ . . . .**	**$ . . . .**

Expenses:	Budgeted	Actual
Salaries	$	$ . . . .
Malpractice insurance	$	$ . . . .
Rent	$	$ . . . .
Utilities	$	$ . . . .
Professional accounting services	$	$ . . . .
Copying costs	$	$ . . . .
Employee benefits	$	$ . . . .
Taxes	$	$ . . . .
Housekeeping	$	$ . . . .
Travel that is not billed to clients	$	$ . . . .
Legal books and periodicals	$	$ . . . .
Access to legal databases such as Lexis	$	$ . . . .
Bar association dues	$	$ . . . .
Office supplies	$	$ . . . .
Equipment, such as computers, office furniture, copiers	$	$ . . . .
Software	$	$ . . . .
Marketing	$	$ . . . .
Total Expenses:	$	$ . . . .
Profit (income – expenses)	$	$ . . . .

trickling in right away. Clients might take two months or longer to actually pay their bills.[5]

Law firms must plan to have sufficient cash on hand to honor their own obligations. During a recession, clients tend to pay their bills less promptly. In response, a firm can bill more frequently (weekly rather than monthly) or specify on its bills that payment is due on receipt (rather than within 30 days).

C. TIMEKEEPING

timekeeping:
The practice of tracking and recording time.

The practice of tracking and recording time spent on various projects is called **timekeeping**. Clients typically are billed according to the number of hours lawyers, paralegals, and others within a firm worked on a project. If the time spent on various tasks for a client is not tracked, bills requesting payment for that time cannot reasonably be sent out.

---

5. *See, e.g., How Small and Midsize Firms Weathered the Storm,* Law.com (Aug. 30, 2010), http://www.law.com/jsp/nlj/PubArticleNLJ.jsp?id=1202471122759.

1. *Tracking Time*

Time should be tracked on a daily basis on a time sheet, which is either manually written on paper or entered into a computer. Accuracy and thoroughness are vital in recording time spent on a legal matter. A law firm typically sets a date by which all time sheets for a given month must be submitted so that bills to clients can be promptly prepared.

Keeping track of every single thing done in a workday can be difficult to get used to. To the extent possible, a timekeeper should record time contemporaneously with the work being performed. Inevitably, though, a lawyer might have some rushed, high-pressure days and may not get around to recording her time. To help reconstruct the tasks performed, keep a handwritten personal calendar identifying work projects. Figure 4-2 shows a sample time sheet.

A law firm may require that time be recorded in 6-minute increments (a tenth of an hour, or .10) or in 15-minute increments (a quarter of an hour, or .25).

What is billable? Time spent researching, whether online or using actual books from a library, is billable, as is time spent reading and analyzing the materials found. Time dedicated to drafting and writing a document should be recorded, as should time spent updating research and checking citations. Time used for correspondence with the client, whether by telephone call, letter, fax, or other means, should be recorded, as should the preparation time for such calls and correspondence. Even time spent on e-mail exchanges should be recorded.

Though not directly billable to clients, time spent on marketing or working on pro bono projects should also be recorded. Firms might have separate requirements for time dedicated to business development or pro bono work. Whether or not the firm records the time, a timekeeper should keep track of the time spent in support of firm activities even when those activities cannot be directly billed to a client. If a timekeeper falls short in billable work, the timekeeper at least can point to other effort that will enhance experience (pro bono work) or eventually generate income for the firm (client development and marketing).

Figure 4.2
Sample Time Sheet

Attorney: _____

Date	Client No./Matter No.	Task	Time
08/01/2013	1743/633084	Prepare complaint	2.00
08/01/2013	1541/000004	Participate in conference call with client and opposing counsel	1.00
08/01/2013	1541/000004	Revise defense strategy	2.50
08/01/2013	1649/790123	Research caselaw on liability for formaldehyde releases	1.75

2. *Billable-Hour Requirements*

Requirements at law firms vary. Attorneys might be required to bill between 1,600 and 2,200 hours per year.[6] Someone who does not meet the firm's requirements could be reprimanded or, in a worst-case scenario, fired. Both lawyers and other timekeepers should monitor their billable hours so that if they fall short in time, they can seek additional work.

3. *Timekeeping Systems*

Today, many large law firms use integrated systems that manage information for many applications, such as billing and accounting, checking conflicts of interest, keeping records, and so forth. Some of these systems are "off the shelf," but some law firms hire consultants or use their own information technology personnel to develop custom-made systems. Law firm practice management software programs constantly evolve along with advances in technology, and new ones are always developed. Some law practice management systems are listed here:

- Abacus Law (http://www.abacuslaw.com)
- Aderant (http://www.aderant.com/products/)
- Amicus (http://amicusattorney.com)
- Elite (http://www.elite.com)
- HoudiniEsq (http://houdiniesq.com)
- Juris (http://www.lexisnexis.com/law-firm-practice-management/juris/)
- Time Matters (http://www.lexisnexis.com/law-firm-practice-management/time-matters/)
- PCLaw (http://www.lexisnexis.com/law-firm-practice-management/pclaw/)
- Rocket Matter (www.rocketmatter.com)
- Tabs3 (http://www.tabs3.com)
- Sage Timeslips (http://na.sage.com/Sage-Timeslips/)

D. CLIENT BILLING

If a bill is not sent to a client, that client likely is not going to just send in a payment. Rather, a bill is prepared, and the billing lawyer reviews it. The billing partner may make some changes to the bill. For instance, a billing partner who believes that a junior associate spent too much time on a task might write off some of the time spent, thus reducing the amount billed to the client.

A firm might establish a billing policy requiring client bills to be prepared as of the fifth of the following month. Time sheets and cost records indicating outlays made on behalf of clients must be submitted for processing by a law firm's

---

6. *See, e.g.*, Building a Better Legal Profession, *An Investigation of the Billable Hour*, LexisNexis Legal newsroom Lexis Hub (Oct. 4, 2012), *available at* http://www.lexisnexis.com/legalnewsroom/lexis-hub/b/careerguidance/archive/2012/10/04/an-investigation-of-the-billable-hour.aspx.

accounting department or other designated person responsible for preparing bills, such as a billing clerk.

A **client activity report** for each active client is generated that specifies the activities performed by attorneys and other timekeepers at the firm, the hours spent on these activities, and the hourly rate of each timekeeper. The **hourly rate** is the amount each timekeeper charges for one hour of work. In setting hourly rates, firms consider a person's expertise, but they also must cover their expenses. So an hourly rate is designed to cover the timekeeper's salary as well as overhead and to generate profit for the firm. The billing partner reviews this report and may deduct any excessive hours before the information in the report is presented in a bill that will be sent to a client.

client activity report: A description of the activities performed by attorneys and other timekeepers at the firm for a specified client, the hours spent on these activities, and the hourly rate of each timekeeper.

hourly rate: The amount a timekeeper charges for one hour of work.

1.   What Exactly Is a Client Charged For?

In addition to being obligated to pay for legal services provided, clients typically are billed for their costs, such as filing fees and process services. The services a law firm provides or uses while offering legal counsel are also billed to the client. Postage and FedEx charges, copying of documents, word processing, travel, and the like are all billed to the client.

2.   Contents of a Bill

Bills contain a description of the services rendered and the amount owed (see Figure 4-3). Some clients require more details than others. While one client might be satisfied with an entry such as "conference call with client," another might specify that the topic of the conference call be indicated on the bill along with its outcome. (Did the client decide to pursue settlement options? Did the client direct the lawyer to prepare to file suit?) Other clients prefer that minimal information be on the bills themselves.

3.   Billing Systems

A firm's billing system software may be able to generate bills as well as productivity reports that can flag poorly performing practice areas or timekeepers who are not meeting their billable-hour requirements. "Good billing software is very flexible and can cost anywhere from just over $100 to as much as $750 per license. Good applications include . . . the ability to undo and reprint billing statements, along with various formats for displaying and transmitting bills (e.g., PDF, HTML, or RTF)."[7] Clients might also be able to specify the precise format they require for billing.

Increasingly, lawyers are turning to electronic billing, or e-billing. E-billing cuts down on paper consumption and postage costs and sends the client's bills electronically. Bills might be e-mailed or uploaded via a client's or a third party's Web site.

---

7. Dee Crocker, *Managing Your Practice: Choices: Law Firm Billing and Accounting Software,* 69 Or. St. B. Bull. 34 (Dec. 2008).

Figure 4.3
Legal Bill

Jones, Kearns, Lewis & Barber
1963 Main Street
Third Floor
Bedford Hills, NY 10507
(914) 555-4321
Federal Tax ID: 06-1234567

January 5, 2013

Pinkmoondust Productions
  ATTN: Hadley Heuess
268 Babbitt Road
Bedford Hills, NY 10507

Our identifying code for this case PM-100467
Invoice number 023

Services Rendered

Atty services rendered		Hours	Amount
12/01/12 LNT	Preparation for conference call with client re strategy for cleaning up Baylis site and conference call with client	1.25	500.00
12/02/12 VLL	Research and identify other potentially responsible parties at Baylis site	2.00	390.00
12/03/12 LNT	Write letters to other potentially responsible parties at Baylis site informing them of cleanup obligations	1.75	700.00
12/10/12 LNT	Strategy session with client re measures to be taken against other responsible parties at Baylis site	.75	300.00

Summary	Hours	Rate	Amount
Lori N. Tripoli	3.75	400.00	1,500.00
Victor L. Laino	2.00	195.00	390.00

Costs advanced	Amount
12/01/12 Photo copy charge	37.25
12/03/12 Postage charge	43.95
Total advanced costs	$81.20
Total current fees and costs	$1,971.20
Prior balance	$0

TOTAL AMOUNT DUE AND PAYABLE   **$1,971.20**

Examples of e-billing systems are listed here:

- DataCert (http://www.datacert.com)
- e-BillingHub (http://www.elite.com/enterprise/ebillinghub/)
- Interbill (http://www.interbill.com)
- Serengeti (http://www.serengetilaw.com/Pages/default.aspx)

E.   FEE AGREEMENTS

Clients are charged in different ways, depending on the agreement the client reached with the lawyer. Some clients agree to legal fees charged on an hourly basis, others agree to pay based on completion of a given task, some agree to an incentives program in which fees are higher if the work is done more quickly or efficiently, and some pay on a contingency basis only if the lawsuit is victorious.

Rule 1.5 of the ABA's *Model Rules of Professional Conduct* specifies that "unreasonable" rates shall not be charged. Model Rule 1.5(b) indicates that fee agreements should be in writing.

The fees themselves generally may not be shared with nonlawyers, such as paralegals, pursuant to Model Rule 5.4. If someone other than the client is paying the client's legal bill, a lawyer may not allow that person to direct the lawyer in rendering legal services. These rules are designed to allow the lawyer independence in making professional judgments.

1.   Hourly Rates

Under an hourly rate agreement, clients agree to pay the firm for each hour spent on a case. Different lawyers bill their time at different rates. New associates' rates are lower than those of seasoned practitioners. The average hourly rate for partners was $369 in 2012, and $242 for associates.[8] Rates can be significantly higher for lawyers at large law firms.

Hourly billing has been heavily criticized as rewarding slowness. With an hourly billing arrangement, someone who performs a task quickly might bill less than someone who plods along.

Given this seemingly valid criticism of hourly rates, why are they still used? In some situations, the amount of time that will be needed isn't clear, such as when major litigation is involved.

Sometimes, a client will agree to pay a **blended rate**, which is a rate based on the legal talent that will be working on a matter. For example, a blended rate might be developed based on a matter to be worked on by a senior partner, several low-level associates, and one paralegal. In some states, the "blend" must apply only to lawyers, not to legal assistants.

blended rate: An hourly rate established based on the legal team that will be working on a matter.

---

8. Leigh Jones, *Revenues Up at Larger Law Firms*, Nat'l L.J., July 29, 2013, http://www.law.com/jsp/nlj/PubArticleNLJ.jsp?id=1202612599398&Revenues_Up_at_Larger_Law_Firms&slreturn=20130631051033.

2. Task-Based Billing

Billing hourly can create inefficiencies. The longer a project takes, the more a lawyer can bill for it. If a lawyer proceeds quickly, she actually earns less for the firm than she would if she took her time. Clients interested in reducing the fees they pay sometimes pursue alternatives to billable-hour arrangements.

One option is to charge a specified amount to perform a given task: $500 to prepare a simple will, for example, or $1,000 for a residential real estate closing. Such a rate structure can encourage a firm to staff a matter efficiently. When alternative arrangements are selected, a very specific engagement letter with the client must be drafted that clearly identifies the agreed-upon billing scenario. A firm should closely track performance under alternative billing arrangements to ensure that it can meet its own income goals.

3. Incentive Billing

Recognizing the inefficiencies inherent in billing based on billable hours, some law firms have moved toward alternative billing arrangements that emphasize performance. For instance, a firm might agree to a lower fixed fee on a trial but arrange to receive a bonus if the client wins the case or if a certain level of settlement is achieved. A client might agree to pay a flat rate for a certain task, but then agree to pay more if the task is completed early, or less if a task is submitted past a specified deadline.

4. Contingent Fees

With a contingent fee arrangement, a fee is paid only if the lawyer wins a lawsuit. The amount is a percentage of the award for damages. If the lawyer loses the suit, no fee is due. Contingent fee arrangements are typically used in personal injury cases or in worker compensation claims. Arrangements are typically made, too, for a fee to be paid in the event that the case is settled before trial or before a verdict is reached. Even though a client will not have to pay attorney fees if the lawyer loses the lawsuit, the client is typically obligated to pay for costs associated with the litigation, such as filing fees.

Model Rules of Professional Conduct Rule 1.5 specifically allows contingent fees except in cases involving domestic relations or in criminal cases. Rule 1.5(c) directs that contingency fees be in writing.

What happens when lawyers who have a contingent fee agreement are fired by the client before a lawsuit is resolved? See the following case for one example.

CAMPBELL V. BOZEMAN INVESTORS OF DULUTH

964 P.2d 41 (Mont. 1998)

JUDGES: JUSTICE JAMES C. NELSON DELIVERED THE OPINION OF THE COURT. WE CONCUR: J. A. TURNAGE, CHIEF JUSTICE, KARLA M. GRAY, WILLIAM E. HUNT, SR., W. WILLIAM LEAPHART, JUSTICES.

OPINION

Justice JAMES C. NELSON delivered the Opinion of the Court.

Jeannie Rosseland Campbell (Campbell) brought an action in the District Court ... to recover damages from Bozeman Investors of Duluth d/b/a Holiday Inn of Bozeman and Patrick Lund for personal injuries she sustained in a motor vehicle collision. Two of Campbell's attorneys in this action, Charming Hartelius (Hartelius) and Gregory Morgan (Morgan), filed a Notice of Lien claiming entitlement, from the proceeds of Campbell's claim, to payment of their costs and attorney fees as well as reimbursement for advances made to Campbell. The District Court found the lien to be valid and awarded judgment in favor of Hartelius and Morgan. From this judgment Campbell appeals; Hartelius and Morgan cross-appeal. We affirm.

The issues, as framed by this Court, are:

Whether the District Court erred in concluding that Hartelius and Morgan are entitled to attorney fees totaling $8800.

Whether the District Court erred in failing to require that Campbell reveal the amount she received as settlement of her claim.

FACTUAL AND PROCEDURAL BACKGROUND

On December 3, 1992, Campbell was seriously injured when her vehicle collided with a van operated by Patrick Lund (Lund). The van was owned by Lund's employer, Bozeman Investors of Duluth d/b/a the Holiday Inn of Bozeman (Bozeman Investors). Bozeman Investors' insurer paid Campbell for the damage to her vehicle as well as $4,000 to $5,000 of her medical bills.

In January 1994, Bozeman Investors' insurer made an unsolicited offer to settle Campbell's claim for the sum of $22,000, less the amounts already paid for medical care and for the damage to Campbell's vehicle. Campbell, who had not yet consulted a physician to determine the extent of the injuries to her back, rejected the offer. On April 29, 1994, Campbell filed a personal injury action against Lund and Bozeman Investors.

Campbell had retained Stephen Pohl (Pohl) to represent her in her personal injury action. However, when Campbell separated from her husband in November 1994, she perceived that there existed a possible conflict of interest with Pohl as Campbell had originally been referred to Pohl by Campbell's mother-in-law for whom Pohl had performed legal services.

Consequently, on December 8, 1994, Campbell entered into a contingent fee agreement with Hartelius and Morgan to render legal services in her suit against Bozeman Investors. The agreement provided that Campbell was to pay Hartelius and Morgan "33-1/3% of any settlement obtained in said case if same is settled at any time prior to instituting suit and 40% of any settlement obtained in said case if same is settled at any time after institution of suit." Pohl provided a complete copy of Campbell's file to Hartelius and Morgan and agreed to wait until the case was resolved to receive reimbursement for costs he expended on Campbell's behalf. Hence, on April 19, 1995, Hartelius and Morgan were substituted as counsel of record.

By this time, Campbell had quit her job and was attending physical therapy on a regular basis. She was also receiving treatment from a surgeon in Billings and was looking into going to a specialist in Minnesota to determine whether she required back surgery.

In April 1995, counsel for Bozeman Investors deposed Campbell. Although neither Hartelius nor Morgan met with Campbell in person before her deposition, Hartelius spoke with her on the phone and attended the deposition. It was determined at the deposition that Bozeman Investors had not been provided with copies of all of Campbell's medical records.

In June 1995, Campbell was examined by Dr. Michael Smith, an orthopedic surgeon in Minneapolis, Minnesota. Dr. Smith indicated that he would perform the necessary surgery on Campbell's back. However, in August 1995, Campbell learned that Medicaid would not pay for an operation performed out-of-state, thus she was forced to seek another surgeon. Campbell contacted Dr. Greg McDowell, a Billings orthopedist, who agreed to perform the surgery.

During this time, Campbell was experiencing financial difficulties since she was not working and had not received any further payments for her medical bills from Bozeman Investors. She had applied for Social Security disability benefits, but was turned down on December 1, 1995. Consequently, Hartelius obtained approval from this Court to loan money to Campbell for her living expenses. To that end, Hartelius loaned her $2,745.29.

On May 6, 1996, Campbell sent a letter to Hartelius and Morgan expressing dissatisfaction with their services and discharging them. Campbell later testified that she became dissatisfied with Hartelius and Morgan because they never wrote to Bozeman Investors' insurer requesting an advance payment for medical costs for surgery, did not request that a trial date be set, and did not adequately advise her about obtaining Social Security disability benefits. Hence, on June 6, 1996, Campbell filed a motion for substitution of counsel, requesting that Pohl be substituted as attorney of record in place of Hartelius and Morgan. The court granted her motion on June 25, 1996.

After they were dismissed by Campbell, Hartelius and Morgan ... filed a Notice of Lien claiming entitlement from the proceeds of Campbell's claim against Bozeman Investors for payment of their costs and attorney fees and requesting reimbursement for the money they had advanced her.

On October 22, 1996, Campbell was examined at the request of Bozeman Investors' attorney by Dr. Peter Wendt, an orthopedic surgeon practicing in Anaconda. A settlement conference was held in December 1996, at the conclusion of which Campbell's personal injury claim against Bozeman Investors was settled. In accordance with the terms of the settlement, the amount of the settlement was kept confidential. On April 3, 1997, a Stipulation and Order of Dismissal was filed by Campbell and Bozeman Investors and the District Court entered its order dismissing with prejudice Campbell's claim against Bozeman Investors.

After the settlement of Campbell's claim, Hartelius and Morgan were reimbursed for the full amount of the costs and advances as itemized in their Notice of Lien, but they did not receive any payment for attorney fees. Instead, Campbell filed a motion for determination of attorney fees and for the release of the lien. . . .

On March 5, 1997, the District Court entered its Findings of Fact and Conclusions of Law wherein the court determined that Hartelius was entitled to a fee of $6,600 and that Morgan was entitled to a fee of $2,200. The court entered judgment in accordance with these findings and conclusions on March 14, 1997.

Campbell appeals from the District Court's judgment regarding attorney fees and Hartelius and Morgan cross appeal.

The District Court concluded that a client's right to discharge an attorney employed under a contingency fee contract is an implicit term of the contract and the client's discharge of the attorney, with or without cause, does not constitute a breach of that contract. The court further concluded that a client who discharges an attorney employed under a contingency fee contract for cause has no obligation to pay a fee to that attorney unless the attorney has substantially performed the services for which he was retained.

On that basis, the court determined that Campbell had not breached the contract by discharging Hartelius and Morgan. Moreover, the court determined that although Hartelius and Morgan were discharged for cause, they substantially performed the services for which they were retained prior to their discharge.

Therefore, they were entitled to a fee limited to the reasonable value of their services. Thus, the court awarded $6600 to Hartelius and $2200 to Morgan.

The standard of review of a district court's conclusions of law is whether the court's interpretation of the law is correct. . . .

First, we must determine whether, as Hartelius and Morgan contend, a client's discharge of his or her attorney is a breach of contract thus entitling the attorney to contract damages. We hold that it is not and does not.

In 1916, the New York Court of Appeals held that a contract under which an attorney is employed by a client has peculiar and distinctive features which differentiate it from ordinary contracts of employment, thus a client may, at any time for any reason or without any reason, discharge his or her attorney. *Martin v. Camp,* 219 N.Y. 170, 114 N.E. 46, 47-48 (N.Y. 1969), *modified,* 220 N.Y. 653, 115 N.E. 1044. Thus, the court reasoned that if the client has the right to terminate the relationship of attorney and client at any time without cause, the client cannot be compelled to pay damages for exercising a right which is an implied condition of the contract. *Martin,* 114 N.E. at 48. The court held that although the attorney may not recover damages for breach of contract, the attorney may recover the reasonable value of the services rendered. *Martin,* 114 N.E. at 48.

A majority of jurisdictions have since adopted the "client discharge rule" as set forth in *Martin.* . . .

Finding considerable merit in the "client discharge rule" as expressed in *Martin, Rosenberg,* and *Olsen,* we follow those jurisdictions in holding that the discharge of an attorney by a client is not a breach of contract and does not give rise to contract damages. Therefore, we affirm the District Court on this issue.

We next must determine whether Hartelius and Morgan are entitled to a fee and on what basis that fee, if any, should be determined. The District Court concluded that Hartelius and Morgan were discharged for cause, however, they substantially performed the services for which they were retained and are thus entitled to a fee based on the reasonable value of the services rendered. Campbell alleges error in the court's determination arguing instead that this Court should formally adopt a rule that an attorney discharged for cause is not entitled to any fee. She contends that we endorsed a similar rule in *Bink v. First Bank West,* 246 Mont. 414, 804 P.2d 384 (1991). However, Campbell's reliance on *Bink* is misplaced.

In *Bink,* we remanded the case to the district court for an evidentiary hearing to determine whether the client discharged his attorney for cause and to determine the amount of attorney fees and costs. We did not, as Campbell suggests, endorse any rule espousing the idea that an attorney discharged for cause is not entitled to a fee and we decline to adopt such a rule now.

Instead, we agree with those jurisdictions that hold that regardless of whether an attorney was discharged with or without cause, that attorney is entitled to a *quantum meruit* recovery for the reasonable value of his services rendered to the time of discharge. *Fracasse v. Brent,* 6 Cal. 3d 784, 494 P.2d 9, 14-15, 100 Cal. Rptr. 385 (Cal. 1972). We note one exception to this general rule, however—situations where the discharge occurs "on the courthouse steps," just prior to settlement and after much work by the attorney. In those cases some reviewing courts have, on appropriate facts, found that the entire fee was the reasonable value of the attorney's services. *Fracasse,* 494 P.2d at 14. Here, however, Hartelius and Morgan were not discharged "on the courthouse steps," and, accordingly, we need not address this exception. Rather, the general *quantum meruit* rule applies.

Moreover, in the case *sub judice,* because we have determined that the general rule applies, it is not necessary for us to entertain a discussion of the reasons *why* Campbell discharged Hartelius and Morgan or whether those reasons constituted "cause." Rather, we review whether the District Court was correct in concluding that the reasonable value of the services rendered by Hartelius and Morgan was $6600 and $2200, respectively.

Hartelius testified at the hearing that he does not normally record his time in contingency fee cases, so he had to reconstruct the time he spent on the case. Thus, he estimated that he spent at least 100 hours on the case, his paralegal spent an additional 50 hours on the case and Morgan spent 22 hours on the case. At the conclusion of the hearing, the parties stipulated that the attorney fees on an hourly basis for Hartelius and Morgan would be $110.

Campbell contends that there was no evidence presented at the hearing to demonstrate the value of the services Hartelius and Morgan performed, thus the evidence was insufficient to award them any fee. Moreover, she contends that the fee should be based on the reasonable value to her of their services. She argues that, because Hartelius and Morgan did not turn her file over to her after she discharged them, their services did not benefit her in the settlement of her case and that her case was settled mainly on the basis of a report from a doctor with whom Hartelius and Morgan had no involvement.

"The amount fixed as attorney fees is largely discretionary with the District Court, and we will not disturb its judgment in the absence of an abuse of that discretion." *Talmage v. Gruss,* 202 Mont. 410, 412, 658 P.2d 419, 420 (1983) (citing *Carkeek v. Ayer,* 188 Mont. 345, 347, 613 P.2d 1013, 1015 (1980)).... Moreover, in *First Security Bank of Bozeman v. Tholkes,* 169 Mont. 422, 429-30, 547 P.2d 1328, 1332 (1976), we set forth several guidelines for a trial court to consider in determining the amount to be awarded as reasonable attorney fees:

> the amount and character of the services rendered, the labor, time and trouble involved, the character and importance of the litigation in which the services were rendered, the amount of money or the value of property to be affected, the professional skill and experience called for, the character and standing in their profession of the attorneys. . . . The result secured by the services of the attorneys may be considered as an important element in determining their value.

We hold that, in the case before us, the District Court did not act arbitrarily, exceed the bounds of reason or ignore recognized principles in determining the amount of attorney fees to be awarded to Hartelius and Morgan. In its Findings of Fact Nos. 27 and 28, the District Court set forth ten specific instances in the record evidencing work performed by Hartelius and Morgan on Campbell's behalf prior to their discharge. The court then applied those facts to the guidelines set forth in *Tholkes* in determining the amount to be awarded as reasonable attorney fees. Furthermore, contrary to Campbell's contention, the court did not award attorney fees based solely on Hartelius' estimate of the number of hours he worked on the case or for the hours he estimated his paralegal worked on the case. Rather, the court determined that a reasonable fee for Hartelius was $6600. Based on the hourly fee of $110 stipulated to by the parties, the court determined that it was reasonable for Hartelius to have put in 60 hours on Campbell's case.

Accordingly, we hold that the District Court did not abuse its discretion in awarding attorney fees to Hartelius in the amount of $6600 and to Morgan in the amount of $2200.

. . .

WHETHER THE DISTRICT COURT ERRED IN FAILING TO REQUIRE THAT CAMPBELL REVEAL THE AMOUNT SHE RECEIVED AS SETTLEMENT OF HER CLAIM

Hartelius and Morgan contend that the District Court should have required Campbell to reveal the amount of the settlement. They argue that the court cannot effectively determine the amount of attorney fees owed until the settlement amount is known. We disagree. The amount of the settlement would only be necessary if the attorney fees were to be based on a percentage of that figure. Since we have already determined that Hartelius and Morgan are entitled only to the value of the services rendered, the amount of the settlement is immaterial.

Accordingly, we affirm the District Court's denial of Hartelius and Morgan's request to force Campbell to disclose the settlement amount.

Affirmed.

5.   Flat Fees

A **flat fee** is an arrangement in which the lawyer agrees to a set price for a particular piece of work. For instance, a price might be set for an uncontested divorce, for a bankruptcy, or for incorporating a business. The lawyer must do the work for the agreed-upon amount no matter how many hours the job takes.

flat fee: A pre-arranged price for a particular piece of work.

6.   Prepaid Legal Services

Some employers, credit unions, and other groups offer an opportunity for their employees or members to have access to legal services at greatly reduced rates through a prepaid legal plan, in which the employee or member is charged a monthly fee and then can obtain legal services as needed for free or at relatively low rates.

7.   Retainers

A **retainer** is an upfront payment made by a client for work that a lawyer will perform in the future. Typically, a lawyer requires payment of a retainer when a client formally agrees to be represented by that lawyer. There are different types of

retainer: An upfront payment made by a client for work that a lawyer will perform in the future.

retainers. A true nonrefundable retainer "is a fee that a lawyer charges the client not necessarily for specific services to be performed but, for example, to ensure the lawyer's availability whenever the client may need legal services."[9] A nonrefundable retainer is considered an earned fee that is not deposited into a lawyer's trust account but that becomes the property of the lawyer—so long as the fee is "reasonable" as required by Model Rule 1.5 and by state ethical rules. Some states have held that nonrefundable retainers are unethical because they limit the ability of a client to fire a lawyer.[10] A refundable retainer "is really payment in advance. Any funds which are part of a refundable retainer are credited against any services performed and any excess must be returned to the client when the attorney's obligation has been fulfilled."[11]

Whether a retainer is refundable or nonrefundable should be clearly explained in the attorney-client agreement.

8.   Court-Awarded Fees

Some statutes provide that a prevailing party may be awarded attorney fees. For example, consider section 505 of the Americans with Disabilities Act:

> In any action or administrative proceeding commenced pursuant to this Act, the court or agency, in its discretion, may allow the prevailing party, other than the United States, a reasonable attorney's fee, including litigation expenses, and costs, and the United States shall be liable for the foregoing the same as a private individual.[12]

Detailed records must be submitted to a court for attorney fees to be awarded in a case.

9.   Statutory Fees

Some states limit the amount that an attorney can earn. For instance, fees for worker compensation claims might be limited to a percentage of the amount of compensation recovered. Similarly, the fee of an attorney appointed by a probate court to be an administrator of an estate may be limited to a percentage of value of the estate.

10.   Referral Fees

Model Rule 7.2(b)(4) allows payment of a referral fee to another lawyer for referring a client so long as the referral agreement is not exclusive and the client is informed of the agreement.

---

9. State Bar of Wisconsin, Opinion E-93-4 Nonrefundable lawyer fees (1998), *available at* http://www.wisbar.org/AM/Template.cfm?Section=Home&TEMPLATE=/CM/ContentDisplay.cfm&CONTENTID=52814.

10. *See, e.g., In re Cooperman*, 187 A.2d 56 (N.Y. App. Div. 1993).

11. Suzan Herskowitz Singer, *Attorney Responsibilities & Client Rights: Your Legal Guide to the Attorney-Client Relationship* 44 (2003).

12. 42 U.S.C. § 12205 (2013).

F.   FEE COLLECTION

Lawyers are not really in the business of bill collection, and attempting to collect money from a long-time client who has suddenly fallen behind in payments can be somewhat stressful. At the same time, however, a firm must make sure that its own cash flow remains in balance so that it will not have to obtain loans to cover shortfalls.

1.   Overseeing the Process

Ideally, a firm may appoint one person to oversee collections and to work with various partners to plan how clients might be pursued. Plans of approach will likely vary—a long-time business client that has slowed payments due to its own recessionary woes will probably not be treated in the same way as an insolvent individual going through a divorce. The amount of money owed can also influence the effort expended in getting paid. An outstanding bill of $100,000 deserves significantly more attention than one of $500. A certain measure of diplomacy is also necessary—a firm that acts in a heavy-handed manner risks losing a possibly valuable client that might be having only short-term problems.

A firm should establish a procedure for dealing with delinquent bills that begins with a follow-up notice, then a follow-up phone call from a member of the support staff to the client's support staff, and then a call from a partner directly to the client.

Such calls need not be combative. The caller might simply note that payment has not been received and indicate that he or she is calling to check whether the client received the bill. The caller can also express concern and ask whether everything is all right. Ultimately, of course, the caller can ask when to expect payment. The firm might also attempt to negotiate a payment plan with a client.

2.   Delinquent Bills

If efforts to collect an overdue bill are not successful, a firm may need to take more drastic measures. The firm might be willing to reduce the amount of a bill in the hope that the client will actually pay the lower figure. Ultimately, a firm may have to file suit against a client for nonpayment of a bill. That risks negative publicity, however, as well as a possible countersuit from the client.

In addition, a firm must consider terminating the representation of a client. Model Rule 1.16(b)(5) allows lawyers to withdraw from representing a nonpaying client, but a court's permission may be necessary if a firm had been representing the client in a lawsuit and had taken substantial action in litigating that suit. A firm may be able to obtain a lien against the client to guarantee payment of the outstanding legal fees.[13]

---

13. *See, e.g., Melnick v. Press,* No. 06-CV-6686 (JFB) (ARL), 2009 U.S. Dist. LEXIS 77609 (E.D.N.Y. Aug. 28, 2009).

G.   CLIENT TRUST FUNDS

A law firm handles more than just its own money; a firm often handles large sums of money for its clients. For example, the check from an award for damages in a personal injury case may be made payable to the client and the attorney, as might a settlement. After the client endorses, or signs, the check, the attorney may deposit such amounts in a client trust account, not in the attorney's or law firm's operating account. Client trust accounts are governed by rules of ethics. A client trust account is a bank account opened by a law firm solely for funds delivered to the firm in its capacity as a fiduciary.

Client trust accounts are required so that a client's money is protected. "Keeping client's funds separate from the attorney's funds protects the client's retainer from the attorney's creditors. Additionally, commingling of funds is often the first step towards conversion of those funds. Lastly, if the funds are commingled and the attorney dies, the funds are at risk of being lost."[14] Client funds and attorney funds may not be commingled. If a lawyer has deposited a client's refundable retainer into a client trust account, the lawyer then withdraws funds from that account when the lawyer has earned a legal fee and deposits that money into the firm's separate account for law firm operations.

States establish rules and programs for interest on lawyers' trust accounts (IOLTA). The interest from these accounts is pooled and used for charitable purchases, such as providing legal aid to indigent people. Most states require lawyers to participate in their IOLTA programs.[15]

H.   ESCROW FUNDS

In addition to placing unearned retainers and money for expenses (such as court costs) that will be incurred in client trust accounts, lawyers sometimes place escrow funds in these accounts as well. Escrow funds are monies that the lawyer is holding on behalf of a client that are to be delivered to a third party when an event occurs. For instance, a lawyer might hold a client's down payment on a piece of property and then transfer that money to the seller when a contract is signed. A divorcing couple might disagree about the disposition of certain money they had; the lawyer for one of the parties might hold that money in a client trust account until the matter is resolved and ownership of the funds is determined.

I.   ACCOUNTING

Given the amount of money a law firm handles and the varied sources from which the money comes, the accounting function within a law practice clearly is

---

14. Kate T. Hlava, *A Survey of Recent Illinois Ethics Law: Professionalism in Practice*, 33 S. Ill. U. L.J. 23, 38 (Fall 2008).

15. IOLTA.org, *IOLTA History*, http://www.iolta.org/grants/item.IOLTA_History (last visited Sept. 11, 2013).

an important one. A firm may have a controller who handles a firm's accounting needs, prepares financial reports and analyses, and manages cash flow. Someone in the firm needs to address the firm's tax issues and also process and pay vendor bills. Large law firms might have an accounting staff to handle the accounting needs of clients, such as the preparation of estate tax returns and of judiciary fiduciary accountings for estates. Some functions might also be outsourced to an accounting firm.

Today, many accounting functions are automated. Examples of software that includes accounting functions are:

- CaseFox (http://www.casefox.com)
- Freshbooks (http://www.freshbooks.com)
- Intuit QuickBooks (http://quickbooks.intuit.com)
- OneSource (http://onesource.thomsonreuters.com)

Some law firms use the Microsoft Excel spreadsheet software that is available in Microsoft Office.

J. SAFEGUARDS

Sadly, theft can be a problem even at a law firm. Low-level employees, long-time trusted secretaries, and even associates and partners themselves are sometimes tempted to take what's not theirs. Consider these examples:

- A law office manager was sentenced to 10-plus years in prison for stealing more than $1 million from the firm across a seven-year time period.[16]
- A law-firm employee stole toner cartridges from a law firm with a value of $375,000 and was later convicted of that crime.[17]
- A lawyer pleaded guilty to stealing more than $300,000 from client trust accounts by having the money transferred to a personal checking account that the firm's accountant believed was a business checking account.[18]
- A paralegal who embezzled $300,000 from a New York law firm then moved to Pennsylvania and allegedly embezzled money from her new law firm employer to pay restitution to the previous firm.[19]
- A securities class action lawyer admitted to taking $9.3 million from client escrow accounts.[20]

---

16. Martha Neil, *Ex-administrator Gets Over 10 Years in $1M Law Firm Theft; All but $237K Was Recovered*, ABA J. online (Aug. 6, 2013), http://www.abajournal.com/news/article/ex-administrator_gets_over_10_years_in_1m_law_firm_theft_all_but_237k_was/.

17. Mary E. Vandenack, *Preventing Theft and Fraud Within Your Law Firm*, 39(5) Law Practice online (Sept./Oct. 2013), http://www.americanbar.org/publications/law_practice_magazine/2013/september-october/finance.html.

18. Press Release, U.S. Attorney's Office, Northern District of Georgia, *Atlanta Attorney Admits Stealing More Than $300,000 from Law Firm Clients* (Aug. 14, 2013), *available at* http://www.fbi.gov/atlanta/press-releases/2013/atlanta-attorney-admits-stealing-more-than-300-000-from-law-firm-clients.

19. Leigh Jones, *Law Firms Make Easy Pickings for Embezzlers*, Nat'l L.J., June 8, 2009, *available at* http://www.nlj.com.

20. *Id.*

Clearly, lawyers must protect themselves and their clients' funds by establishing procedures and safeguards designed to thwart such crimes. Even a trusted person may be the one who is stealing money, so firms must install safeguards for long-time, dedicated lawyers and staff. Checks and balances are clearly vital. Audits should be performed regularly and reviewed to prevent theft. Inventory of supplies should be taken, and duties involving financial operations should be divided so that no single person controls incoming or outgoing payments. For instance, checks above a certain amount might be signed by more than one person. A staffer responsible for purchasing supplies should not be the same person who takes inventory of them or issues payment for them.

CHECKLIST

- A budget helps a firm plan for revenues and expenses. Even major law firms have declared bankruptcy. It is vital that a law firm pursue sound financial practices.
- A law firm must manage its cash flow. Steps can be taken to increase cash flow during economic hard times.
- Timekeepers at a firm must track and record the time they devote to work. Clients are billed for the time dedicated to their legal matters.
- Law firms require that attorneys and others meet specified billable-hour requirements.
- Clients are typically billed based on the hourly rate of a lawyer and other timekeepers at a firm. Some firms use alternative billing methods, such as task-based billing or incentive billing. Contingent fee arrangements are typically made in litigation involving money damages. Contingency fees are barred in cases that involve domestic relations or crimes.
- Attorneys must make collection efforts when clients do not pay their bills promptly. In extreme cases, a firm might file suit against a delinquent client or withdraw from representation of the client.
- Money that belongs to clients is deposited in a law firm's client trust fund, which is separate from the firm's operating account for its own business. Interest on lawyers' trust accounts is typically managed by a state program and used for charitable purposes, such as legal aid.
- A firm should institute proper accounting procedures and install safeguards to protect against theft.

VOCABULARY

blended rate (87)
budget (81)
client activity report (86)
flat fee (95)
hourly rate (86)

income budget (83)
net profit (83)
operating budget (83)
realization rate (83)
retainer (95)
timekeeping (83)
time-to-billing percentage (81)
variance reporting (83)

CAREER PREPARATION TIPS

When considering prospective employers, you will want to assess the financial soundness of the organization to the extent that you can. Do your due diligence: Research lawsuits the employer has been involved in—search for media coverage and for disciplinary actions. Also try to learn about turnover at the organization and look to any recent changes in office space (whether downsizing or upsizing). In an interview, you might inquire directly about an organization's finances, or be more circuitous (e.g., "How has the firm weathered economic challenges? How has the firm remained competitive in these challenging times? Does the firm have any merger plans? How many lawsuits has the firm won in the past year?").

If you are already considering employers that you would like to work for, you might start following them now so you can remain abreast of their activities. You might set up a Google alert so that you will be notified by e-mail of any additions about the organization on Internet Web pages.

IF YOU WANT TO LEARN MORE

ABA Commission on Interest on Lawyers' Trust Accounts. http://www.abanet.org/legalservices/iolta/home.html

The American Prepaid Legal Services Institute is a nonprofit clearinghouse for the prepaid legal services industry. http://www.aplsi.org

The American Bar Association's Model Rules of Professional Conduct are accessible online. http://www.americanbar.org/groups/professional_responsibility/publications/model_rules_of_professional_conduct.html

News about electronic billing is provided by www.ebillingnews.com

Information about IOLTA programs may be found at www.iolta.org

READING COMPREHENSION

1. Why is the billable-hour system falling out of favor?
2. If a client is charged a blended rate, who benefits more: the law firm, or the client?
3. Read the excerpt from *Campbell v. Bozeman Investors of Duluth* in this chapter. What kind of agreement was at stake in this case? What is the "client discharge rule"? Was the outcome of the case fair? Would you still consider the outcome of the case fair if you learned that the settlement amount was $2 million? How can attorneys protect themselves if a client fires them and shortly thereafter settles a case?
4. As the client of a law firm, which type of billing arrangement would you prefer?
5. What are some ways that law firms are susceptible to embezzlement?

DISCUSSION STARTERS

1. Suppose you go on a job interview and are told that you are required to bill 2,000 hours per year. Would you try to negotiate that figure?
2. Suppose your supervising attorney pulls you aside and tells you that you are not meeting your billable-hour requirements. What would you do?
3. Should a law firm pay bar association dues for its attorneys?
4. Why might some law firm clients prefer that bills contain only general information rather than specific details?
5. In what circumstances would someone other than a client pay that client's legal bill? What ethical considerations might arise in such cases?
6. Find one recent case in your state in which a lawyer was professionally disciplined for mismanaging client funds. What did the lawyer do? What punishment did the lawyer receive? Do you consider that punishment fair?
7. Research your state's rules on retainers. What types of retainers does your state allow? Do the rules specify whether a particular type of retainer is to be placed in a client trust account or in the lawyer's operating account?
8. Find one recent court decision in your state involving a law firm or lawyer that filed a lawsuit against a client over payment of fees. How much money was outstanding? Did the lawyer or the law firm win the case? Did the client file a countersuit? How much do you think the law firm spent litigating the matter?
9. Look up your state's rules on nonrefundable retainer agreements. Does your state allow them? Should nonrefundable retainer agreements be permissible? Whom do such agreements protect? Do they hurt anyone?

CASE STUDIES

1. Suppose your supervising partner has asked you to research new time-keeping systems for your law firm, which has three partners, seven associates, four paralegals, and three legal secretaries. Which "off the shelf" software is best suited for the firm? What factors should be considered when choosing a software package? Compare and contrast the features of commercially available software and their prices.

2. You work in the accounting department of a large law firm that has 600 lawyers in five offices around the United States. The firm has corporate and litigation departments, and its clients are primarily businesses (both large and small ones). You have been asked to research new billing software for the firm. What software is commercially available, and what features might your firm be specifically interested in? How might your billing software needs differ from those of a two-lawyer firm dedicated to family law?

3. Consider the list of expenses in the sample law firm budget in Figure 9-1. During an economic downturn, which expenses would you try to reduce? How can a law firm prepare for future downturns during periods of economic growth?

4. Suppose you are a prospective client with a personal injury suit that could result in an award of damages up to $1 million. You are considering signing a contingent fee agreement. Look up sample contingency fee agreements. Which provisions of a contingency fee agreement would you definitely want to include?

5. Your supervising attorney is interested in advertising your law firm on sites like Groupon (http://www.groupon.com), which offer daily deals to prospective customers. Could the law firm's payment to a site like Groupon be considered an inappropriate referral fee payment to a nonlawyer? Is there a potential for any other ethics rules to be violated through the use of sites like Groupon for attorneys?

6. Compare and contrast annual revenue and profits per partner of three major law firms, and also research turnover at the firm in the last year. Did major practice groups join or leave? Which of the firms seems to be most financially stable and why? What questions might you ask during a job interview with the firm that seems to have the weakest financials?

7. Research the bankruptcies of two major law firms, Dewey & LeBoeuf and Howrey. What contributed to their collapses? How did the firms conduct themselves in the months preceding their bankruptcy filings? What other litigation occurred when the firms collapsed? How did partners at these firms fare? What happened to nonlawyer employees? How might these firms have taken measures to avoid bankruptcy?

CHAPTER

5

File Management

CHAPTER OUTCOMES

By the end of this chapter, a student will be able to:

- Set up a new client file
- Establish and operate a filing system
- Draft a file retention policy
- Develop a file-destruction plan
- Write a conflict-of-interest waiver

Even a sole practitioner needs a system for accessing client files. Papers—or computer files—can quickly become voluminous and disorganized in offices both large and small. Paralegals and legal secretaries may need to pull information from the files. Without a system for organizing and maintaining the files, a law office can quickly—and devastatingly—devolve into chaos. Lawyers tend to represent more than one client at a time, and any given client may have more than one **client matter**, a legal problem needing resolution. There may be files on the client's divorce, the client's will, the client's real estate transactions. All of this material—whether in paper or digital format—must be easily accessible when needed.

client matter: A client's legal problem; the subject of a given law firm representation.

People within the firm who are responsible for handling and maintaining files must understand the office's filing methods so that documents can be quickly retrieved. For instance, should a business client named A Better Baker be filed under *A* or under *B*? How should a file with a client name 21st Century Gold be placed? Under *T* for 21? Suppose a client is a real estate developer and the firm handles transactions for a number of different properties. Should client matters be filed under street number? Under the name of the street? Under the name of the apartment complex? Should all clients be assigned unique numbers and their materials filed by number?

Unless the firm has established a system, lawyers and others in the office may have difficulty accessing information when they most need it. Similarly, unless someone regularly maintains the files, client information will soon be in disarray. The potential for mayhem only increases as the law firm expands and more people need authorized access to information in files. When law firms merge, consideration must be given to how files will be handled and how different filing systems will be managed. Plans for turning over files either to clients or to another practitioner should be in place in case a law firm dissolves.

A.   OPENING A NEW FILE

Whenever a prospective client comes into the office for a consultation, a file on that person or business should be created, or "opened," even if the client ultimately opts to use another firm or declines to be represented for any other reason. Meeting notes should be placed in the file. A client intake form should be completed, and a conflict of interest check should be conducted. A sample client intake form is shown in Figure 5.1. Information identified on the form, such as names of

Figure 5.1
Sample Client Intake Form

CLIENT INTAKE FORM

Name: _____
Other names known as: _____
Home address: _____
Work address: _____
Where should bills and other correspondence be sent? _____
Phone numbers:
Office: _____ Cell: _____ Home: _____
Email_____
_____
Is your e-mail address a work e-mail address, or a personal e-mail address? _____

How would you like us to correspond with you? Specify by order of preference.
E-mail
Call (specify number)
Text (specify number)
Employer: _____
Occupation: _____
Driver's license (state and number): _____
Social Security number: _____
Insurance information: _____
Name of insurance agent: _____
Type of insurance: _____
Policy number: _____
Why are you seeking legal advice?
_____
Are there any other parties involved?
_____
Name _____
Relationship _____
Have you been served with any papers in this case?
_____
What documents do you have concerning this case?
_____
Are there any witnesses to this case?
_____
What would you like to have happen?
_____
What is the urgency of this matter?
_____
Have you consulted other lawyers about taking this case?
_____
How did you learn about this law firm?
_____
If from a referral, obtain name and contact information.
_____

DATE: _____

ATTORNEY: _____

Figure 5.2
Sample Conflict of Interest Search Form

CONFLICT OF INTEREST SEARCH FORM

Client Number/Matter Number: _____

Client Name: _____

Address: _____

For individual clients:

Identify name of client, name of businesses owned by client, name of client's spouse, any other names client has been known by, name of businesses in which client is an executive, a shareholder, a principal, a partner, or a director.

_____

_____

For corporate clients:

Identify affiliates, parent companies, names of executive officers, shareholders who own more than 10 percent of stock, partners, and directors.

_____

_____

Lenders: Identify the name of client lenders if pertinent.

_____

Adverse parties: Identify all potential adverse parties.

_____

Conflict of interest search undertaken by _____

Date: _____

Attorney assigned to matter: _____

Date search results provided to attorney: _____

prospective witnesses and names of people affiliated with the prospective client, should be entered electronically into a database so potential conflicts can be easily identified, especially if future prospective clients list some of the same names.

If the prospective client wishes to retain the firm, or whenever a current client wishes to hire the firm to handle a new matter, a conflict of interest check must be performed. If a conflict is identified, a waiver of the conflict of interest might need to be obtained before the firm can represent the prospective client. If a conflict cannot be overcome, then the firm will be unable to represent the prospective client. In any event, a record should be kept of what transpired. A record that a conflict of interest search was initiated must be established, and the outcome of that search and any further action taken properly recorded. To initiate conflict of interest searches, a conflict of interest search form should be completed (see Figure 5.2).

Conflicts of interest can easily arise, as illustrated in the following case.

ABUBAKAR V. COUNTY OF SOLANO

**No. Civ. S-06-2268 LKK/EFB, 2008 U.S. Dist. LEXIS 12173
(E.D. Cal. Feb. 4, 2008)**

JUDGES: LAWRENCE K. KARLTON, SENIOR JUDGE
OPINION BY: LAWRENCE K. KARLTON

Opinion

ORDER

This is a Fair Labor Standards Act (FLSA) action for uncompensated overtime wages and other relief brought by various correctional officers against their employer, Solano County. Plaintiffs have filed a motion to disqualify defendant's attorneys, one of whom allegedly established an attorney-client relationship with nine of the plaintiffs in this action while representing the county in a separate suit. The court resolves the matter upon the parties' papers and after oral argument. For the reasons explained below, the court denies the motion.

I. Background

This is an FLSA action filed in October 2006 by Solano County correctional officers. The complaint alleges that the county failed to pay overtime for certain pre- and post-shift activities. First Am. Compl. (FAC) P 1. At present, there are approximately 160 plaintiffs in the action. Mr. Terence Cassidy and Mr. John Whitefleet of the law firm of Porter Scott represent the county.

A. Events Giving Rise to Asserted Conflict of Interest

In April 2007, the county retained one of these same attorneys, Mr. Cassidy, to represent it in another action filed in this district, *Todd v. County of Solano*, No. 07-CV-726 FCD/EFB. Decl. of Terence Cassidy ("Cassidy Decl.") P 5. *Todd* is a currently pending class action arising from the strip search policies and practices of the Solano County Adult Jail.

In connection with that case, on October 10, 2007, Mr. Cassidy requested that the Sheriff's Department coordinate meetings with the officer-witnesses identified in the *Todd* defendants' mandatory initial disclosures. *Id.* P 6. The following day, on October 11, 2007, Mr. Cassidy met with a total of approximately fifteen officers. *Id.* P 8. He met with them in groups of four or five for approximately forty-five minutes to an hour and fifteen minutes each. *Id.*

During each meeting, Mr. Cassidy explained that he was representing the county in a lawsuit regarding its strip search policies and practices. *Id.* P 8. He also volunteered to represent the officers for the specific and limited purpose of defending them as witnesses in the *Todd* case and for purposes of depositions. *Id.* During the meetings, Mr. Cassidy and the officers discussed the operating procedures regarding strip searches of inmates at the main jail. *Id.* Not discussed, according to Mr. Cassidy, was this case, nor the officers' wages, overtime, or compensation. *Id.* P 9. In addition, Mr. Cassidy maintains that he did not obtain any information from the officers regarding strip searches that could not have been obtained through deposition. *Id.* P 8.

Of the approximately fifteen officers who met with Mr. Cassidy, nine were plaintiffs in this suit.

B. Events After Officer Meeting

Later in the day after the meetings had concluded, Mr. Cassidy realized for the first time that some of the officers with whom he had met might also be plaintiffs in this action. Cassidy Decl. P 10. Upon confirming that his suspicions were accurate, Mr. Cassidy immediately informed plaintiffs' counsel. *Id.* Both parties then conducted research on the ethical obligations under the circumstances. *Id.*

Approximately a week later, Mr. Cassidy wrote to each of the nine officers to inform them that he had "a conflict of interest in representing [them] as [] witness[es] in the *Todd* case." Carr Decl., Ex. C. This correspondence was copied to counsel. Cassidy Decl. P 11.

On November 6, 2007, plaintiffs sent Mr. Cassidy a written letter requesting that he (and all other Porter Scott attorneys, including Mr. Whitefleet) voluntarily recuse themselves from continued representation of the county in this action. *Id.*, Ex. A. Then, on November 12, 2007, plaintiffs contacted Mr. Whitefleet about potentially adding a new plaintiff. Decl. of John Whitefleet P 7. At that point, Mr. Whitefleet informed plaintiffs that given the recusal request, and in an abundance of caution, Porter Scott would not be conducting any further activity on the case. *Id.*

On November 15, 2007, Mr. Cassidy explained in writing the reasons why he felt that recusal was not required under the circumstances. Cassidy Decl., Ex. B. Plaintiffs did not respond to this correspondence; instead, on December 10, 2007, they inquired about the inspection of documents that had previously been scheduled for that date (before Mr. Cassidy's meeting with the nine officer plaintiffs). *Id.* P 9. Defendant stated that it would not produce documents because the conflict of interest issue appeared to remain pending. Carr Decl., Ex. D. Plaintiffs responded that defense counsel was improperly conditioning the production of documents, as well as its stipulation to add new plaintiffs, upon a waiver of the conflict of interest issue. Carr Decl. P 15.

Following this exchange, plaintiffs filed a motion to compel on December 18, 2007. The magistrate judge assigned to this case ruled that if the present motion to disqualify were denied, the county would have 30 days to produce the documents, and that if the present motion were granted, the county would have 30 days to produce the documents from the date it obtained new counsel.

II.   DISCUSSION

Motions to disqualify are decided under state law. *See In re County of Los Angeles,* 223 F.3d 990, 995 (9th Cir. 2000); L.R. 83-180(e) ("[T]he Rules of Professional Conduct of the State Bar of California . . . are hereby adopted as standards of professional conduct in this court."). Whether an attorney should be disqualified is within the discretion of the trial court. . . . Disqualification, however, is a drastic remedy that courts should hesitate to impose unless necessary. . . . An appearance of impropriety by itself is generally not sufficient to warrant disqualification. . . .

Here, plaintiffs argue that defense counsel violated two California Rules of Professional Conduct. First, plaintiffs maintain that defense counsel violated the rule against concurrent representation of adverse interests. *See* Cal. Rules of Prof'l Conduct 3-310(C) (stating that an attorney "shall not, without the informed written consent of each client . . . [r]epresent a client in a matter and at the same time in a separate matter accept as a client a person or entity whose interest in the first matter is adverse to the client in the first matter"). Second, plaintiffs contend that defense counsel violated the rule prohibiting ex parte contact with represented parties without consent. *See* Cal. Rules of Prof'l Conduct 2-100(A) (stating that an attorney "shall not communicate directly or indirectly about the subject of the representation with a party the member knows to be represented by another lawyer in the matter" without obtaining that lawyer's consent).

A. WAIVER

As an initial matter, defendant argues that plaintiffs have waived any right to move to disqualify. In general, waiver occurs where one evinces the intention to relinquish a right, or engages in conduct so inconsistent with that right as to induce a reasonable belief that it has been relinquished. . . . "Implied waiver, especially where it is based on conduct manifestly inconsistent with the intention to enforce a known right, may be determined as a matter of law where the underlying facts are undisputed." *Oakland Raiders v. Oakland–Alameda County Coliseum, Inc.*, 144 Cal. App. 4th 1175, 1191, 51 Cal. Rptr. 3d 144 (2006).

Here, defendant argues that plaintiffs have impliedly waived the right to seek disqualification based upon their conduct. Specifically, defendant points to the fact that after plaintiffs' initial recusal request and defendant's response (on November 6 and 15, 2007, respectively), plaintiffs did not pursue the conflict issue any further but instead pressed forward with its request for production of documents (on December 10, 2007). In defendant's view, it is inconsistent to argue that there has been an ethical violation warranting disqualification but then demand that defense counsel continue litigating the case.

Plaintiffs, on the other hand, maintain that unless the very utterance of an ethical objection operates as an automatic stay of all proceedings, Mr. Cassidy and Mr. Whitefleet still had a continuing duty to represent the county, which included responding to discovery requests. In addition, plaintiffs contend that their conduct has been no more inconsistent than defendant's position that there has been no ethical violation but that it has no obligation to honor its discovery obligations pending a resolution of the ethical objections.

. . .

Throughout this entire dispute, plaintiffs consistently maintained the position that they were not waiving the conflict of interest issue—and defendant was aware of this fact. Given this context, plaintiffs' conduct in pressing forward with discovery would not induce a reasonable belief that plaintiffs were relinquishing their rights. More fundamentally, the conduct at issue—a request for production of documents—is not sufficiently clear to constitute implied waiver. . . . This is not a case, for example, where a party knowingly refrained from raising a grounds for disqualification, . . . or where a party unreasonably delayed in raising the objection. . . . Rather, plaintiffs timely expressed their opinion that defense counsel should be disqualified from this action. Accordingly, the court finds that plaintiffs have not waived the right to bring the present motion.

B. CONFLICT OF INTEREST

1. *Concurrent Versus Successive Adverse Representations*

Turning to the merits, plaintiffs first argue that Mr. Cassidy created a conflict of interest by representing clients with adverse interests: the county, in this action, and the officers, in *Todd*. Conflicts of interest may arise in one of two ways. First, an attorney may successively represent clients with adverse interests. *Flatt v. Superior Court*, 9 Cal. 4th 275, 283, 36 Cal. Rptr. 2d 537, 885 P.2d 950 (1994). Under those circumstances, the chief fiduciary value at jeopardy is that of confidentiality. Accordingly, the legally relevant question is whether there is a substantial relationship between the former and subsequent representations; if so, access to confidential information by the attorney in the course of the first representation is presumed and disqualification in the second representation is required. *Id.* at 283.

Second, an attorney's duty of loyalty may be violated when he or she simultaneously represents clients with adverse interests, which is what plaintiffs contend happened here. Under this second set of circumstances, the chief fiduciary value at stake is not one of confidentiality but that of loyalty. *Id.* at 284 ("The primary value at stake in cases of simultaneous or dual representation is the attorney's duty—and the client's legitimate expectation—of loyalty, rather than confidentiality."). Accordingly, there is no requirement that the two representations be substantially related. Instead, unless an exception applies,[1] "the rule of disqualification in simultaneous representation cases is a per se or 'automatic' one." *Id.* at 285. Merely converting a present client into a former client is, under the aptly-named "hot potato rule," insufficient to cure the conflict. *Id.* at 288.

2. Existence of Attorney-Client Relationship

In analyzing the conflict of interest issue, the initial question that must be answered is whether Mr. Cassidy formed an attorney-client relationship with the nine plaintiff officers during the meeting.[2] *See Civil Service Commn. v. Superior Court,* 163 Cal. App. 3d 70, 76–77, 209 Cal. Rptr. 159 (1984) ("Before an attorney may be disqualified . . . because his representation . . . is adverse to the interest of a current or former client, it must first be established that the party seeking the attorney's disqualification was or is 'represented' by the attorney in a manner giving rise to an attorney-client relationship.").

Under the California Supreme Court's decision in *SpeeDee Oil,* the formation of an attorney-client relationship for conflict of interest purposes turns on "whether and to what extent the attorney acquired confidential information." *People ex rel. Dept. of Corporations v. SpeeDee Oil Change Systems, Inc.,* 20 Cal. 4th 1135, 1148, 86 Cal. Rptr. 2d 816, 980 P.2d 371 (1999). "An attorney represents a client—for purposes of a conflict of interest analysis—when the attorney knowingly obtains material confidential information from the client and renders legal advice or services as a result." *Id.* When one seeking legal advice consults with an attorney and secures that advice, an attorney-client relationship is presumed. *Id.* An attorney-client relationship may be formed even when the conversation

---

1. These exceptions include instances where an attorney "immediately withdraws from an unseen concurrent adverse representation which occurs by 'mere happenstance,'" *Florida Ins. Guaranty Assn. v. Carey Canada, Inc.,* 749 F. Supp. 255, 261 (S.D. Fla. 1990), and where the attorney played no role in creating the conflict of interest, such as when a corporate client is acquired by another company. . . . Also, as contemplated by the text of Rule 3-310(C), no disqualification is required where there is informed written consent by both clients. Cal. Rules of Prof'l Conduct 3-310(C). . . .
. . . I need not reach the issue of whether an exception applies given that I ultimately conclude that no attorney-client relationship was formed for conflict of interest purposes. . . .
2. Not all courts have framed this requirement in terms of whether an attorney-client relationship has been formed. For example, other courts have required "standing" to bring disqualification motions, which is conferred by "a breach of the duty of confidentiality owed to the complaining party, regardless of whether a lawyer-client relationship existed." *DCH Health Services Corp. v. Waite,* 95 Cal. App. 4th 829, 832, 115 Cal. Rptr. 2d 847 (2002) (noting that a lawyer may be disqualified after improper contacts with an opposing party's expert witness); *see also Am. Airlines v. Sheppard, Mullin, Richter, & Hampton,* 96 Cal. App. 4th 1017, 1033-34, 117 Cal. Rptr. 2d 685 (2002) (holding that conflict may arise from an attorney's relationship with a non-client where confidential information has been disclosed or there is an expectation that the attorney owes a duty of fidelity); *Colyer v. Smith,* 50 F. Supp. 2d 966, 971 (C.D. Cal. 1999) (holding that non-clients have standing to raise serious ethical breaches). The difference in approach, however, is oftentimes "largely semantic." *Dino v. Pelayo,* 145 Cal. App. 4th 347, 353, 51 Cal. Rptr. 3d 620 (2006) (finding that so long as "some sort of confidential or fiduciary relationship" existed, disqualification motion is proper).

between the lawyer and client is brief, or where there has been no fee agreement or retainer. *Id.*

As noted above, the primary fiduciary value at stake in concurrent representation cases is that of loyalty rather than confidentiality, but the court must nevertheless consider whether Mr. Cassidy obtained confidential information for the limited purpose of ascertaining whether an attorney-client relationship was formed.[3] Plaintiffs have submitted the declarations of two of the nine officers who met with Mr. Cassidy. Both officers declared that the discussion with Mr. Cassidy at the October 11, 2007 meeting "generally involved the operating procedures regarding strip-searches of inmates in the jails." Decl. of David Holsten ("Holsten Decl.") P 6; Decl. of Thomas Schlemmer ("Schlemmer Decl.") P 6. They also stated that Mr. Cassidy discussed the general aspects of a deposition. Holsten Decl. P 7; Schlemmer Decl. P 7. Neither officer, however, stated that they divulged confidential information. Mr. Cassidy has also affirmed that the officers did not disclose confidential information, and that he did not render any legal advice during the meeting. Cassidy Decl. P 8. Plaintiffs respond that the nine officers had a reasonable belief that Mr. Cassidy was their attorney, based on both his verbal promise to represent them as witnesses, as well as his subsequent letter terminating any attorney-client relationship with the officers. Carr Decl., Ex. C ("[W]e hereby withdraw our representation of you as a witness in the *Todd* case."). But the "reasonableness" of their beliefs ultimately turns on a question of law: when is an attorney-client relationship formed for conflict of interest purposes? Under *SpeeDee Oil*, the answer is whenever confidential information is disclosed. Here, the silence of the officer declarations on that issue is telling. While certainly not dispositive, the short length of the meetings (approximately one hour), combined with the fact that Mr. Cassidy did most of the talking, also supports the inference that no confidential information was disclosed.[4]

Moreover, the court's present finding dovetails with the practical reality that any harm suffered by plaintiffs is likely minimal. Even if the nine officers believed that Mr. Cassidy was their attorney, Mr. Cassidy disabused them of this belief a week later when he sent his letter. This absence of practical harm is juxtaposed against the serious consequences that would flow from disqualification, including financial burdens on the county and interference with its choice of counsel.

Accordingly, the count finds that plaintiffs never formed an attorney-client relationship with Mr. Cassidy for conflict of interest purposes.

C. EX PARTE CONTACTS

Plaintiffs next argue that Mr. Cassidy violated the rule against communicating with a represented party without the consent of that party's lawyer. Cal. Rules of Prof'l Conduct 2-100(A) ("While representing a client, a member shall not

---

3. This initial focus on whether confidential information has been disclosed is therefore somewhat anomalous. Nevertheless, the relationship between an attorney and a client must mature to a sufficiently serious stage before courts will intervene to protect a would-be client's trust in his or her attorney — particularly with the harsh remedy of disqualification. The disclosure of confidential information may not be a perfect barometer of that maturation, but it is not an irrational line to draw. In any event, this court is bound to follow the California Supreme Court's holding in *SpeeDee Oil*.

4. Although plaintiffs argue that the exchange of confidential information may be presumed where the two actions are substantially related, *Civil Service Commn.*, 163 Cal. App. 3d at 79, that is not the case here, *see infra* n.5, and this presumption applies in successive as opposed to concurrent adverse representation cases.

communicate directly or indirectly about the subject of the representation with a party the member knows to be represented by another lawyer in the matter, unless the member has the consent of the other lawyer.").

Here, both officers have stated that strip searches were performed "prior to and/or immediately after the end of the scheduled work shift without compensation" and that strip searches constitute part of their overtime claim in this action. Schlemmer Decl. P 11; Holsten Decl. P 11. Curiously, there is no allegation in the complaint that the plaintiffs conducted strip searches as part of their uncompensated overtime work.[5] *See* FAC PP 38-39 (discussing pre- and post-shift activities, such as obtaining assignment information, gathering paperwork, logging in/out of computers, returning keys, and briefings). Nevertheless, plaintiffs need not recite every single fact in support of their claims, *see* Fed. R. Civ. P. 8 (requiring only a "short and plain statement of the claim"), and the present complaint can be fairly read to encompass strip searches.

Mr. Cassidy's October 11, 2007 meeting therefore violated the rule against ex parte communication. But, given that his communication was obviously inadvertent, and that no confidential information was disclosed during this contact, the harsh penalty of disqualification would not be appropriate.

Generally, disqualification for ex parte communication is only appropriate where the misconduct will be certain to have "continuing effect" on the judicial proceedings. *See Marcum v. Channel Lumber Co.*, No. 94-2637, 1995 U.S. Dist. LEXIS 3799, 1995 WL 225708, at *2 (N.D. Cal. Mar. 24, 1995); *Chronometrics, Inc. v. Sysgen, Inc.*, 110 Cal. App. 3d 597, 607, 168 Cal. Rptr. 196 (1980). Here, plaintiffs argue that they are prejudiced by virtue of the fact that Mr. Cassidy had the opportunity to examine the credibility of the nine officer plaintiffs. They contend that where an employer fails to record time and keep proper records, an employee's testimony is relevant to proving damages. *See, e.g., Brock v. Seto*, 790 F.2d 1446 (9th Cir. 1986). But this same credibility assessment can also be made during the course of depositions. *See Marcum*, 1995 U.S. Dist. LEXIS 3799, 1995 WL 225708, at *2. ("Nothing was discussed which could not have been learned through [] depositions."). More fundamentally, it does not rise to the level prejudice warranting disqualification.

III.   CONCLUSION

For the reasons explained above, the motion to disqualify (Dock. No. 64) is DENIED.

IT IS SO ORDERED.

When a firm does take on a new client, a memo or form announcing that fact should be sent to the firm's managing partner, other lawyers who need to know about the representation, the attorneys responsible for handling the client's matter, and the firm's accounting office. Essentially, when a firm gets a new client, appropriate people must be informed so that the client is provided with the service he needs. The firm must also make sure that the client is billed for the services the firm provides and that the client pays for those services. None of this can

---

5. Although the court need not resolve the issue of whether there was a substantial relationship between Mr. Cassidy's representation of the county in this action and his brief representation of the officers in *Todd*, the omission of any mention of strip searches in the complaint in this case would counsel against such a finding.

happen unless information about the client is entered into the firm's filing and accounting systems.

B. CONTENTS OF CLIENT FILES

Lawyers might speak about "opening a new client file," but they really mean that a series of standard files are prepared whenever a new client retains the firm or a prospective client contacts the firm with a potential case. Although little more than the client intake form, the results of a conflict of interest search, and notes from meetings and conversations might be placed in a prospective client's file if that contact does not ultimately retain the firm, more information—and a greater number of files—is prepared for a new client or a new client matter.

The standard set of files to be prepared for any new client depends on the type of case involved—criminal, divorce, hazardous waste site cleanup, and so forth. A primary file on the client should contain basic information about the client and the terms of the firm's retention. Such a file would likely include basic information on a new client sheet stapled inside the file itself:

* Name and contact information for the client
* Date the matter was opened
* Date of any relevant statute of limitations
* Fee agreement terms
* Billing statement requirements
* Legal team information
  - Name of the originating attorney (attorney who brought the client to the firm)
  - Name of the lawyers assigned to work on the case
* Results of a conflict of interest check

This form would also contain an entry, to be filled in later, when a matter is closed, or concluded.

A copy of the engagement letter should also be included in the client file. The engagement letter itself might explain the firm's file retention policy. For instance, it may indicate that files will be returned to the client after a specified period of time, or that files are automatically destroyed after ten years.

During the course of representation, any number of actual file folders will be used. An index of files should be created. There may be standard hierarchy ones for all clients and for certain types of matters. For instance, a standard set of files for all clients might include:

* Attorney-Client Correspondence
* Third-Party Correspondence
* Meeting Notes

For an individual type of matter, standard files are also generated. For instance, for divorce, standard files created might be Court Documents, Mediation, Financial Information, Depositions, Transcripts, Settlement, Custody

Agreement. Within each of those categories, there may be subcategories. For example, files might be labeled Court Documents—Complaint; Court Documents—Answer, Court Documents—Response, and so on. How many files, and how specifically each file is labeled, will depend on the size of the case and the scope of the representation. Original documents might be kept in specially labeled files and copies of those documents placed in other files as needed. Files on litigation might include a case cover sheet documenting the progress of the litigation, such as dates pleadings were filed, dates discovery was conducted, and dates of hearings and trials. Opposing parties and their lawyers might also be identified. These cover sheets are meant to make use of the file easier for the attorney, paralegal, or other employee who needs materials found in the files.

Materials in each file are typically filed in reverse chronological order, with the most recent document on top. All correspondence received by a law firm is logged, and the date a document is received is noted on the document, typically with the initials of the person who logged the document into the firm's master log.

C.   FILE MANAGEMENT SYSTEMS

Files must be carefully maintained, both so clients can be serviced well by lawyers and because lawyers owe a duty of confidentiality to the client. A single client might generate hundreds of actual file folders within a law firm. Multiply that by 10 clients, or 100, or 1,000, and the potential for chaos is easy to understand. For that reason, careful attention must be paid to labeling and organizing files so that people who need them can retrieve them and have easy access to them. At the same time, though, files must be protected so that no one with unauthorized access views them.

1.   Filing Conventions

As important as having a well-organized filing system is communicating the organization of that system to members of the law firm office who are responsible for maintaining and using the files. Ideally, training of law office personnel should be conducted periodically. At the very least, a written explanation of a firm's filing system should be maintained and distributed to employees who work with the files.

An **alphabetic filing system** is one in which files are stored alphabetically, by last name of individuals or by business name of corporate clients. In a **numerical filing system**, a unique number is assigned to each client and an additional number is assigned to each client matter. An **alphanumeric filing system** combines elements of both. For instance, a responsible attorney's initials might be included in a matter number, or an abbreviation for the type of matter involved might be included. An environmental matter might be slugged ENV; a criminal case might be labeled CRIM. Law firm personnel responsible for creating files must be aware of the firm's naming conventions. For ease of use, folders in which documents are stored might be assigned a unique color based on the type of matter or, if the law firm is small enough, the lawyer handling the case. Colored file labels might also be used for similar reasons.

alphabetic filing system: A system in which files are stored alphabetically, by last name of individuals, or by business name of corporate clients.

numerical filing system: A system in which a unique number is assigned to each client and an additional number is assigned to each client matter.

alphanumeric filing system: A system that combines elements of both alphabetic and numerical filing systems.

A master list of files should be maintained, along with the opening and closing dates of the files, the storage location of the files, and the destruction date of the files.

Numbered files should be filed sequentially, first by client code and then by matter code. Firms using an alphabetic filing system should place files in alphabetical order. Files in firms using an alphanumeric system should have materials beginning with numbers, from lowest to highest, and then in alphabetical order. Files themselves are filed according to the "unit" on each file. For example, a file might be labeled *Bedford Bakery*. Unit 1 in this file is *Bedford*, and Unit 2 is *Bakery*. In a file labeled *3 Big Brothers Construction*, Unit 1 is *3*, Unit 2 is *Big*, Unit 3 is *Brothers*, and Unit 4 is *Construction*. Individuals are identified on files with last name first, so a client named Ada B. Codding would have a filed labeled *Codding, Ada B.* Unit 1 is *Codding*, Unit 2 is *Ada*, Unit 3 is *B.* These files would be placed in the following order in a filing cabinet:

3 Big Brothers Construction
Bedford Bakery
Codding, Ada B.

In what order should the following files be placed?

Bedford Bakery
Laino, Victor Lorenzo
Laino, Victor L.
The Laino Group, Ltd.
A Smarter Vegan Frozen Foods
Heuess-Barber, Hadley
Heuess, Helen
Heuess Baker, Amara
Mt. Kisco Medical Associates
Mount Kisco Hospital
3 Big Brothers Construction
L. Tripoli & Sons
The George Washington University

A look at the list demonstrates the need for certain filing conventions. How should the word *The* be handled when it begins a company name? What if the word *A* begins the company name? What if a company's name includes an ampersand rather than the word *and*? Where should a file for a client with a hyphenated name be filed? If an organization's formal name includes an abbreviation, should a document be filed using the abbreviation or the complete word?

Many firms observe the following conventions:

- When an organization's name begins with the word *The*, file the material using the second word in the name. In creating a file label, the word *The* is placed at the end of the label, not the beginning: George Washington University, The

- When an organization's name begins with the word *A*, file under *A*.

- When an individual's name is included in an organization's name, file according to the first unit in the name: L. Tripoli & Sons is filed under *L*.
- When an organization's name includes an ampersand, file as if the word *and* appeared in place of the ampersand.
- When an organization's formal name includes an abbreviation, file according to the abbreviation.
- If a client's name is hyphenated, ignore the hyphen and treat the hyphenated name as a single unit.
- If a client's name begins with a numeral, such as *3*, file in numerical order if the firm uses an alphanumeric system. Files begin with 1, 2, 3, and then proceed to alphabetical order for clients whose names begin with letters. If the firm uses an alphabetical system, file in the appropriate place alphabetically. A client's name that begins with the numeral *3* is filed under the letter *T*.

With these conventions and following an alphanumeric system, the files in the list above should be placed in the following order using the file names given below:

3 Big Brothers Construction
A Smarter Vegan Frozen Foods
Bedford Bakery
George Washington University, The
Heuess Baker, Amara
Heuess, Helen
Heuess-Barber, Hadley
L. Tripoli & Sons
Laino, Victor L.
Laino, Victor Lorenzo
Laino Group, Ltd., The
Mount Kisco Hospital
Mt. Kisco Medical Associates

Ultimately, the filing conventions that any given firm uses will vary by firm. The important point is that conventions be established and effectively communicated. A firm might also adapt standard naming conventions to its own needs. For instance, a firm that handles a high volume of real estate transactions might organize the files according to the address of the building involved, such as 123 Park Avenue, 45 Cheswell Way, and so on. Naming conventions for files involving street addresses might be modified so that addresses with hyphenated numbers, such as 305-315 West 57 Street, are filed under the first number before the hyphen. File systems can be adapted to fit the needs of the law firm.

centralized file system: An arrangement in which all the files are located in one file room.

2. *Storage and Tracking*

The location of files must be tracked so that a file can be easily found if someone needs to access it. Firms that have a **centralized file system** keep all their files in

decentralized file system: Also called a local filing system, an arrangement in which files are in various locations in an office, such as with individual attorneys or specific departments.

one file room. In a **decentralized file system**, files are placed in various locations in an office, such as with individual attorneys or specific departments. A decentralized file system is also referred to as a *local filing system*. However files are located and stored, their placement in certain areas must make sense for the law firm. An office map indicating where files are located should be created and posted at useful points throughout the firm.

Bar coding is a method in which files are tracked using a bar code assigned to each file. The bar code must be scanned into a computer when someone removes the file from the repository. The name of the person withdrawing the file is recorded in the computer as well, perhaps with a firm identification bar code assigned to that individual. Bar coding systems make tracking files easy. Reports can be generated indicating where various files are. Bar code systems can also be used for recording the time when someone begins work on a file. Even with a bar code system, a file should have a label indicating the file name (client number and matter number or client name and subject name of the file).

bar coding: A method that tracks files using a bar code assigned to each file.

Even where bar coding is not used, a file checkout system must be established. Files might be signed out from a central repository, or large, brightly colored cards (similar to cards used to check out library books) might be inserted in the location from which the file was taken. The person who took the file records his or her name and location on the card along with the date the file was removed.

Paralegals are often responsible for maintaining files. They should never purge material from a file unless given explicit instructions from an attorney to do so. Even seeming irrelevant materials, such as scribbled-on sticky notes or handwritten pages, may contain something relevant for the lawyer working on the case.

Firms must establish procedures for marking documents to be placed in certain files. For instance, each lawyer might have a "To File" box that is regularly checked by a secretary or paralegal. Lawyers might write the client number and matter number on the top-right corner of a document along with the name of the file in which the document is to be placed.

Lawyers tend to like to have their frequently used materials around them. They don't want to have to walk up three floors to a central location to sign out a file. Typically, active files on which lawyers are regularly working are stored in or near their offices or near those of their secretaries. Active files that are not being worked on are stored in their designated storage area. When files are closed, they are typically deposited in a centralized location or moved off-site for longer-term storage.

Files are too voluminous to be maintained indefinitely. There's no real need to keep a file on-site for a client who saw the firm for a single matter ten years ago. Files for closed matters might be returned to the client or sent into storage at an off-site facility, and they might be destroyed after a certain number of years. Before a paper file is destroyed, though, a firm might opt to store digital copies of the materials in the file.

3.   *Paperless Files*

Lawyers and those who work for them can appreciate the space-saving advantages of paperless files. If records are digitized rather than printed out on paper, far less office real estate needs to be dedicated to storing them. Digital files, which can be searched by name or by key word, provide easier access to attorneys, paralegals, and others within the office who need access to the materials. Electronic files might also be created as backups to paper files.

A firm must have a scanner to transfer paper files to digital form, typically a PDF, or portable document format. A firm should also establish conventions for retaining the originals of certain documents, such as contracts, wills, and deeds. These conventions might be modified as courts expand their willingness to accept electronic versions of certain materials.

Even if a firm still relies extensively on paper files for must client records, a number of computer files are generated as lawyers and others prepare documents related to a client's matter. For example, ten drafts of a document may be prepared before it is finalized.

A firm should establish protocols for naming digitized documents and newly created electronic files. In addition, the personnel who create such files may add appropriate key words to the metadata in these files so that the materials can be easily searched and retrieved. **Metadata** is information embedded in an electronic file about the creation and modification of that file. Examples of metadata are key words and dates that files were edited.

Although metadata is very useful for retrieving data, firms must also take care not to transmit such data when documents are provided to others outside the firm. Confidential information can sometimes be inadvertently transmitted in metadata. Metadata can be removed, or "scrubbed" from documents using software. Ethical rules on metadata and an attorney's obligation with respect to it vary by state.[1]

metadata: Information embedded in an electronic file about the creation and modification of that file.

A firm must establish naming conventions for directories and files so that these materials can easily be retrieved by those in the firm who need them. For instance, a firm might determine that the date on each document must precede every file name within a client and matter file in a computer. A computerized version of a letter might be named as follows:

06062013 ltr fr LTripoli to VLaino

If the firm has procedures set up and educates its personnel on appropriate naming conventions, documents can be retrieved easier and more quickly.

4.   *File Ownership*

If a client fires a lawyer, typically, the attorney has an obligation to provide the client's file to the client. State requirements vary, though, as to whether the file must be provided if the client still owes the lawyer money. Rule 1.15(a) of the ABA's *Model Rules of Professional Conduct* obligates lawyers to safeguard property that belongs to clients.

Some states allow lawyers to hold on to client files until their fees are paid. For instance, in Nevada, "an attorney who has been discharged by his client shall, upon demand and payment of the fee due from the client, immediately deliver to the client all papers, documents, pleadings and items of tangible personal property which belong to or were prepared for that client."[2]

---

1. *See, e.g.,* ABA Law Practice Division Legal Technology Resource Center, *Metadata Ethics Opinions Around the U.S., available at* http://www.americanbar.org/groups /departments_offices/legal_technology_resources/resources/charts_fyis/metadatachart.html (last visited Sept. 13, 2013).

2. Nev. Rev. Stat. Ann. § 7.055(1) (2013).

Whether a client is entitled to the return of an entire file or only some of its contents also varies by state.[3]

A firm might prevent later disputes by including a standard file retention policy provision in its retainer agreement about the contents of files and the charges associated with maintaining files or returning them to the client. The policy should clearly specify when a firm will destroy files after a matter is closed. Whether a lawyer can charge a client to prepare and deliver the contents of the client's file varies by state.[4]

If a lawyer leaves a law firm, it should be clarified whether the lawyer or the original law firm is responsible for retaining the client files. A firm's employment or partnership agreement might clarify this, as might a retainer agreement with the client.[5] The client should be informed who is retaining the files.

5.   *Proper Disposal of Files*

Whether paper or electronic, proper precautions must be taken to safely dispose of information marked for deletion in files. Sensitive materials could easily get into the wrong hands. Lawyers and people who work for them must take measures to ensure that confidential information is not disclosed inappropriately. Consider, for example, the following case.

DISCIPLINARY COUNSEL V. SHAVER
904 N.E.2d 883 (Ohio 2009)

JUDGES: MOYER, C.J., AND PFEIFER, LUNDBERG STRATTON, O'CONNOR, O'DONNELL, LANZINGER, AND CUPP, J.J., CONCUR.

OPINION
Per curiam.

Respondent, David Brian Shaver of Pickerington, Ohio, Attorney Registration No. 0036980, was admitted to the practice of law in Ohio in 1986. The Board of Commissioners on Grievances and Discipline recommends that we publicly reprimand respondent, based on findings that he failed to properly dispose of confidential client files and other materials, in violation of the Rules of Professional Conduct. We agree that respondent committed professional misconduct as found by the board and that a public reprimand is appropriate.

Relator, Disciplinary Counsel, charged that respondent had violated *Model Rules of Professional Conduct* Rules 1.6(a) (prohibiting, with exceptions not relevant here, a lawyer from revealing information relating to the representation of a client) and 1.9(c)(2) (prohibiting, with exceptions not relevant here, a lawyer who has formerly represented a client from revealing information relating to

---

3. *See, e.g.,* Maine Board of Overseers of the Bar, Opinion #187 (Nov. 5, 2004), http://www.maine.gov/tools/whatsnew/index.php?topic=mebar_overseers_ethics_opinions&id=89446&v=article.

4. *See, e.g., Sage Realty Corp. v. Proskauer Rose Goetz & Mendelsohn LLP,* 9 N.Y.2d 30, 38 (1997).

5. *See, e.g.,* Maine Board of Overseers of the Bar, Opinion #201 (Nov. 1, 2010), http://www.maine.gov/tools/whatsnew/index.php?topic=mebar_overseers_ethics_opinions&id=152001&v=article.

that representation). A panel of board members considered the case on the parties' stipulations, found the cited misconduct, and recommended the public reprimand proposed by the parties. The board adopted the panel's findings of misconduct and recommendation.

MISCONDUCT

At all times relevant to this case, respondent served as the mayor of Pickerington. In the spring of 2007, respondent moved his law office from a Columbus Street location to another location in that city. He continued to lease the garage behind the Columbus Street address, storing an estimated 500 boxes of records in that space on a month-to-month basis.

In late June 2007, the owner of the Columbus Street property sold the garage and advised respondent to remove the records from it. The new owner and her tenant took possession shortly thereafter and immediately began preparing the space for their businesses. In early July 2007, respondent brought a crew to assist him in removing the many boxes. He took some boxes with him, placing them in a moving truck; but he put some boxes in a nearby dumpster and left approximately 20 other boxes beside the dumpster.

The new tenant, who had worked as a paralegal for a law office, had misgivings about the propriety of respondent's disposal method. She examined the contents of several of the boxes left by the dumpster and realized that they contained client materials including confidential information. Concerned that those boxes might not be taken away with the others in the dumpster and that client confidences might be compromised, the tenant and her husband returned them to the garage later that evening.

Upon receiving notice that respondent had left not only the boxes of client records but also furniture and computers in the garage, the former owner paid to have those items hauled away. Neither of the property owners nor the new tenant contacted respondent again about his failure to remove all the contents of the garage. An anonymous tipster, however, contacted a television station about the incident, and the tip led to television news and newspaper stories.[1]

Respondent admitted that he failed to ensure the proper disposal of client files, records, and related materials. The panel and board thus found him in violation of *Model Rules of Professional Conduct* Rules 1.6(a) and 1.9(c)(2). We accept these findings of misconduct.

SANCTION

In recommending a sanction for this misconduct, the panel and board weighed the aggravating and mitigating factors of respondent's case. See BCGD Proc. Reg. 10(B). The panel and board found no aggravating factors. Mitigating factors were respondent's history of public service and the absence of a prior disciplinary record. See BCGD Proc. Reg. 10(B)(2)(a).

We accept the board's recommendation of a public reprimand. Respondent is hereby publicly reprimanded for his violations of *Model Rules of Professional Conduct* Rules 1.6(a) and 1.9(c)(2). Costs are taxed to respondent.

Judgment accordingly.

---

1. A television reporter took two boxes of files to her office for the story but has since turned them over to relator.

To properly dispose of papers, a firm might purchase a shredder. Originals of some documents may be returned to the client. To properly scrub, or delete, electronic records, a firm might need to hire an information technology consultant to ascertain that material is permanently deleted and cannot be retrieved.

CHECKLIST

- A client may retain a law firm to handle more than one matter.
- Materials relevant to a client's representation are stored in a client file, which may be in paper format, digital format, or some mix of the two.
- Files must be properly maintained, organized, and easily retrievable.
- A new file is opened for prospective clients and when current clients hire the firm to handle an additional matter. Conflicts of interest checks must be performed whenever a prospective client wishes to hire the firm and when a current client asks the firm to handle an additional matter.
- A record that a conflict of interest search was initiated must be established, and the outcome of that search and any further action taken properly recorded.
- A firm might be able to obtain a waiver from a client who presents a conflict of interest.
- A standard set of files should be prepared for each new client.
- Given the vast number of documents that can be generated for a single client, a firm must have a file management system in place. Files must be labeled and organized so that they are easily retrievable.
- Numbered files should be filed sequentially, first by client code and then by matter code. Firms that use an alphabetic filing system place files in alphabetical order. Firms that use an alphanumeric system file materials beginning with numbers, from lowest to highest, and then in alphabetical order. Files themselves are filed according to each "unit" on the file.
- Files for closed matters may be returned to the client or put in storage at an off-site facility, and they may eventually be destroyed after a certain number of years. Before destroying a paper file, a firm might opt to store digital copies of the materials in the file.
- Digital files, which can be searched by name or by key word, can provide easier access to attorneys, paralegals, and others in the office who need the materials. Electronic files might also be created as backups to paper files.
- Although metadata is useful to lawyers and others as they retrieve and use electronic files, precautions should be taken to remove such data, as appropriate, so that confidential information is not inadvertently disclosed to outsiders when electronic documents are disseminated outside the firm.
- Lawyers who are fired by clients generally have an obligation to give the client's file back to the client. Some states allow lawyers to hold on to client files until their fees are paid.

- The firm's file retention policy should be provided to clients in the retainer agreement. The policy should clearly specify when a firm will destroy files after a matter is closed.
- Model Rule 1.15(a) obligates lawyers to safeguard property that belongs to clients.
- Whether files are paper or electronic, proper precautions must be taken to safely dispose of information marked for deletion in files.

VOCABULARY

alphabetic filing system (115)
alphanumeric filing system (115)
bar coding (117)
centralized file system (117)
client matter (p. 253)
decentralized file system (117)
metadata (118)
numerical filing system (115)

CAREER PREPARATION TIPS

File management really depends on good organization. Develop and enhance your own organizational skills by applying some of the concepts learned in this chapter to your personal life. You might practice scrubbing metadata from personally created documents and set up naming and filing conventions for your own personal documents and records. Consider how different versions of the same documents should be named. Focus, too, on easy, quick retrievability of documents.

IF YOU WANT TO LEARN MORE

International Legal Technology Association. http://www.iltanet.org
   Legal files case and matter management software. http://www.legal-files.com/
   PDF for Lawyers is a blog about PDFs. http://www.pdfforlawyers.com
   The American Bar Association's Model Rules of Professional Conduct are accessible online. http://www.americanbar.org/groups/professional_responsibility/publications/model_rules_of_professional_conduct/model_rules_of_professional_conduct_table_of_contents.html

READING COMPREHENSION

1. When must a client intake form be filled out?
2. If a firm identifies a conflict of interest after conducting a search, what should the firm do?
3. Read the excerpt from *Abubakar v. County of Solano*. Why did the plaintiffs in the case believe a lawyer representing the defendant had a conflict of interest? Did the court agree that there was a conflict of interest? How might the lawyer have avoided litigation over this alleged conflict of interest?
4. Prepare file name labels for each of the clients listed here, and then place the file names in alphabetical order:
     Pinky Ring Jewelers, Co.
     Pink Moon Dust Paper Products
     Pinkmoondust Petroleum
     Pink Moon, Inc.
     Pink, Moon & Rainbow
     A Pink Moon
     Leon A. "Pinky" Pink
     Priscilla Pink
     Patty-Ann Pink Potter
     Patricia Pink
     Patrick B. Pink
     Amy Pink-Fink
     Amy Pink Fasselback
     Amy Jo Pinfass
     Pink Holding Corp.
     The Pink and Blue Babywear Co.
     Pink & Blue Baby Bottles, Inc.
     Leon A. "Pinky" Pink, Jr.
     Leon A. "Pinky" Pink, III
     Leon A. "Pinky" Pink, IV
     Lori World
     Lori's World Roller Rink
     The World of Lori Stationery Co.
     Lori Wayne
     Lorri Wade
     L'Ree Wooster
     L. R. Wooster-Brewster
     Lawrence Wooster-Brewster
     Lorenzo Wooster-Brewster
     Lauri Wooster Brewster
     Lorri B. Wooster
     Lori Wooster Brewster
     City of Wooster
     Pink House Trailer Park
     Little Pink Houses Toy Co.
     Pinkerton Fire Arms

Pickled Pink Plateware Corp.
A Pinker Pink Party House
The Pink Family Trust
What filing conventions did you use in ordering the files?

5. Under what circumstances should files be destroyed?

DISCUSSION STARTERS

1. Review the client intake form in Figure 5.1. How might this form be improved?

2. Consider the case of *Disciplinary Counsel v. Shaver*. Why was the lawyer involved in the controversy being professionally disciplined? How might that lawyer have avoided the situation? What impact might the disciplinary proceeding have had on the lawyer's client base? If you had hired that lawyer to work on one of your matters and you found out about the disciplinary action, what would you do? What would you tell your friends and colleagues about the lawyer? What impact do you suppose this disciplinary proceeding had on the lawyer's practice? Ultimately, the lawyer was just publicly reprimanded. Does that seem to imply that improper disposal of client records is not a significant infraction?

3. What set of standard files should be prepared for the following?
    a personal bankruptcy case?
    a closing on a house for an individual client?
    an immigration case involving deportation?
    a landlord-tenant dispute?
    a car accident case?

4. Create a one-page filing conventions sheet to be posted by each filing station in a law firm. The sheet should identify the 25 most significant filing conventions used by the firm.

5. Research your jurisdiction's ethical rules on metadata in electronic files. How can a lawyer in your jurisdiction take care not to violate rules on metadata?

6. Research language that should be included in a file retention policy. Craft an appropriate file retention provision for inclusion in a retainer agreement that complies with professional conduct rules in your jurisdiction.

7. Look up a recent legal decision or disciplinary action involving an attorney conflict of interest. Consider whether and how a better file management system might have prevented the problem from arising.

CASE STUDIES

1. Cynthia Smith wants to retain your firm to handle her divorce from Mark Jones. A conflict of interest search reveals that, 15 years ago, the firm represented Mark Jones's business partner in a civil suit brought against the partner stemming from a car accident he'd had during nonbusiness hours. Does this pose a conflict of interest for the firm? Why or why not? Suppose the firm had represented the business partner in a divorce proceeding. Would a conflict of interest exist then?

2. Mariel Carter and Jennifer Hayes wish to hire your firm to incorporate their business, Sew Little Time, a yarn retailer. Your firm represents the landlord of the building where their yarn shop is located. The landlord is the defendant in a criminal case in which he was charged with driving while intoxicated. Does the representation of the landlord prevent the firm from representing Carter and Hayes? Draft a letter from the firm asking the landlord to waive any conflict of interest.

3. You work for a ten-lawyer, single-office law firm in your state, and you have been charged with drafting the firm's file destruction policy. What factors should be considered before files are destroyed? How should files be destroyed?

4. Research shredders and their capacities and abilities, and make recommendations about which one to purchase for a sole practitioner.

5. Your firm must either place 2,000 boxes of documents in off-site storage or create electronic images of all the documents. Compare and contrast the merits of each option, including the costs. Which do you recommend? Why?

6. You are a paralegal at a law firm charged with maintaining client files. You realize you just accidentally shredded the last will and testament of a firm client, who died last week. What do you do?

7. Suppose you are a paralegal at a law firm that represents a famous singer. A reporter for a major newspaper calls you and asks whether the firm represents the singer. You explain that you cannot disclose whether or not the firm represents the singer. The reporter then says that she found a copy of the singer's recording contract in a trash bin in your office building and wants to confirm that the singer will earn $10 million for her next album. What should you say?

CHAPTER
6

Docket Management

CHAPTER OUTCOMES

By the end of this chapter, a student will be able to:

- Explain calendaring
- Specify information needed to make a calendar entry
- Identify ethical implications of incompetent docket management
- Understand and apply different methods for determining deadlines
- Compare and contrast features of different case management programs

A law firm should have a system in place for tracking and overseeing each case that the firm is involved in on behalf of a client. Lawyers must appear in court, at depositions, in conferences, at informal meetings. Sometimes, they need the additional support of paralegals or others in a law firm. Of course, activities involving litigation are not the only ones lawyers are involved in. They are also working on other matters not necessarily destined for court—contracts, mergers and acquisitions, compliance counseling, commenting on proposed regulations, and so on. Without a procedure in place to track who is doing what, where, when, and by what deadline, a firm's business can easily become chaotic given the number of clients, client matters, and professional activities with which lawyers and support staff are involved.

A. CALENDARING

At the very least, a firm should have a **master calendar** listing all of the litigation-related activities (such as filing deadlines and hearing dates) scheduled for lawyers and staff at the firm. Some firms also track other important client events that are not involved in litigation, such as real estate closings, deadlines for submitting comments on proposed rulemakings, and the like. Reminders about upcoming due dates should also be entered in a calendar.

master calendar: A calendar on which important dates for an entire law firm are recorded.

Calendar systems provide lawyers with advance notice of due dates for matters requiring legal action. The advance notice is provided by "ticklers" that identify that an action date is approaching. The "tickler" can be preset to the amount and frequency of notices, i.e., a single (e.g., 10 day or 7 day) notice or multiple (e.g., 30 day, 7 day, 1 day) notices. Calendar systems help insure that the lawyer's attention and the client's file are brought together sufficiently in advance of the date action is required so that a conscientious lawyer does not fail to do the work. Calendar systems cannot ensure good work, but they permit lawyers the opportunity to do good work through appropriate time management. Not surprisingly, insurers are true believers in the efficacy of calendaring, and it is inconceivable that a policy would be written today for a firm that did not have a calendaring system and trained personnel and office procedures to insure that it is implemented properly.[1]

calendaring:
The act of recording important information on a calendar.

As simple as **calendaring** seems to be, about one-sixth of malpractice claims are attributable to calendar, deadline, and time-management mistakes.[2] Consider the following case involving a single attorney.

DANIELS V. SACKS

No. E041543, 2008 Cal. App. Unpub. LEXIS 6316 (Cal. Ct. App. July 29, 2008)

JUDGES: GAUT, J.; MCKINSTER, ACTING P. J., MILLER, J. CONCURRED.
OPINION BY: GAUT

OPINION

Defendant Dennis Michael Sacks appeals a default judgment entered on May 31, 2006, in favor of plaintiff Clifford R. Daniels in the amount of $228,896.52. Defendant, an attorney who represented himself in this matter, contends the trial court abused its discretion in denying his motions to set aside the default judgment. He claims default was entered due to defendant's and his staff's inadvertence.

We conclude there was no abuse of discretion in denying defendant's motions to set aside default. . . . We affirm the judgment.

Unless otherwise noted, all statutory references are to the Code of Civil Procedure.

FACTUAL AND PROCEDURAL BACKGROUND

On November 16, 2004, plaintiff filed a complaint for damages against defendant. The complaint contained the following causes of actions: (1) negligence— legal malpractice; (2) intentional breach of fiduciary duty; (3) negligent breach of fiduciary duty; and (4) unjust enrichment.

Plaintiff alleged in his complaint that he and defendant entered into an agreement, which was partially oral and partially written, whereby defendant was to

---

1. James M. Fischer, *External Control over the American Bar,* 19 Geo. J. Legal Ethics 59, 76-77 (Winter 2006).

2. Dan Pinnington, *Avoid a Malpractice Claim Using Time Management Tools,* 38(3) Law Prac. online, May/June 2012, http://www.americanbar.org/publications /law_practice_magazine/ 2012/may_june/avoid-a-malpractice-claim-using-time-management-tools.html.

provide plaintiff with legal services consisting of recovering proceeds due plaintiff from a foreclosure trustee company, after the foreclosure sale of plaintiff's home. Plaintiff further alleges defendant committed legal malpractice and breached his fiduciary duty owed to plaintiff by not disclosing to plaintiff that the trustee was required to release to plaintiff those funds from the foreclosure sale of plaintiff's home that exceeded the mortgage and liens on plaintiff's home. Defendant charged plaintiff an unconscionable fee for legal services since recovery of the funds was certain and required very little work. By not disclosing this to plaintiff, defendant allegedly tricked plaintiff into executing an unconscionable contingency fee agreement. Defendant was thus unjustly enriched in the amount of at least $40,000 paid for legal fees.

Plaintiff further alleged in his complaint that in a separate matter defendant agreed to defend plaintiff in an unlawful detainer action, arising from plaintiff renting back his foreclosed home from the new owner for 60 days after the foreclosure. Defendant negligently defended plaintiff in the unlawful detainer action by failing to obtain a rental agreement in writing, which resulted in plaintiff being locked out of his home.

Defendant failed to file a timely answer to plaintiff's first amended complaint. Accordingly, plaintiff filed a request for entry of default, which the trial court entered on April 29, 2005.

On May 4, 2005, defendant filed a motion to set aside entry of default. Defendant's notice of motion stated the motion was brought under section 473.1 and was based on surprise, mistake or excusable neglect. Defendant attached his own nonsensical declaration stating, "Counsel for Plaintiff inadvertently missed the deadline to respond to defendant's Cross-Complaint, but has moved quickly to correct the error so that no prejudice should have occurred as to Defendant. [P] Plaintiff has attached his proposed Answer to Cross-Complaint clearly indicating a probability of successfully defeating t[sic], other than where both Complaint and Cross-Complaint are seeking virtually the same causes and the same results as to the Dissolution of Partnership, Partition of Real Estate, and Accounting."

On June 13, 2005, the trial court denied defendant's first motion without prejudice to defendant refiling his motion, noting the motion was incomprehensible. Defendant acknowledged the motion cited the wrong code section and needed to be redrafted.

In defendant's third attempt to set aside the default, on August 12, 2005, defendant filed an ex parte application for an order shortening time for a hearing on his refiled motion to set aside default pursuant to section 473.2. Defendant asserted he inadvertently missed the deadline to respond to plaintiff's complaint due to his heavy case load. The trial court denied defendant's ex parte application without prejudice to refiling the motion. The court noted there was no section 473.2 statute and the motion therefore needed to be corrected and refiled.

On August 22, 2005, defendant refiled his ex parte application to shorten time for hearing defendant's motion to set aside default pursuant to section 473. Defendant stated in his attached declaration that he was representing himself in the case and inadvertently missed the deadline to respond to plaintiff's complaint due to his heavy case load. Defendant requested shortened notice "due to impending default judgment." Plaintiff filed opposition.

On September 14, 2005, the trial court denied defendant's motion without prejudice. The trial court explained it was denying the motion because merely stating defendant did not timely respond to plaintiff's amended complaint was too general: "The excuse, i.e., heavy case load, is very non specific."

On October 21, 2005, defendant again filed an application for an order shortening time, along with a fourth notice and a motion to set aside default pursuant to section 473. Defendant erroneously stated in his notice of motion that attached to his motion was a proposed demurrer and motion to strike the amended complaint. Rather, defendant attached a proposed "answer to complaint." Defendant asserted he inadvertently missed the deadline to respond to plaintiff's complaint due to failing "to properly calendar the date for the response to the first amended complaint." The court set the motion for a hearing on November 29.

After plaintiff filed opposition, defendant filed additional points and authorities, asserting that the motion was brought under section 473. Defendant argued in his supplemental points and authorities that his secretary erroneously and improperly calendared the hearing date for the demurrer of the original complaint, and therefore failed to notify defendant of the due date for the response. Defendant's secretary, Minerva Soto, provided a declaration attached to the supplemental points and authorities, stating defendant informed her of the due date for filing a response to the amended complaint but Soto inadvertently failed to properly calendar the date, resulting in entry of default against defendant.

Plaintiff filed supplemental opposition. Plaintiff argued in his opposition and supplemental opposition that defendant's motion to set aside default was in effect an improper, untimely motion for reconsideration.

On November 29, 2005, the trial court denied defendant's motion to set aside the default. . . . The court . . . noted that defendant initially failed to provide in his earlier motion sufficient details explaining why he missed the filing deadline due to a heavy case load. Then, not until his supplemental brief in his fourth motion did he attach his secretary's declaration and blame the failure to file a timely response on his secretary. This contradicted his previous declarations and there was no explanation as to why he did not provide his secretary's declaration sooner.

On December 9, 2005, defendant filed a motion for reconsideration of the November 29 ruling denying his motion to set aside default. . . . Defendant did not state in his motion any grounds for granting reconsideration.

Defendant, however, attached his own declaration stating that he inadvertently failed to calendar properly the deadline to file a response to the amended complaint. When his office received the amended complaint, his secretary brought it to his attention but defendant was in the middle of another matter. He told his secretary to calendar the response date and bring the amended complaint back to him later. She neglected to do so. Defendant explained in his declaration that, because defendant's office is so busy, he relies on his staff to calendar matters. His calendaring system failed in this instance. Defendant further stated in his declaration the factual basis for his defense in the case.

On January 9, 2005, the trial court continued defendant's motion for reconsideration and because plaintiff claimed he had not been served with defendant's motion. The trial court also permitted plaintiff to file opposition. Thereafter, plaintiff filed opposition.

On January 26, 2006, the trial court denied defendant's motion for reconsideration and entered judgment on May 31, 2006. The trial court noted during the hearing on January 26, that defendant had not complied with the requirements of section 1008. There were no new facts or law, including no new facts explaining why defendant did not provide his secretary's supporting declaration earlier.

DEFICIENT RECORD AND FAILURE TO CITE CLERK'S TRANSCRIPT

We begin by noting that defendant's appellate brief is in violation of *California Rules of Court*, Rule 8.204(1)(C) in that it contains no citations to the record on appeal. Furthermore, defendant violated *California Rules of Court*, Rules 8.120 and 8.122, by failing to request in his notice to prepare the clerk's transcript the following documents: (1) the underlying complaint, (2) amended complaint, and (3) April 29, 2005, request and entry of default. These are court documents that are critical to defendant's appeal. The exclusion of these documents, as well as the failure to cite to the court record, are sufficient grounds alone to dismiss defendant's appeal or return the appellate brief for corrections. (*Cal. Rules of Court*, Rules 8.276, 8.204(e)(2).)

In addition, defendant's appellate brief violates *California Rules of Court*, Rule 8.204(a)(2), in that it does not: "(A) State the nature of the action, the relief sought in the trial court, and the judgment or order appealed from; (B) State that the judgment appealed from is final, or explain why the order appealed from is appealable; and (C) Provide a summary of the significant facts limited to matters in the record."

Despite these significant deficiencies in defendant's appeal, which impede our ability to review efficiently and decide the matter, we nevertheless will disregard defendant's noncompliance and decide the appeal on the merits. Plaintiff has assisted us in the review of this matter by augmenting the record to include the complaint and amended complaint. In addition, the register of actions contains sufficient additional information upon which to decide this appeal. (*Cal. Rules of Court*, Rule 8.204(e)(2)(C).)

MOTIONS TO SET ASIDE DEFAULT JUDGMENT

Defendant contends the trial court abused its discretion in denying his motions to set aside default. We disagree.

. . .

DISCUSSION

Defendant argues that his supporting declaration attesting to his mistake in not filing a timely response was all that was required for the court to grant his motion to set aside default, particularly since he was diligent in seeking relief and the courts favor trial on the merits, as opposed to default judgments. We conclude the trial court did not abuse its discretion in denying defendant's five motions seeking to set aside default.

IRST AND SECOND MOTIONS

As to defendant's first and second motions to set aside default, it is quite clear the trial court did not abuse its discretion in denying them. The first motion was incomprehensible. The second motion, while somewhat comprehensible, was based on incorrect statutory authority. For this reason, the trial court denied the motion without prejudice and indicated that defendant could refile his motion.

THIRD MOTION

The trial court's denial of defendant's third motion to set aside default was also not an abuse of discretion. Defendant's excuse was that he failed to file a response to the amended complaint due to his heavy case load. The courts have routinely rejected this as a valid excuse for setting aside a default judgment.

As stated in *Martin v. Taylor*, 267 Cal. App. 2d 112, 117 (1968), "The 'busy attorney' reason for delay has been almost uniformly rejected by the courts as a ground for failure to seek relief from a default within a reasonable time. For example, in *Smith v. Pelton Water Wheel Co.*, 151 Cal. 394 (1907), the delay was only four months—the defendant pleaded that his attorney was ill for over two months and under the pressure of 'other business' for some weeks thereafter— yet the court held the reason was insufficient ground for granting relief under section 473. In *Schwartz v. Smookler*, 202 Cal. App. 2d 76, the defendant delayed moving to set aside a default for three and a half months and the attorney alleged 'pressure of other business in my office.' The court held this did not constitute legal justification for the delay."

Here, such an excuse is even less persuasive since defendant was representing himself and thus he was directly responsible for failing to file his own response to the amended complaint.

The court in *Martin* explained that "The reason 'press of business' is not usually accepted as a ground for relief under section 473 is found in *Willett v. Schmeister Manufacturing Co.*, 80 Cal. App. 337 at 340: 'Nor is unusual press of business a legal excuse. To accept this as a legal justification for the failure to comply with the statute would be to discourage diligence in the prosecution of appeals and establish a precedent that might lead to vexatious delays.' [P] Moreover, there is some indication here that defendants themselves were inexcusably negligent." (*Martin v. Taylor, supra*, 267 Cal. App. 2d at 117.) This is the case here. Defendant, representing himself, had full knowledge that he was required to respond to the amended complaint and failed to do so.

FOURTH MOTION

Realizing the press of business was not an adequate basis for setting aside the default, defendant filed his fourth motion, claiming he failed to file a timely response because his secretary failed to calendar the due date properly. The trial court did not abuse its discretion in rejecting this excuse as well, since it was completely different from defendant's original press-of-business excuse and defendant failed to provide any justification for failing to mention previously his new excuse.

FIFTH MOTION

As to defendant's fifth attempt to set aside default, defendant brought a motion for reconsideration of the trial court's November 29, 2005, ruling denying his motion to set aside default. We first note that there is a split of authority over whether orders denying reconsideration (§ 1008) are appealable. . . . Some courts have held that motions for reconsideration are appealable only if the underlying orders are appealable and if the reconsideration motions are based on new or different facts. . . .

The trial court's order denying defendant's reconsideration motion is not appealable for the simple reason that the motion was not based on new or different facts. For the same reason, even assuming it is appealable, there was no abuse of discretion in denying the motion for reconsideration. There was no explanation as to why defendant initially said he failed to file a timely response because of the press of business, and then in his supplemental brief filed in connection with his fourth motion he asserted for the first time that his secretary was responsible for the omission. We do not find compelling defendant's explanation that his initial excuse and most recent excuse were compatible and that his most recent explanation merely elaborated on his initial press-of-business excuse.

We conclude there was no abuse of discretion in the trial court denying defendant's four motions to set aside default and motion for reconsideration.

DISPOSITION

The judgment is affirmed. Plaintiff is awarded his costs on appeal.

No matter what size a law firm, someone at the firm should be designated to record appointments and deadlines on a master calendar. At some firms, calendaring events and filing and tracking documents can be a full-time job.

Today's law firms tend to use computerized calendars, which make changing entries and printing out daily, weekly, and monthly calendars very easy. Thus, lawyers—and sometimes trusted paralegals—might update and maintain their own entries on the master calendar rather than submitting requests to calendar clerks to update the system.

As modifications to the calendar are made, lawyers and staff must be alerted to the revisions. Some firms use electronic calendars but keep a paper backup as well. No matter what sort of calendar is used, updating the calendar on a daily basis and actually referring to it are vital. A calendar can be perfectly up to date, but unless a lawyer takes a look at it, the calendar will be of little use.

At a minimum, entries in a master calendar should include the following information:

- time of event
- location of event
- name of case
- client name and matter
- short description of the entry
- name or initials (depending on firm size) of the firm's lawyers and/or staff involved in the event

So, an entry for June 6 might look like this:

10 a.m.
Westchester County Courthouse
Conference Room 3
Ciavardini v. Fox Run
Lorenzo Ciavardini—personal injury case
Settlement conference with defendant and magistrate
LNT, VLL, H2H

As entries are added to or revised, appropriate personnel within the firm should be alerted to the changes. This might be done by circulating an updated paper version of the calendar, by e-mail, or by automatically generated communications that inform personnel of the modification.

Firms that identify lawyers and staff using their initials should have a system in place in case two or more people at the firm have the same initials. A firm might assign a number as the middle initial for a person with the same initials who is hired later. So, a lawyer named Harry Alders Haight would be identified with the initials HAH. When a new lawyer named Hadley Alison Heuess joins the firm, she will be identified with the initials H2H. When a paralegal named Henderson Aimes Hill joins, he will be identified as H3H. Consistency in entering lawyer and staff identities is important, especially in large firms. Care must be taken to accurately identify people who go by nicknames. Someone named Robert T. Jones who goes by "Bob" must still be identified by the first initial of his given name to avoid confusing him with Brian T. Jamison, a lawyer whose first initial is B.

personal calendar: A calendar maintained for an individual's own use.

Lawyers' and staff members' **personal calendars** may contain more detailed information about "officially" calendared events along with activities, such as bar association luncheons, speaking engagements, and continuing legal education classes, that may not merit inclusion on the master calendar that is widely circulated to members of the firm and staffers in need of it. In addition to fleshing out entries on the master calendar in an individual one, entries for other important deadlines involving legal action that may not be in litigation (such as a deadline for submitting comments on proposed rulemaking to a government agency) should be made in an individual calendar.

Calendaring practices vary by firm and even by attorney. A lawyer who is very comfortable using technology may have no problem using an individual calendar that is computerized. One who is not quite so technically savvy may prefer to maintain a paper-calendar backup. Most important, calendars should not be limited to "one set of eyes"—if they are, it is easy to overlook or forget about an important deadline. A lawyer, her paralegal, and her legal secretary should check entries in the firm's master calendar that pertain to matters the lawyer is working on. The human element involved in calendaring and alerting appropriate people to significant events cannot be overlooked.

B.   DOCKET CONTROL

docket: A list of matters in litigation; caseload.

Whereas an individual calendar contains networking meetings, client meetings, scheduled conference calls, and other matters, master calendars tend to identify major events in litigation with which the firm is involved. Keeping close track of matters in litigation, or a firm's **docket,** is especially important, because failure to make an appearance or to meet a deadline can have serious repercussions, both for a client and for the lawyer who made a mistake. A client might automatically lose a case because her lawyer neglected to file an answer on time.

1.   Deadlines

Automated docketing programs can incorporate court rules by, for instance, calculating a response date if one is required within 14 days of receipt of a document. Computerized docketing programs can also generate reminders about important upcoming deadlines. Such computer programs are also valuable because they can easily generate reports identifying activities by lawyer, by date, by practice group, by case, and so forth. Automated docketing programs can often be synchronized with smartphones and tablets (small handheld computers such as the iPad). Using an automated calendar can result in lower malpractice insurance premiums.[3] Automated docketing programs are not without their drawbacks, though. They can be expensive for small firms and pose management challenges for very large firms practicing in multiple jurisdictions.[4]

No matter what type of calendar (automated or paper) a firm uses, of necessity, a firm must establish a process for making entries into the master calendar. The firm might generate a docket request form to ask that an item be added to the firm's master calendar. At minimum, the form should identify the requester, the responsible attorney, the case name, the event being scheduled, and the client and matter numbers. The law firm must establish a process for entering the data on the forms into the computer and for verifying that the information was entered accurately.

If the firm does not have an automated calendar program that calculates dates, someone must do so manually. A **trigger date** is the date that launches the time clock. For instance, suppose an answer must be filed within 30 days from the filing of a complaint; then the trigger date is the filing date. Care must be taken to distinguish between events that are triggered upon the filing of a document and those that are triggered upon the receipt of a document. A **deadline** is the date on which a specified document is due. A **mailing date** is the date on which a document must be sent in order to be received by a deadline. A **default date** is the date an opposing party will be considered to have defaulted if an answer is not filed by the appropriate deadline.

The person calculating a deadline must know how a given court establishes various deadlines. Some courts calculate deadlines by calendar days; other courts calculate deadlines using workdays (days when the court is open) and do not include weekends, holidays, and other days when the court is closed (such as election day). Federal, state, and local court rules can vary significantly, and the person responsible for calculating due dates must take great care in determining the dates. Federal Rules of Civil Procedure Rule 6 governs how time is computed in federal district courts (see Figure 6.1 on page 146). The calculations vary somewhat for federal appeals courts (see Figure 6.2). A state statute specifying that workdays are to be used when calculating deadlines is presented in Figure 6.3.

Review the calendar in Figure 6.4. If a document was due 14 calendar days from a trigger date on December 1, the document would have to be filed by December 15 in a court that uses calendar days to calculate deadlines. In a state court that uses workdays, however, the document would not have to be filed until December 16 (because weekends and other days when the court is closed are excluded). The trigger date is not included in the calculation; begin counting on the next day.

trigger date: The date that launches a specified amount of time by which another event must occur.

deadline: The date on which a specified document is due.

mailing date: The date on which a document must be sent in order to be received by a deadline.

default date: The date an opposing party will be considered to have defaulted if an answer is not filed by the appropriate deadline.

---

3. *See, e.g.,* Gerald J. Hoenig, *Selecting Practice Management Software, a Daunting Task,* 22 Prob. & Prop. 57 (Oct. 2008).

4. *See, e.g.,* Joseph C. Scott, *Test Your Court Calendaring IQ,* 51 Orange County Law. 35 (May 2009).

Figure 6.1
Federal Rules of Civil Procedure

Rule 6: Computing and Extending Time; Time for Motion Papers

(a) Computing Time. The following rules apply in computing any time period specified in these rules, in any local rule or court order, or in any statute that does not specify a method of computing time.

(1) *Period Stated in Days or a Longer Unit.* When the period is stated in days or a longer unit of time:

(A) exclude the day of the event that triggers the period;

(B) count every day, including intermediate Saturdays, Sundays, and legal holidays; and

(C) include the last day of the period, but if the last day is a Saturday, Sunday, or legal holiday, the period continues to run until the end of the next day that is not a Saturday, Sunday, or legal holiday.

(2) *Period Stated in Hours.* When the period is stated in hours:

(A) begin counting immediately on the occurrence of the event that triggers the period;

(B) count every hour, including hours during intermediate Saturdays, Sundays, and legal holidays; and

(C) if the period would end on a Saturday, Sunday, or legal holiday, the period continues to run until the same time on the next day that is not a Saturday, Sunday, or legal holiday.

(3) *Inaccessibility of the Clerk's Office.* Unless the court orders otherwise, if the clerk's office is inaccessible:

(A) on the last day for filing under Rule 6(a)(1), then the time for filing is extended to the first accessible day that is not a Saturday, Sunday, or legal holiday; or

(B) during the last hour for filing under Rule 6(a)(2), then the time for filing is extended to the same time on the first accessible day that is not a Saturday, Sunday, or legal holiday.

(4) *"Last Day" Defined.* Unless a different time is set by a statute, local rule, or court order, the last day ends:

(A) for electronic filing, at midnight in the court's time zone; and

(B) for filing by other means, when the clerk's office is scheduled to close.

(5) *"Next Day" Defined.* The "next day" is determined by continuing to count forward when the period is measured after an event and backward when measured before an event.

(6) *"Legal Holiday" Defined.* "Legal holiday" means:

(A) the day set aside by statute for observing New Year's Day, Martin Luther King Jr.'s Birthday, Washington's Birthday, Memorial Day, Independence Day, Labor Day, Columbus Day, Veterans' Day, Thanksgiving Day, or Christmas Day;

(B) any day declared a holiday by the President or Congress; and

(C) for periods that are measured after an event, any other day declared a holiday by the state where the district court is located.

(b) Extending Time.

(1) *In General.* When an act may or must be done within a specified time, the court may, for good cause, extend the time:

(A) with or without motion or notice if the court acts, or if a request is made, before the original time or its extension expires; or

(B) on motion made after the time has expired if the party failed to act because of excusable neglect.

(2) *Exceptions.* A court must not extend the time to act under Rules 50(b) and (d), 52(b), 59(b), (d), and (e), and 60(b).

(c) Motions, Notices of Hearing, and Affidavits.

(1) *In General.* A written motion and notice of the hearing must be served at least 14 days before the time specified for the hearing, with the following exceptions:

(A) when the motion may be heard ex parte;

(B) when these rules set a different time; or

(C) when a court order—which a party may, for good cause, apply for ex parte—sets a different time.

(2) *Supporting Affidavit.* Any affidavit supporting a motion must be served with the motion. Except as Rule 59(c) provides otherwise, any opposing affidavit must be served at least 7 days before the hearing, unless the court permits service at another time.

(d) Additional Time After Certain Kinds of Service. When a party may or must act within a specified time after service and service is made under Rule 5(b)(2)(C), (D), (E), or (F), 3 days are added after the period would otherwise expire under Rule 6(a).

Source: **Fed. R. Civ. P. 6**

In addition to filing deadlines, statutes of limitations dates should be included as calendar entries. A **statute of limitation** bars lawsuits after a certain period of time after the occurrence of the activity (such as a car accident) that gave rise to the legal action. The time after which an action is time-barred varies by the type of claim involved. See Figure 6.5 for a sample statute of limitations.

The importance of maintaining and updating a calendar cannot be overstated.

statute of limitation: A law barring lawsuits after a certain period of time after the activity (such as a car accident) that gave rise to the legal action occurred.

2. *Reminders*

Because deadlines can be missed even when they are properly noted on a calendar, firms post reminders, or **ticklers,** to alert lawyers to upcoming deadlines.

tickler: A reminder about an upcoming deadline.

Figure 6.2
Federal Rules of Appellate Procedure

Rule 26: Computing and Extending Time

(a) Computing Time. The following rules apply in computing any time period specified in these rules, in any local rule or court order, or in any statute that does not specify a method of computing time.

(1) Period Stated in Days or a Longer Unit. When the period is stated in days or a longer unit of time:

(A) exclude the day of the event that triggers the period;

(B) count every day, including intermediate Saturdays, Sundays, and legal holidays; and

(C) include the last day of the period, but if the last day is a Saturday, Sunday, or legal holiday, the period continues to run until the end of the next day that is not a Saturday, Sunday, or legal holiday.

(2) Period Stated in Hours. When the period is stated in hours:

(A) begin counting immediately on the occurrence of the event that triggers the period;

(B) count every hour, including hours during intermediate Saturdays, Sundays, and legal holidays; and

(C) if the period would end on a Saturday, Sunday, or legal holiday, the period continues to run until the same time on the next day that is not a Saturday, Sunday, or legal holiday.

(3) Inaccessibility of the Clerk's Office. Unless the court orders otherwise, if the clerk's office is inaccessible:

(A) on the last day for filing under Rule 26(a)(1), then the time for filing is extended to the first accessible day that is not a Saturday, Sunday, or legal holiday; or

(B) during the last hour for filing under Rule 26(a)(2), then the time for filing is extended to the same time on the first accessible day that is not a Saturday, Sunday, or legal holiday.

(4) "Last Day" Defined. Unless a different time is set by a statute, local rule, or court order, the last day ends:

(A) for electronic filing in the district court, at midnight in the court's time zone;

(B) for electronic filing in the court of appeals, at midnight in the time zone of the circuit clerk's principal office;

(C) for filing under Rules 4(c)(1), 25(a)(2)(B), and 25(a)(2)(C) — and filing by mail under Rule 13(b) — at the latest time for the method chosen for delivery to the post office, third-party commercial carrier, or prison mailing system; and

(D) for filing by other means, when the clerk's office is scheduled to close.

(5) "Next Day" Defined. The "next day" is determined by continuing to count forward when the period is measured after an event and backward when measured before an event.

(6) "Legal Holiday" Defined. "Legal holiday" means:

(A) the day set aside by statute for observing New Year's Day, Martin Luther King Jr.'s Birthday, Washington's Birthday, Memorial Day, Independence Day, Labor Day, Columbus Day, Veterans' Day, Thanksgiving Day, or Christmas Day;

(B) any day declared a holiday by the President or Congress; and

(C) for periods that are measured after an event, any other day declared a holiday by the state where either of the following is located: the district court that rendered the challenged judgment or order, or the circuit clerk's principal office.

(b) Extending Time. For good cause, the court may extend the time prescribed by these rules or by its order to perform any act, or may permit an act to be done after that time expires. But the court may not extend the time to file:

(1) a notice of appeal (except as authorized in Rule 4) or a petition for permission to appeal; or

(2) a notice of appeal from or a petition to enjoin, set aside, suspend, modify, enforce, or otherwise review an order of an administrative agency, board, commission, or officer of the United States, unless specifically authorized by law.

(c) Additional Time after Service. When a party may or must act within a specified time after service, 3 days are added after the period would otherwise expire under Rule 26(a), unless the paper is delivered on the date of service stated in the proof of service. For purposes of this Rule 26(c), a paper that is served electronically is not treated as delivered on the date of service stated in the proof of service.

Source: **Fed. R. App. P. 26**

Figure 6.3
State Statute on Computing Time Periods

Oregon Rules of Civil Procedure

Rule 10: Time

A. COMPUTATION

In computing any period of time prescribed or allowed by these rules, by the local rules of any court or by order of court, the day of the act, event, or default from which the designated period of time begins to run shall not be included. The last day of the period so computed shall be included, unless it is a Saturday or a legal holiday, including Sunday, in which event the period runs until the end of the next day which is not a Saturday or a legal holiday. If the period so computed relates to serving a public officer or filing a document at a public office, and if the last day falls on a day when that particular office is closed before the end of or for all of the normal work day, the last day shall be excluded in computing the period of time within which service is to be made or the document is to be filed, in which event the period runs until the close of office hours on the next day the office is open for business. When the period of time prescribed or allowed (without regard to section C. of this rule) is less than 7 days, intermediate Saturdays and legal holidays, including Sundays, shall be excluded in the computation. As used in this rule, "legal holiday" means legal holiday as defined in ORS 187.010 and 187.020. This section does not apply to any time limitation governed by ORS 174.120.

Source: **Or. R. Civ. P. 10**

Figure 6.4
Sample Calendar

November 2010

S	M	Tu	W	Th	F	S
	1	2	3	4	5	6
7	8	9	10	11	12	13
14	15	16	17	18	19	20
21	22	23	24	25	26	27
28	29	30				

December 2010

January 2011

S	M	Tu	W	Th	F	S
						1
2	3	4	5	6	7	8
9	10	11	12	13	14	15
16	17	18	19	20	21	22
23	24	25	26	27	28	29
30	31					

Sunday	Monday	Tuesday	Wednesday	Thursday	Friday	Saturday
			1	2	3	4
5	6	7	8	9 STATE ELECTIONS-STATE COURTHOUSE CLOSED	10	11
12	13	14	15	16	17	18
19	20	21	22	23	24 FEDERAL HOLIDAY STATE HOLIDAY	25 CHRISTMAS
26	27	28	29	30 STATE HOLIDAY	31 FEDERAL HOLIDAY STATE HOLIDAY	Jan. 1-NEW YEAR'S DAY

Automated calendars can also send e-mail reminders automatically or display pop-up boxes on a computer. Apps for smartphones can synchronize with a lawyer's automated calendar. A tickler for any given event might be set at 30 days, 14 days, 7 days, and the day before a deadline. Some firms even color code their ticklers, so events might reach "red alert" level as the date of a deadline gets closer.

Ultimately, the responsibility for meeting deadlines rests with the lawyer. But, inevitably, lawyers still miss deadlines. When they do, they might face a

Figure 6.5
Sample Statute of Limitations

New York Civil Practice Law and Rules 214 (2013)

§214. Actions to be commenced within three years: for non-payment of money collected on execution; for penalty created by statute; to recover chattel; for injury to property; for personal injury; for malpractice other than medical, dental or podiatric malpractice; to annul a marriage on the ground of fraud.

The following actions must be commenced within three years:

1. an action against a sheriff, constable or other officer for the non-payment of money collected upon an execution;

2. an action to recover upon a liability, penalty or forfeiture created or imposed by statute except as provided in sections 213 and 215;

3. an action to recover a chattel or damages for the taking or detaining of a chattel;

4. an action to recover damages for an injury to property except as provided in section 214-c;

5. an action to recover damages for a personal injury except as provided in sections 214-b, 214-c and 215;

6. an action to recover damages for malpractice, other than medical, dental or podiatric malpractice, regardless of whether the underlying theory is based in contract or tort; and

7. an action to annul a marriage on the ground of fraud; the time within which the action must be commenced shall be computed from the time the plaintiff discovered the facts constituting the fraud, but if the plaintiff is a person other than the spouse whose consent was obtained by fraud, the time within which the action must be commenced shall be computed from the time, if earlier, that that spouse discovered the facts constituting the fraud.

malpractice lawsuit from the client whose deadline was overlooked. Even if the client does not sue the lawyer, the client is likely to fire the lawyer.

Although people may agree that "everyone makes mistakes," courts are not necessarily so forgiving of casual errors. In certain circumstances, a court will forgive a lawyer's calendaring error if the court finds there has been "excusable neglect." Excusable neglect is defined as:

> a failure—which the law will excuse—to take some proper step at the proper time (esp. in neglecting to answer a lawsuit) not because of the party's own carelessness, inattention, or willful disregard of the court's process, but because of some unexpected or unavoidable hindrance or accident or because of reliance on the care and vigilance of the party's counsel or on a promise made by the adverse party.[5]

Simply making a mistake, or failing to catch the mistake of a staff person, generally will not absolve the lawyer before a court:

> Lawyers must assume that courts will treat the failure to read rules, failure to understand rules and failure to properly apply rules as *in*excusable neglect. Few courts are likely to hold otherwise where a lawyer delegates responsibility for rules

---

5. Black's Law Dictionary 1061 (2004).

interpretations to non-lawyer staff. The bottom line is that lawyers must be responsible for reading appropriate rules and deciding upon appropriate deadlines, even if the task of calendaring such deadlines and ministerial acts designed to ensure compliance are delegated to non-lawyers.[6]

Of course, there is an exception to every rule. Consider the following case, where a court did allow a lawyer who had missed a deadline to obtain an extension of time. Notice the reasons for the mistake that the lawyer provided.

PINCAY V. ANDREWS
389 F.3d 853 (9th Cir. 2004)

COUNSEL: Neil Papiano and Patrick McAdam, Iverson, Yoakum, Papiano & Hatch, Los Angeles, California, for the plaintiffs-appellants.

David Boies and Robert Silver, Boies, Schiller & Flexner, LLP, Armonk, New York, for the defendants-appellees.

Judges: Before: Mary M. Schroeder, Chief Judge, Alex Kozinski, Pamela Ann Rymer, Andrew J. Kleinfeld, Sidney R. Thomas, Barry G. Silverman, M. Margaret McKeown, Ronald M. Gould, Marsha S. Berzon, Johnnie B. Rawlinson, and Consuelo M. Callahan, Circuit Judges. Opinion by Chief Judge Schroeder; Concurrence by Judge Berzon; Dissent by Judge Kozinski.

OPINION BY: MARY M. SCHROEDER

OPINION

This appeal represents a lawyer's nightmare. A sophisticated law firm, with what it thought was a sophisticated system to determine and calendar filing deadlines, missed a critical one: the 30-day time period in which to file a notice of appeal under Federal Rule of Appellate Procedure 4(a)(1)(A). The rule, however, provides for a grace period of 30 days within which a lawyer in such a fix may ask the district court for an extension of time, and the court, in the exercise of its discretion, may grant the extension if it determines that the neglect of the attorney was "excusable."[1] Here an experienced trial judge found excusable neglect, and the appellee asks us to overturn that ruling.

The underlying dispute began in 1989 when Laffit Pincay, Jr. and Christopher McCarron (Pincay) sued Vincent S. Andrews, Robert L. Andrews, and Vincent Andrews Management Corp. (Andrews) for financial injuries stemming from alleged violations of the Racketeer Influenced and Corrupt Organizations Act (RICO) and California law. In 1992, a jury returned verdicts in Pincay's favor on both the RICO and the California counts. Pincay was ordered to elect a remedy, and he chose to pursue the RICO judgment. This judgment was reversed on appeal on the ground that the RICO claim was barred by the federal statute of limitations. *Pincay v. Andrews*, 238 F.3d 1106, 1110 (9th Cir. 2001). On remand,

---

6. Douglas R. Richmond, *Neglect, Excusable and Otherwise*, 2 Seton Hall Cir. Rev. 119, 136 (Fall 2005).

1. The rule provides in relevant part: "The district court may extend the time to file a notice of appeal if: (i) a party so moves no later than 30 days after the time prescribed by this Rule 4(a) expires; and (ii) . . . that party shows excusable neglect or good cause." Fed. R. App. P. 4(a)(5)(A).

Pincay elected to pursue the remedy on his California law claim. Judgment was entered in his favor on July 3, 2002.

Andrews's notice of appeal was due 30 days later, but a paralegal charged with calendaring filing deadlines misread the rule and advised Andrews's attorney that the notice was not due for 60 days, the time allowed when the government is a party to the case. *See* Fed. R. App. P. 4(a)(1)(B). Andrews's counsel learned about the error when Pincay relied upon the judgment as being final in related bankruptcy proceedings, and Andrews promptly tendered a notice of appeal together with a request for an extension within the 30-day grace period. By that time the matter had been in litigation for more than 15 years. Everyone involved should have been well aware that the government was not a party to the case, and any lawyer or paralegal should have been able to read the rule correctly. The misreading of the rule was a critical error that, had the district court viewed the situation differently, would have ended the litigation then and there with an irreparably adverse result for Andrews. The district court, however, found the neglect excusable and granted the motion for an extension of time to file the notice of appeal.

Pincay appealed to this court, and a majority of the three-judge panel concluded that Andrews's attorney had improperly delegated the function of calendaring to a paralegal, and held that the attorney's reliance on a paralegal was inexcusable as a matter of law. . . . It ordered the appeal dismissed. The dissent would have applied a more flexible and deferential standard and affirmed the district court. . . .

A majority of the active non-recused judges of the court voted to rehear the case en banc to consider whether the creation of a per se rule against delegation to paralegals, or indeed any per se rule involving missed filing deadlines, is consistent with the United States Supreme Court's leading authority on the modern concept of excusable neglect, *Pioneer Investment Services Co. v. Brunswick Associated Ltd. Partnership*, 507 U.S. 380, 123 L. Ed. 2d 74, 113 S. Ct. 1489 (1993). We now hold that per se rules are not consistent with *Pioneer*, and we uphold the exercise of the district court's discretion to permit the filing of the notice of appeal in this case.

The *Pioneer* decision arose in the bankruptcy context and involved the "bar date" for the filing of claims. The Court in *Pioneer* established a four-part balancing test for determining whether there had been "excusable neglect" within the meaning of Federal Rule of Bankruptcy Procedure 9006(b)(1). The Court also reviewed various contexts in which the phrase appeared in the federal rules of procedure and made it clear the same test applies in all those contexts. The *Pioneer* factors include: (1) the danger of prejudice to the non-moving party, (2) the length of delay and its potential impact on judicial proceedings, (3) the reason for the delay, including whether it was within the reasonable control of the movant, and (4) whether the moving party's conduct was in good faith. 507 U.S. at 395.

In this case, the district court analyzed each of the *Pioneer* factors and correctly found: (1) there was no prejudice, (2) the length of delay was small, (3) the reason for the delay was carelessness, and (4) there was no evidence of bad faith. It then concluded that even though the reason for the delay was the carelessness of Andrews's counsel, that fact did not render the neglect inexcusable. The district court relied on this court's decision in *Marx v. Loral Corp.*, 87 F.3d 1049 (9th Cir.

1996), in which we affirmed an order granting an extension of time in a case that involved an attorney's calendaring error.

Because the panel majority decided the case in part on the issue of delegation of calendaring to a paralegal, we consider that issue first. This issue was not presented to the district court, and it was raised *sua sponte* by the three-judge panel.

In the modern world of legal practice, the delegation of repetitive legal tasks to paralegals has become a necessary fixture. Such delegation has become an integral part of the struggle to keep down the costs of legal representation. Moreover, the delegation of such tasks to specialized, well-educated non-lawyers may well ensure greater accuracy in meeting deadlines than a practice of having each lawyer in a large firm calculate each filing deadline anew. The task of keeping track of necessary deadlines will involve some delegation. The responsibility for the error falls on the attorney regardless of whether the error was made by an attorney or a paralegal. We hold that delegation of the task of ascertaining the deadline was not per se inexcusable neglect.

The larger question in this case is whether the misreading of the clear rule could appropriately have been considered excusable. . . .

. . .

In this case the mistake itself, the misreading of the Rule, was egregious, and the lawyer undoubtedly should have checked the Rule itself before relying on the paralegal's reading. Both the paralegal and the lawyer were negligent. That, however, represents the beginning of our inquiry as to whether the negligence is excusable, not the end of it. The real question is whether there was enough in the context of this case to bring a determination of excusable neglect within the district court's discretion.

We therefore turn to examining the *Pioneer* factors as they apply here. The parties seem to agree that three of the factors militate in favor of excusability, and they focus their arguments on the remaining factor: the reason for the delay. Appellee Andrews characterizes the reason for the delay as the failure of a "carefully designed" calendaring system operated by experienced paralegals that heretofore had worked flawlessly. Appellant Pincay, on the other hand, stresses the degree of carelessness in the failure to read the applicable Rule.

We recognize that a lawyer's failure to read an applicable rule is one of the least compelling excuses that can be offered; yet the nature of the contextual analysis and the balancing of the factors adopted in *Pioneer* counsel against the creation of any rigid rule. Rather, the decision whether to grant or deny an extension of time to file a notice of appeal should be entrusted to the discretion of the district court because the district court is in a better position than we are to evaluate factors such as whether the lawyer had otherwise been diligent, the propensity of the other side to capitalize on petty mistakes, the quality of representation of the lawyers (in this litigation over its 15-year history), and the likelihood of injustice if the appeal was not allowed. Had the district court declined to permit the filing of the notice, we would be hard pressed to find any rationale requiring us to reverse.

Pioneer itself instructs courts to determine the issue of excusable neglect within the context of the particular case, a context with which the trial court is most familiar. Any rationale suggesting that misinterpretation of an unambiguous rule can never be excusable neglect is, in our view, contrary to that instruction. "The right way, under *Pioneer*, to decide cases involving ignorance of federal rules is with an 'elastic concept' equitable in nature, not with a per se rule." *Pincay v. Andrews*, 351 F.3d 947, 953 (9th Cir. 2003) (Kleinfeld, J., dissenting).

We are also mindful that Rule 4 itself provides for leniency in limited circumstances. It could have been written more rigidly, allowing for no window of opportunity once the deadline was missed. Many states' rules provide for an extension of the time for filing a notice of appeal under few, if any, circumstances. . . . The federal rule is a more flexible one that permits a narrow 30-day window for requesting an extension, and the trial court has wide discretion as to whether to excuse the lapse.

We understand several of our sister circuits have tried to fashion a rule making a mistake of law per se inexcusable under Rule 4. We agree that a lawyer's mistake of law in reading a rule of procedure is not a compelling excuse. At the same time, however, a lawyer's mistake of fact, for example, in thinking the government was a party to a case and that the 60-day rule applied for that reason, would be no more compelling.

We are persuaded that, under *Pioneer*, the correct approach is to avoid any per se rule. *Pioneer* cautioned against "erecting a rigid barrier against late filings attributable in any degree to the movant's negligence." 507 U.S. at 395 n.14. There should similarly be no rigid legal rule against late filings attributable to any particular type of negligence. Instead, we leave the weighing of *Pioneer*'s equitable factors to the discretion of the district court in every case.

We hold that the district court did not abuse its discretion in this case. Therefore, the district court's order granting the defendant's motion for an extension of time to file the notice of appeal is AFFIRMED. The merits of the appeal are before the three judge panel in appeal number 02-56491. The panel should proceed to decide that appeal.

C. CASE MANAGEMENT

Although the concepts are related, case management is broader than docket control and includes cases and client matters as well as calendars, notes, time reports, documents, and other materials. Such a system really is practice management software that helps lawyers organize and track many of the materials they generate or use in support of their work for clients.

case management systems: Law firm management programs that include information about lawsuits involving clients and other client matters, along with other documents, calendars, lawyers' notes, and timekeeping elements.

Case management systems may be customized for an individual firm. Off-the-shelf systems are also available. A case management system is helpful to attorneys and their staffs only if people within the firm know how to use the system and how to update and maintain it. Training on the system is vitally important for support staff as well as for attorneys. Law firm leadership must also consistently send a message that the case management system is important to the ultimate success of the firm and should be updated and referred to often.

CHECKLIST

- A law firm should have a system in place for tracking and overseeing each case that the law firm is involved in on behalf of a client.
- A master calendar lists all of the litigation-related activities (such as filing deadlines, hearing dates, and the like) scheduled for lawyers and staff at the firm. Some firms also track other important client events that are not part of litigation.
- Lawyers and staff also maintain their own personal calendars, which tend to flesh out entries on the master calendar with which they are involved and include other activities not listed in the master calendar, such as bar association luncheons, continuing legal education classes, and so forth.
- Automated docketing programs can incorporate court rules and calculate response dates.
- Whether or not a calendar or docket control program is computerized, it must be constantly updated and referred to.
- If the firm does not have an automated calendar program that calculates dates, someone must calculate dates manually. A trigger date is the date that launches the time clock. Care must be taken to distinguish between events that are triggered upon the filing of a document and events that are triggered upon the receipt of a document. A deadline is the date on which a specified document is due. A mailing date is the date on which a document must be sent in order to be received by a deadline. A default date is the date an opposing party will be considered to have defaulted if an answer is not filed by the appropriate deadline.
- The person calculating a deadline must know how a given court establishes various deadlines. Some courts calculate deadlines by calendar days; other courts calculate deadlines using workdays (days when the court is open) and do not include weekends, holidays, and other days when the court is closed (such as election day).
- The responsibility for meeting deadlines rests with the lawyer.
- When lawyers miss deadlines, they might face a malpractice lawsuit from the client whose deadline was overlooked. Even if the client does not sue the lawyer, the client is likely to fire the lawyer.
- Lawyers who miss deadlines might blame their staff for their error.
- Courts are not necessarily forgiving of casual errors. In certain circumstances, a court may forgive a lawyer's calendaring error if the court finds there has been "excusable neglect."

VOCABULARY

calendaring (127)
case management systems (144)

deadline (134)
default date (134)
docket (134)
mailing date (134)
master calendar (p. 279)
personal calendar (133)
statute of limitation (139)
tickler (139)
trigger date (134)

CAREER PREPARATION TIPS

You don't need to be working in the legal field to develop your docket management skills. Apply the principles you have learned here to your personal life, to your volunteer activities, or to your current career. Practice calendaring events and setting up ticklers. For instance, suppose you were invited to a wedding to take place in two months. You might set that up, and then calendar certain tasks (and set up accompanying ticklers) that you need to accomplish, such as returning the response card, purchasing a gift, making travel arrangements, buying a wedding outfit, and so on. Become familiar with free or low-cost software and applications that can aid you in the management of your personal docket.

IF YOU WANT TO LEARN MORE

Association of Legal Administrators. www.alanet.org
    National Institute for Trial Advocacy. http://www.nita.org
    Texas Lawyers' Insurance Exchange Self-Audit Docket Control Evaluation. http://www.tlie.org/prevention/self-audit-docket.php
    Calendar/docket management/case management software:
    http://www.abacuslaw.com
    http://www.activecollab.com
    http://www.amicusattorney.com
    http://basecamphq.com
    http://www.aderant.com/products/aderant-compulaw/
    http://www.deadlines.com
    http://www.elite.com
    http://www.lawfirmadvisor.com
    https://www.ma3000.com
    http://www.perfectpractice.com
    http://www.projectpier.org
    http://www.elite.com/prolaw/
    http://www.theombudsman.com/wp_site/

READING COMPREHENSION

1. What is the difference between a master calendar and a personal calendar?
2. What types of events are recorded in a master calendar?
3. What information should be included in an entry in a master calendar?
4. Who is responsible for maintaining a master calendar?
5. What does a calendar clerk do?
6. What is the difference between calendar days and workdays, and why is this difference important for calendaring events?
7. Will courts allow lawyers to file documents after deadlines have passed?
8. What factors does a court consider in assessing whether a lawyer should be allowed to file a document after a deadline has been missed?
9. What are some drawbacks to automated calendaring and case management systems?

DISCUSSION STARTERS

1. Review *Daniels v. Sacks.* Who brought the lawsuit? What excuses did the defendant give for his failure to meet important deadlines? Why didn't the court accept those excuses?
2. Compare *Pincay v. Andrews.* Who did the lawyer who missed the important deadline blame for the error? Did the court accept the lawyer's excuse? What was the result of the case? In what ways is this case similar to *Daniels v. Sacks?* In what ways is it different? Why do you suppose the U.S. Court of Appeals for the Ninth Circuit decided *Pincay* as it did? Who was the attorney who represented the defendants/appellees? At what firm did the lawyer who made the mistake work? Do you think the law concerning mistakenly missed deadlines is evolving? Do you think the law is changing for the better? Do you think lawyers should delegate calendaring responsibilities to staff?
3. Lawyers seem to blame their paralegals or other staff when they miscalculate deadlines or miss important deadlines. Why do you suppose they do that? How might a paralegal or other staff person protect himself from such an accusation? What should a staff person do if she realizes that she miscalculated an important deadline and the law firm failed to take action by the "real" deadline?
4. Do you think the U.S. Court of Appeals for the Ninth Circuit in *Pincay* displayed favoritism toward the lawyer who had made the mistake? Why do you think the lawyer's law firm was not mentioned in the body of the decision? How might you find out at what law firm the lawyer worked at the time the mistake was made? If you think favoritism did

occur, what does that tell you about the importance of a law firm's reputation and a lawyer's good relationship with judges and court clerks?
5. What do you consider to be the difference between excusable negligence and inexcusable negligence?
6. How might docket management skills be transferred to organizations other than law firms?

CASE STUDIES

1. Suppose you work for a single-office, three-lawyer general practice firm. Identify three case management programs that the firm might purchase. What features of each program would work well for the firm? Are there a lot of superfluous features that the firm might not need or use? Compare and contrast the programs, and recommend one the firm should buy.
2. Suppose you work for a major law firm with 1,500 lawyers in ten offices: seven in the United States, one in London, one in Hong Kong, and one in Dubai. Identify three case management programs that the firm might purchase. What features of each program would work well for the firm? Are there a lot of superfluous features that the firm might not need or use? Compare and contrast the programs, and recommend one the firm should buy.
3. How are court deadlines computed in your state's courts? Look up your state's statute on computation. Is the statute clearly written? Could it be improved to eliminate possibilities for errors?
4. You are the docket clerk at a law firm, and you must calculate the deadlines for the following items. Use the calendar in Figure 6.4 in calculating the deadlines.
     Answer due 15 days after a complaint's filing on Dec. 3 in federal court
     Answer due 15 days after a complaint's filing on Dec. 3 in state court
     Appeal due in federal court seven days after court's decision was filed on Dec. 23
     Appeal due in state court seven days after court's decision was filed on Dec. 23
     Complaint to be filed in federal court by statute of limitations deadline on Dec. 30
     Complaint to be filed in state court by statute of limitations deadline on Dec. 9
     What ticklers for each of these items would you add to the calendar?
5. You are the docket clerk at a law firm, and you must enter the following items on your firm's master calendar. Prepare a calendar with each of these entries; include only pertinent material.
     Smith v. Jones oral argument on Dec. 20
     Second U.S. Circuit Court of Appeals
     11:30 A.M.

Client: Samantha Strahern, who filed an amicus curiae brief on
  behalf of respondent Jones
Attorneys: Carrie Diane Kearns, Juana Marie Lopez, George Mario
  Letterer
Paralegal: Mindy Starr Osmond

Dec. 20
Apple v. Dell
answer due
Second U.S. Circuit Court of Appeals
Client: Wilhelmina Dell
Attorneys: Carrie Diane Kearns, Juana Marie Lopez
Paralegal: Mindy Starr Osmond

Dec. 20
response to motion for summary judgment due
Dell v. Smith Bank
Client: Wilhelmina Dell
Attorneys: Juana Marie Lopez, George Mario Letterer
Paralegal: Mindy Starr Osmond

Dec. 20
deadline for any appeal to be filed
Dell Holding Co. v. Dell
Client: Wilhelmina Dell
Attorney: Mark Landers Christian
Paralegal: Marcia Lynne Cheney
contract claim

Keller v. Keller
conference with mediator on Dec. 21
2 P.M.
Westchester County Courthouse
Room 8
Client: Ryan Keller (plaintiff)
Attorney: Mark Landers Christian
Paralegal: Marcia Lynne Cheney
divorce action

Dec. 15
Simonetti v. Garfunkle
jury selection
Monroe County Courthouse
Courtroom 10
Client: Justicia Simonetti
Attorney: Mark Landers Christian
personal injury case

6. What ticklers for each of these events should also be added to the mas-
    ter calendar? What other information, if any, should be added to the
    master calendar for each of these entries? What additional

information, if any, should be added to the personal calendars of each of the people involved in these activities?

7. Research "help wanted" ads for docket/calendar/case management clerks in your area. Are many positions available? What pay levels are given? Would you like to be a docket/calendar/case management clerk? Do you think there's much promotion potential for someone with that job?

CHAPTER

7

Knowledge and Records Management

CHAPTER OUTCOMES

By the end of this chapter, a student will be able to:

- Distinguish between knowledge management and records management
- Describe the elements of a records management system
- Identify ethical issues associated with knowledge and records management
- Propose means to prevent ethical violations from occurring

Think about all of the information that arrives at a law firm every single day, whether by delivery, e-mail, regular mail, messenger, FedEx or UPS, phone, voice mail, or download from the Internet. Much of that information must be retained, remembered, followed up, and retrieved at some future date. **Records management** is the process in which all of these materials are organized, handled, and stored. As tedious as supervising a paper trail (much of which is no longer actually on paper but is in various electronic forms) might seem to some people, it's a vitally important responsibility. Without some sort of system in place, a law firm's business—its very reason for existence—can easily go astray. Think for a moment about a private individual's life. A person probably has established his or her own systems for dealing with the information that arrives each day: She might place bills received in the mail into a basket for handling before the end of the month, she might enter appointments on a family calendar, she might listen to voice mail messages after she comes home from work and then return calls later in the evening, she might place paychecks that arrive directly into her wallet for later deposit at her bank. If she stops doing any of these activities, bills can pile up, utilities can be turned off, appointments can be missed, friends and family can become mad, and, in short, chaos ensues.

Law firms are constantly barraged by an overwhelming amount of information. It is very easy for some to slip away, to be overlooked, accidentally discarded, or simply forgotten. Law firms must establish their own practices for handling all of the information they receive, they must educate their lawyers and staff about the practices, and they must make sure that the practices are followed accurately. If they are not, the same negative events that can happen to an individual can happen to a law firm: Bills can pile up, utilities can be turned off, appointments

records management: The process by which materials containing information are organized, handled, and stored.

can be missed, clients can become mad, and chaos ensues. Sometimes clients sue their lawyers for malpractice. Then the law firm's reputation suffers, it loses clients and fails to attract more of them, and, in a worst-case scenario, the law firm might become insolvent and shut down.

Ultimately, of course, just about everyone at a law firm must be responsible for managing the firm's records in some way. Documents must be retrievable, and the system for managing them must be understood and used by everyone at the firm. A law office manager, an information technology employee, a records administrator, or even a librarian employed by the firm might be responsible for developing, implementing, and enforcing a records management program.

Dealing efficiently and effectively with records is no small matter for a law firm. Think of the many activities that take place on any given day at a law firm: Lawyers prepare work products for clients, paralegals conduct research, prospective clients visit the firm, new employees begin their first day on the job, practice groups depart, marketers place advertisements about the firm, payroll is met, the rent is paid, the utilities remain on, and so on. All of these activities must occur seamlessly on an ongoing basis. The ability to function well begins with a strong records management system.

A. WHAT IS RECORDS MANAGEMENT?

Records management is a broader activity than file management and docket management. Records management really refers to systems a law firm establishes to manage all of the materials it receives. One useful definition of records describes them as

> books, papers, maps, photographs, machine readable materials, or other documentary materials, regardless of physical form or characteristics, made or received . . . or in connection with the transaction of . . . business and preserved or appropriate for preservation . . . as evidence of the organization, functions, policies, decisions, procedures, operations, or other activities . . . or because of the informational value of data in them.[1]

File management and docket management may be considered subsets of records management, although in some ways they overlap. File management refers primarily to client files, whereas docket management involves mostly the actual lawsuits a firm is involved in on behalf of clients. Records management encompasses files, dockets, and all of the other records flowing through a firm.

Dealing with records can be very costly. Hours and hours might be dedicated to creating record management policy, procuring software for managing it, implementing the policy, training staff on records management, arranging for physical storage space, and hiring a record destruction service.

---

1. 44 U.S.C. § 3301 (2013).

Remember that more than **"front-office" activities**—which support the law practice itself—are included in records management. **"Back-office" activities**, such as accounting, human resources, marketing, and facilities management, also generate plenty of records that have to be protected from inappropriate disclosure.

A records management policy developed by a firm should identify the various types of records that are being tracked, establish handling requirements for each type, determine who has access to various types of records, and safeguard the handling of records. Arrangements must also be made for storage, whether electronic, physical on-site, or long-term off-site storage. A records destruction policy and procedure should also be an element of a records management policy.

"front-office" activity: Work that supports the law practice itself.

"back-office" activity: Work that deals with the business administration side of the law firm.

1.   Records Retention

Records retention—the length of time an item is kept—should be an element of any records management policy. Some records must be kept for a certain number of years as specified by statute. For instance, tax laws and unemployment insurance laws might require that records be available for a certain number of years. It's a good idea to retain other records as well. Remember that law firms today are not static entities. People are constantly moving into and out of them—working there for a period of time and then departing. The institutional memory that might have existed in firms of a century ago, when lawyers tended to stay at a single firm for their entire professional lives, does not exist today— unless a well-developed records management policy is set up to preserve it. For instance, although a firm might not be legally required to maintain records about its advertising campaign in perpetuity, the firm still might want to keep them. Five years, 10 years, 15 years from now, firm employees are not likely to remember approaches the firm tried today that backfired, or slogans that were considered and rejected. As even more time goes by, the firm might want to preserve these records for use in a firm history.

records retention: The length of time a piece of information should be kept.

The important point is that a firm must set up a policy for records retention, and its employees must then follow that policy. Areas must be designated for the storage of records on-site, either in a centralized records room or at decentralized areas near lawyers and personnel who will frequently use them. Procedures for shipping records to off-site storage and for accessing those records in off-site storage must also be established.

Records retention policy will likely vary for client files as opposed to administrative files of the law firm. Here are some examples of administrative records a law firm is likely to have:

- payroll data
- health insurance information
- employee files
- records on job applicants
- performance evaluations
- contracts
- hiring letters
- offer letters
- background checks

- information about salaries
- references
- vacation request forms
- information on garnishments
- disability claims
- attendance records
- time cards for staff
- recruiting materials
- family and medical leave materials
- accounts payable
- accounts receivable
- affirmative action/diversity information
- discrimination claims
- benefits information
- independent contractor records
- data on marketing efforts
- research on prospective clients
- insurance carriers, policies, and premiums
- workers' compensation claims
- material safety data sheets
- Occupational Safety and Health Administration information
- injury reports
- retirement policies

In addition, a firm is likely to establish its own databases, or storehouses of knowledge, on legal subjects that lawyers and others at the firm frequently research. These databases may include templates and copies of work the firm has done for other clients. For instance, a real estate firm is unlikely to draw up a new contract of sale for every single real estate transaction. It will likely use a template or pull up samples of contracts prepared for similar clients and then customize individual parts. Publicly available documents might also be stored in these databases, such as comments on proposed regulations, complaints, answers, and so on.

cloud computing: Use of remote servers for data and management allowing users to access data from any computer with an Internet connection (rather than programs and other materials being stored directly on one's personal computer or internal network).

A records retention policy must address how all of these different types of records are to be handled and retained and must also specify when they are to be destroyed. Such a policy should identify the people who are responsible for determining the records' fate.

Of necessity, technology plays a role here. Increasingly, more records are electronic. Technological developments are likely to affect a firm's records management policies, especially as phenomena like **cloud computing**—which uses remote servers for data storage and management rather than programs and other materials for storage directly in one's personal computer—become more accepted and mainstream.

Practical matters must also be attended to. As anyone who has worked for a law firm knows, there is likely to always be at least one lawyer at a firm who has a "leaning tower of Pisa" inbox, with documents piled almost to the tipping point. Lawyers may not spend a whole lot of time managing records they keep in their own offices, and these can fall into disarray. Actual storage space—meaning filing cabinets—can be highly coveted within a firm, and lawyers, paralegals, and others sometimes battle in an effort to stake out convenient storage space. A records management procedure, which clearly sets out how any newly available storage space is to be parceled out, can alleviate some of these disturbances.

A law firm must have appropriate materials for storing all of these records: filing cabinets, file folders, labels, bar coding systems, and such. Unfortunately, these supplies do not just magically appear when a lawyer or paralegal needs them. Someone at the firm must be responsible for ordering and reordering them and for monitoring new developments that will make records management easier.

Perhaps the most important attribute of any records management system is being able to find a document when you need it.

2. *Indexing and Records Retrieval*

One sign that a firm has a less than optimal records managements system is when paralegals or legal secretaries have to call former lawyers and other employees asking where they left certain files. Simply put, a firm must have a records management system in place, and the firm's leaders must make sure people are aware of it! Also important is cataloging information so that it can be retrieved easily. Probably all of us have had the experience of using a book with a poorly crafted index—one with few entries, where seemingly obvious topics are omitted, and information cannot be easily found. No matter how punctilious a firm is in logging in new documents and storing them promptly, its efforts will be of little use if the very people who must access the information are unable to locate it.

Records may be organized in a number of ways: by subject matter, by practice area, by author, by a unique number assigned to the record, by client and matter number, by other numbers assigned to materials generated within the firm, and so on. An index of these categories and subcategories should be created, and guidelines on how to categorize various types of documents must be established. An index is "a structured hierarchy of terms developed for the purpose of locating specific objects within a larger collection."[2] In short, an index is essentially a map to all of a firm's records. It largely resembles an outline and becomes increasingly detailed.

What does this mean for the law office manager or the records manager, if the firm has one? Someone needs to set up the system and then implement it. Employees must be trained in using the system, and someone must follow up to make sure that materials are properly categorized so that the system is actually useful. Remember that records are retrieved for different purposes. For instance, a paralegal might be looking for a specific deed the law firm has worked on. Alternatively, the paralegal might be looking for copies of all deeds that have a certain phrase in them or that are in a certain geographic area. Users of the records management system must be able to retrieve very specific information as well as more general information.

Of necessity, much of the information—and the index itself—is stored electronically. Key words can be assigned to electronic records, and even to paper ones, to make them more easily retrievable. When key words are assigned to a document, consistent terms must be used. For example, a search engine might

---

2. George C. Cunningham & John C. Montaña, *The Lawyer's Guide to Records Management and Retention* 120 (2006).

not retrieve a document to which the key word *Superfund* had been spelled *Super Fund*. The search engine would not retrieve a search for the key word *radioactive* if the word *nuclear* had been assigned to a document itself. Conventions must be established for assigning key words and for spelling them. For example, a search engine might be unable to retrieve a document labeled *N.Y. D.E.C.* if someone had searched for *NYDEC*.

Naming conventions should be established for documents. Here, too, there are many methods. Documents might be slugged first by client name and matter and then by document type, version, the initials of the person who wrote the most recent revision, and the date. For example, the following are some document names:

- ManhattanNetworkInc-NYCtransactions-305E86St9JWcontractofsale-LNT-06152010
- PinkmoondustProductions-Connecticutstore-interiordesigncontract-v2-VLL-04302009
- GreggFarms-roadsidestandfranchise-storespecs-v4-RSD-06062010

The ability to track documents is vital. Untold hours could be wasted drafting a new work product from scratch when a prior effort is not remembered or recovered. Earlier projects can serve as templates for later ones. New contracts are not written each time a client needs an agreement drawn up; a lawyer or staff person begins with a prototype and then tailors it to the individual client's needs.

Not only must a firm's lawyers be able to locate documents previously prepared by themselves or by others at the firm, but also knowing who worked on those materials can also be enormously helpful. The lawyer can then consult these earlier drafters, as needed, for suggestions and input about various elements of a document. Why did they craft a phrase a certain way? Why was a standard clause omitted? Unless a later user can retrieve this earlier work, much valuable insight may well be lost.

3. *Record Destruction*

At some point, certain records are no longer needed. The trick is deciding what is unnecessary and when it becomes unnecessary. No one wants to deliberately destroy an important document. A firm should develop a records destruction policy in which records are reviewed periodically and slated for destruction provided that such measure is approved. For instance, a records clerk might identify certain materials that have been unused for a period of time, such as ten years, then circulate a list of materials to lawyers and others in the firm who once worked on them, and indicate that, unless there is an objection, the records will be destroyed on a certain date. Even if there is no objection, a lawyer should review the records to be destroyed. Other firms might choose to take greater precautions and require a lawyer to sign a request for records destruction.

If the records at issue are client files, the client should be informed that the firm no longer wishes to store the records for the client. The firm should offer to deliver the files to the client and should explain that if the client does not get back in touch with the firm by a certain date about the disposition of the files, the files will then be destroyed.

Factors to consider before files are destroyed include whether the statute of limitations period on any prospective malpractice claim has run and whether a case involves an unsatisfied judgment.

Certain documents should be retained, such as wills, files on a structured settlement if the settlement is not yet final, deeds, and other vital documents.

Precautions should be taken in actually destroying the documents, whether they are in digital form or in hard copy. Papers should not merely be deposited in garbage cans; they should be shredded first. Electronic files can often be recovered even if someone hits the "delete" key. A disk wiping program or other technological approach should be taken to permanently erase the existence of a file from a computer.

4.   Lawyer and Staff Training

Personnel at law firms need to be told how to handle records. If they are not properly trained, documents will not be properly recorded, acted upon, filed, stored, retrieved, or disposed of, and a law firm will struggle as lawyers and others waste valuable time trying to find materials or to "reinvent the wheel" and generate new documents needlessly.

Undoubtedly, learning about records management procedures can be a bit tedious. Lawyers have a tendency to delegate such responsibilities to their support staff. Lawyers might put off going to training classes themselves or attend only briefly. New law clerks at large firms may be given no training and may have no idea where work they generate should be stored or how it should be filed. This is a mistake. How expensive is it on a day-to-day basis as they hunt for materials? Top-down demonstrations that records management is a vital activity for everyone at the firm are necessary in order for both lawyers and staff people to take the chore seriously.

Not only must everyone at the firm be trained on records management, but also a records supervisor must conduct quality control activities to make sure that materials are properly recorded and managed. A firm that is lax in its records management will find itself in disarray and exposed to malpractice lawsuits.

If a firm opts to delegate records management responsibilities to a revolving team of paralegals or other staffers, not much attention may be paid to quality control. Documents must still be retrievable when the primary person responsible for managing them is not in the office. To get people to follow appropriate records management procedures, the procedures should be user friendly, easy to explain, and easy to learn and use.

To encourage lawyers and staff people to take records management duties seriously, a firm might provide them with an opportunity to have input into its records management procedures. The suggestions of staff, in particular, should be sought. After all, they are the people who most often manage records. Lawyers must delegate appropriate records management tasks. Why should a lawyer who charges $500 per hour organize files when a files clerk making $40 per hour can do the task more efficiently? Even though staffers are likely to be better acquainted with records management tasks, lawyers must still be able to retrieve information, especially after-hours when support staff have gone home.

B. RECORDS MANAGEMENT SYSTEMS

Every law firm must have a records management system—a standardized means for recording, using, retaining, and destroying materials that can be taught to and used by others and revised as needed. Mail and packages must be appropriately routed, faxes must be delivered to the right person, client lists must be maintained, client contact information must be updated, copies of complaints or answers or other documents filed in a lawsuit must be responded to, documents associated with being in business must be addressed: utility bills, credit card bills, information about health insurance and claims, information about workers' compensation. The information coming into a firm must be organized and tracked so it can be followed up on, used, stored, and retrieved when necessary.

The need for duplicating some records must be addressed. If a letter from a client to a partner arrives, does a secretary log that letter into a master list of documents? Does she deliver it directly to the partner's inbox, or does she make a copy for the associate who is also working on the case? Does she place a copy of the letter in a client file? Does she scan a copy of that letter so it can be stored electronically? Who will follow up to determine that a response to the letter is sent?

So many different types of documents come into a firm that a clear line of authority must be established. Some materials must be circulated and acted upon or responded to, while others must be stored for future reference. Will all bills received be directed to the head of the accounting department? Or should they instead be routed to an overseeing partner, who will review them before forwarding them to accounting?

Although many records are stored electronically, these items, too, must be tracked and acted upon or stored appropriately so they can be easily retrieved at a future date. A firm's chief information officer may be closely involved with electronic records management, and a firm's librarian may share responsibilities for establishing and maintaining the firm's records management system. If a staff person is out of the office or on leave, others in the office must be able to maintain the records management system with no, or minimal, interruption. A system is necessary so that decision making is uniform: One person who is handling a document will route it to the appropriate destination just as another person who is handling it will.

A records management system can ensure an orderly business process. Without such a system, lawyers risk some fairly negative consequences. They can be subject to court sanctions and to legal malpractice claims.[3] Through the use of routing forms and software, records can be organized and stored. Using software will allow people to retrieve documents by key word and by other searchable features.

Before a records management system is established, modified, or expanded, an audit should be conducted to determine how records are used and managed

---

3. *See, e.g.*, Anthony E. Davis & David J. Elkanich, *The Risk Management Challenges of Record Retention and Destruction—Developing Records Management Policies That Protect Both Law Firms and Their Clients,* 19 A.B.A Prof. Law. 1 (2008).

and where problems currently exist. A new or modified system can correct failures associated with earlier ones the firm used.

Firms might either use commercially available software or have a custom-developed system created. In deciding whether to choose an "off-the-shelf" product or pay for someone to personalize one, a law firm should consider the following questions:

- How easily can the product be integrated with other systems, such as the firm's calendar or docket control system?
- How popular is the product? Are other users, especially other law firms, pleased with the product, or does it contain serious flaws?
- Are upgrades frequently and regularly available? Are they free, or is there a charge?
- How reputable is the company selling or developing the software? Is the company likely to be in existence and to create future generations of the product?
- How easily will new employees be able to learn and use the system successfully? What is the likelihood they will already be familiar with it?
- Is technical support available, and what does it cost?
- What does the product itself cost?

C.   THE IMPORTANCE OF KNOWLEDGE MANAGEMENT

Just as file management and docket management are subsets of records management, records management itself is a subset of the broader **knowledge management.** Knowledge refers both to explicit knowledge (that which is easily articulated and recorded) and to tacit knowledge (the knowledge that is in people's heads, such as insights).

Tacit knowledge—the sort that is unspoken—can be exceedingly valuable to a lawyer's practice. For instance, a firm might have, on behalf of a client, a copy of an application for a wetlands permit that it filed with a state department of environmental management. That is a record (explicit knowledge). The client might want to know when the application will be approved or, if it is not, when requests for additional information will be made. The state agency might not yet be able to provide a formal date for when it will make its decision or seek additional materials. A lawyer at the firm might know someone who works in the wetlands program who might be able, via a phone call, to found out whether this particular permit application will be deemed complete soon, or if additional information is likely to be sought. The agency contact might even be able to provide an informal time frame for when the agency will respond to the applicant. The lawyer with the contact could be in another office and might not even work in a firm's environmental group. Perhaps the lawyer went to graduate school with the state agency contact. The ability to determine that the firm and this particular lawyer have this resource—and the ability to retrieve and use it when appropriate—is knowledge management. Other lawyers at a firm might know that a certain judge likes to golf on Wednesdays or that another judge is very formal and prefers that lawyers who appear before him dress very conservatively.

knowledge management: The means by which knowledge is provided to allow people to perform their jobs.

Knowledge management—via databases, SharePoint sites, intranets, and so forth—can provide a means to record, retrieve, and share this information. This is especially important for large firms with multiple offices.[4]

> The fundamental problem of managing knowledge has been with the profession since the earliest legal proceedings at Westminster, through the print era and has carried forward into the digital age. It is a challenge that lawyers will face far into the future. The prevailing modes of information transfer that are available to lawyers often dictate the methods we choose to preserve knowledge. In the early days of Anglo-American law practice, lawyers relied on being physically present and utilized their memory or their capacity for note taking as a way of building expertise. With the advent of the printing press, text became the dominant method for acquiring and preserving knowledge. Now, at what are still the early stages of the digital age, new tools of knowledge management are available to us. Our methods may change, but the problem remains the same.
>
> The challenge of finding new and better ways to develop, retain, and share expertise has never been more pressing.[5]

Knowledge should be organized, retrievable, shared, and maintained so that it remains even when there are departures from the firm. A firm should provide both internal knowledge management for information to be used by lawyers and staff, and client-facing knowledge management so that pertinent and appropriate information can be shared with specific clients. In setting up knowledge management systems, firms should be aware that some lawyers prefer to protect their knowledge. They feel their value to the firm might diminish if their insights are widely disseminated within the firm. Steps should be taken to reward lawyers and others for sharing their information to prevent this sort of knowledge hoarding.

D. ETHICAL ISSUES

Like client files, many records must be properly safeguarded and protected from inadvertent disclosure. Personnel files contain sensitive information that should not be treated casually. Similarly, a firm is unlikely to want outsiders to know its income, expenditures, and the draw each partner gets. The same precautions accorded client files should also be given to firm records. Sensitive material in those files should be safeguarded and confidentiality maintained.

1. Security

A firm should delineate clear lines of access to certain records. A random paralegal should not be able to access a senior associate's health care reimbursement claims. Should a summer associate be able to obtain every partner's home phone

---

4. *See, e.g.,* Robert Denney, *Can All the Multinational Firms Survive?*, 63 The Advoc. (Texas) 27 (Summer 2013).

5. Conrad Johnson & Brian Donnelly, *If Only We Knew What We Know*, 88 Chi.-Kent L. Rev. 729, 729-30 (2013) (footnote omitted).

number and address? Should a new hire be able to access all prospective client intelligence data? Access to various types of information should be limited.

Protection of records may require the use of data encryption and passwords. A large firm that has an information technology employee should be able to discover potential problems with a records management system easily. For instance, an inquiry might be made if someone tries to access or duplicate thousands of files.

Precautions should likewise be taken when disposing of old records. Sensitive materials should not simply be placed in a wastebasket. Confidential materials should be shredded. A disk-wiping program should be used to rid old computers of sensitive data.

Appropriate precautions must also be taken to preserve records currently in use. Electronic records should be protected with antivirus software that is regularly updated. A firm should also have a procedure to alert appropriate people and take action should a security breach occur. Clear lines of authority should specify the people to be notified of a security breach, and decision-making authority should be established. Who decides whether the police should be notified of a security breach? It is best to anticipate such crises before they actually occur so lawyers and employees will understand their responsibilities if an unfortunate situation arises.

Likewise, a firm must have a disaster plan in place. If a fire or flood occurs in the office, the firm must be able to recover and to begin operating again as soon as possible. Electronic copies of vital records should be made and backed up at a remote location, so if an in-house computer service is destroyed, copies of the documents can still be recovered. Lawyers learned the importance of disaster planning after the 9/11 terrorist attacks on the World Trade Center in New York City. Several major law firms were housed in and around the World Trade Center. Buildings that were not destroyed by the attack were closed for a period of time after the attack occurred. Some firms had realized the importance of backing up important documents after the first attack on the World Trade Center in 1993.[6]

In addition to plans for a disaster, plans should be made for the disposition of records should the law firm dissolve or, in the case of a sole practitioner, should an attorney become incapacitated.

2.   *When Lawyers Leave Law Firms*

In this age of mobility and transition, law firms merging, practice groups departing, and associates leaping from firm to firm, a law office must have a clear policy addressing the ownership of records that do not belong to clients. A lawyer who is thinking about leaving a firm may surreptitiously make copies of documents, such as sample forms, publicly available information that the firm has obtained, and prospective client intelligence. The lawyer might intend to take these materials with him or her to a new law firm. If leadership at a firm becomes aware that a lawyer, or practice group, may be departing, the firm might want to limit access

---

6. *See, e.g.,* Jonathan D. Glater, *After the Attacks: The Records; Corporate Paper Trails Lie Buried in Soot,* N.Y. Times, Sept. 13, 2001, *available at* http://www.nytimes .com/2001/09/13/business/after-the-attacks-the-records-corporate-paper-trails-lie-buried-in-soot.html?scp=6&sq=law%20firm%20records%20&st=nyt&pagewanted=1.

to records. Ideally, a computerized records management system would flag instances of massive duplication of records and be able to identify such activities by user. A lawyer who is leaving may well begin to copy materials before he or she has given formal notice of departure.

Consider the following case involving lawyers who moved from one firm to another.

GIBBS V. BREED, ABBOTT & MORGAN
271 A.D.2d 180 (N.Y. App. Div. 2000)

OPINION

MAZZARELLI, J.

Plaintiffs Charles Gibbs and Robert Sheehan are former partners of Breed, Abbott & Morgan (BAM) who specialize in trust and estate law. They withdrew from BAM in July 1991 to join Chadbourne & Parke (Chadbourne), and brought this action for monies due to them under their BAM partnership agreement. Defendants asserted various counterclaims alleging that plaintiffs breached their fiduciary duty to BAM. The counterclaims were severed and tried without a jury. Plaintiffs appeal from the trial court's determination that, in the course of both partners' planning and eventually implementing their withdrawal from BAM, they breached their fiduciary duty to the partnership.

From January 1991 until July 1991, plaintiffs were the only partners in the trusts and estates department (T/E) at BAM; plaintiff Gibbs was the head of the department. A third partner, Paul Lambert, had been the former head of the department, and he had obtained many, if not most, of the department's clients. In 1989 he had left the firm to become the United States Ambassador to Ecuador and was still on leave in 1991. Lambert intended to return to the firm upon completion of his term as ambassador. The BAM trusts and estates department also employed three associate attorneys, Warren Whitaker (fifteenth year), Austin Wilkie (fourth year), and Joseph Scorese (first year); two accountants, Lois Wetzel and Ellen Furst; and two paralegals, Lee Ann Riley and Ruth Kramer.

Gibbs had become dissatisfied with BAM, and in January 1991 he began interviews to locate a new affiliation. He also approached Sheehan to persuade him to move with him. Sheehan and Gibbs subsequently conducted a number of joint interviews with prospective employers. In May 1991, Ambassador Lambert visited BAM, and Gibbs told him that he had been interviewing. Lambert relayed this information to the other partners. In early June, plaintiffs informed the executive committee that they had received an offer from two firms: McDermott, Will & Emory and Bryan Cave.

On June 19, 1991, both plaintiffs informed Stephen Lang, BAM's presiding partner, that they had accepted offers to join Chadbourne. Lang asked Gibbs not to discuss his departure with any of the T/E associates, and Gibbs agreed not to do so. On June 20, 1991, Lawrence Warble, a BAM partner who was named temporary head of the T/E department, met with its associates and nonlegal personnel to inform them that plaintiffs were leaving the firm.

On June 24, 1991, Gibbs and Sheehan sent Chadbourne a memo listing the names of the personnel in the T/E department at BAM, their respective salaries, their annual billable hours, and the rate at which BAM billed out these employees to clients. The memo included other information about the attorneys, including the colleges and law schools they attended and their Bar admissions. This list had been prepared by Sheehan on April 26, 1991, months before the partners announced they were leaving. Sheehan specifically testified that the memo was prepared in anticipation of discussions with prospective firms, and both Gibbs and Sheehan testified at trial that the recruitment of certain associates and support personnel was discussed with different firms between March and May, as the partners were considering various affiliations. While Gibbs and Sheehan were still partners at BAM, Chadbourne interviewed four BAM employees that Gibbs had indicated he was interested in bringing to Chadbourne with him. On June 27, 1991, plaintiffs submitted their written resignations. Before Gibbs and Sheehan left BAM, they wrote letters to clients served by them, advising that they were leaving BAM and that other attorneys at BAM could serve them. These letters did not mention the fact that the two partners were moving to Chadbourne. Although the partnership agreement required 45 days' notice of an intention to withdraw, BAM waived this provision upon plaintiffs' production of their final billings for work previously performed.[1] Gibbs left BAM on July 9, 1991, and Sheehan left on July 11, 1991, both taking various documents, including their respective "chronology" or desk files.[2] With the assistance of his chronology file, Gibbs began to contact his former clients on July 11, 1991. On July 11th, Chadbourne made employment offers to Whitaker, Wilkie, Wetzel, and Riley. Wilkie, Wetzel, and Riley accepted that same day; Whitaker accepted on July 15, 1991. In the following weeks, 92 of the 201 BAM T/E clients moved their business to Chadbourne.

After hearing all the testimony and the parties' arguments, the trial court determined that Gibbs' actions in persuading his partner Sheehan to leave BAM, "and the way in which the leave was orchestrated, were done, at least partially, with the intention of crippling BAM's trusts and estates (T/E) department," (181 Misc 2d 346, 348) and constituted a breach of loyalty to BAM. The court also found that Gibbs and Sheehan had breached their fiduciary duties to BAM by sending Chadbourne the April 26, 1991 memo detailing personal information about the individuals in the T/E department at BAM, because this gave Chadbourne a competitive advantage in offering employment to other members of the department. Finally, the court found that Gibbs and Sheehan breached their fiduciary duties to BAM by taking their chronology files with them to Chadbourne. Specifically, the court concluded that by taking their respective chronology files, the partners "to a large degree hobbled their former partners in their

---

1. AM did not attempt to prepare a joint letter with Gibbs and Sheehan, announcing their departure, as recommended by the American Bar Association (ABA) Committee on Ethics and Professional Responsibility (*see* ABA Comm. on Ethics & Prof'l Responsibility, Informal Op. 1457 [1980]).

2. The "chronology" or desk files contained copies of every letter written by the respective attorneys during the previous years. The letters included those written to adversaries about pending legal matters, letters written to clients, and letters written to others about ongoing BAM matters. These letters were duplicates of those kept in BAM's regular client files, but defendants allege that due to the fact that the files are arranged chronologically, active matters are more easily referenced. The original correspondences, left with the firm, have been filed by client and are dispersed throughout the department.

effort to rebuild the Trusts and Estates department, in order to maintain a viable department, and in their ability to serve clients without undue disruption."

With respect to damages, the court concluded that both Gibbs and Sheehan were entitled to recover their share of BAM profits accruing until the end of July 1991, and that Sheehan was entitled to the remainder of his capital account with the firm. Although there was no evidence that the partners had improperly solicited former BAM clients, the court found that despite BAM's efforts to mitigate damages by hiring a new partner and two associates into the T/E department, that department suffered financial losses as a result of plaintiffs' conduct, and concluded that it was entitled to recover lost profits for a reasonable period following plaintiffs' departure. The court directed that lost profits be calculated from July 1991, when the partners left the firm, to November 1993, when BAM dissolved. Gibbs and Sheehan were held jointly and severally liable for $1,861,045. The court also awarded defendants prejudgment interest and attorneys' fees. The court's liability finding should be modified, the damage award vacated, and the matter remanded for a determination of the financial loss, if any, occasioned by plaintiffs' disloyal act of supplying competitors with BAM's confidential employee data.

The members of a partnership owe each other a duty of loyalty and good faith, and "[a]s a fiduciary, a partner must consider his or her partners' welfare, and refrain from acting for purely private gain" (*Meehan v. Shaughnessy*, 404 Mass. 419, 434, 535 N.E.2d 1255, 1263). Partners are constrained by such duties throughout the life of the partnership and "[t]he manner in which partners plan for and implement withdrawals . . . is [still] subject to the constraints imposed on them by virtue of their status as fiduciaries" (Robert Hillman, *Loyalty in the Firm: A Statement of General Principles on the Duties of Partners Withdrawing from Law Firms*, 55 Wash. & Lee L. Rev. 997, 999 [1998]). According the trial court's findings on issues of fact and credibility appropriate deference, we uphold that portion of the court's liability determination which found that plaintiffs breached their fiduciary duty as partners of the firm they were about to leave by supplying confidential employee information to Chadbourne while still partners at BAM. However, we find no breach with respect to Gibbs' interactions with Sheehan, or with respect to either partner's removal of his desk files from BAM.

Defendants did not establish that Gibbs breached any duty to BAM by discussing with Sheehan a joint move to another firm, or that Sheehan's decision was based upon anything other than his own personal interests. In addition, while in certain situations "[A] lawyer's removal or copying, without the firm's consent, of materials from a law firm that do not belong to the lawyer, that are the property of the law firm, and that are intended by the lawyer to be used in his new affiliation, could constitute dishonesty, which is professional misconduct under [Model] Rule 8.4 (c)" (DC Bar Legal Ethics Comm. Op. 273, at 192), here, the partners took their desk copies of recent correspondence with the good faith belief that they were entitled to do so.

Contrary to the finding of the trial court, and applying the principle that "[t]he distinction between motive and process is critical to a realistic application of fiduciary duties" (Hillman, *op. cit.* at 999), we find no breach of duty in plaintiffs taking their desk files. These were comprised of duplicates of material maintained in individual client files, the partnership agreement was silent as to these documents, and removal was apparently common practice for departing attorneys.

However, the record supports the court's finding that both partners committed a breach of their fiduciary duty to the BAM partners by supplying Chadbourne, and presumably the other partnerships they considered joining, with the April 26, 1991 memorandum describing the members of BAM's T/E department, their salaries, and other confidential information, such as billing rates and average billable hours, taken from personnel files. Moreover, a closer examination of the record does not support the dissent's conclusion that these partners did not engage in surreptitious recruiting. The partners may not have discussed with firm employees the possibility of moving with them prior to June 20, 1991, but they indicated to Chadbourne the employees they were interested in prior to this date, and Gibbs specifically testified that he refrained from telling one of his partners, to whom he had a duty of loyalty, about his future plans to recruit specific associates and support staff from the partnership.

There is no evidence of improper client solicitation in this case, nor is it an issue on this appeal. Although the analogy could be useful in concluding that Gibbs did not breach his fiduciary duty to the partnership by working with Sheehan to find a new affiliation, the fiduciary restraints upon a partner with respect to client solicitation are not analogous to those applicable to employee recruitment. By contrast to the lawyer-client relationship, a partner does not have a fiduciary duty to the employees of a firm which would limit his duty of loyalty to the partnership. Thus, recruitment of firm employees has been viewed as distinct and "permissible on a more limited basis than . . . solicitation of clients" (Hillman, *op. cit.* at 1031). Prewithdrawal recruitment is generally allowed "only after the firm has been given notice of the lawyer's intention to withdraw" (*ibid.*).

However, here Sheehan prepared a memo in April of 1991, well in advance of even deciding, much less informing his partners of his intention to withdraw. There is ample support in the record for the trial court's finding that the preparation and sending of the April 26, 1991 memo, combined with the subsequent hiring of certain trusts and estates personnel, constituted an egregious breach of plaintiff's fiduciary duty to BAM. Moreover, it is not speculative to infer more widespread dissemination given Sheehan's trial testimony that the memo "was prepared in connection with talking to other firms," and that "he was sure the subject of staffing was discussed at firms other than Chadbourne." Sheehan's disclosure of confidential BAM data to even one firm was a direct breach of his duty of loyalty to his partners. Because the memo gave Chadbourne confidential BAM employment data as well as other information reflecting BAM's valuation of each employee, Chadbourne was made privy to information calculated to give it an unfair advantage in recruiting certain employees.

While partners may not be restrained from inviting qualified personnel to change firms with them, here Gibbs and Sheehan began their recruiting while still members of the firm and prior to serving notice of their intent to withdraw. They did so without informing their partners that they were disseminating confidential firm data to competitors. Their actions, while still members of the firm, were intended to and did place BAM in the position of not knowing which of their employees were targets and what steps would be appropriate for them to take in order to retain these critical employees. The dissent's analysis, that once the firm was notified of the partners' departure, there was no breach of fiduciary duty, is flawed. The breach occurred in April of 1991 and could not be cured by any after-the-fact notification by the fiduciary who committed the breach that he was withdrawing from the firm. Chadbourne still had the unfair advantage of the confidential information from the April 1991 memo, and still had the upper hand, which was manifested by its ability to tailor its offers and incentives to the BAM recruits.

Contrary to the dissent, I would characterize the memo distributed to prospective competitors as confidential. The data was obtained from BAM personnel files which Sheehan had unique access to as a BAM partner. The dissent's statement that such financial information is generally known to "headhunters" is without foundation. While the broad outlines of the partners' profits at a select number of large New York firms and the incremental increases in the base compensation of young associates at some firms are published in professional publications such as the New York Law Journal, or known to some recruitment firms, the available figures often vary substantially from the actual compensation received by specific individuals.

For example, the BAM partnership agreement, which is included in the record, reveals that the approximately 40 partners in the firm earn substantially different percentages of the firm's earnings. No professional publication would be privy to these financials. With respect to the specific associates and support staff whose compensation was disseminated in the April 1991 memo, the information disclosed to Chadbourne incorporated these individuals' bonuses. Bonus payments are confidential, often voted by the partnership, based upon the unique quality of an individual's work, the number of hours billed, and many other intangible factors. These lump-sum payments often constitute a substantial portion of an associate's salary, and the payments are certainly not available to the public. Finally, support staff also receive bonuses paid to them at the discretion of the individual partners, from their personal accounts. This information is highly individualized and also privileged. Sheehan abused his fiduciary duty to the partnership by accessing personnel files to obtain the actual gross compensation of the associates and support staff he and Gibbs wished to bring with them, including bonuses, and disclosing this information to Chadbourne.

Moreover, the memo contained more than a list of salaries. It itemized each of the employee's annual billable hours, and the rates at which BAM billed these employees out to their clients, information which was not otherwise publically available. These facts go directly to a potential employee's value and were accessible only to members of the BAM partnership. Selected partners providing BAM's confidential information, which they were able to obtain by virtue of their position as fiduciaries, to Chadbourne was an act of disloyalty to their partnership. The confidential information placed Chadbourne, as a competing prospective employer, in the advantageous position of conducting interviews of the associates and support staff with more knowledge than any firm could obtain through independent research, as well as providing it with information BAM partners did not know it had, thereby prejudicing their own efforts to retain their associates and support staff.

The calculation of damages in cases such as this is difficult. "[B]reaches of a fiduciary relationship in any context comprise a special breed of cases that often loosen normally stringent requirements of causation and damages" (*Milbank, Tweed, Hadley & McCloy v. Chan Cher Boon*, 13 F.3d 537, 543 [2d Cir. 1994]; *see Wolf v. Rand*, 258 A.D.2d 401). This is because the purpose of this type of action "is not merely to *compensate* the plaintiff for wrongs committed . . . [but also] 'to *prevent* them, by removing from agents and trustees all inducement to attempt dealing for their own benefit in matters which they have undertaken for others, or to which their agency or trust relates'" (*Diamond v. Oreamuno,* 24 N.Y.2d 494, 498 [emphasis in original], quoting *Dutton v. Willner,* 52 N.Y. 312, 319). However, the proponent of a claim for a breach of fiduciary duty must, at a minimum, establish that the offending parties' actions were "a substantial factor" in causing an identifiable loss (*Millbank, Tweed, Hadley & McCloy v. Chan Cher Boon, supra* at 543; *see 105 E. Second St. Assocs. v. Bobrow,* 175 A.D.2d 746 [awarding amount of loss sustained by reason of the faithless fiduciary's conduct]).

A reasonable assessment of lost profits has been deemed an appropriate measure of damages in cases where there was evidence that the fiduciary improperly solicited clients to move with him or her (*see Meehan v. Shaughnessy, supra,* 404 Mass. at 435, 535 N.E.2d at 1264), or where the fiduciary's acts could otherwise be connected to a subsequent loss of business (*see Duane Jones Co. v. Burke,* 306 N.Y. 172, 192; *Bruno Co. v. Friedberg,* 21 A.D.2d 336, 341; *see also Wolf v. Rand, supra* at 402 [lost profits awarded where defendants in closely held corporation misappropriated company profits to themselves]). Here, the court based its damage award on what it believed to be a series of disloyal acts. Defendants did not establish how the only act of plaintiffs which this Court finds to be disloyal, that of supplying employee information to Chadbourne, in and of itself, was a substantial cause of BAM's lost profits (*see Stoeckel v. Block,* 170 A.D.2d 417 [no demonstration that the decline in defendant's business was attributable to plaintiffs' alleged wrongful conduct during the term of their employment]). We therefore vacate the court's award to defendants of the total profits lost by BAM between the time of plaintiffs' departure in July 1991 and BAM's dissolution in November 1993, and remand for consideration of the issue of whether plaintiffs' disloyal act of sending Chadbourne the April 26, 1991 memorandum was a significant cause of any identifiable loss, and, if so, the amount of such loss.

Accordingly, the order, Supreme Court, New York County (Herman Cahn, J.), entered October 1, 1998, which, after a nonjury trial on defendants' counterclaims, determined that plaintiffs had breached their fiduciary duty to defendants, should be modified, on the law, to limit such conclusion to the act of disseminating confidential employee information, and otherwise affirmed, without costs. Order, same court and Justice, entered on or about June 29, 1999, which, to the extent appealed from as limited by the parties' briefs, directed that defendants shall recover $1,861,045, plus prejudgment interest, on their counterclaims, should be reversed, on the law, without costs, the damage award vacated, and the matter remanded for recalculation of damages in accordance with this Opinion.

CONCUR BY: SAXE (IN PART)

Dissent by: SAXE (In Part)

E.   SPECIAL-INTEREST AREA: E-MAIL

Rule 1.6 of the ABA's *Model Rules of Professional Conduct* directs lawyers to ensure that their communications regarding representation of clients are confidential. A law firm should take precautions to protect its e-mail communications. A firm should draft an e-mail policy addressing the use of e-mail and its handling and storage. Such a policy might specify that all e-mail messages should have a confidentiality notice indicating that the message is intended for only a specified recipient. The policy might also standardize how e-mail messages should be "slugged," or named, in the "Re" line so they can be tracked easily and retrieved later.

A system for storing e-mail messages should be established. Will e-mail messages be filed according to client and matter? Will certain ones be directed to others for follow-up? How will such correspondence be logged and tracked? E-mail messages might also be separated into subject matter files with copies stored in client files. Ideally, any e-mail system will have a search capability. If an e-mail program is incapable of storing large volumes of material, then options for storing and retrieving older e-mail messages should be explored.

Care must be taken not to misdirect e-mail messages by, for instance, hitting "Reply all" when responding to a message, if that is not the sender's intention. "Reply all" might be disabled or "Reply sender" might be made the default option. Caution should also be exercised when an e-mail program automatically fills in an addressee's name after a few letters have been typed in the "To" box. A message can easily be misdirected simply because two people have names that begin with the same letters.

Access to e-mail messages should be appropriately limited through the use of passwords, firewalls, and antivirus software. At the same time, such protections should be monitored and checked that they are allowing necessary correspondence to be received.

CHECKLIST

- A law firm must have a records management system in place to deal with all the materials it receives on a daily basis.
- A firm's record management policy should identify the various types of records that are being tracked, establish handling requirements for each type, determine who has access to various types of records, and safeguard the handling of different types of records.
- A firm should also have a broader knowledge management system that incorporates both explicit knowledge, such as records, and tacit knowledge, such as lawyers' insights about judges. The information in a knowledge management system should be retrievable and able to be shared both internally and with clients, as appropriate.
- Arrangements must also be made for knowledge and records storage, whether electronic, physical on-site, or long-term off-site storage.
- A records destruction policy and procedure should also be an element of a records management policy.
- The firm's leadership should support the firm's knowledge and records management systems and ensure that other lawyers and employees are aware of them and contribute to them.
- An index identifying the categories by which records are organized must be created and maintained.

- Users of the knowledge and records management systems must be able to retrieve very specific information as well as more general information.
- Key words can be assigned to electronic records, and even to paper ones, to make them more easily retrievable.
- Conventions must be established for assigning key words and for spelling them.
- Through the use of routing forms and software, records can be organized and stored. Using software allows documents to be retrieved by key words and other searchable features.
- Before a records management system is established, modified, or expanded, an audit should be conducted to determine how records are used and managed and where problems exist.
- Records must be protected so that sensitive or confidential information is not accessible by inappropriate people within or outside the firm.
- Law firms should have a disaster preparedness plan in place and should also provide for the disposition of records should the law firm dissolve or, in the case of a sole practitioner, should an attorney become incapacitated.
- Given the amount of correspondence by e-mail today, a firm should also have a policy in place to protect e-mail correspondence and to store and retrieve it.

VOCABULARY

"back-office" activity (152)
cloud computing (153)
"front-office" activity (152)
knowledge management (159)
records management (p. 305)
records retention (152)

CAREER PREPARATION TIPS

Much of the knowledge that you are acquiring as you work your way through this textbook can be applied and used in a future career in the legal field. As you gain knowledge and insight about the legal market and those who work in it, you might want to organize it into your own personal knowledge management system. Rather than taking notes on paper by hand, you might want to take notes electronically using your computer so that you can file these notes and retrieve them easily at some future point. As you take other courses about law and the legal industry, you can add to your knowledge management system so that you will be better prepared when you are seeking a position in the legal field and going on job interviews. Learn how to assign key words to documents and to store them in various places in your computer or in the cloud so that they can be retrieved easily at some future point.

IF YOU WANT TO LEARN MORE

ABA Law Practice Division. http://www.americanbar.org/groups /law_practice.html

Association of Legal Administrators Legal Management Resource Center. http://www.alanet.org/research/directory.asp

Association of Records Managers and Administrators. http://www.arma.org

Florida Bar, Member Services, Law Office Management Assistance Service (LOMAS). http://www.floridabar.org/LOMAS

U.S. National Archives and Records Administration. http://www.archives.gov

A2J Author, a software tool to assist pro se litigants that allows courts and others to create guided interviews to help these litigants complete forms. http://www.a2jauthor.org/drupal/ or http://www.youtube.com /a2jauthor

HotDocs, a document generation platform that includes document generation interviews so a client can provide much information himself. http://www.hotdocs.com

---

READING COMPREHENSION

1. How does records management differ from file management and docket management?
2. Which is more challenging to record, explicit knowledge or tacit knowledge?
3. What equipment is needed for records management?
4. For how long should a law firm retain records?
5. How does an index help support a law firm's record management system?
6. When should client files be destroyed?
7. Who is responsible for records management at a law firm?
8. What are some precautions that can be taken to protect physical records?
9. What are some precautions that can be taken to protect electronic records?
10. Who owns law firm records that do not belong to the law firm's clients?
11. How can the confidentiality of e-mail messages be protected?

DISCUSSION STARTERS

1. Consider the documents you have stored in your own computer. Would a stranger be able to retrieve a paper you had written for one of your courses? Would the stranger be able to determine which version was the final one if you had drafted more than one? How do you name documents?

2. Consider e-mail messages slugged with the following words:

   Us
   Today's Meeting
   Thanx
   Snuggy Bear v. Puffinstuff Expert Witness

   a. Which one is the most informative?
   b. Which one is too casual?
   c. Which ones are appropriate for lawyer-client correspondence?
   d. Which ones are appropriate for paralegal-client correspondence?

3. Consider the following types of administrative records a law firm is likely to have in its possession. Who should have access to each type of record, and why?
   - payroll records
   - health insurance information
   - employee files
   - forms completed by job applicants
   - performance evaluations
   - contracts
   - hiring letters
   - offer letters
   - background checks
   - information about salaries
   - references
   - vacation request forms
   - information on garnishments
   - disability insurance claims
   - attendance records
   - time cards for staff
   - recruiting materials
   - family and medical leave materials
   - accounts payable
   - accounts receivable
   - affirmative action/diversity information
   - discrimination claims
   - benefits information
   - independent contractor records
   - data on marketing efforts
   - research on prospective clients
   - insurance carriers, policies, and premiums
   - workers' compensation claims

- material safety data sheets
- Occupational Safety and Health Administration information
- injury reports
- information on retirement benefits

4. Suppose you had to teach a four-hour seminar on your law firm's records management policy to new hires, both lawyers and support staff. What areas would you cover? How would you make the seminar interesting? How would you ensure that the new hires follow the records management policy?

5. Review the excerpt from *Gibbs v. Breed, Abbott & Morgan* in the chapter. Who brought the lawsuit? Why? What was the court's holding in the case? Do you think the decision was correctly decided? Did any aspect of the decision surprise you? How did the dissenting opinion differ from the majority one?

6. Look up and read *Pace v. United Services Automobile Assn.*, No. 05-cv-01562-LTB-MJW, 2007 U.S. Dist. LEXIS 49425 (D. Colo. July 9, 2007). Why did the plaintiff's counsel in the case fail to appear for a settlement conference? What excuse for their failure to appear did they provide to the court? Was this an adequate excuse? What was the result of their failure to appear?

CASE STUDIES

1. Suppose you work for the law firm that represented the plaintiffs in *Gibbs v. Breed, Abbott & Morgan* (see the excerpt in this chapter). What key words would you assign to the case so that the opinion would be retrievable in your firm's electronic database? If you were setting up client files for these plaintiffs, what would you name the files? Create a master list of files, and then create an index for those files.

2. Imagine that you are an information manager at a major law firm that wants to expand the tacit knowledge in its knowledge management system as the firm has expanded and has many lawyers in multiple offices around the globe. Develop a questionnaire for attorneys and staff to complete that will provide useful, tacit knowledge. Consider specifically how questions might be phrased to provide more thorough, candid responses. Also research change management plans and develop a change management plan appropriate for the legal field to persuade lawyers and others to contribute regularly to the knowledge management system.

3. Consider all of the subjects discussed in this chapter and establish naming conventions for them. For instance, should the phrase "records management" include an *s* on the end of records, or should there be no *s*? Should the law firm Breed, Abbott & Morgan be identified by that name, by the name Breed Abbott and Morgan, by the initials BAM, or by the initials B.A.M.? Write a short naming conventions

manual including the letters *A* through *Z* for which names or words should be standardized.

4. Research several commercially available records management systems programs. Compare and contrast their features. Which would work best in a firm with 10 or fewer lawyers? Which would work with a 30-lawyer firm that has offices in three states? Which would work with a 1,000-lawyer firm that has seven offices in the United States and eight other offices around the world? The programs you might research include Accutrac, Elite, FileSurf, iManage, LegalKey, ProLaw, and Worldox.

5. Find a recent newspaper account of a lawyer or law firm employee who got into trouble involving e-mail. What activity is covered in the newspaper account? How might this situation have been avoided? What would your reaction to this account be if you were a client of this particular firm? In what way should the lawyer or law firm employee have been reprimanded for getting into this trouble?

CHAPTER
8

Office Productivity Software

OBJECTIVES

→ **Survey** types of office productivity software that can increase the effectiveness of a legal practice.

→ **Examine** Microsoft's Word in detail and compare it with other word processing software, especially for generating and managing legal documents like pleadings and briefs.

→ **Determine** how **spreadsheet** software like Microsoft's Excel can make it easier for a legal practice to manage numerical data efficiently and accurately, such as for tracking time spent on a client's case.2

→ **Evaluate** slide show presentation software, like Microsoft's PowerPoint or OpenOffice.org's Impress, for use in a legal practice.

→ **Assess** the utility of free office productivity software such as OpenOffice.Org and Google Docs in a law office.

INTRODUCTION

Software commonly used in a law office can increase productivity by simplifying the steps needed to create and edit documents. This, in turn, can generate savings that could be passed along to clients in the form of reduced fees.

A. COMMON FEATURES OF SOFTWARE

1. Bars and Ribbons and Pulldowns

The **graphic user interface (GUI)** of software describes how information will look on a computer screen. One approach to organizing those visual cues (sometimes called **buttons**) involves grouping them in a **toolbar** (or a **ribbon**), particularly by function. Users can often customize the number and kind of features available with a toolbar or ribbon. A user in a law firm could, for example, include a button for quick access to software used for a real estate closing or for generating a petition for bankruptcy.

2.   *Suites*

Software makers appreciate that customers might prefer to have software applications that mesh well with one another. For example, Microsoft's suite, MS Office, integrates software that has, among other features, word processing, spreadsheets, Internet browsing, and the creation of slide shows. Of course, a suite, or bundle, of applications will cost less than if a law firm had to buy a license for each application.

B.   MICROSOFT OFFICE SUITE

The preeminent office productivity suite, Microsoft Office, has an array of software most commonly used in any business. While Microsoft updates Office every few years, the company tends to have the same features in its software. This review will use the 2007 version of Office.

1.   *Word 2007*

A common feature of Office software is the Microsoft graphic in the upper left-hand corner of the screen.

a.   Office Button

In Word, clicking on the Office button will reveal a pulldown submenu of commonly used functions, such as to close a document, or the following:

→ **New:** Not only can a user create a blank document, but Word also provides templates for different types of documents. For example, a law firm could create a template that contains standard language in a services contract for a new client. A link to Microsoft Office Online provides access to additional templates.
→ **Open:** Here the user obtains access to documents by file name or in a particular folder.
→ **Save, Save As:** Not only can a user save a copy of a document, but via Save As the user can save it in a different format, such as PDF (protected document format), which limits options for subsequently altering it.
→ **Print:** Options for printing a document include being able to select printers, like those in a firm's networked computers.
→ **Prepare:** Before a user distributes a document, like a non-compete agreement, the user can select who can access the agreement or limit changes that recipients can make.
→ **Send:** In addition to the opportunity to send a document as an e-mail, a user could also send it as a fax via the web (where that service is available).
→ **Publish:** Here, for example, the user could post a commentary about a recent U.S. Supreme Court decision on a blog, or store a document on a server so that others may access it.

Figure 8.1
Microsoft Word—Microsoft Word with submenu

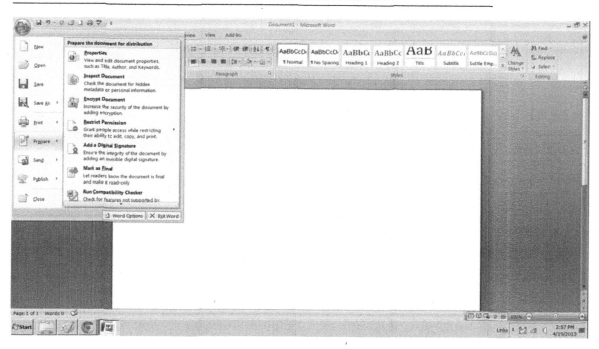

Figure 8.2
Microsoft Word—Microsoft Word with submenu: the Prepare link

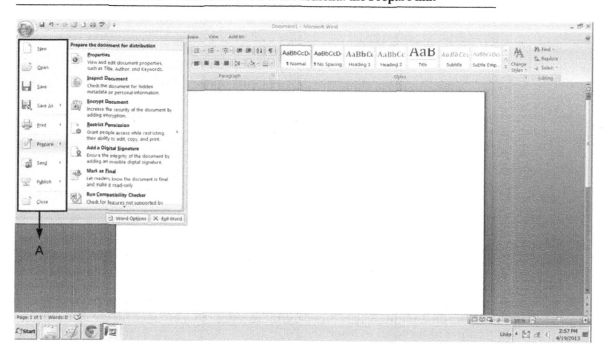

Figure 8.3
Microsoft Word—Prepare options in Word

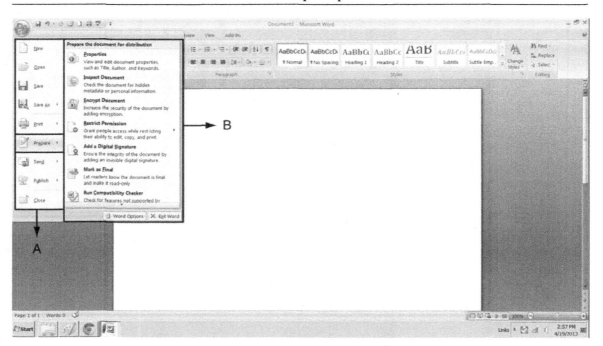

→ **Word Options:** This button is on the bottom of the menu. Clicking this button opens a submenu where a user may personalize a copy of Word, like adding or deleting features, such as for proofreading.

b.   Tabs

Tabs, like those along the top of manila folders, serve as the way of using particular features of the software. Under each tab, options get sorted in labeled subsections, as seen in the boxes entitled Editing or Font, under the Home tab.

i.   *Home tab*

A user will find, under the Home tab, the following boxes: Clipboard, Font, Paragraph, Styles, and Editing.

I.   Clipboard

The Clipboard box contains buttons for cutting and pasting material. Via a submenu, a user could, for example, open a box on the side that contains material that has been cut, like a disclaimer of warranty. To insert that disclaimer later in the document, a user needs only to move the browser arrow onto the disclaimer and click it to insert it.

Figure 8.4
Microsoft Word—Home tab

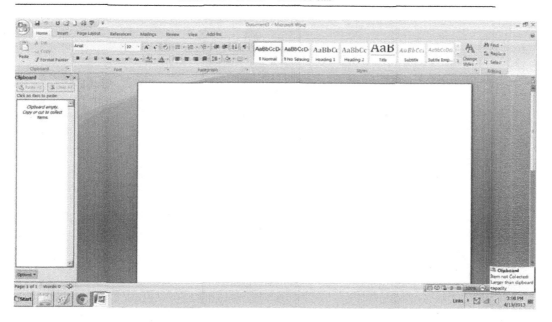

Figure 8.5
Microsoft Word—Home tab: Clipboard option

Figure 8.6
Microsoft Word—Clipboard option submenu

II.   Font

The Font box allows the user to manipulate the appearance of the typeface. Some courts only accept documents that use the Courier typeface, with a font size of 12, and the user can easily change the typeface and font here. Using the bottom row's buttons means putting content into italics or underlining. Clicking the double-headed arrow in the corner will open a submenu with other options, such as inserting double-strike lines over typed material.

Figure 8.7
Microsoft Word—Home tab: Font box

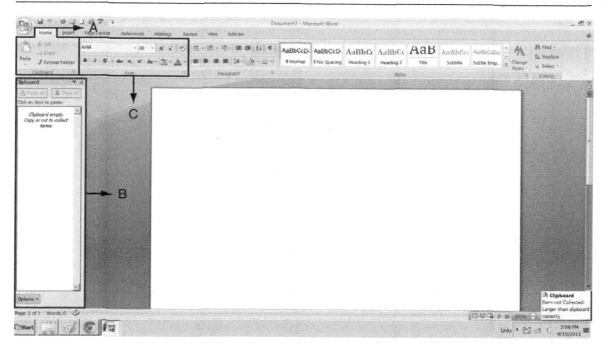

III.   Paragraph

The adjacent Paragraph box provides users with buttons, along the top, for inserting bullet points or numbers, as well as to indent and sort text. Buttons on the bottom make it easy for a user to center, justify content, or have text run flush to either margin. Also, a user can change the line spacing of the text, as well as add different types of borders.

Figure 8.8
Microsoft Word—Home tab: Paragraph box

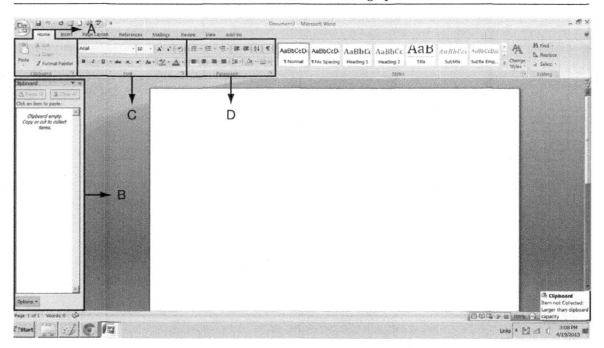

IV.   Styles

Over the past few decades, courts have established requirements regarding aspects of a legal brief. This might mean using only 8 1/2" x 11" paper (because the old 8 1/2" x 14" "legal size" required special file cabinets), with one-inch margins. Briefs might have a page limit and require a certain typeface or font.

An easy way to meet these requirements would involve setting up a style. The Styles box provides users with a way to create styles that can be applied with a click of a button. Style templates called Quick Style come as presets which the user can quickly modify.

Figure 8.9
Microsoft Word—Home tab: Styles box

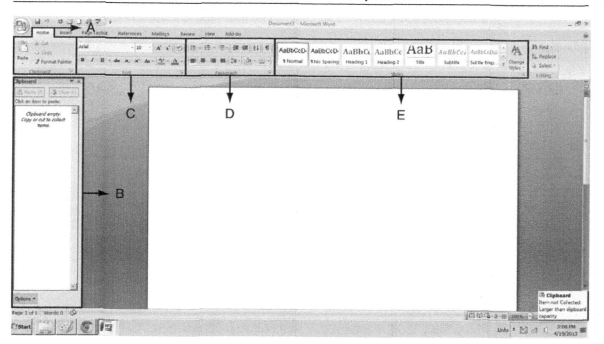

V. Editing

A user will want the freedom to move around the document quickly. The last box, Editing, contains links to go to a page in the document and to find and/or replace content.

Figure 8.10
Microsoft Word—Home tab: Editing box

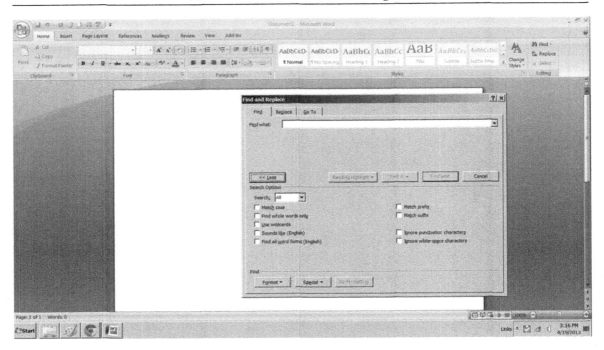

Figure 8.11
Microsoft Word—Home tab: Editing box

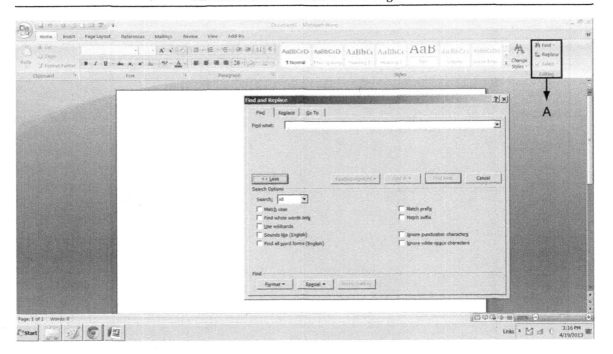

Figure 8.12
Microsoft Word—Home tab: Editing box, Find options, Find and Replace submenu

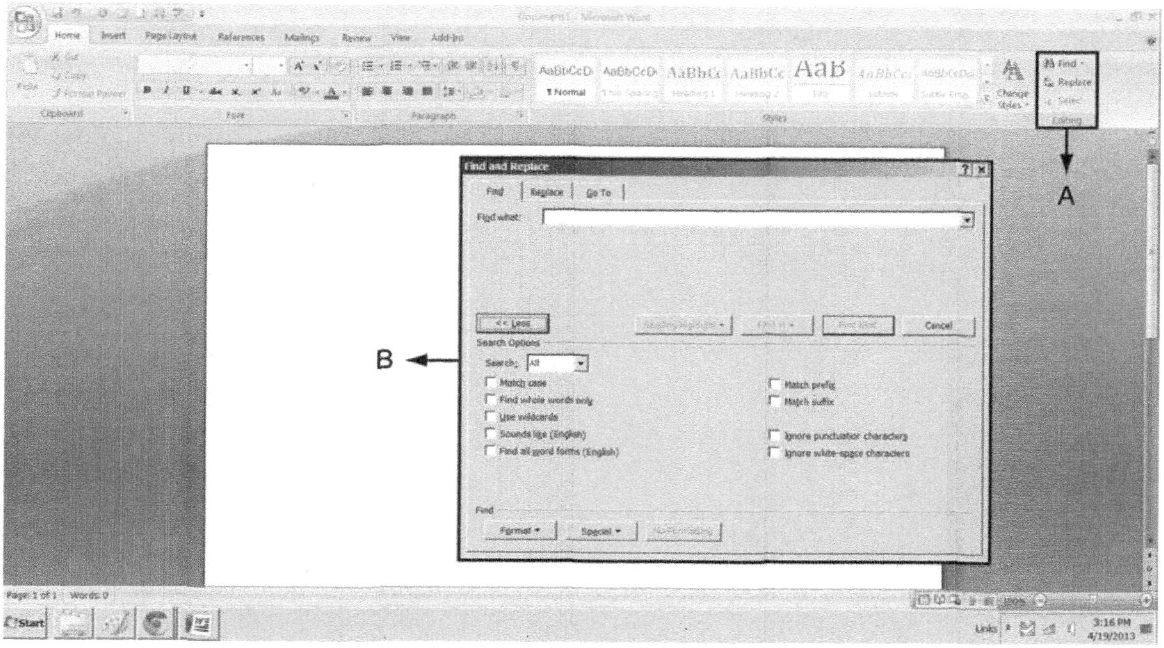

The Find link, when clicked, opens to a submenu with Find, Replace, and Go To tabs, as well as buttons. The user can find and/or replace letters, numbers, punctuation, functions (like a page break), or special characters (like the section symbol §). The Go To tab allows the user to move around the document, whether to a page, heading, or predesignated location, called a bookmark.

ii. Insert tab

The Insert tab provides a user with the chance to add a number of nontextual features, such as tables, pictures, or hyperlinks, as well as allowing the editing of headers and footers.

I. Pages

Here, the user can insert a blank page or a page break and use templates to create a cover page.

II. Tables

This box makes it possible to create and insert tables, including Excel spreadsheets. If a plaintiff will suffer reduced earnings in the future because of an injury, a table could describe how much that plaintiff will not earn in successive years. Also, a user can convert text into a table.

Figure 8.13
Microsoft Word—Insert tab: Table box, Table button options, Insert Table submenu, 977 table displayed

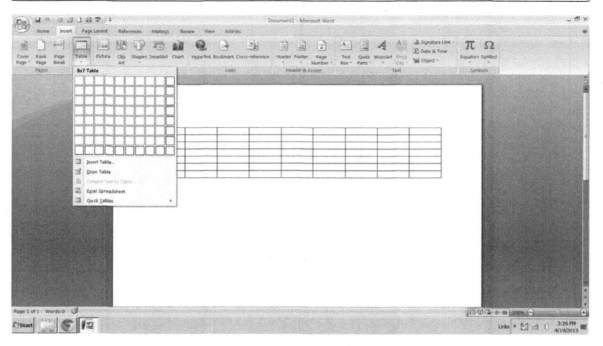

III.   Illustrations

Illustrations can make it easier to describe, for example, the layout of an intersection where cars collided. Here, a user can insert:

→ Pictures in formats such as a bitmap and JPEG, depicting the post-accident condition of the vehicle in which that plaintiff was riding;
→ **Clip art:** small, simple graphics that come with Word;
→ Shapes such as lines, arrows, and other figures, with an option to create effects like shadowing;
→ Smart art: additional graphic styles that show how a process unfolds, such as the flow of traffic on a highway; and
→ Charts, using columns, lines, bars, or a pie chart, perhaps to show how to apportion damages among multiple defendants.

Figure 8.14
Microsoft Word—Insert tab

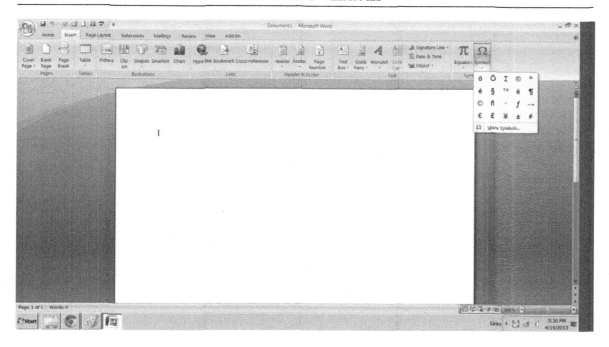

Figure 8.15
Microsoft Word—Insert tab: Illustrations box

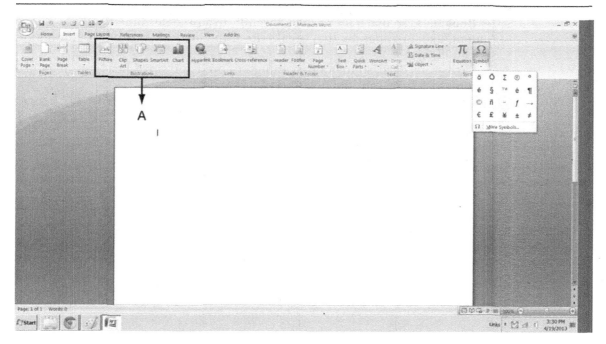

Figure 8.16
Microsoft Word—Insert tab: Links box

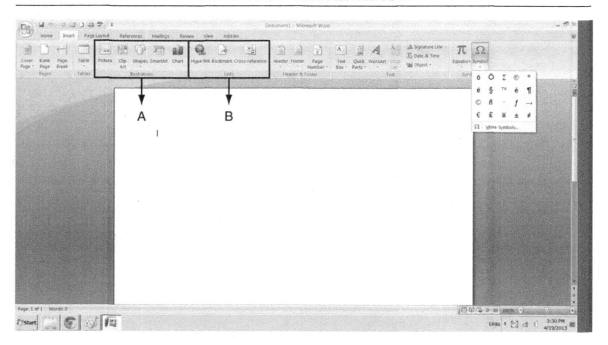

IV.   Links

In this box, a user can insert a:

→ **Hyperlink,** a connection to a web page;
→ **Bookmark,** so that a user can go instantly to a predetermined point in a document, like an appendix that breaks down the medical expenses of an injured plaintiff; and
→ **Cross-reference,** so that a user can go to predetermined headings in a document, such as an introduction or conclusion.

Figure 8.17
Microsoft Word—Insert tab: Header and Footer box

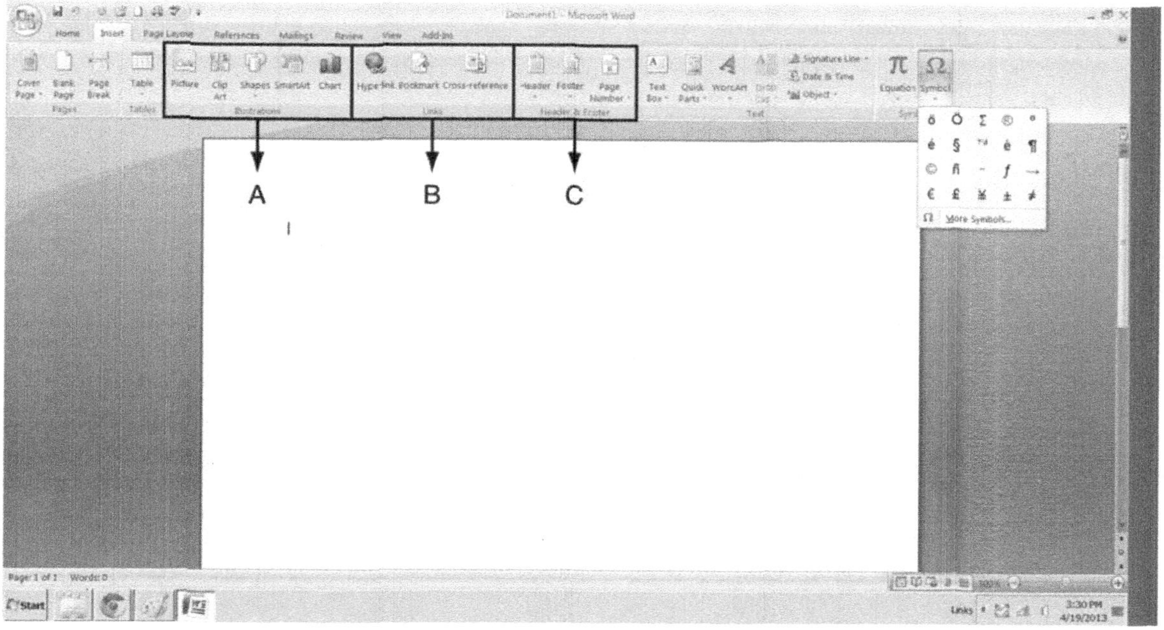

V.   Header and footer

By running a header on a multipage letter, a reader can figure out instantly the sequence of the pages. For a brief, a footer contains the information about the order of the pages. The real benefit of the software occurs when a paralegal inserts or deletes content, because the software will automatically adjust headers and footers to accommodate such a change.

VI.   Text

This box allows the user to insert different, specialized kinds of content in order to reflect the date and time, and to have it update over several days as changes are made. Or, in a trademark dispute, a user may need to insert the art for the trademark, even when the art came from a different type of document.

Figure 8.18
Microsoft Word—Insert tab: Text box

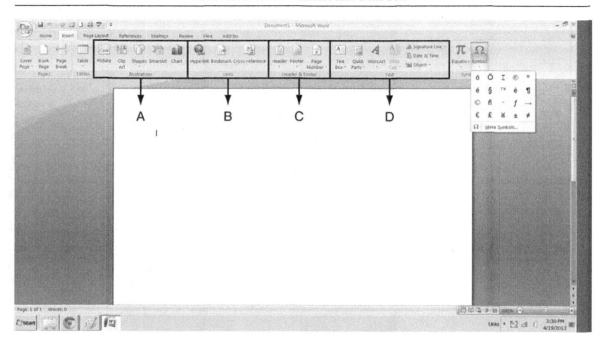

VII.   Symbols

Symbols such as ™ or © immediately alert a reader to a claim of legal right in a trademark or a copyright. Buttons, here, make it possible to insert those and other symbols into the text. Also, if needed, the user could include letters used in the Cyrillic alphabet, commonly used in Eastern European languages. For sales made with a business located in a member state of the European Union (EU), the user can insert the symbol for the monetary unit, the euro: €.

Figure 8.19
Microsoft Word—Insert tab: Symbol box, Symbol button

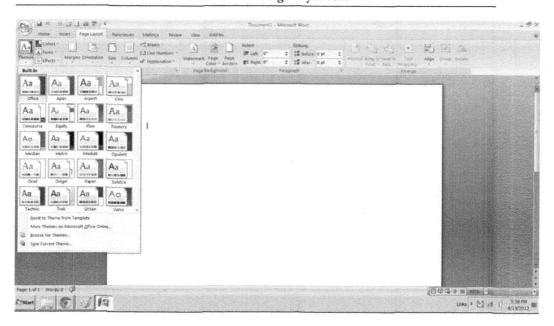

iii. Page layout tab

A law firm might want to keep its client current about changes in the firm. Because a newsletter can convey that information, the software contains options for presenting that information in a more appealing format.

Figure 8.20
Microsoft Word—Page Layout tab

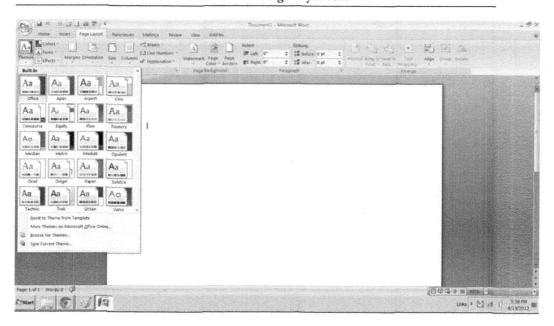

Figure 8.21
Microsoft Word—Page Layout tab

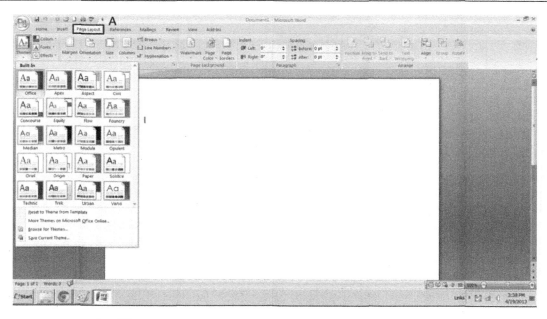

I.   Themes

Here, a user could choose a theme for such a newsletter. A theme allows the user to select a specific color scheme for the material and adjust the size and nature of the words, known as the font. Also, a user could choose graphics that alert the reader to the importance of the information.

Figure 8.22
Microsoft Word—Page Layout tab: Themes box, Themes button, Built-in

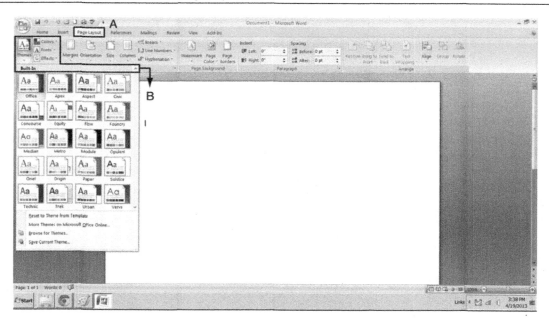

II. Page setup

When people created letters using a typewriter, they could adjust the margins or insert tabs manually. Here the user can make similar adjustments to the image on the monitor. That means not just adjusting margins, but also:

Figure 8.23
Microsoft Word—Page Layout tab: Page Setup

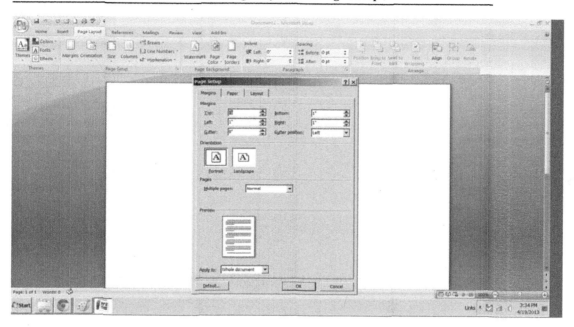

Figure 8.24
Microsoft Word—Page Layout tab: Page Setup box

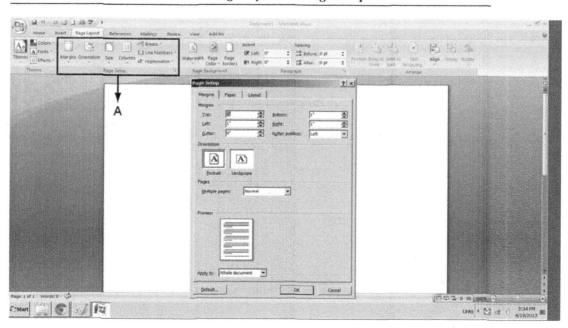

Figure 8.25
Microsoft Word—Page Layout tab: Page Setup box, Margins button

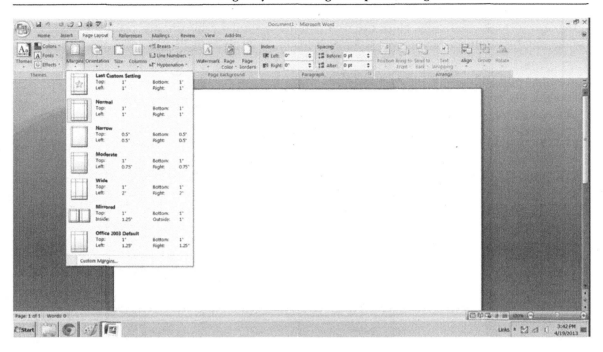

→ Selecting the size of the electronic page in a documents, such as $8\frac{1}{2}'' \times 11''$;

Figure 8.26
Microsoft Word—Page Layout tab: Page Setup box, Margins button, Custom Margins link, Paper tab

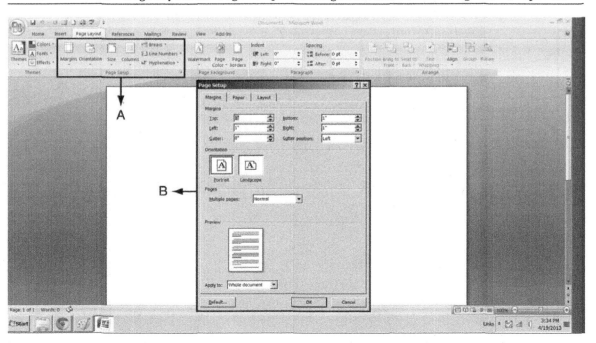

→ Choosing the orientation of the electronic page, such as portrait or landscape;
→ Inserting columns, including an option for multiple columns, such as the annual change in an injured plaintiff's earnings;

Figure 8.27
Microsoft Word—Page Layout tab: Page Setup box, Line Numbers link

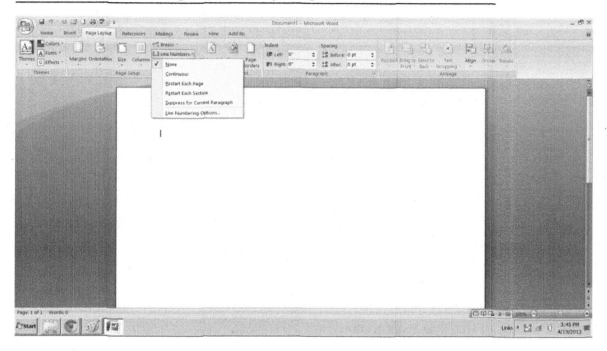

→ Making page or section breaks;
→ Using line numbers; and
→ Adjusting hyphenation.

Figure 8.28
Microsoft Word—Page Layout tab: Page Background box

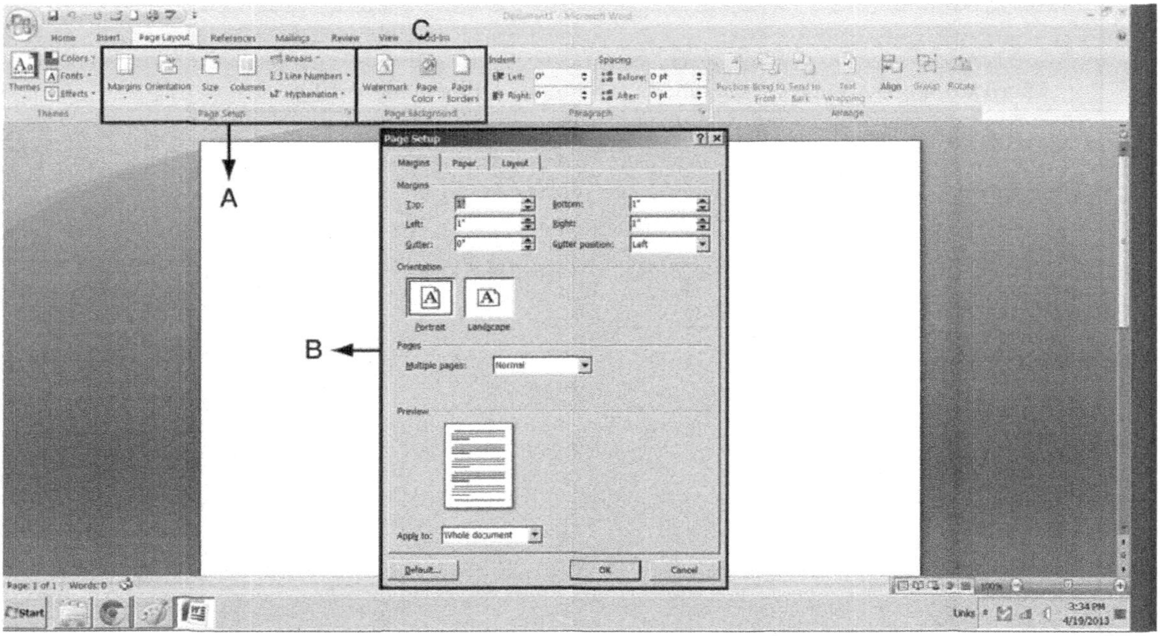

III.   Page background

A client might ask a firm to draft a contract. As the firm and client make changes to the contract, using a watermark could identify the document as a "Draft," so as to reflect this process while not obscuring the provisions of the contract. The user may also select a page color and borders.

IV.   Paragraph

Here, a user can insert a large amount of quoted material, known as a block quote, and set the format for that quote. This might happen in a dispute about a specific provision in a contract. Options here include setting indents, and whether to insert spaces, of varying length, before and after a paragraph.

Figure 8.29
Microsoft Word—Page Layout tab: Paragraph box

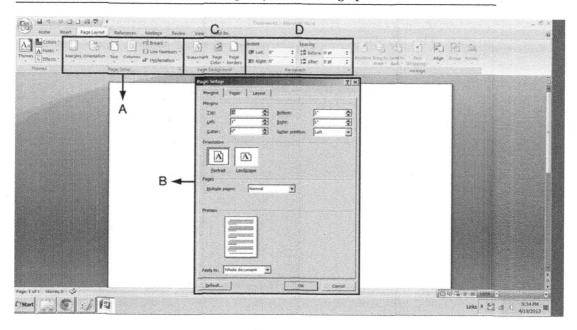

V.   Arrange

The presentation, or layout, of material can make it easier for a reader to understand what a user wants to say. Here, the user can arrange the layout of text, so that in a newsletter to clients text can wrap around an image, for example.

Figure 8.30
Microsoft Word—Page Layout tab: Arrange box, Align button

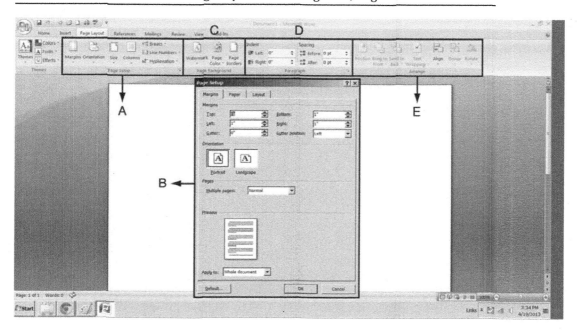

iv.   References tab

To make a legally persuasive argument, an attorney may need to refer to the case law, statutory law, or regulations that support the point that the lawyer wants to make. This tab allows the user to manage those references.

Figure 8.31
Microsoft Word—References tab

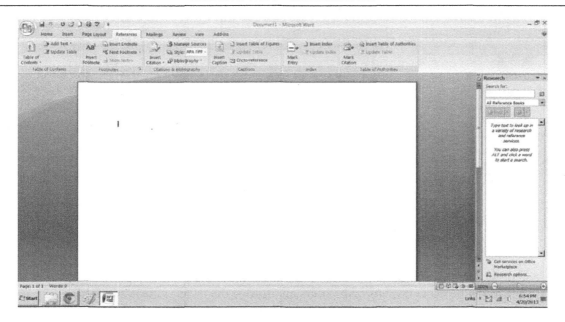

Figure 8.32
Microsoft Word—References tab

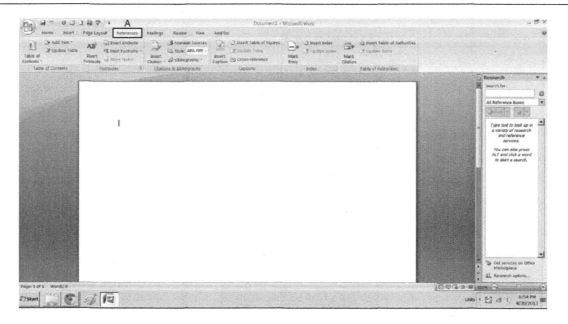

Figure 8.33
Microsoft Word—References tab: Table of Contents box

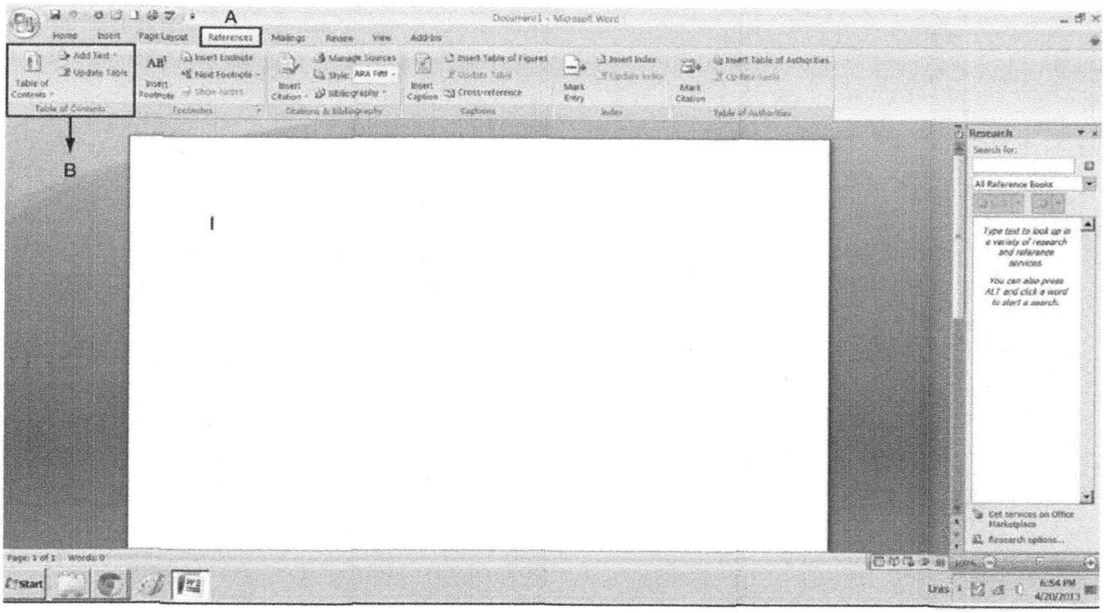

I. Table of Contents

Especially with appellate briefs, a table of contents has to show where certain important information, such as the case law used in the brief, appears in the document.

II. Footnotes

Where an attorney is making a legally persuasive argument in a brief, but wants to make a point not directly related to the argument, the lawyer will use a footnote. Because one of the benefits of software involves making the work of a user easier, the buttons here will properly place a footnote. Best of all, the software will automatically adjust the placement of a footnote if the attorney wants to add or delete material, an otherwise time-consuming process if done manually, such as before the advent of word processing software.

Figure 8.34
Microsoft Word—References tab: Footnotes box

III.   Citations and bibliography

One way to make an argument more persuasive in a brief involves referring to appropriate case law, statutes, regulations, or other authority, by including a citation. Critically, the citation for the legal reference has to conform to the specific style commonly used in the American legal field, the "Blue Book" format. Although this software can style a citation into a format used in research papers or periodicals, it will not automatically put a case citation into "Blue Book" format. It can, however, compile a list of references, in the form of a bibliography.

Figure 8.35
Microsoft Word—References tab: Citations and Bibliography box

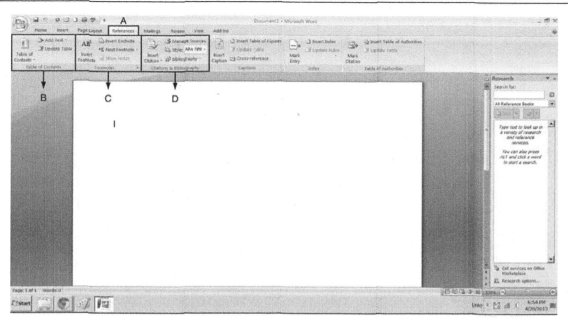

The user can also search for references from sources such as Microsoft's Bing search engine.

Figure 8.36
Microsoft Word—References tab: Citations and Bibliography box, Insert Citation button, Search Libraries submenu

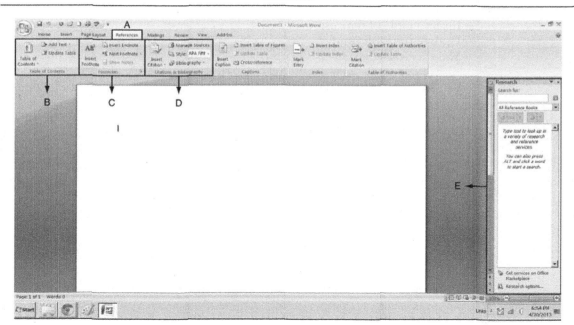

Figure 8.37
Microsoft Word—References tab: Captions box

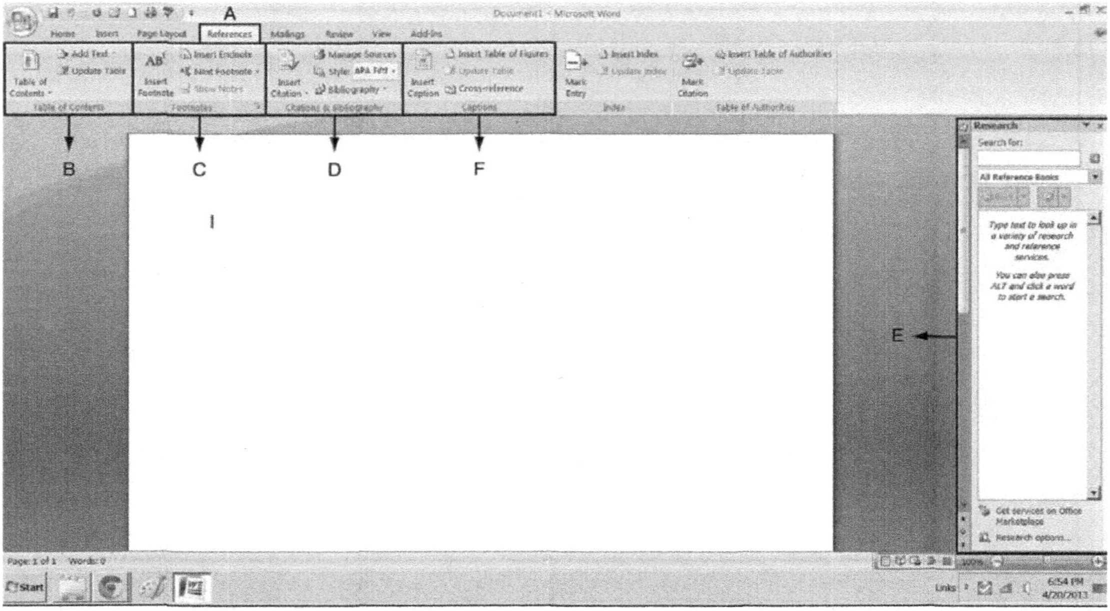

IV.   Captions

In a dispute regarding a patent, often a question arises about "original art" which relates to important graphic information. This box offers options to:

→ Generate captions for such graphics;
→ Insert a table of figures;
→ Update the table; and
→ Make a cross-reference.

V.   Index

One way that a lawyer could share his or her expertise would involve writing a text. The author could use this option to create an index. This involves going through the manuscript and designating the level of importance of information, so that the software can generate an index. For example, the index for this book has as a heading Microsoft Office, with subordinate headings for Word and for Excel.

Figure 8.38
Microsoft Word—References tab: Index box

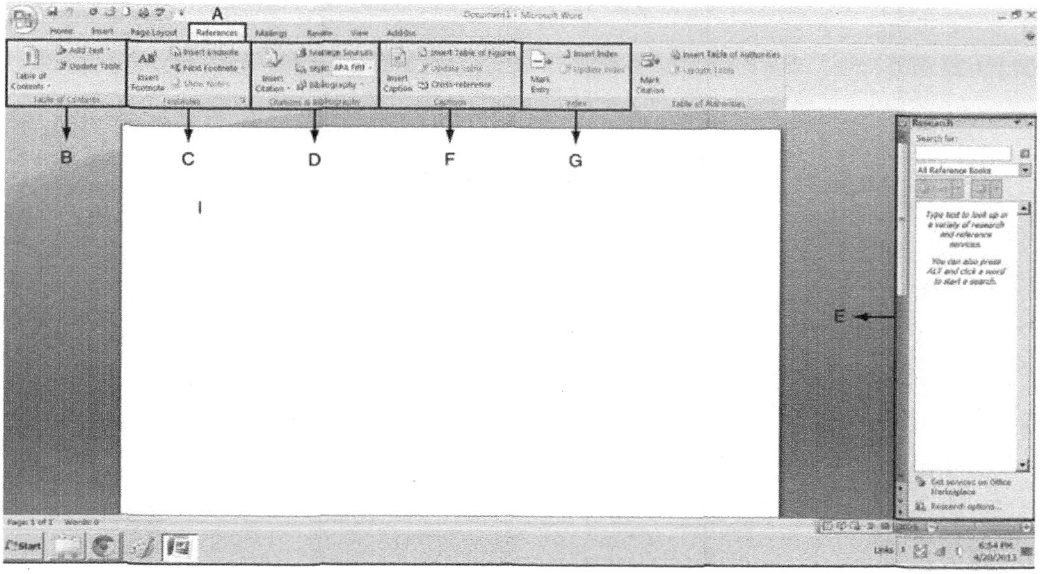

VI. Table of Authorities

Rules of appellate courts generally require that an appellate brief include a listing of all sources of law mentioned in a brief, called a table of authorities. The last box makes it possible to create a table of authorities.

Figure 8.39
Microsoft Word—References tab: Table of Authorities box

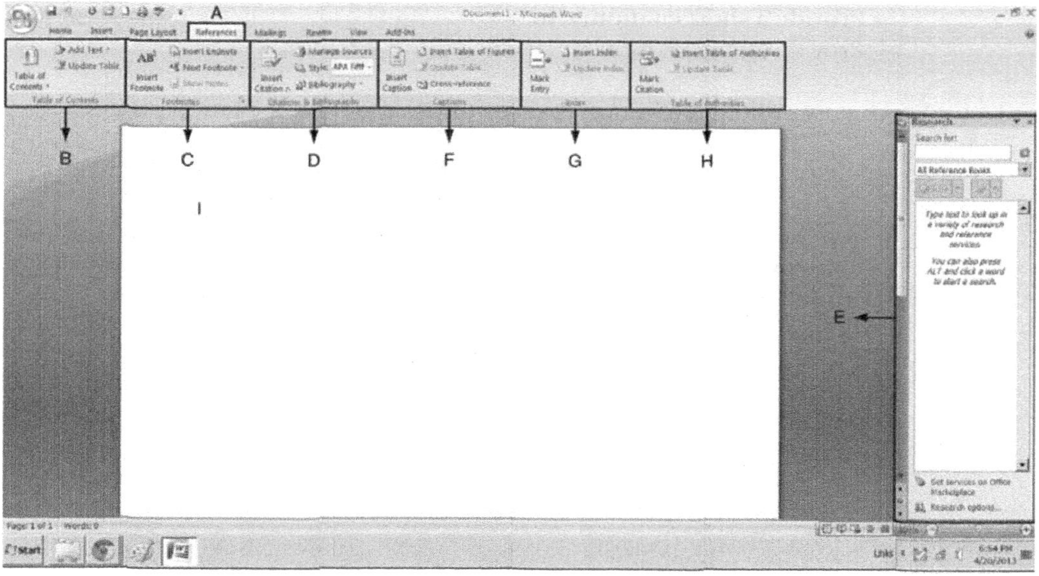

Figure 8.40
Microsoft Word—References tab: Table of Authorities box, Mark Citation submenu

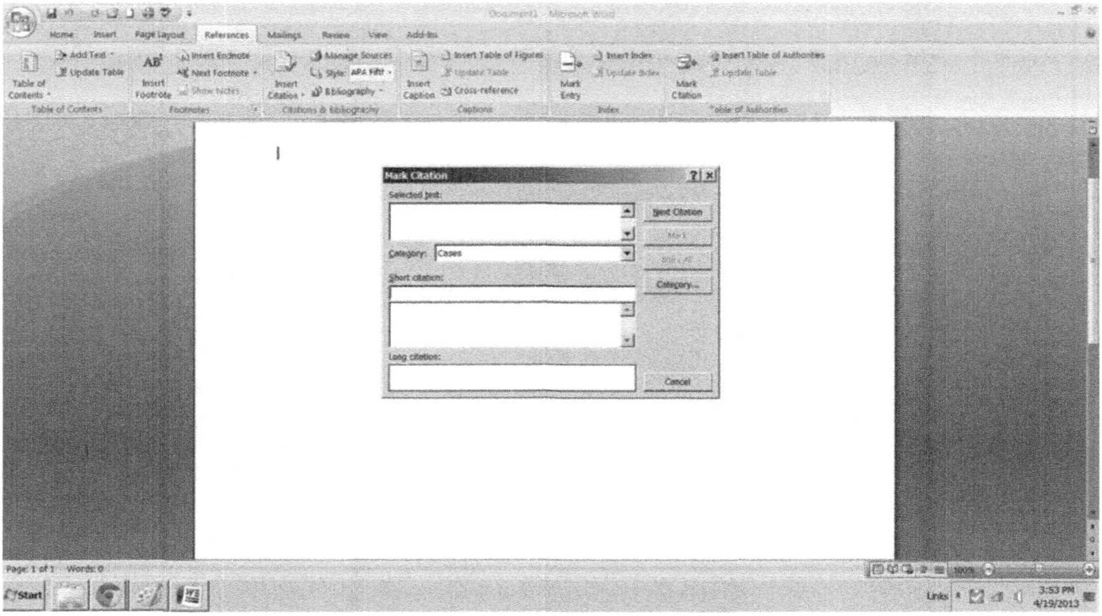

Mark Citation

When the user clicks this option, a submenu entitled Mark Citation opens with the following features to:

→ Select the text that will be included in a table of authorities;
→ Categorize this citation (also possible using an adjacent button);
→ Provide a short citation; and
→ Provide a long citation.

The user will find a button that continues this type of citation process.

Insert Table of Authorities

When the user clicks this option, a submenu entitled Table of Authorities opens to a tab by that name; several other inactive tabs also appear. These are accessible in other boxes, such as the one for generating an index.

Figure 8.41
Microsoft Word—References tab: Table of Authorities box, Table of Authorities submenu

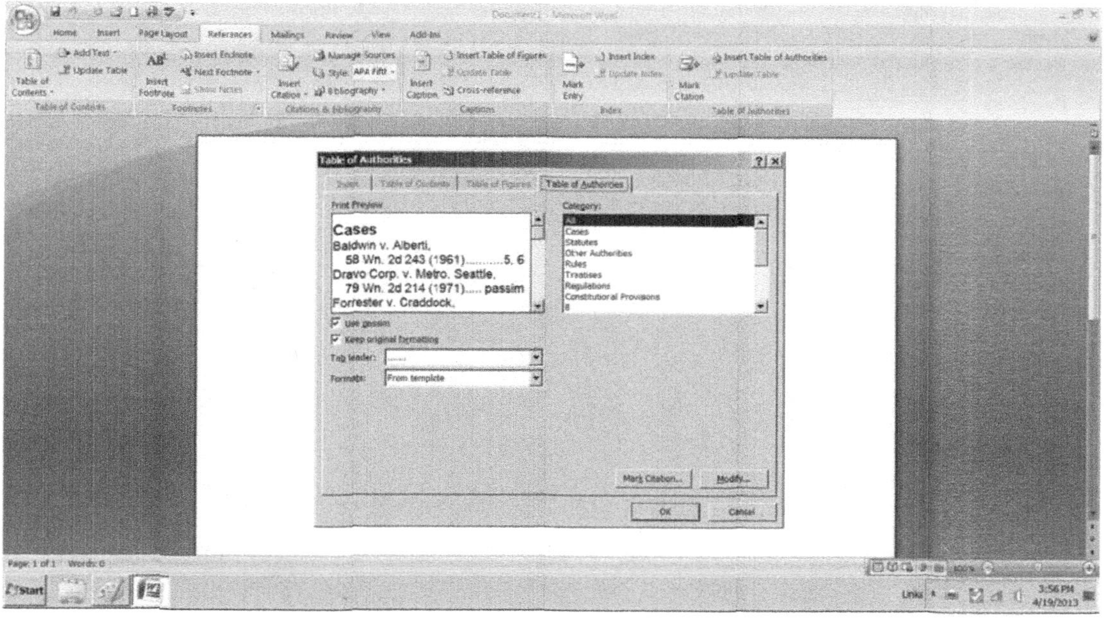

This submenu provides the user with:

→ The ability to see how a table of authorities will look;
→ Another opportunity to categorize authorities;
→ The chance to note whether an authority is mentioned *passim* (that is, in passing);
→ The choice to keep original formatting;
→ The option to select a tab header (with choices just like those mentioned above); and
→ The option to determine the formatting header (with choices just like those mentioned above).

Here the user has buttons to Mark Citations and to Modify. This box also contains an option to update the table of authorities automatically when changes occur in the text of the document.

v. Mailings tab

Under this tab heading, a user can generate different types of mailings. For example, this could mean drawing client names and addresses from a database to print out envelopes for a mailing about the addition of a new attorney to a firm.

Figure 8.42
Microsoft Word—Mailings tab

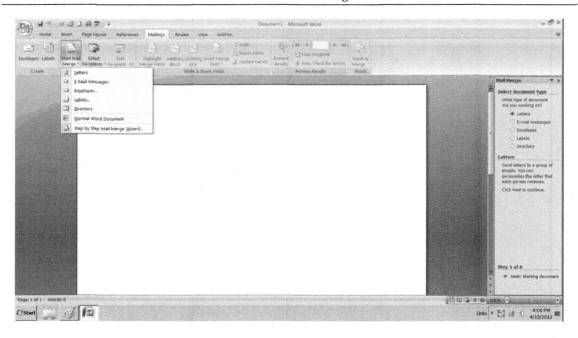

Figure 8.43
Microsoft Word—Mailings tab

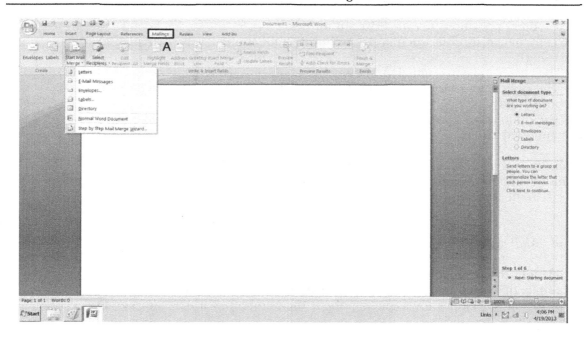

Figure 8.44
Microsoft Word—Mailings tab: Create box

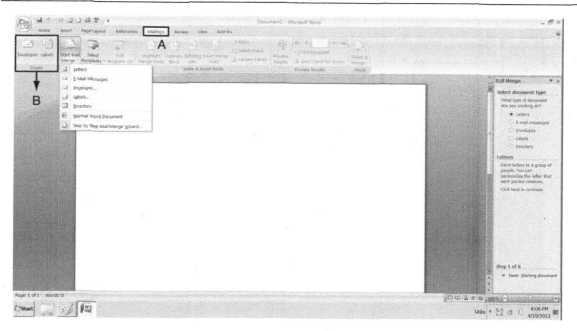

I. Create

Here, the user can draw on a list of names and addresses to generate envelopes and labels. Options can include setting the position of the envelopes in the printer and generating a single label or a sheet of labels.

II. Mail merge

The software can guide a user, via a Mail Merge **Wizard,** on how to generate envelopes and labels from an existing list of addresses. In addition to making it possible to generate labels and envelopes, a user could merge a list of clients' e-mail addresses with an announcement of the addition of a new employee in order to notify clients instantly about this significant change to a law firm.

Figure 8.45
Microsoft Word—Mailings tab: Start Mail Merge box

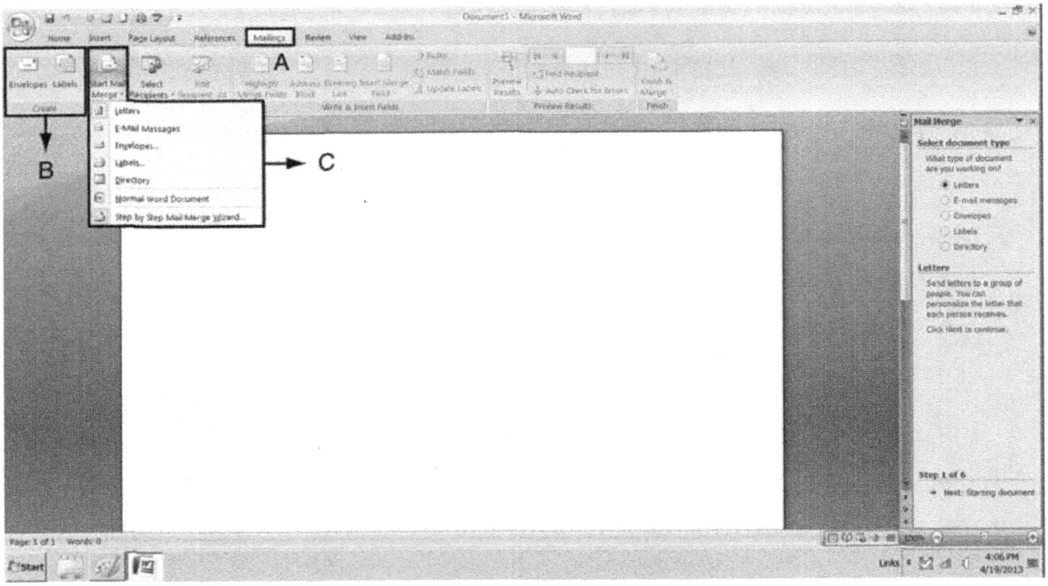

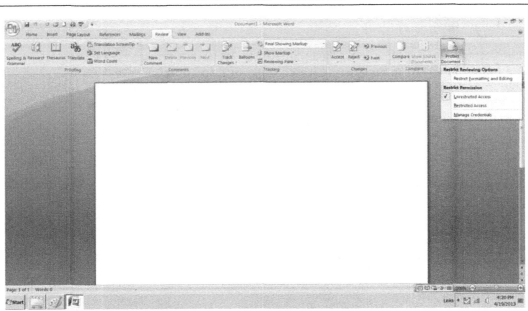

vi.   Review tab

Because documents issued by a law firm can have a significant impact, the software provides options to improve upon the quality of a document's content.

Figure 8.46
Microsoft Word—Review tab

Figure 8.47
Microsoft Word—Review tab

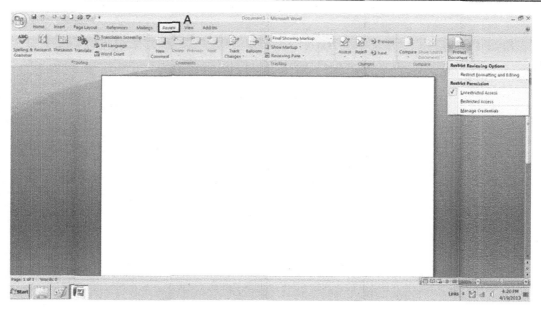

I.   Proofing

Software can simplify the checking of spelling and even identify potential mistakes in grammar. Other options include generating a word count, determining whether a document will exceed a court's page-length requirements for a brief, or translating text.

Figure 8.48
Microsoft Word—Review tab: Proofing

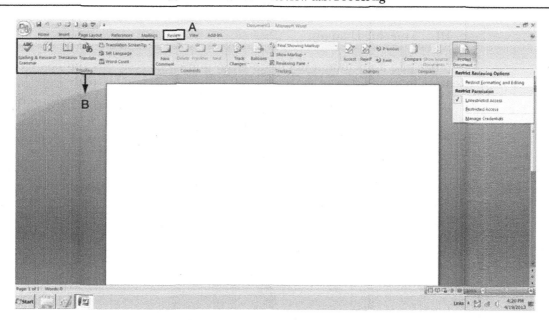

Figure 8.49
Microsoft Word—Review tab: Comments box

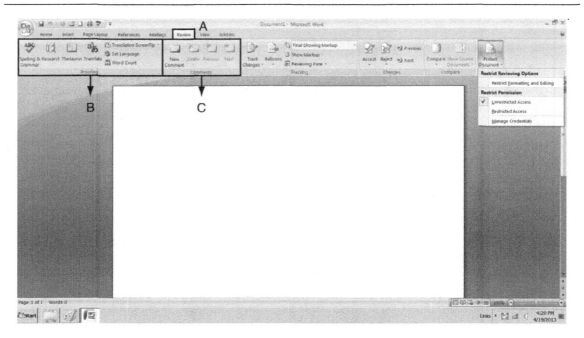

II.   Comments

Members of a law firm might need to review a document to offer their insights or opinions. Here, they can insert comments without altering the document's appearance. Given the possibility of input from several reviewers, the user can assign a particular color for each reviewer's input or indicate where to place the comments, such as in a marginal area of the document.

III.   Tracking changes

Because a document might undergo numerous revisions and changes, this feature helps the user to see the history and types of changes made.

Figure 8.50
Microsoft Word—Review tab: Tracking box, Track Changes button

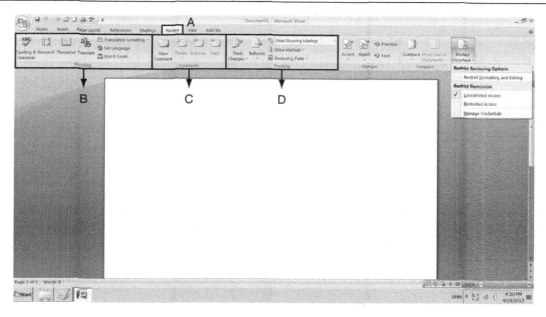

IV. Changes

Here, the option exists to accept or reject a change, such as whether to include a disclaimer in a document regarding the title to property for sale.

Figure 8.51
Microsoft Word—Review tab: Changes box

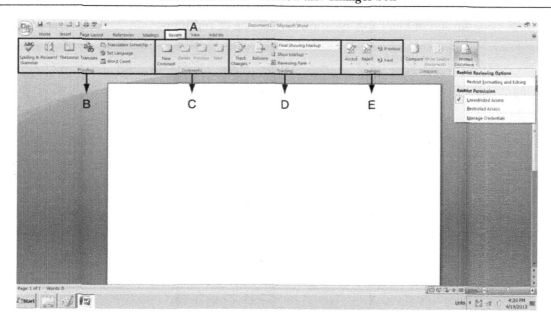

Figure 8.52
Microsoft Word—Review tab: Compare box

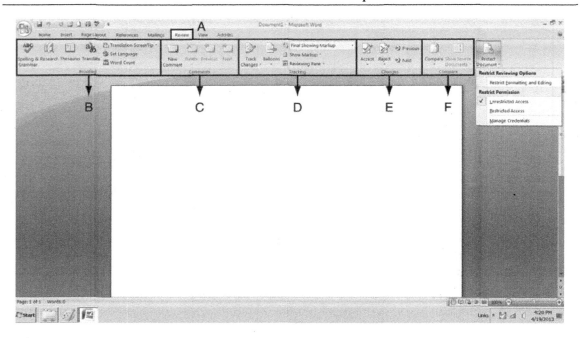

V.   Compare

a.   Compare and combine

Another way to look at changes involves comparing versions of a document. The software can quickly identify differences in otherwise similar documents. Doing this manually, by underlining differences between versions of a document in red or black ink, is called **blacklining** or **redlining.**

b.   Using Compare

To start this process, clicking the button will open up the following submenu.

Figure 8.53
Microsoft Word—Review tab: Compare box, Compare submenu

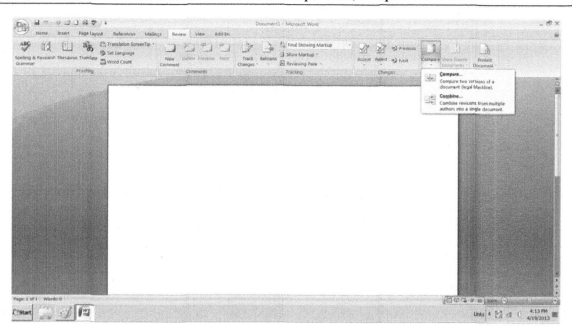

Clicking on the Compare link will produce this submenu.

Figure 8.54
Microsoft Word—Review tab: Compare box, Compare submenu, Compare link, Compare documents

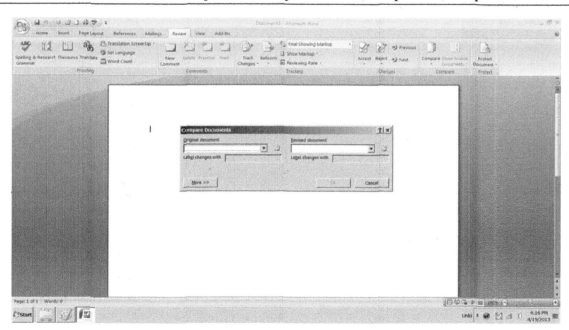

Here, the user has the option to:

→ Select an original and revised version of the baseline document;
→ Choose how to identify changes in the two;
→ Determine the criteria to be used in the comparison from a long list that may, for example, include looking at tables or commas;
→ Indicate where to put the results—in the baseline or other documents, or into a new document—with indications identifying the changes.

The user then can combine changes made by reviewers into one document and have the same options available as with the Compare function.

VI.   Protect document

A law firm could send a client a draft of a prenuptial agreement without allowing the client to make a change to the electronic version of the agreement. The software can protect the agreement or portions of it from alteration.

Figure 8.55
Microsoft Word—Review tab: Protect Document box, Protect Document button, submenu

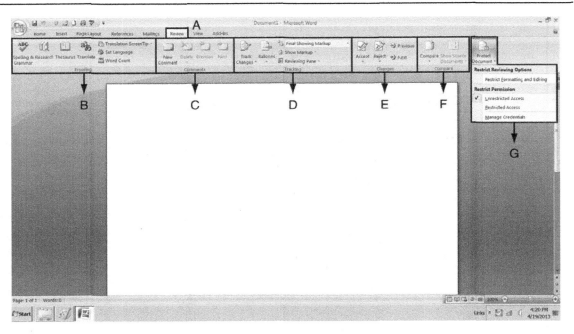

Figure 8.56
Microsoft Word—Review tab: Protect Document box, Protect Document button, submenu Restrict Formatting and Editing options, Information Rights Management service option

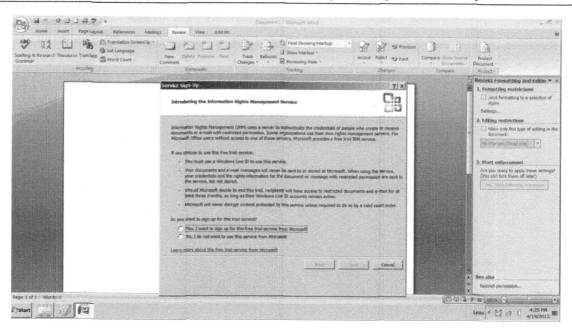

Consider this possibility: for the sake of speed, a firm and a client could each make revisions to a purchase and sale agreement stored in a central location on a Microsoft **server.** By activating the free Information Rights Management service available through Microsoft, the firm could limit access to the agreement, or provide limited access to portions of this contract.

vii.   View tab

Understanding how a document, like a newsletter, might look to clients, could make it more appealing for clients to read. The last tab on the standard Word screen makes it possible to see, but not change, how content will look.

Figure 8.57
Microsoft Word—View tab

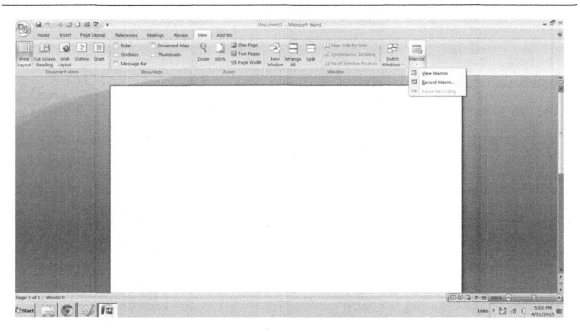

Figure 8.58
Microsoft Word—View tab

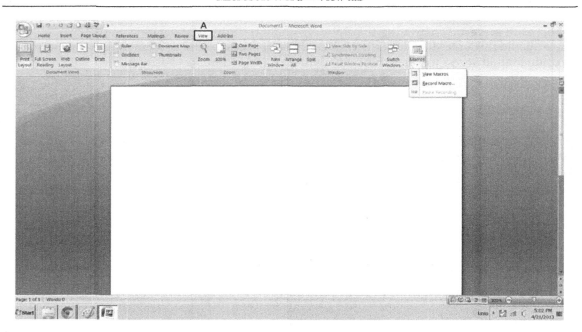

Figure 8.59
Microsoft Word—View tab: Document Views box

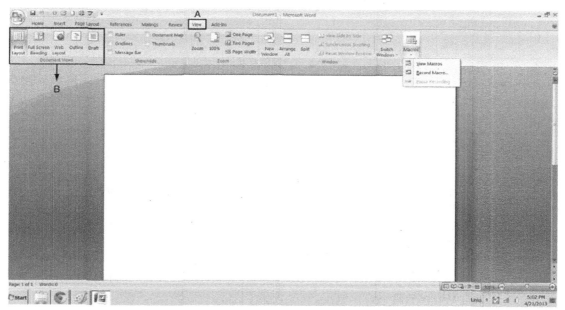

I.   Document views

Here, the views reveal how different content will look when printed out as a book or posted on the Web. Submenus, accessible via a toolbar, allow the user to look up words while reading or page through the document.

II.   Show/Hide

With this box, a user can have a ruler appear at the top of the screen to show the placement of tabs and margins, impose gridlines on the text, or provide small graphic images, called **thumbnails,** which represent the placement of pages in a document.

Figure 8.60
Microsoft Word—View tab: Show/Hide box

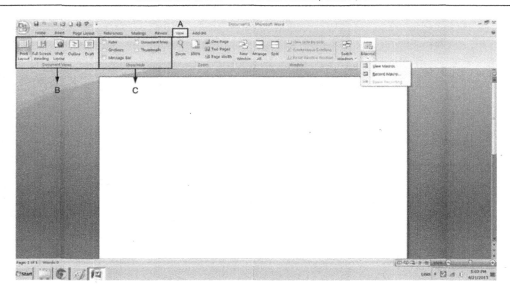

III.   Zoom

This box allows a user to magnify the screen image, have it expand, or adjust its layout to fit on adjacent pages.

Figure 8.61
Microsoft Word—View tab: Zoom box

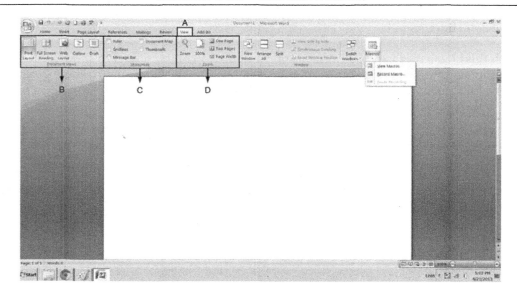

Figure 8.62
Microsoft Word—View tab: Window box

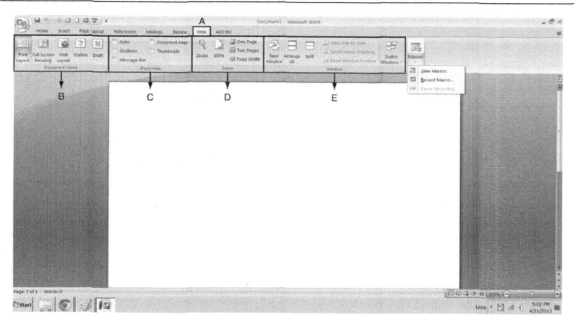

IV. Window

One way to look at multiple documents simultaneously would involve opening them in multiple windows. Using the options in this box makes it possible to arrange those multiple windows on the screen.

V. Macros

A **macro,** in this context, is a very simple computer program. By creating a macro, a user could automate the performance of an activity. For example, since clients who get billed by the hour need to get accurate expense statements, a user could create a macro that lists those expenses typically associated with a client's case. The user also can find and edit macros.

Figure 8.63
Microsoft Word—View tab: Window box, Macros button, submenu

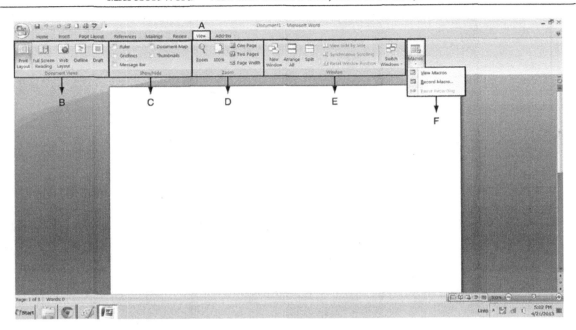

2.   Excel

Software that took advantage of the speed and accuracy of a personal computer's microprocessor demonstrated the benefit of having computers in the workplace. For example, spreadsheet software could perform calculations and eliminate errors. Even better, a user could change data and see the results instantly. So, if a client wants a firm to create a trust fund for the client's child, the firm could show how changing the amount of money put into the fund would change the amount that a child would receive as a monthly payment.

a.   Features

i.   Grids, cells, and sheets

The Excel screen has a gridwork of lines like that of graphing paper.

Figure 8.64
Microsoft Excel—Home tab: gridwork of cells

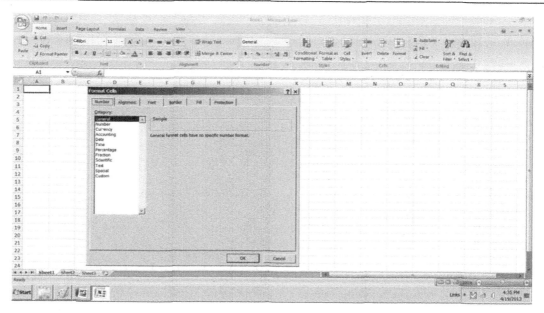

The **cell** serves as the basic unit of operation in Excel. When preparing a divorce agreement, a user could take a year's worth of electrical bills, enter them into individual cells, and calculate an average, to estimate some of the cost for running a household where children will reside.

The grids exist on sheets. **Sheets** are the Excel version of a page in Word. A collection of sheets is called a **workbook.**

Figure 8.65
Microsoft Excel—Home tab: cell

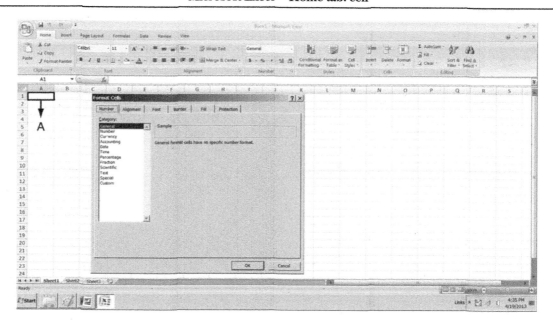

Figure 8.66
Microsoft Excel—Sheet 1 tab: bottom of start page

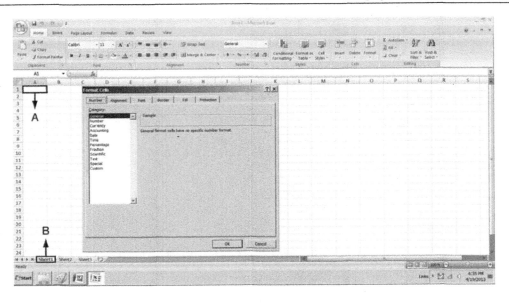

ii. *Function box*

The function box may best demonstrate what spreadsheet software can do. By using the function box, users can create their own formula for manipulating information in cells. For example, the user could create and insert a formula that makes it possible to project a business's growth based on information contained in cells, such as anticipated expenses.

Figure 8.67
Microsoft Excel—Function box

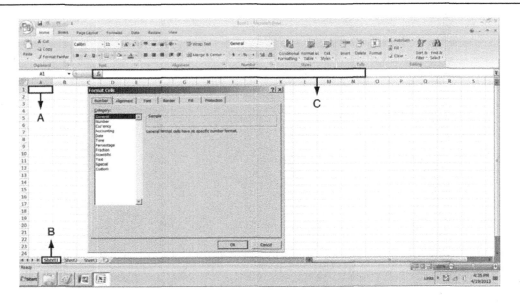

b.   Tabs

Microsoft uses the metaphor of a manila folder's tab to organize different software functions. Not surprisingly, then, many of the same tab headings appear for organizing functions, like in other Microsoft software.

i.   *Home tab*

Like the Home tab in Word, this contains similar boxes for further organizing applications. The first two—Clipboards and Font—have the identical buttons, links, and functions as in Word.
Boxes unique to Excel contain the following:

I.   Alignment

a.   Positioning material in a cell

By using buttons in this box, a user can align content in a cell relative to a margin, putting the data at the top, middle, or bottom.
The user can also rotate that data at an angle, such as a right angle. This would give the user another way of identifying characteristics of data, like monthly bills that fall closest to the end of a month, if a law firm needed to generate projections about the annual costs for running a business.

Figure 8.68
Microsoft Excel—Home tab: Alignment box

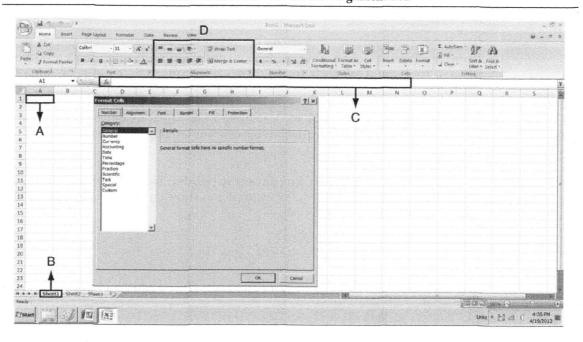

Figure 8.69
Microsoft Excel—Home tab: Alignment box, top row, Angle of Content button submenu,
Format Cells options

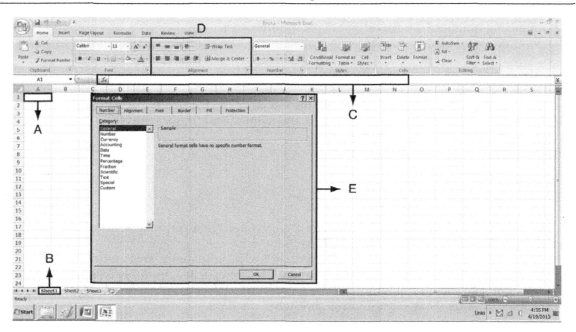

b.   Formatting of a cell

Formatting data in a cell allows the user to make adjustments quickly to the data. If a firm doing business in the European Union needed to determine its costs, a user could switch between those costs expressed as Euros or American dollars.

Also, a user can alter the font, create or alter a border, fill in cells with colors so as to quickly show the costs of operating a law office in different parts of the world, and password-protect data to prevent subsequent alteration.

c.   Combining cells

The Merge and Center link makes it possible to combine information in cells. This could allow a user, for example, to show cumulative changes in business costs over different intervals.

Figure 8.70
Microsoft Excel—Home tab: Alignment box, bottom row, Merge and Center button submenu

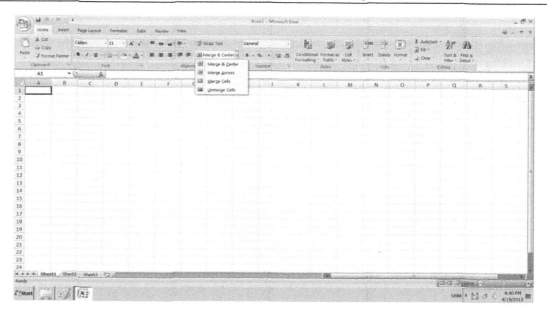

II.   Styles

Manipulating the way that data appears in cells could make it easier to show changes in operating costs for a client's different business offices. Options in the Styles box let the user alter the presentation of data in cells.

Figure 8.71
Microsoft Excel—Home tab: Styles box

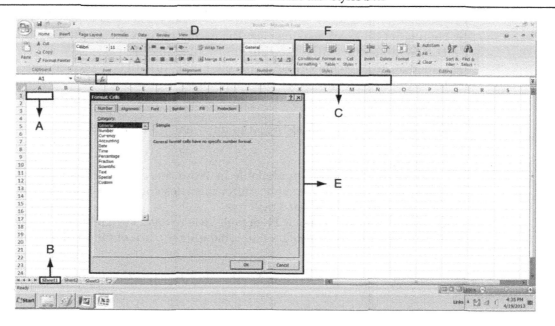

Figure 8.72
Microsoft Excel—Home tab: Styles box, Conditional Formatting button and submenu

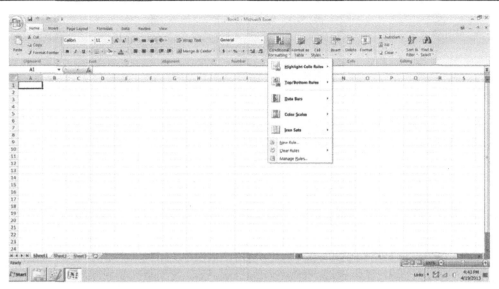

a.   Conditional formatting

Excel makes it possible to apply different rules to cells. For example, a business may not have the option to deduct from annual income taxes the complete cost of acquiring equipment in a year, but must do that over time. Conditional formatting gives the user the ability to apply different rates of deducting the costs for different classes of equipment over time. Given the volatility of tax law, the user can adjust those rules when Congress votes to change the rate at which a business may deduct the expense of purchasing the equipment on the business's annual tax returns. In addition to presenting data graphically, some of the following affect the presentation of data.

→ Highlight Cell Rules, making clear the nature of rules that apply to cells;
→ Top/Bottom Rules, about sorting information in cells;
→ Data Bars, to depict information in cells in the form of bars on a graph;
→ Icon sets, to select the color and shape of icons that will reflect certain values (as a number or percentage), using a graphic image in a "traffic light" pattern; and
→ Manage Rules, which would apply to the cells.

b.   Format as table

As with the Styles option available in Word, here the user can set styles for the table or portions of the table. Different styles could represent the different types of annual expenses that a firm has.

Also, the user can assign a new **Pivot table** style to data. Pivot table is a proprietary application of Microsoft, designed for changing the presentation of data.

Figure 8.73
Microsoft Excel—Home tab: Styles box, Format as Table button and submenu

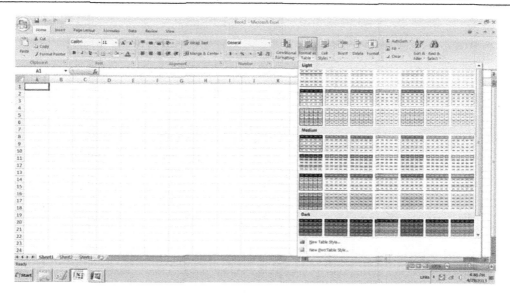

c.   Cell styles

Similarly, the user can select features of a cell, such as title or headings. For example, titles could identify different firm-related expenses, like salary or rent.

Figure 8.74
Microsoft Excel—Home tab: Styles box, Format as Table, Cell styles

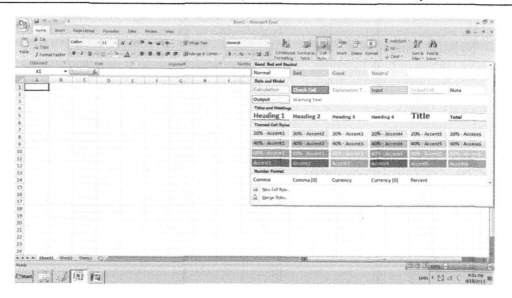

Figure 8.75
Microsoft Excel—Home tab: Cells box

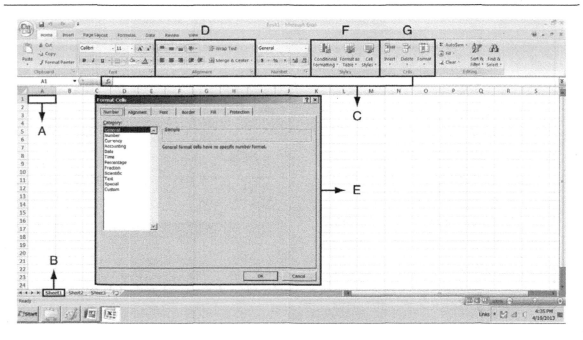

III.   Cells

This box allows the user to alter portions of a table, like having to combine a year's average expenditures on computer technology, with other years. Other operations available here include:

→ Inserting or deleting cells, rows, columns, or a sheet;
→ Formatting of cells;
→ Hiding or making visible cells; and
→ Organizing sheets, such as moving them or renaming them.

IV.   Editing

In Word, clicking the Σ (the capital Greek letter sigma) button makes it possible to add up figures. This button, in Excel, also allows a user to perform mathematical calculations and to:

Figure 8.76
Microsoft Excel—Home tab: Editing box

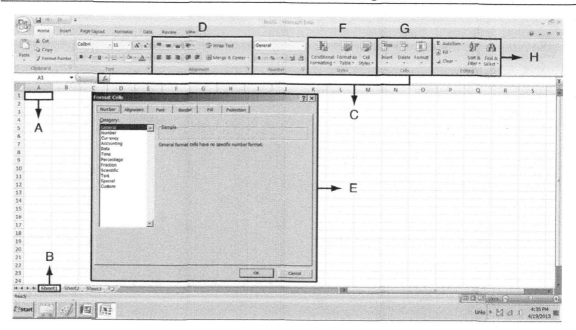

→ Continue a pattern among cells;
→ Clear formatting, content, and comments;
→ Sort and filter information; and
→ Find and select, such as looking for differences or formulas.

ii.   Insert tab

I.   Content

As in Word, the user can insert illustrations, a Pivot table, or a chart.

II.   Charts

This box makes it possible for a user to depict cell data as:

Figure 8.77
Microsoft Excel—Insert tab: Charts box

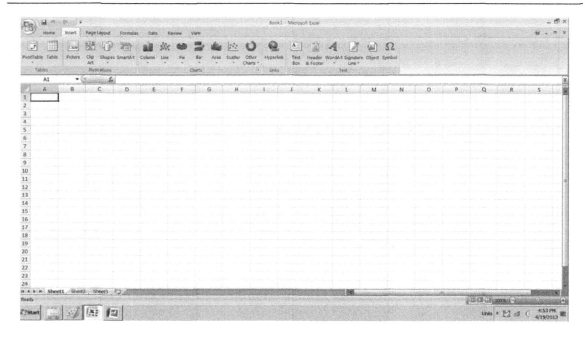

→ Columns;
→ Lines;
→ Pie charts;
→ Bar graphs;
→ An area, or;
→ Scattergrams.

Taking a client's projections for growth, the user could present this data graphically as lines or columns.

iii.   Page layout tab

Here, much like in Word, the user can adjust the:

→ Page Setup, regarding the presentation of data on sheets;
→ Scale to Fit, to adjust the width and height of a printout; or
→ Sheet Options, including whether to include gridlines on the printout.

Figure 8.78
Microsoft Excel—Page Layout tab

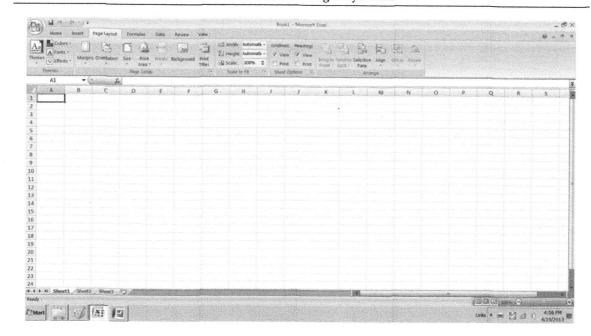

iv.   Formulas tab

Under this tab, a user can create or use existing formulae. For example, if a business's assets decline in value at a particular rate, a user could create a formula that can show the pace at which physical assets like equipment lose their value over time.

Figure 8.79
Microsoft Excel—Formulas tab

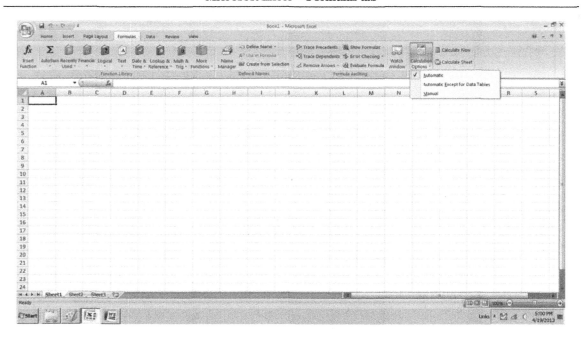

Figure 8.80
Microsoft Excel—Formulas tab

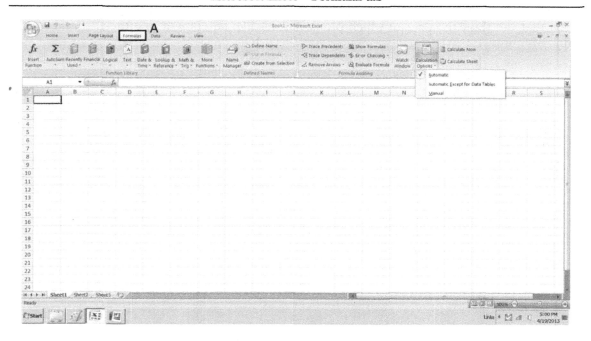

Figure 8.81
Microsoft Excel—Formulas tab: Function Library box

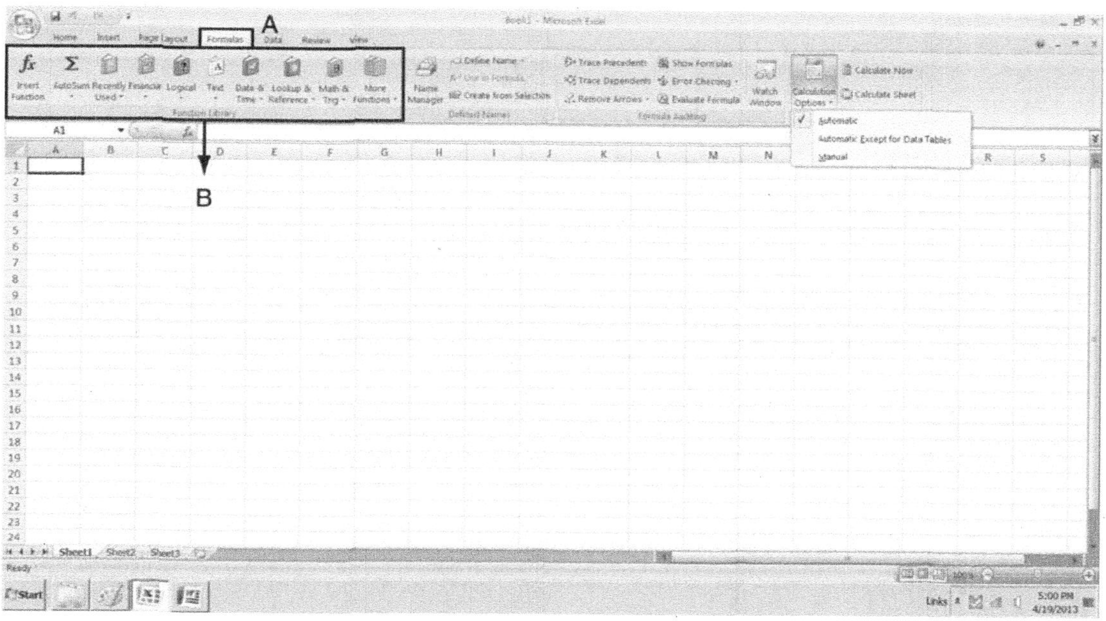

I. Function Library

This box provides a user with different types of functions, such as financial formulae. Once selected, the function shows up in the function bar, adjacent to the *fx* symbol in the bar just below the ribbon, as seen in Figure 2-81.
Buttons under this tab allow a user to:

→ Calculate the percentage yield of a bond daily, weekly, or annually, using Financial;
→ Add up information, via Auto Sum (Σ);
→ Calculate financial formulae, such as yield, price, or rate;
→ Engage logical functions, such as those involving "if-then" statements, via Logical;
→ Manage text strings, in order to be able to convert content to text;
→ Convert information into the date-time code used by Excel;
→ Obtain information about the location of a cell or areas of cells, under Lookup and Reference;
→ Perform mathematical calculations or trigonometric functions like sine or cosine; and
→ Employ functions related to statistics and engineering, among others.

For example, a law firm representing a joint enterprise created for a large public works project might need to use many of these in order to predict expenses or estimate costs.

Figure 8.82
Microsoft Excel—Formulas tab: Defined Names box

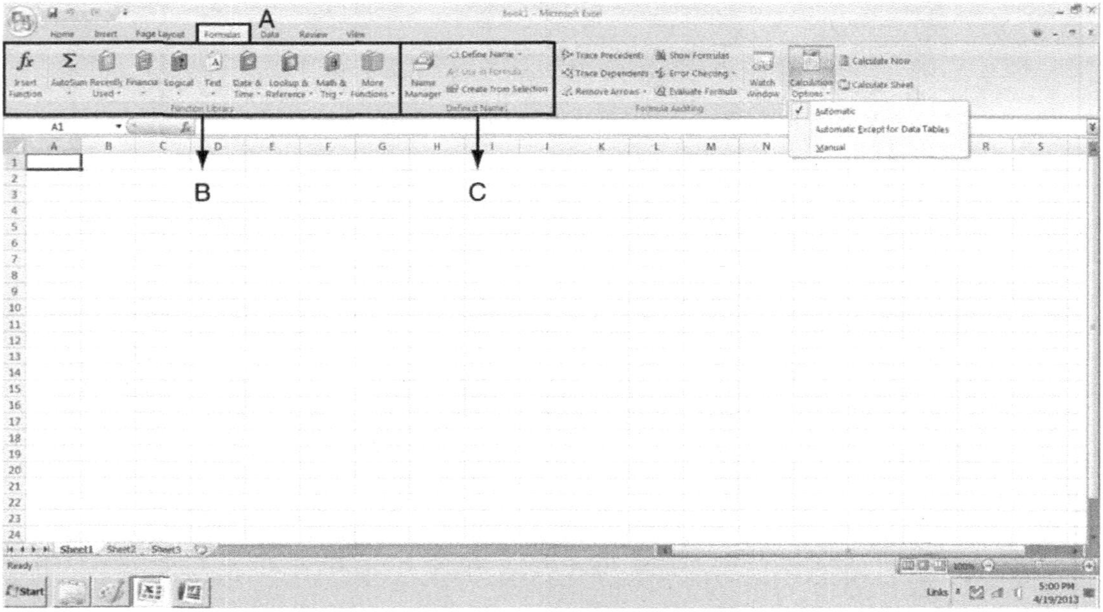

II.   Defined Names

This box allows the user to manipulate names in a document, such as for associating a value for a name, like the fixed rate of decline in value of a class of assets over time.

III.   Formula Auditing

If a firm created a formula to project an average increase in rent for office space, the result might be wildly beyond what was expected. To check why the software produced this clearly erroneous outcome, a user has buttons here for helping to figure out why a formula did not produce the expected results.

Figure 8.83
Microsoft Excel—Formulas tab: Formula Auditing box

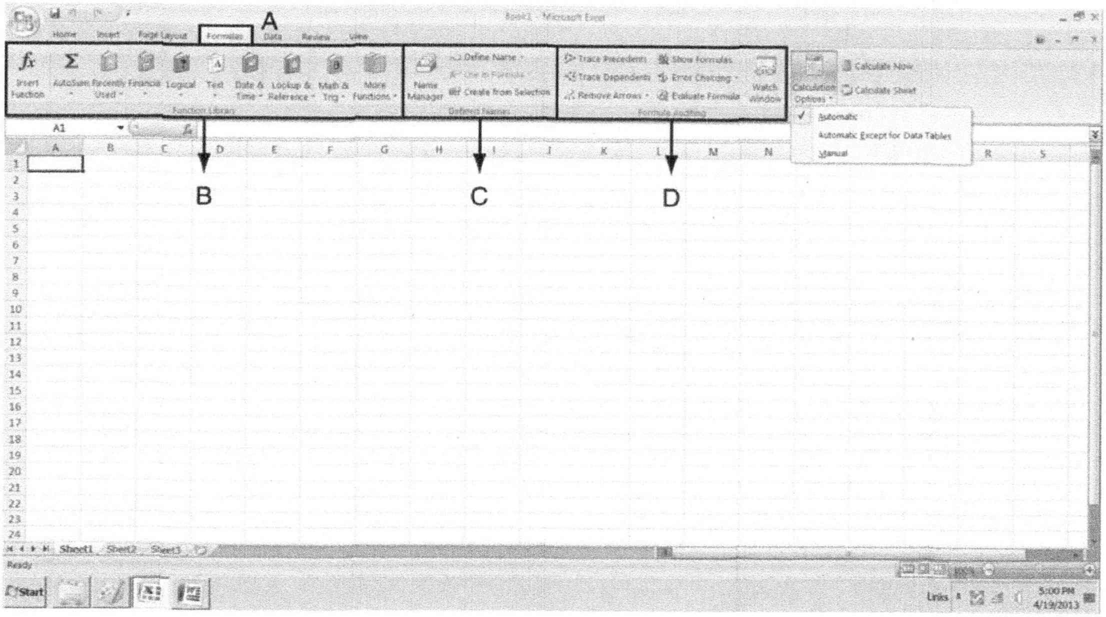

Another available function in this box, called Watch Window, allows a user to open a separate window that remains open no matter where in the workbook the user is. This way, a user can monitor the results in a window on selected cells when the user changes values elsewhere on a sheet.

IV. Calculation

The user can instruct the software, via buttons in this box, how to do calculations in order to run:

Figure 8.84
Microsoft Excel—Formulas tab: Calculation box, Calculation Options button submenu

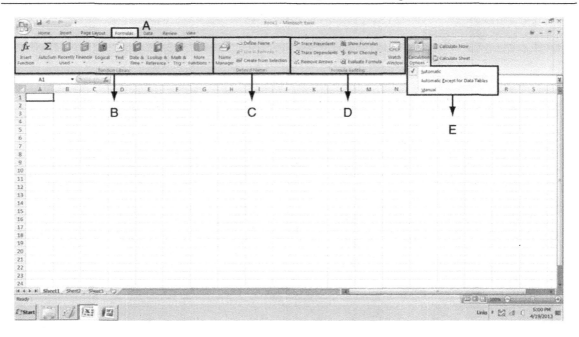

→ Automatically or manually;
→ Without data tables; and
→ Only for a sheet.

This could allow a firm, representing a grievously injured client, to project cost-of-living increases needed for a lifetime of the client's care because of the severity of the client's injuries.

v.   Data tab

Here, a user can use and manage data.

Figure 8.85
Microsoft Excel—Data tab

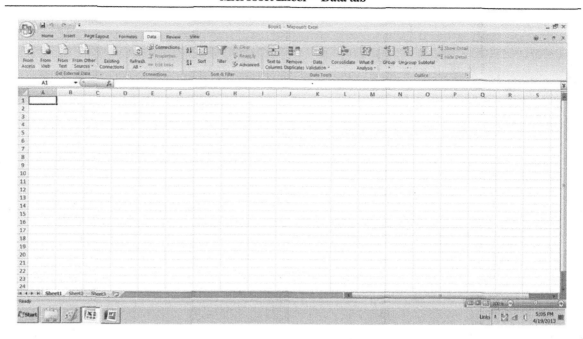

Figure 8.86
Microsoft Excel—Data tab

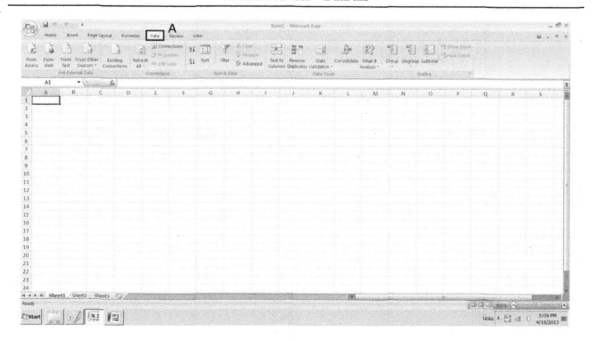

Figure 8.87
Microsoft Excel—Data tab: Get External Data box

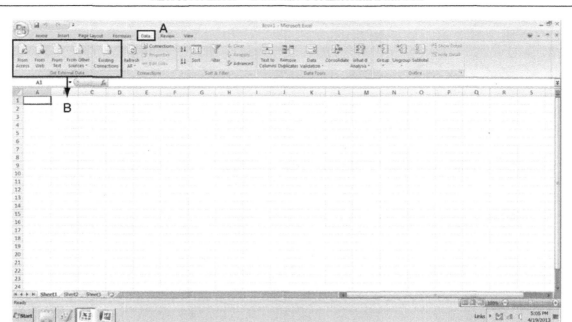

I.   Get External Data

The data can come from an array of sources, like:

→ **Access,** Microsoft's database software;
→ The web; and
→ An **SQL** server.

II.   Connections

The user can adjust or manage cell connections in the workbook. For example, this would allow a firm to show how changes in the design of a client's new house will increase the projected costs of construction.

Figure 8.88
Microsoft Excel—Data tab: Connections box

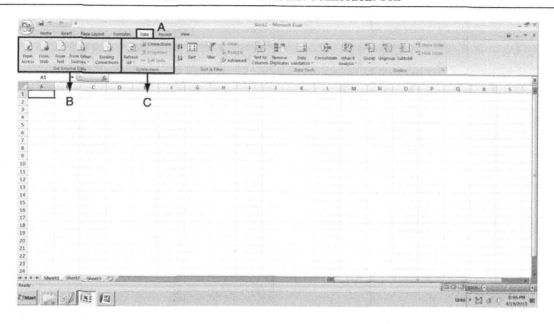

III.   Sort & Filter

Not only can a user organize data here, but a user could sort a corporation's projected expenses for a year, whether a one-time cost or an annual cost.

Figure 8.89
Microsoft Excel—Data tab: Sort and Filter box

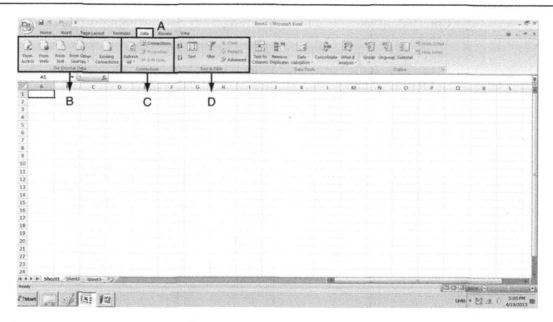

Figure 8.90
Microsoft Excel—Data tab: Data Tools box

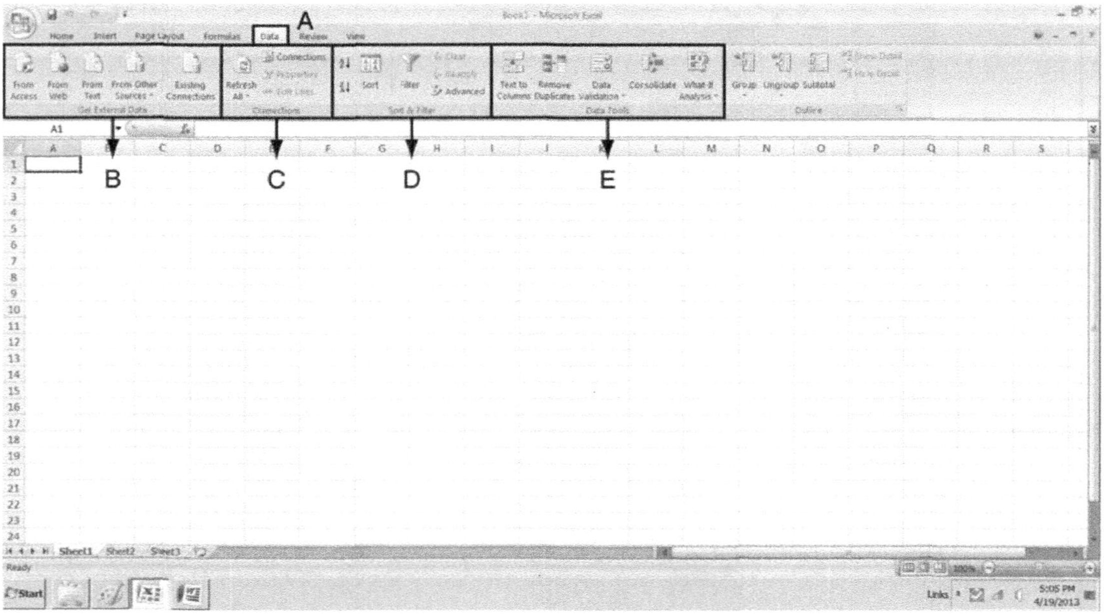

IV.   Data Tools

Buttons in the Data Tools box make it possible for a user to:

→ Separate the contents of a cell into columns (similar to a feature in Word for
   putting text into columns);
→ Consolidate values from multiple ranges of cells into a single, new range;
→ Validate data, which can:
     → Prevent the entry of invalid data into a cell;
     → Check that the correct values were used; and
     → Identify invalid data.

Because a business's operating costs can change with the addition of a new client
or a loss of business, these tools allow a user to:

→ Conduct a "what if" analysis, so that a firm could anticipate an increase in the
   costs of employment if it signs on a big, multinational communications firm,
   for example;
→ Use a scenario manager, in order to predict costs if there is a sudden economic downturn; and
→ Alter data tables, to reflect a change in a firm's policy about how to calculate
   billable hour rates.

Figure 8.91
Microsoft Excel—Data tab: Outline box

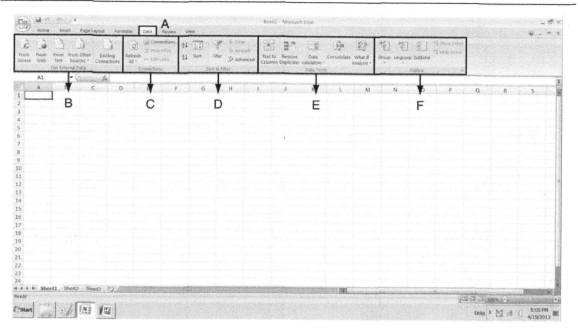

V. Outline

A question of law may exist of whether a client's expenses can be deducted from income taxes for a single business year. Via the buttons here, expenses can be grouped with similar kinds of expenditures depending on whether they can be deducted over time or in a year.

vi. Review tab

In addition to allowing a user to choose actions like those in the corresponding box in Word, the user can:

Figure 8.92
Microsoft Excel—Review tab: Changes box

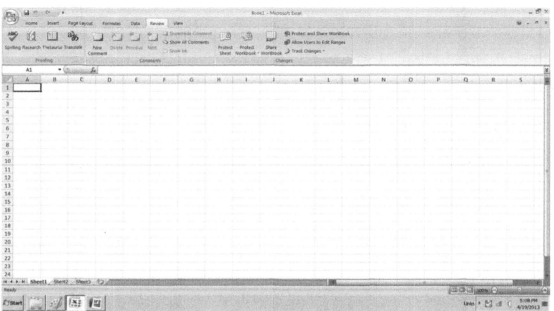

→ Password-protect the contents of a sheet or a workbook;
→ Designate those with the authority to alter data; and
→ Accept or reject changes.

3.   PowerPoint

A slide show presentation can visually convey to a client the impact of an adverse court ruling in a client's case. Because of the difference in impact that graphic information has over text, Microsoft's slide show presentation software, Power-Point, may get used as often as Word or Excel.

Using tabs like those in Word and Excel across the top of the screen, the user can select a title and subtitle for a slide, such as "annual expenditures," and then a "breakdown of costs" by month.

Figure 8.93
Microsoft PowerPoint

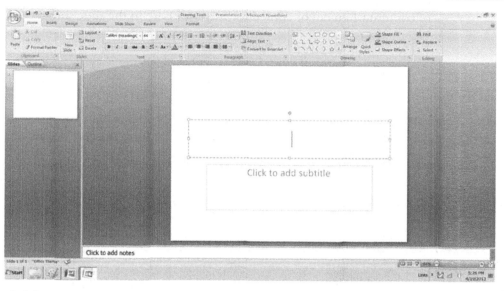

On the left-hand screen, the user has a box that shows the positioning of the slides. This allows a user to change the sequence of the slides via a drag-and-drop option or to see how the slides will look in an outline format.

a.   Home Tab

The Home tab, here, has many of the same boxes in Word and Excel. For example, the Editing box has the same features as that box in Word and Excel.

Figure 8.94
Microsoft PowerPoint—Home tab

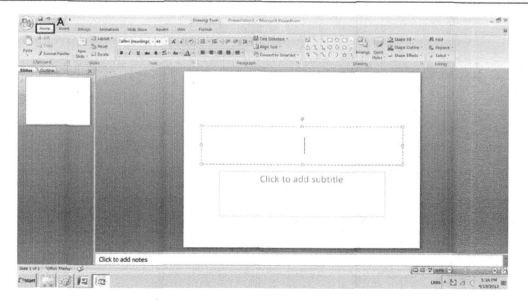

Some boxes might differ slightly:

→ The Clipboard box has a link to Format Painter, for preserving the formatting of content when cut or copied for use elsewhere in the slide show.

Figure 8.95
Microsoft PowerPoint—Clipboard box

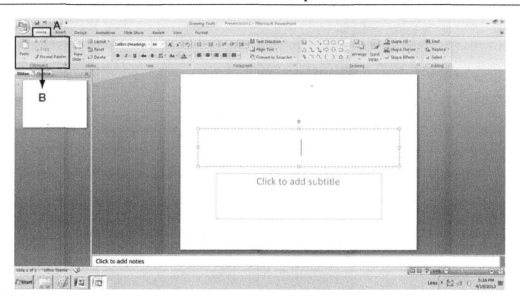

→ The Font box has a button for adding a shadow to text, so that it can stand out on the slide.

Figure 8.96
Microsoft PowerPoint—Font box: Text Shadow button

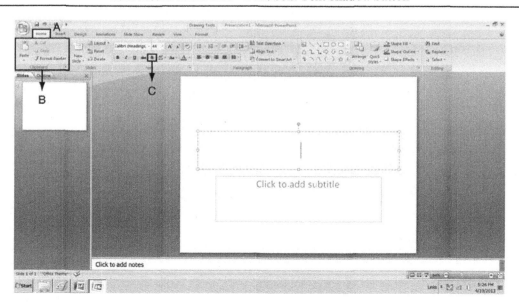

→ The Paragraph box has a link to convert text in a slide into SmartArt.

Figure 8.97
Microsoft PowerPoint—Paragraph box: Convert to SmartArt button

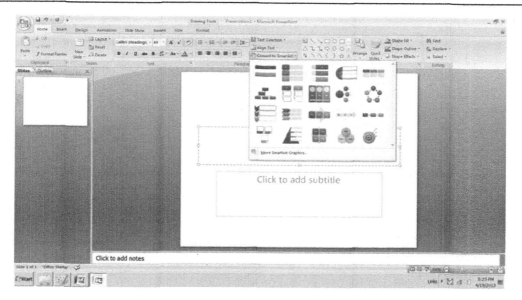

Some boxes reflect the unique possibilities for creating a slide show.

i.   Slides

The Slides box, to the immediate right of the Clipboard box, has buttons for generating and for altering features of slides.

Figure 8.98
Microsoft PowerPoint—Home tab: Slides box

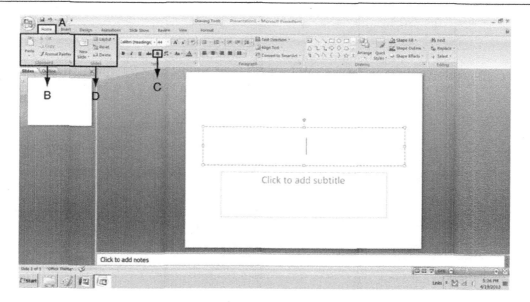

Figure 8.99
Microsoft PowerPoint—Home tab: Slides box, New Slide button submenu

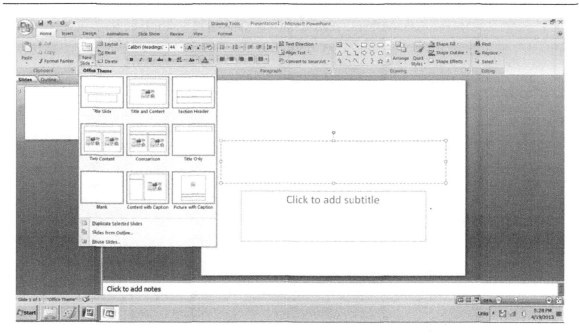

For example, when creating a slide, a user can choose different layouts for presenting the content of a slide. These can include Two Content, which has a narrow header at the top and adjacent blocks for inserting text. Using a Picture with Caption layout allows a user, for example, to present the image of a house along with its square footage and the size of the house's lot. Links at the bottom allow for easy duplication and reuse of slides, as well as to take slides from saved outline files. Other links make it easy for the user to start over, to delete a slide, or to alter the layout of its content.

ii.   Drawing

Because the presentation of information visually can have a significant impact, a user has options for the use of graphic images which can involve inserting ready-made shapes, like those available in Word. A submenu offers a host of other such shapes.

Figure 8.100
Microsoft PowerPoint—Home tab: Drawing box

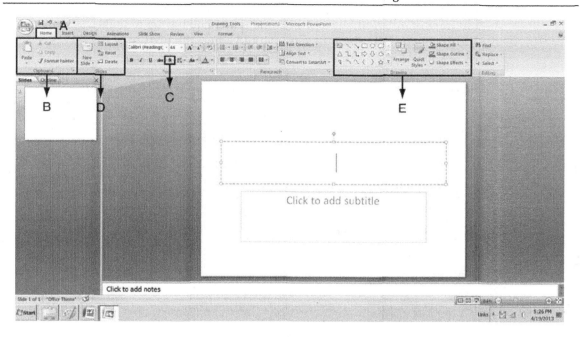

Figure 8.101
Microsoft PowerPoint—Home tab: Drawing box, submenu of ready-made graphics

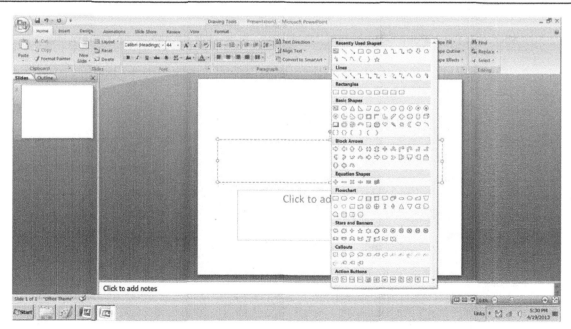

Options allow a user to change the capacity of a shape to hold an image, and to vary the lighting and texture of the content of a shape. This could highlight differences to an arrow shape depicting a range of cost increases, based upon different rates of inflation, that a firm could anticipate having to make.

Via the Shape Fill submenu, a user could adjust the texture of the fill.

Figure 8.102
Microsoft PowerPoint—Home tab: Drawing box, Shape Fill link submenu

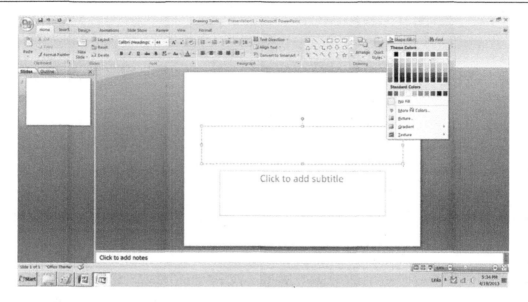

Figure 8.103
Microsoft PowerPoint—Home tab: Drawing box, Shape Fill link submenu, Texture link

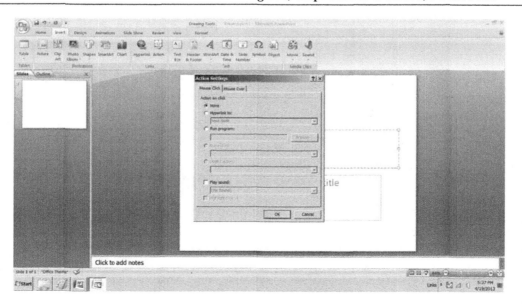

The user could also, through the link at the bottom of the previous submenu, further edit the nature of the fill used in order to:

→ Select the type of material to fill a shape;
→ Decide to vary the width of a line, or to depict it as dashes;
→ Use effects like shadowing or 3-D;
→ Adjust the transparency of a shape; or
→ Insert a picture or text.

b.   Insert Tab

In addition to being able to insert material as in Word and Excel, such as pictures or text, a user can include images that can enhance the quality of the presentation.

Figure 8.104
Microsoft PowerPoint—Insert tab

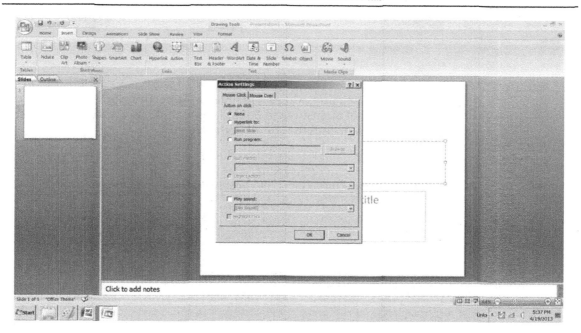

Figure 8.105
Microsoft PowerPoint—Insert tab

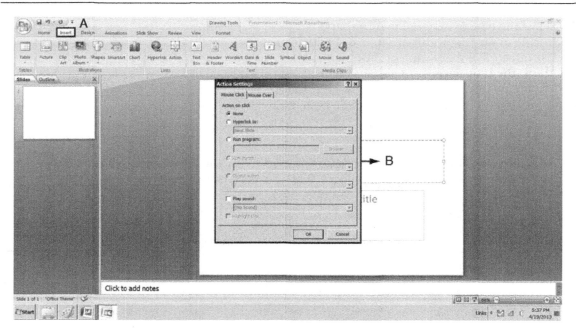

For a presentation to a jury, where a plaintiff is suing an insurance company for breach of the terms of an insurance policy, a user could insert animation, such as a graphic of a car crash, and the sound of the crash.

Figure 8.106
Microsoft PowerPoint—Insert tab: Links box, Action button submenu

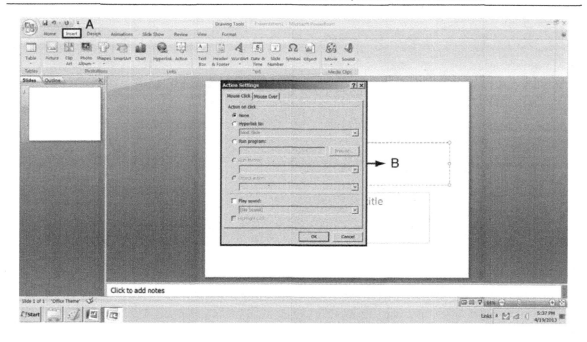

Figure 8.107
Microsoft PowerPoint—Insert tab: Media Clips box

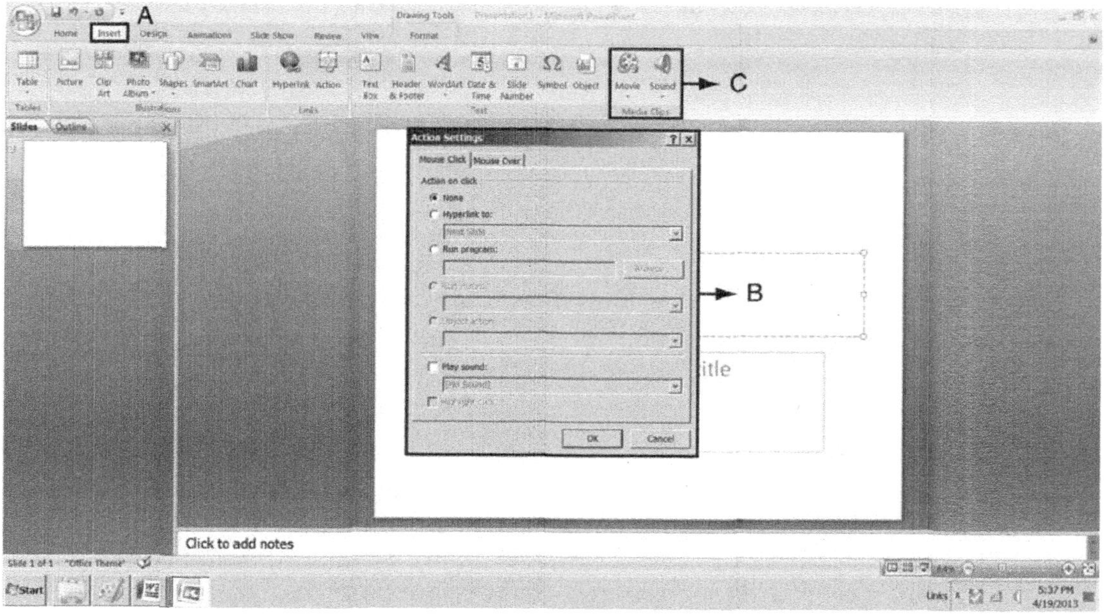

Also, a user can insert media clips, such as a segment from a local television news program that talks about the number of accidents that have happened at a bad curve in a road.

c.   Design Tab

Just as in Word, the user can orient a slide to the portrait or landscape positions. In landscape, a user would have more room to magnify the text of a specific provision in a contract in a lawsuit about a breach of that contract.

Figure 8.108
Microsoft PowerPoint—Design tab

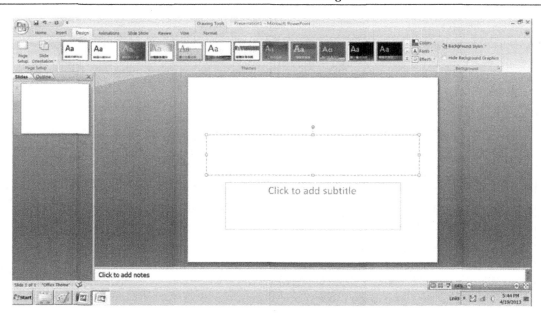

d. Animations Tab

The use of animation allows a user to tap into the full power of the software, making a presentation more dynamic than if the slide merely contained text and graphics.

Figure 8.109
Microsoft PowerPoint—Animations tab

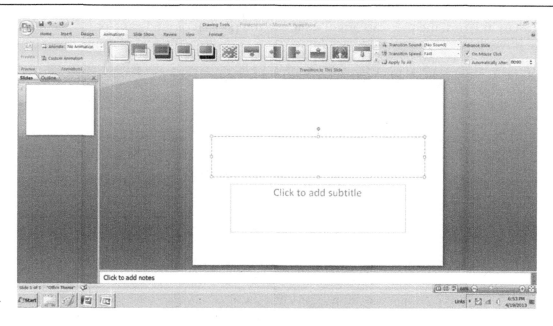

Figure 8.110
Microsoft PowerPoint—Animations tab

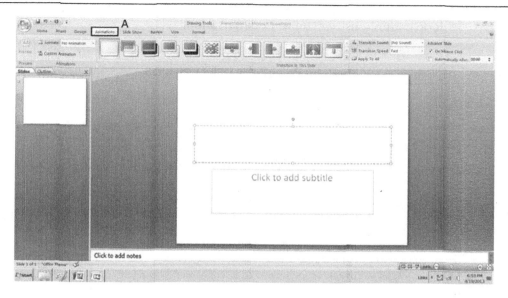

The user can also:

→ Modify the animation, controlling when it should start and end, as when to begin a video clip of the beating of a plaintiff at the hands of a defendant;
→ Adjust the transition, so that one slide may fade away as another appears; and
→ Select sounds that play during a transition, such as applause or a drumroll.

Figure 8.111
Microsoft PowerPoint—Animations tab: Translation to This Slide box

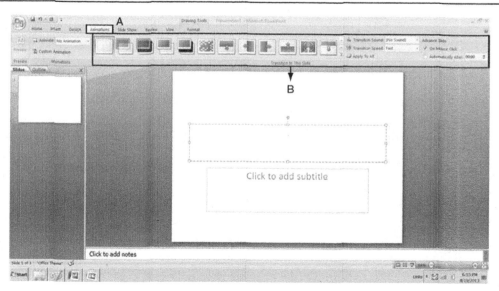

e.   Slide Show Tab

Options in the Start the Slide Show box allow the user to have the slide show loop continuously or run without narration.

Figure 8.112
Microsoft PowerPoint—Slide Show tab

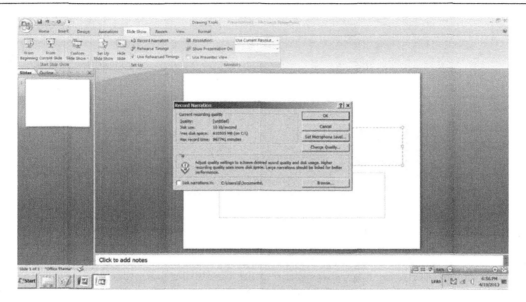

Figure 8.113
Microsoft PowerPoint—Slide Show tab

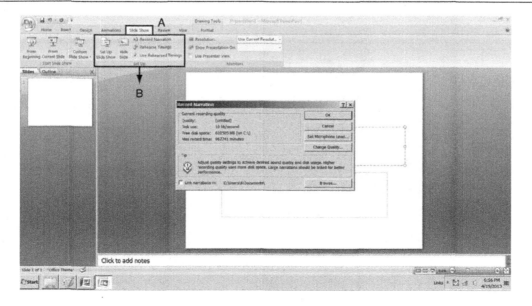

The next box provides the user with options for setting up the slide show. Those options include recording narration that will run during the slide show. For example, when presenting a slide show about a plaintiff's injuries from a car crash, the plaintiff can talk about the pain associated with those injuries.

Figure 8.114
Microsoft PowerPoint—Slide Show tab: Setup box

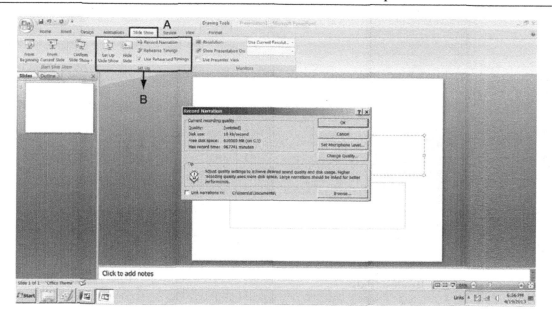

Figure 8.115
Microsoft PowerPoint—Slide Show tab: Setup box, Record Narration link submenu

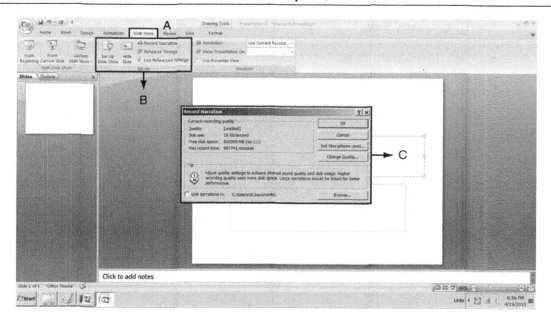

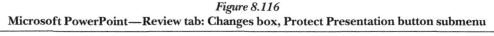

Figure 8.116
Microsoft PowerPoint—Review tab: Changes box, Protect Presentation button submenu

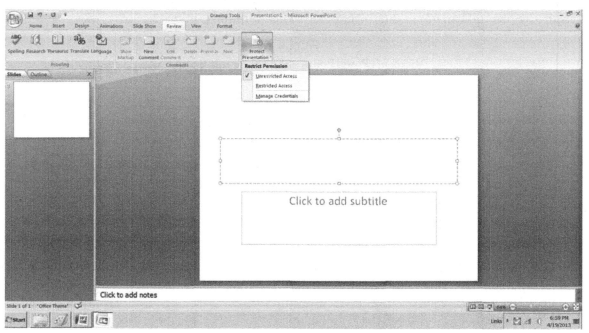

f.   Review Tab

As with the Review tab in Word, a user can proofread text and insert comments. Also, the user can protect the contents from unauthorized alteration.

g.   View Tab

In addition to having the same options as the View tab in Word, like Show/Hide and Zoom, a user can see how the presentation will look.
Buttons allow the user to:

Figure 8.117
Microsoft PowerPoint—View tab: Presentation Views box

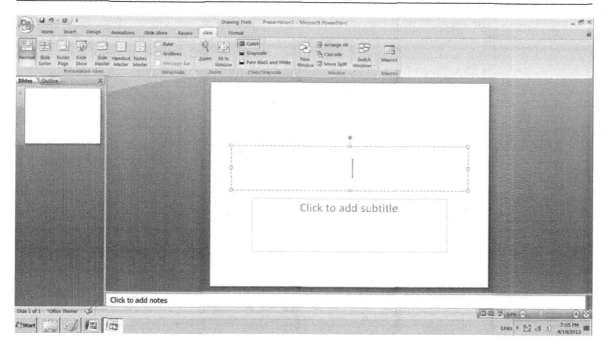

→ Look at a normal presentation of the show;

→ Use a slide sorter to rearrange the sequence of slides;

→ Edit the notes that only the presenter will see during the presentation, such as a reminder to a presenter about the elements that make up a tort for negligence;

→ Select the style for the slides, including the design and layout of master slides, which serve as a style template for subsequent slides; and

→ Choose the design and layout of the slides when printed as a handout.

C.   OPENOFFICE.ORG

The free software suite put out by OpenOffice.org, which uses the open-source Unix operating system, has many of the same features available in the Microsoft Office suite. One trend in the creation of free software involves making it "open source," where the creators disclose all the underlying computer code that makes the software work. As a result, people might create different, free versions of, for example, office productivity software. Often, users might provide revisions and fixes to correct occasional glitches in the free software. Also, the community of users may modify the software to run on different OSs, including Microsoft's Windows and Apple's Mac OS.

A legal practice might want to use free software to manage costs, since updates could also be free. Given the wide base of users for many types of free software, it likely will ensure the continuing accessibility of the content with newer versions of the software.

Because the software applications available at OpenOffice.org approximately correspond to those in Microsoft's Office suite, an Office user might quickly learn how to use this free software. Freeware like OpenOffice.org may not come with technical support, something available with Office. People may provide such support for a fee, or, some might provide free support.

1. *Writer*

Writer, the word processing software in the OpenOffice.org suite, shares many of the features of Word. For example, this suite uses tabs, like those in Word, to sort out categories of software functions. Writer has toolbars instead of the ribbon used in Word, with rows of similar buttons, as well as a drop-down link for customizing the toolbar.

Figure 8.118
Writer default view

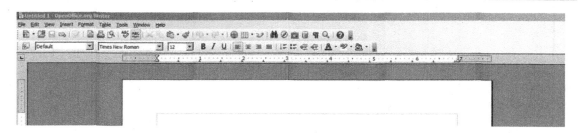

Figure 8.119
Writer Toolbar—top level, drop-down link

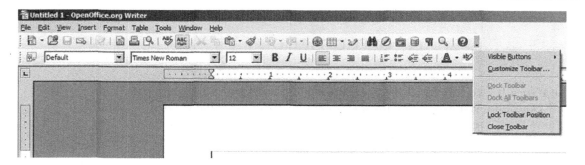

Familiar tabs and functions in Writer include:

→ Edit, as well as the option to block the undo or restore features;

Figure 8.120
Writer Edit tab

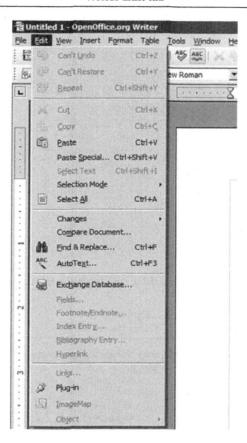

→ View, which also can control the addition of content;

Figure 8.121
Writer View tab

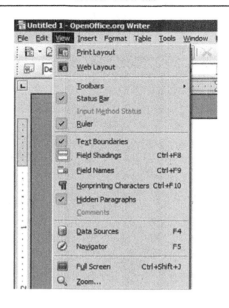

→ Insert, including the ability to add a movie or a sound;

Figure 8.122
Writer Insert tab

→ Table;

Figure 8.123
Writer Table tab

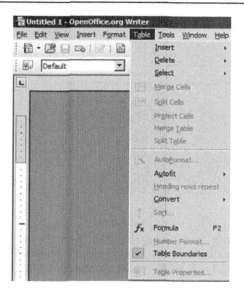

→ Tools, including spelling and grammar checking; and

Figure 8.124
Writer Tools tab

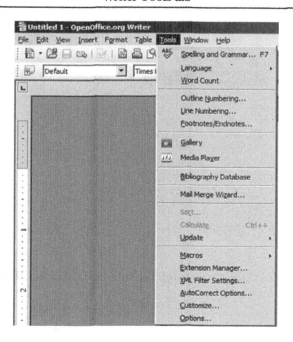

→ Help.

Figure 8.125
Writer Help tab

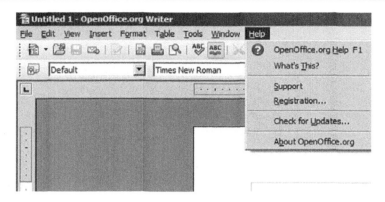

Writer also uses wizards, which provide step-by-step guidance in using a feature of the software. For example, these could make it possible to use an address book for generating an e-mail using Microsoft **Outlook** or Mozilla's **Thunderbird.**

Figure 8.126
Writer File Tab—Wizards link submenu

Many of the keyboard shortcuts available in Word, such as CTRL-S (to save), will also work in Writer.

Figure 8.127
Base—Database Wizard page

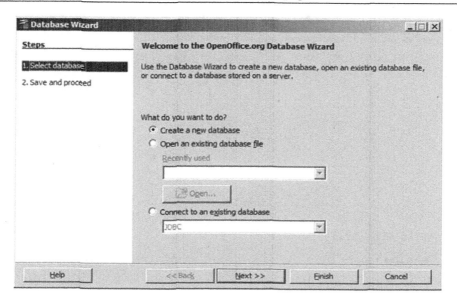

2. Base

The database software for OpenOffice.org is Base. A law office's database could include all data associated with representing clients, such as client contact information. It roughly corresponds to the Access database application in the Microsoft Office suite.

3. Calc

Calc, OpenOffice.org's spreadsheet software, roughly corresponds to the Excel software in the Microsoft Office suite. For example, a user might find it just as easy to add up litigation expenses for inclusion in a bill to a client as when using Excel.

Figure 8.128
Calc

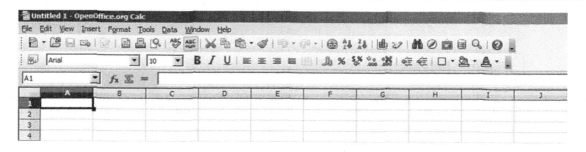

Figure 8.129
Math start page

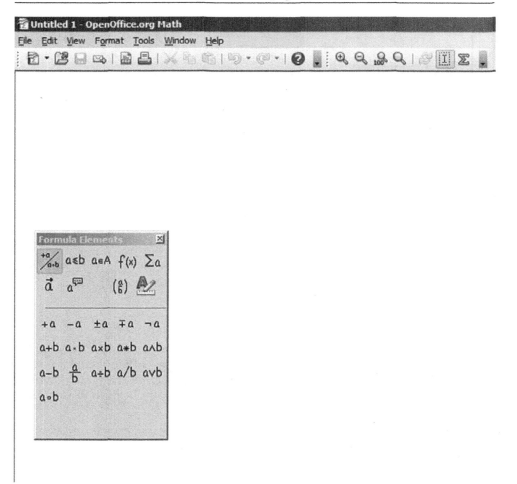

4.   Math

With Math, OpenOffice.org gives a user the option to do calculations without the grid used in Calc. Math users can insert formula elements, such as operators or functions, with a single click. Using a formula makes it easy to generate a graphic representation of the math process for subsequent insertion into any of the other applications available in OpenOffice.org.

5.   Impress

Impress, the OpenOffice.org version of Microsoft's PowerPoint software, contains many of the same options for the creating and editing of a slide show. Slight differences include an option to enter data points on a slide and to keep the data points at a specific position in the slide.

Figure 8.130
Impress start page

6.   *Draw*

OpenOffice.org has Draw, software that allows for drawing. It approximately corresponds to the Microsoft Word application, Paint.

Figure 8.131
Draw start page

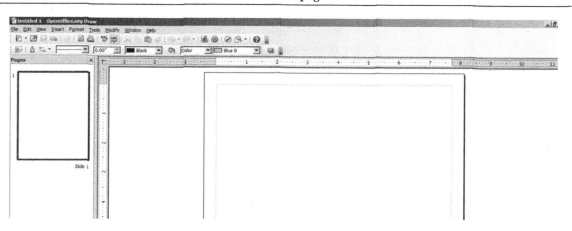

D.   GOOGLE DOCS

1.   *Software in the Cloud*

Google Docs is a type of free software that involves **cloud computing.** As noted earlier, the concept of **Software as a Service (SaaS),** also known as cloud computing, allows a user to edit and save documents using software stored on a server. This would allow a lawyer to obtain and/or modify a brief or pleading stored online by using any computer with Internet access. Google Docs comes with one gigabyte of free storage, with the option to buy more storage for an annual fee.

2.   *Features*

Google Docs has features akin to those in Microsoft's Office suite and OpenOffice.org's business productivity software, such as presentation and spreadsheet software. Microsoft's Office Suite and OpenOffice.org may have an advantage over Google Docs because of the wider array of applications they contain.

a.   Access

Typing www.google.com/docs into a browser brings the user to the log-in to a free Google Account.

Figure 8.132
Google Docs sign in

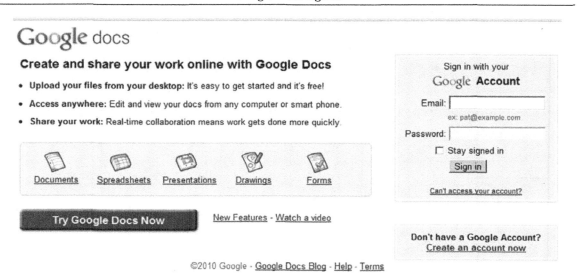

b.   The First Screen

The first screen of Google Docs shows a menu of documents stored there. From here, a user could create a new word processing document, slide show presentation, or spreadsheet.

Figure 8.133
Google Docs start page

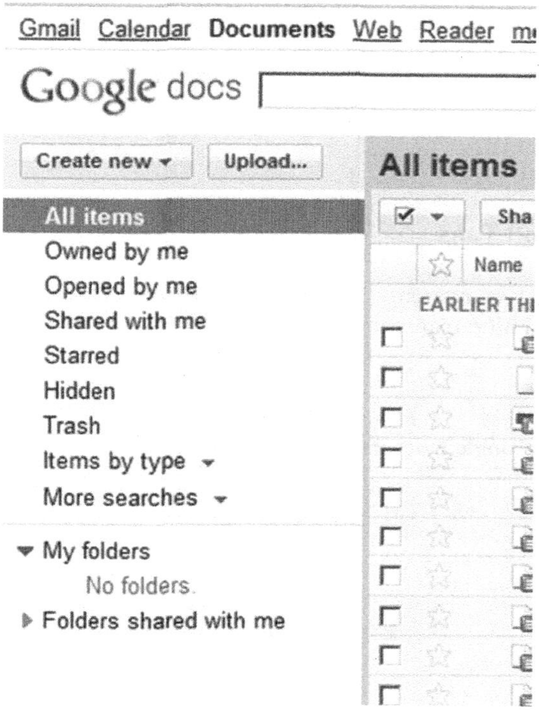

c. Search

Because this is from Google, a user has the option to search for documents. A lawyer could find, among a series of briefs, one that mentions a particular statute.

Figure 8.134
Google Docs start page—Search Docs box

d. Link

Along the top of the web page, Google Docs also has links to applications like Gmail.

Figure 8.135
Google Docs start page — links

e.   Toolbar and Tabs

Beneath this row appears a toolbar with tabs that correspond to those in Word and OpenOffice.org, such as File, Edit, View, Insert, Format, Table, Tools, and Help.

Figure 8.136
Google Docs start page — toolbar

E.   CONCLUSION

Office productivity software can make a business operate more efficiently. Suites, which are integrated bundles of such software, make it easier for a user to exploit the full processing capacity of a computer, regardless of the nature of the license or operating system. Word processing technology goes beyond mere typing to provide a number of options on how to design and use a document. Spreadsheet software increases the ease with which a business can assess a range of information often related to the efficient operation of a business. Slide show software can more effectively convey information in a presentation to enhance clarity. A user can purchase a license to the very popular Microsoft Office suite, with frequent updates and readily available help, or use free software like OpenOffice.org or Software as a Service, like Google Docs.

F.   TERMS

Access
Blacklining
Buttons
Cell
Clip art
Cloud computing
Graphic user interface (GUI)

Hyperlink
Macro
Outlook
PDF (protected document format)
Pivot table
Redlining
Ribbon
Servers
Sheet
Slide
Software as a Service (SaaS)
Spreadsheet software
SQL
Suite
Tabs
Thumbnails
Thunderbird
Toolbar
Wizard
Workbook

G.   HYPOTHETICALS

1.   Generating a table of cases

Have students generate a table of cases from the following quote, from *Citizens United v. Federal Election Commission,* 130 S. Ct. 876, 886-890 (2010):

> Limits on electioneering communications were upheld in *McConnell* v. *Federal Election Comm'n,* 540 U.S. 93, 203-209, 124 S. Ct. 619, 157 L. Ed. 2d 491 (2003). The holding of *McConnell* rested to a large extent on an earlier case, *Austin* v. *Michigan Chamber of Commerce,* 494 U.S. 652, 110 S. Ct. 1391, 108 L. Ed. 2d 652 (1990). *Austin* had held that political speech may be banned based on the speaker's corporate identity.
>
> In this case, we are asked to reconsider *Austin* and, in effect, *McConnell.* It has been noted that "*Austin* was a significant departure from ancient First Amendment principles," *Federal Election Comm'n* v. *Wisconsin Right to Life, Inc.,* 551 U.S. 449, 490, 127 S. Ct. 2652, 168 L. Ed. 2d 329 (2007) *(WRTL)* (Scalia, J., concurring in part and concurring in judgment). [. . .]
>
> Citizens United is a nonprofit corporation. [. . .]
>
> In January 2008, Citizens United released a film entitled *Hillary: The Movie.* We refer to the film as *Hillary.* It is a 90-minute documentary about then-Senator Hillary Clinton, who was a candidate in the Democratic Party's 2008 Presidential primary elections. *Hillary* mentions Senator Clinton by name and depicts interviews with political commentators and other persons, most of them quite critical of Senator Clinton. *Hillary* was released in theaters and

on DVD, but Citizens United wanted to increase distribution by making it available through video-on-demand.

[...]

Before the Bipartisan Campaign Reform Act of 2002 (BCRA), federal law prohibited—and still does prohibit—corporations and unions from using general treasury funds to make direct contributions to candidates or independent expenditures that expressly advocate the election or defeat of a candidate, through any form of media, in connection with certain qualified federal elections. 2 U.S.C. § 441b (2000 ed.); see *McConnell, supra,* at 204 and n. 87, 124 S. Ct. 619, 157 L. Ed. 2d 491; *Federal Election Comm'n* v. *Massachusetts Citizens for Life, Inc.,* 479 U.S. 238, 249, 107 S. Ct. 616, 93 L. Ed. 2d 539 (1986) *(MCFL).* [...]

Citizens United contends that § 441b does not cover *Hillary,* as a matter of statutory interpretation, because the film does not qualify as an "electioneering communication." § 441b(b)(2). Citizens United raises this issue for the first time before us, but we consider the issue because "it was addressed by the court below." *Lebron* v. *National Railroad Passenger Corporation,* 513 U.S. 374, 379, 115 S. Ct. 961, 130 L. Ed. 2d 902 (1995).

[...]

Prolix laws chill speech for the same reason that vague laws chill speech: People "of common intelligence must necessarily guess at [the law's] meaning and differ as to its application." *Connally* v. *General Constr. Co.,* 269 U.S. 385, 391, 46 S. Ct. 126, 70 L. Ed. 322 (1926).

[...]

On what we might call conventional television, advertising spots reach viewers who have chosen a channel or a program for reasons unrelated to the advertising. With video-on-demand, by contrast, the viewer selects a program after taking "a series of affirmative steps": subscribing to cable; navigating through various menus; and selecting the program. See *Reno* v. *ACLU,* 521 U.S. 844, 867, 117 S. Ct. 2329, 138 L. Ed. 2d 874 (1997).

While some means of communication may be less effective than others at influencing the public in different contexts, any effort by the Judiciary to decide which means of communications are to be preferred for the particular type of message and speaker would raise questions as to the courts' own lawful authority. Substantial questions would arise if courts were to begin saying what means of speech should be preferred or disfavored. And in all events, those differentiations might soon prove to be irrelevant or outdated by technologies that are in rapid flux. See *Turner Broadcasting System, Inc.* v. *FCC,* 512 U.S. 622, 639, 114 S. Ct. 2445, 129 L. Ed. 2d 497 (1994).

2. Using the compare function in Word

A prospective client seeks legal advice over a possible copyright infringement. This prospective client says that an unscrupulous agent passed along a first draft of a chapter on word processing software, who then published a book allegedly containing content from the first draft. The lawyer has doubts that a well-established publishing firm would do that and wants to see whether the prospective client's claim has any merit. In particular, the lawyer has asked you to compare a paragraph in the prospective client's manuscript with that of the publication, using Word.

A. Here's the prospective client's original paragraph:

Since an office may use software for word processing, for generating financial reports or for communication, some such as Microsoft have bundled together the software that a business might have a need to use. Microsoft Office's suite, for example, integrates software that does word processing, spreadsheets, Internet access, and slide show presentations, at a minimum. An integrated bundle or suite of software, then, may mean having information in a format that lends itself to easy use by other software from the software manufacturer. Of course, the bundle as a group will cost less than if the office would separately buy a license to each application.

B. Here's a paragraph from the publication:

Software makers understand how customers might prefer to have software that meshes well with one another. For example, Microsoft's suite, MS Office, integrates software that does word processing, spreadsheets, Internet browsing, and the creation of slide shows, at a minimum. Of course, the bundle as a group will cost less than if the business would separately buy a license for each application.

Show the results, explaining what they mean.

3. Prepare a PowerPoint slide show. For each bullet-pointed item, create a separate slide, using appropriate graphics, appearing below the content.

[Aside: to copy a graphic from a Microsoft document, have the image on the screen. Using CTRL-PrtSc will capture the image. Paste the image into Painter, usually available with a Microsoft OS. In Painter, options exist for cropping out that information not part of the graphic to be saved.]

Like a typewriter, word processing software will, at a minimum, have the capacity to manipulate:

→ Spacing
→ Font
→ Style
→ Margins
→ Italics, bold face, underlining (or any combination of the three)
→ Subscript
→ Superscript
→ Insert a symbol
→ Indent
→ Center
→ Flush left or right
→ Insert bullet points or numbers
→ Generating page numbers, headers, or footers

4. As part of a divorce, the couple will maintain the marital residence, for the raising of children. The following constitutes the financial information that you have available, for a six month period:

Gas: February, $292.41; March, $314.13; April, $209.91; May, $163.15; June, $77.36

Electric: January, $78.24; February, $81.24; March, $37.18; April, $62.32; May, $65.92; June, $89.07

Water: March, $124.45; June, $149.34

Cable: January, $174.72, February, $167.44; March, $167.44; April, $174.72; May, $174.72; June, $174.72

Using Excel, answer the following:

a. What are average costs for electricity, per month?
b. What are average costs for cable, per month?
c. What are average costs for water, per month?
d. For gas, used for heating and to heat water, you do not have information for January. What are average costs for gas, for those five months? Use that figure as an estimate for gas costs for January. What are average costs for gas, for those six months?

5. Create company letterhead, using Google Docs. This is for the firm Cahoone, Lamb and Murray, LLP, with offices at 1 Beacon Street, Suite 101, Peabody, Massachusetts 01960. They have a website, www.Cahoone-LambLLP.com, and a telephone number, 978-555-1212. The lawyers are David Cahoone, Scott Lamb, and Susan Murray. Identify yourself on the letterhead as a paralegal.

Use one of the graphics available after doing a search for "legal graphics," at the top of the letterhead. The software will automatically annotate the source for the image, although using such a graphic would not typically be appropriate without having paid a licensing fee for its use.

When done composing this document, download a copy of it as a PDF file.

CHAPTER

9

Practice-Specific Software

OBJECTIVES

→ **Review** the process involved in generating appropriate documents for a bankruptcy filing so that a debtor/petitioner can reach a settlement with creditors for a discharge of debts in order to obtain a fresh start.

→ **Examine** the documents used in creating and operating a corporation, such as Articles of Incorporation, resolutions, and the appropriate reports that would have to be filed with the state.

→ **Proceed** through the steps involved for completing a federal HUD-1 form, used when financing a purchase of residential property.

→ **Determine** what assets and obligations a court would need to consider to arrive at a financial settlement in a divorce.

→ **Identify** and process information needed to generate an accurate accounting of a trust.

→ **Gather** information necessary for estate planning and for the generation of additional useful documents.

INTRODUCTION

Upon graduation from law school, lawyers may have the ability to practice any kind of law but might find it easier to have a specialty. Increasingly, areas of law have developed such complexity that a lawyer has to watch for daily changes in the law so as to serve the interests of clients diligently and conscientiously. Software about a specific legal topic can make it easier to operate a legal practice. This chapter showcases types of practice-specific software.

A. BANKRUPTCY

Bankruptcy can mean that a client, whether individually (and a spouse) or as a business, has more debts than **assets** (**property** or savings) and seeks help, under federal law, to get a fresh start. A court-approved distribution of debtor/

petitioner's assets to the **creditors** likely means that the creditors typically will get only partial payment of the debt. Bankruptcy software can help a lawyer gather and organize the client's information to prepare a petition in bankruptcy so that a client can get relief from those debts.

1. In General

a. Terms

The client, as the **debtor/petitioner,** owes money to creditors. To obtain a fresh start, the client has to request, or petition, for bankruptcy protection. A **trustee,** appointed by the bankruptcy court, will oversee the distribution of the debtor/petitioner's assets to creditors. Upon completion of that process, the debtor/petitioner obtains a **discharge in bankruptcy.** This means that the debtor/petitioner no longer has a legal obligation to repay creditors beyond what they had received from the bankruptcy court. All assets that the debtor/petitioner has available for distribution to creditors are known as the **estate.**

A discharge in bankruptcy, involving the distribution of all of a debtor/petitioner's assets, save for some exemptions, is known as **liquidation.** Alternatively, the debtor/petitioner could ask for **reorganization,** which involves setting a schedule to repay some or all debts. If the debtor/petitioner has a job, reorganization could mean that part of the paycheck goes toward paying off the debt; creditors could get more of the moneys owed would have to wait to get that money.

b. Type of Petition

A debtor/petitioner would start by filing a voluntary petition for a discharge in bankruptcy. Sometimes creditors, like suppliers to a department store, can force the department store, as debtor, into bankruptcy by filing an involuntary petition. This increases the chances that the creditors will get some payment for the debt, avoiding the possibility that the debtor uses up all the assets before filing for bankruptcy. Software will generate a completed version of a petition for voluntary bankruptcy, available at: http://www.uscourts.gov/uscourts/RulesAndPolicies/rules/BK_Forms_Current/B_001.pdf.

c. Software

This exploration of software for filing for bankruptcy uses National Law-Forms Bankruptcy Case Software, available at www.nationallawforms.com. All images taken from this software are copyrighted by the creator of such images and inclusion of such images in this text does not constitute any claim of copyright in them. Other such software comes from the publisher of this text, Wolters Kluwer, at www.bestcase.com/, as well as from www.ezfiling.com/ and www.bankruptcysoftware.com/, among others.

d.   Electronic Filing

Courts increasingly prefer to receive documents as electronic files because this:

→ Cuts down on the space used for storing paper documents;
→ Makes it easier to search the data files; and
→ Can make it easy to generate copies.

Because the client has to file a paper version of the petition, the output generated by the software can come in the form of a text or a PDF, per the requirements of the federal court. Blank versions of these forms also appear at http://www.uscourts.gov/FederalCourts/Bankruptcy.aspx.

2.   *Content*

Information in support of the petition appears in documents called **pages, schedules,** and **exhibits.**

a.   Familiar Tabs

The makers of this software created an interface similar to the ribbon used with Microsoft's Office Suite. This includes familiar tabs such as File, Edit, and Help.

Figure 9.1
National LawForms Bankruptcy Case Software—start screen

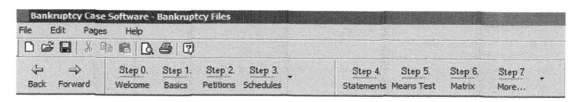

b.   Pages Tab

The Pages tab contains links to begin the preparation of a petition for bankruptcy protection.

Figure 9.2
National LawForms Bankruptcy Case Software—Pages tab

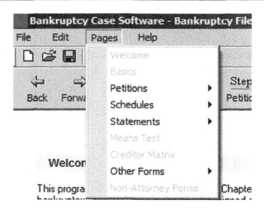

i.   Voluntary petition link

I.   Page 1

Via the Petitions link, a law firm preparing a voluntary petition for a client needs to indicate the:

Figure 9.3
National LawForms Bankruptcy Case Software—Pages tab: Petitions link, Voluntary petition, Page 1

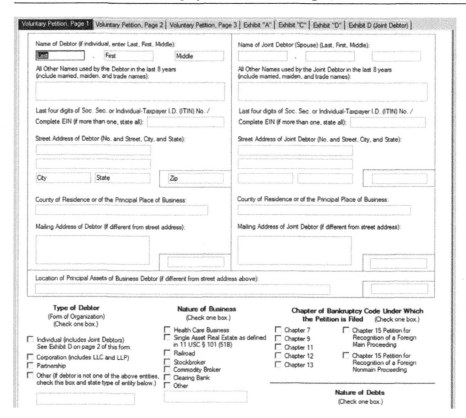

→ Type of debtor, since the debts and assets of a person can dramatically differ from that of a business;
→ Type of petition, for
  →Reorganization (**Chapter 11** of the **Bankruptcy Code** for a business or **Chapter 13** for an individual); or
  →Liquidation (**Chapter 7**);
→ Type of **liabilities,** like a **mortgage** or credit card debt; and

Figure 9.4
National LawForms Bankruptcy Case Software—Pages tab: Petitions link, Voluntary petition, Page 1, Preliminary information

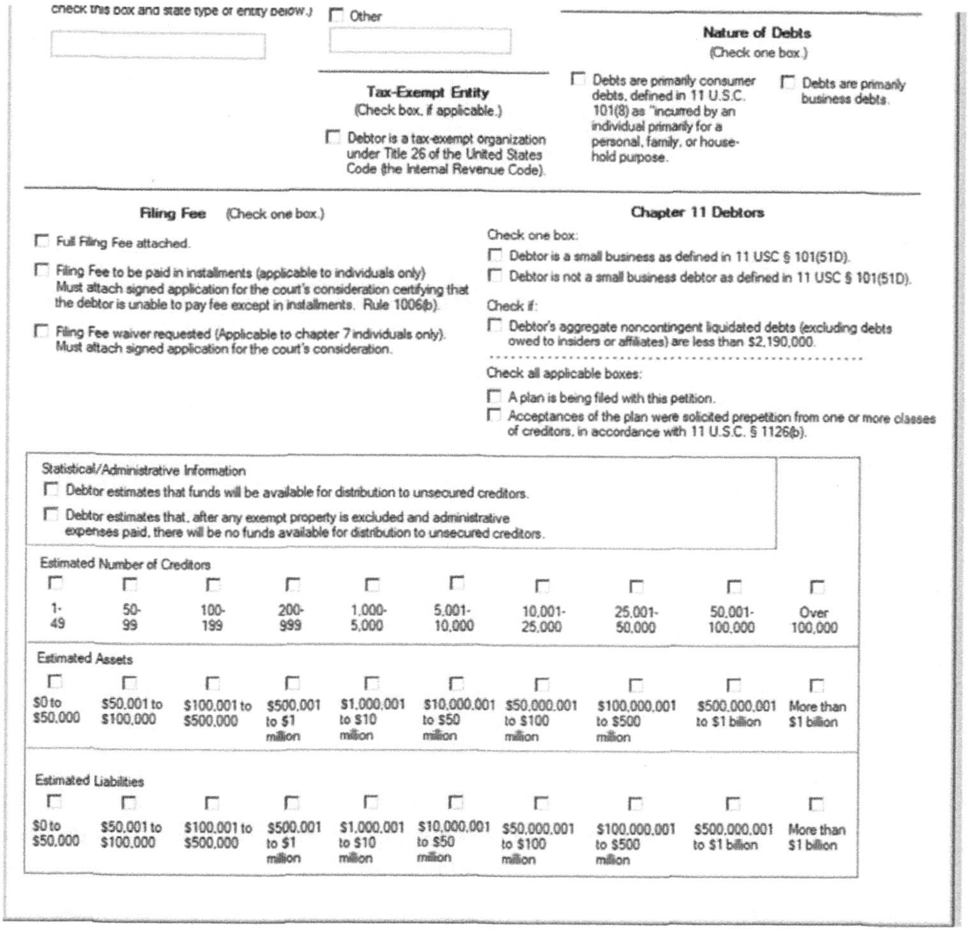
check this box and state type of entity below.) ☐ Other

Nature of Debts
(Check one box.)
☐ Debts are primarily consumer debts, defined in 11 U.S.C. 101(8) as "incurred by an individual primarily for a personal, family, or house-hold purpose.
☐ Debts are primarily business debts.

Tax-Exempt Entity
(Check box, if applicable.)
☐ Debtor is a tax-exempt organization under Title 26 of the United States Code (the Internal Revenue Code).

Filing Fee (Check one box.)
☐ Full Filing Fee attached.
☐ Filing Fee to be paid in installments (applicable to individuals only) Must attach signed application for the court's consideration certifying that the debtor is unable to pay fee except in installments. Rule 1006(b).
☐ Filing Fee waiver requested (Applicable to chapter 7 individuals only). Must attach signed application for the court's consideration.

Chapter 11 Debtors
Check one box:
☐ Debtor is a small business as defined in 11 USC § 101(51D).
☐ Debtor is not a small business debtor as defined in 11 USC § 101(51D).
Check if:
☐ Debtor's aggregate noncontingent liquidated debts (excluding debts owed to insiders or affiliates) are less than $2,190,000.
Check all applicable boxes:
☐ A plan is being filed with this petition.
☐ Acceptances of the plan were solicited prepetition from one or more classes of creditors, in accordance with 11 U.S.C. § 1126(b).

Statistical/Administrative Information
☐ Debtor estimates that funds will be available for distribution to unsecured creditors.
☐ Debtor estimates that, after any exempt property is excluded and administrative expenses paid, there will be no funds available for distribution to unsecured creditors.

Estimated Number of Creditors

☐	☐	☐	☐	☐	☐	☐	☐	☐	☐
1-49	50-99	100-199	200-999	1,000-5,000	5,001-10,000	10,001-25,000	25,001-50,000	50,001-100,000	Over 100,000

Estimated Assets

☐	☐	☐	☐	☐	☐	☐	☐	☐	☐
$0 to $50,000	$50,001 to $100,000	$100,001 to $500,000	$500,001 to $1 million	$1,000,001 to $10 million	$10,000,001 to $50 million	$50,000,001 to $100 million	$100,000,001 to $500 million	$500,000,001 to $1 billion	More than $1 billion

Estimated Liabilities

☐	☐	☐	☐	☐	☐	☐	☐	☐	☐
$0 to $50,000	$50,001 to $100,000	$100,001 to $500,000	$500,001 to $1 million	$1,000,001 to $10 million	$10,000,001 to $50 million	$50,000,001 to $100 million	$100,000,001 to $500 million	$500,000,001 to $1 billion	More than $1 billion

→ Identity of creditors, like banks, individuals, credit card companies, or a government.

II.   Page 2

Additional necessary information includes:

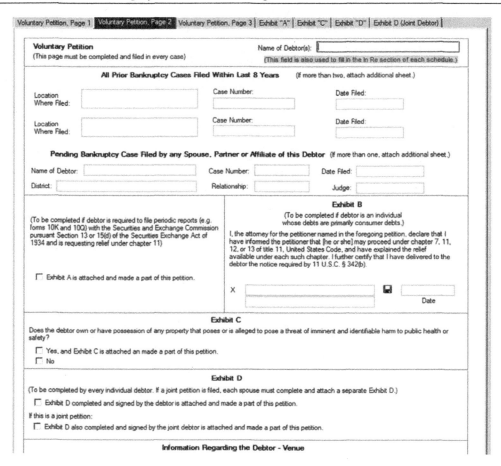

Figure 9.5
National LawForms Bankruptcy Case Software—Pages tab: Petitions link, Voluntary petition, Page 2

→ Whether and what other bankruptcy cases the client might be involved with;

→ If the federal Securities and Exchange Commission (SEC), which oversees corporations that have made available **stock** for sale to the public, has been notified;

→ Identifying property that could pose an imminent public safety threat, like propane tanks (as noted in Exhibit C); and

→ A statement where an individual debtor/petitioner (and a spouse, if married and filing jointly) **attests** to the accuracy of the information in this petition (Exhibits B and D).

III.   Page 3

Besides learning about all debtors/petitioners, the bankruptcy court judge will need to know whether a non-attorney completed the petition for the client, an option available under the law.

Figure 9.6

National LawForms Bankruptcy Case Software—Pages tab: Petitions link, Voluntary petition, Page 3

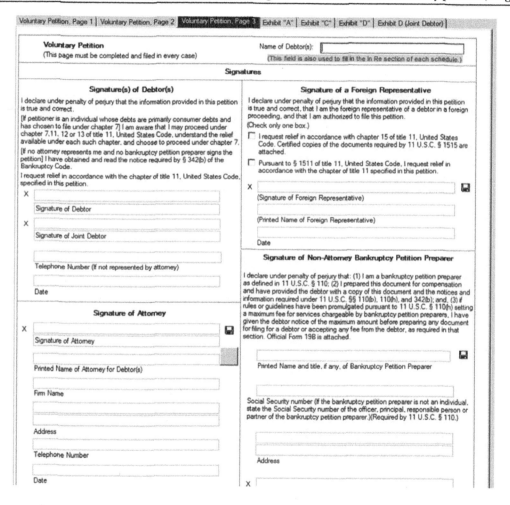

IV.   Exhibits A through D

These documents, which would accompany the petition, would include:

→ A list of assets, such as stock (Exhibit A);

Figure 9.7

National LawForms Bankruptcy Case Software—Pages tab: Petitions link, Voluntary petition, Exhibit A

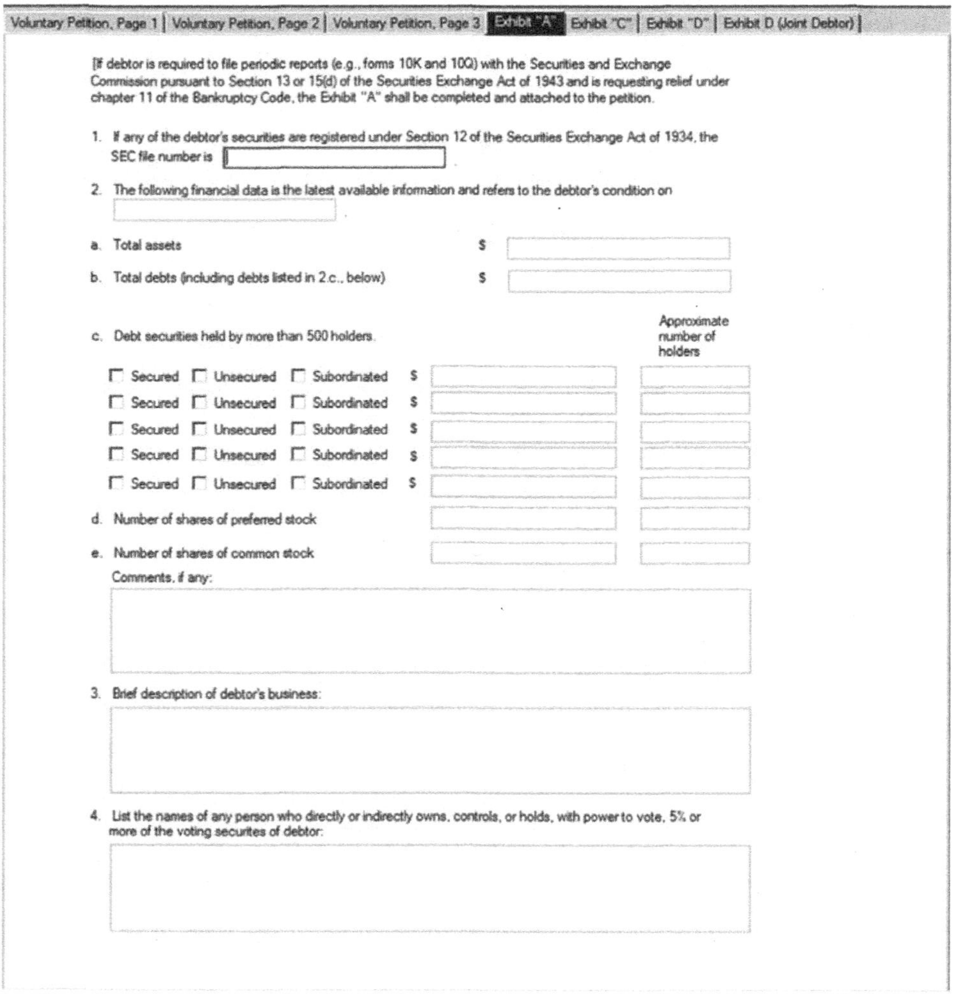

Voluntary Petition, Page 1 | Voluntary Petition, Page 2 | Voluntary Petition, Page 3 | Exhibit "A" | Exhibit "C" | Exhibit "D" | Exhibit D (Joint Debtor)

[If debtor is required to file periodic reports (e.g., forms 10K and 10Q) with the Securities and Exchange Commission pursuant to Section 13 or 15(d) of the Securities Exchange Act of 1943 and is requesting relief under chapter 11 of the Bankruptcy Code, the Exhibit "A" shall be completed and attached to the petition.

1. If any of the debtor's securities are registered under Section 12 of the Securities Exchange Act of 1934, the SEC file number is

2. The following financial data is the latest available information and refers to the debtor's condition on

a. Total assets $

b. Total debts (including debts listed in 2.c., below) $

c. Debt securities held by more than 500 holders. Approximate number of holders

☐ Secured ☐ Unsecured ☐ Subordinated $

☐ Secured ☐ Unsecured ☐ Subordinated $

☐ Secured ☐ Unsecured ☐ Subordinated $

☐ Secured ☐ Unsecured ☐ Subordinated $

☐ Secured ☐ Unsecured ☐ Subordinated $

d. Number of shares of preferred stock

e. Number of shares of common stock

Comments, if any:

3. Brief description of debtor's business:

4. List the names of any person who directly or indirectly owns, controls, or holds, with power to vote, 5% or more of the voting securites of debtor:

→ Interests in real estate, such as land, and personal property, such as an automobile (Exhibit C); and

Figure 9.8

National LawForms Bankruptcy Case Software—Pages tab: Petitions link, Voluntary petition, Exhibit C

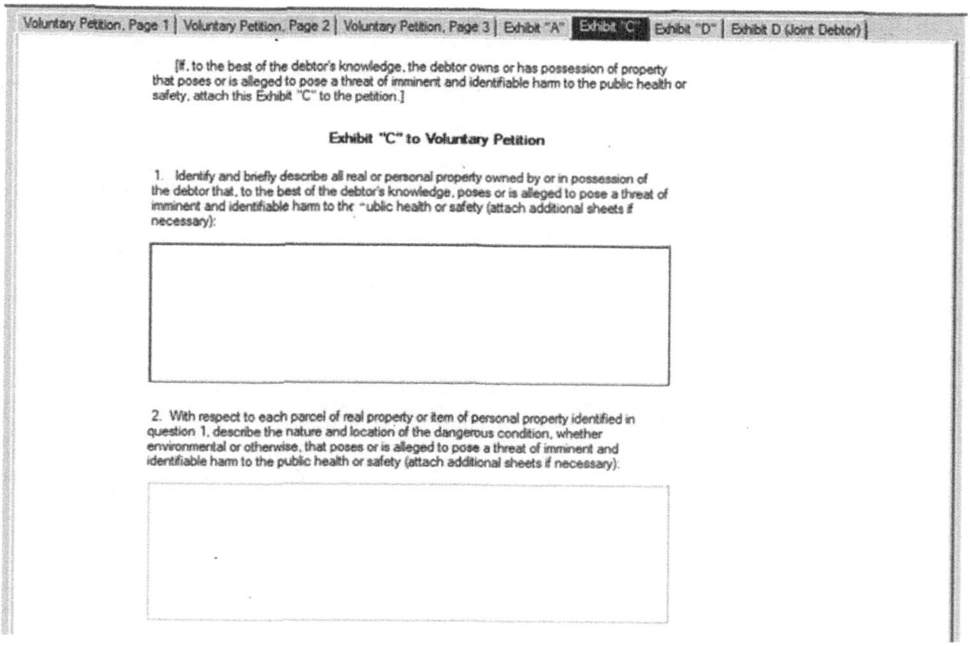

| Voluntary Petition, Page 1 | Voluntary Petition, Page 2 | Voluntary Petition, Page 3 | Exhibit "A" | Exhibit "C" | Exhibit "D" | Exhibit D (Joint Debtor) |

[If, to the best of the debtor's knowledge, the debtor owns or has possession of property that poses or is alleged to pose a threat of imminent and identifiable harm to the public health or safety, attach this Exhibit "C" to the petition.]

Exhibit "C" to Voluntary Petition

1. Identify and briefly describe all real or personal property owned by or in possession of the debtor that, to the best of the debtor's knowledge, poses or is alleged to pose a threat of imminent and identifiable harm to the public health or safety (attach additional sheets if necessary):

2. With respect to each parcel of real property or item of personal property identified in question 1, describe the nature and location of the dangerous condition, whether environmental or otherwise, that poses or is alleged to pose a threat of imminent and identifiable harm to the public health or safety (attach additional sheets if necessary):

→ A statement by the debtor/petitioner of meeting the educational requirements for filing for bankruptcy (Exhibit D), since federal law requires a debtor/petitioner to take classes on debt management before qualifying for a discharge in bankruptcy.

Figure 9.9
National LawForms Bankruptcy Case Software—Pages tab: Petitions link, Voluntary petition, Exhibit D

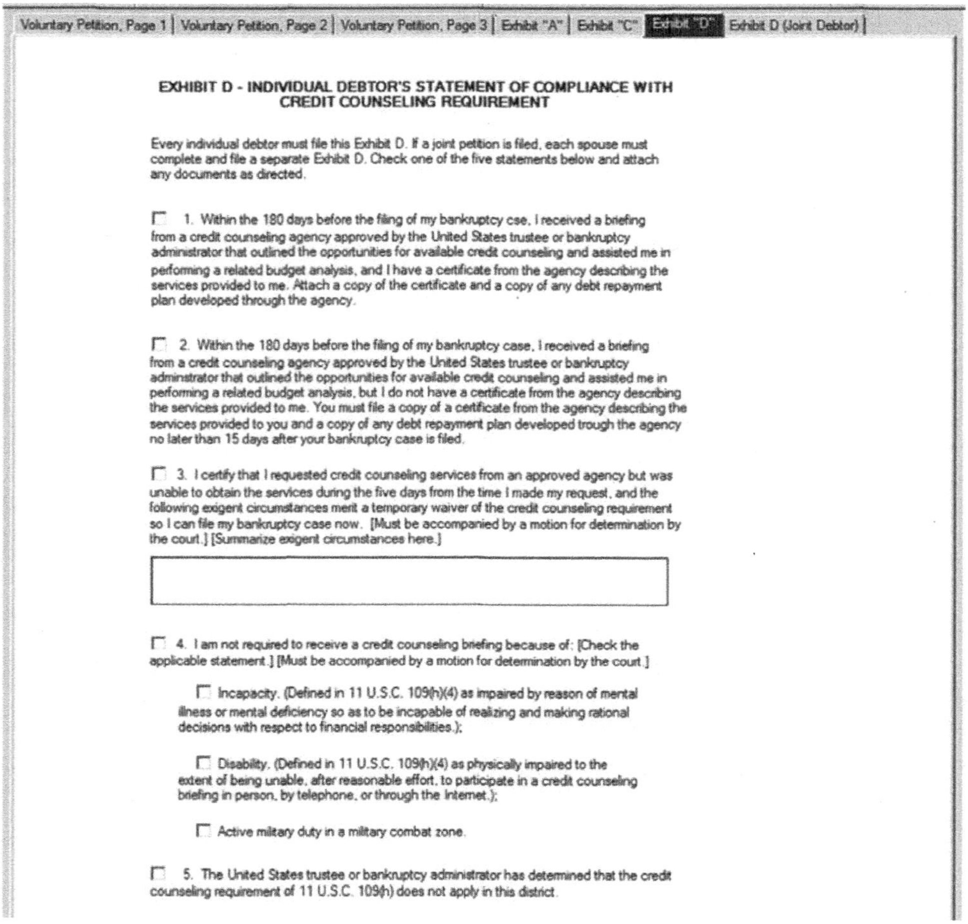
Voluntary Petition, Page 1 | Voluntary Petition, Page 2 | Voluntary Petition, Page 3 | Exhibit "A" | Exhibit "C" | Exhibit "D" | Exhibit D (Joint Debtor)

EXHIBIT D - INDIVIDUAL DEBTOR'S STATEMENT OF COMPLIANCE WITH CREDIT COUNSELING REQUIREMENT

Every individual debtor must file this Exhibit D. If a joint petition is filed, each spouse must complete and file a separate Exhibit D. Check one of the five statements below and attach any documents as directed.

☐ 1. Within the 180 days before the filing of my bankruptcy cse, I received a briefing from a credit counseling agency approved by the United States trustee or bankruptcy administrator that outlined the opportunities for available credit counseling and assisted me in performing a related budget analysis, and I have a certificate from the agency describing the services provided to me. Attach a copy of the certificate and a copy of any debt repayment plan developed through the agency.

☐ 2. Within the 180 days before the filing of my bankruptcy case, I received a briefing from a credit counseling agency approved by the United States trustee or bankruptcy administrator that outlined the opportunities for available credit counseling and assisted me in performing a related budget analysis, but I do not have a certificate from the agency describing the services provided to me. You must file a copy of a certificate from the agency describing the services provided to you and a copy of any debt repayment plan developed trough the agency no later than 15 days after your bankruptcy case is filed.

☐ 3. I certify that I requested credit counseling services from an approved agency but was unable to obtain the services during the five days from the time I made my request, and the following exigent circumstances merit a temporary waiver of the credit counseling requirement so I can file my bankruptcy case now. [Must be accompanied by a motion for determination by the court.] [Summarize exigent circumstances here.]

☐ 4. I am not required to receive a credit counseling briefing because of: [Check the applicable statement.] [Must be accompanied by a motion for determination by the court.]

☐ Incapacity. (Defined in 11 U.S.C. 109(h)(4) as impaired by reason of mental illness or mental deficiency so as to be incapable of realizing and making rational decisions with respect to financial responsibilities.);

☐ Disability. (Defined in 11 U.S.C. 109(h)(4) as physically impaired to the extent of being unable, after reasonable effort, to participate in a credit counseling briefing in person, by telephone, or through the Internet.);

☐ Active military duty in a military combat zone.

☐ 5. The United States trustee or bankruptcy administrator has determined that the credit counseling requirement of 11 U.S.C. 109(h) does not apply in this district.

ii. Schedules

In addition to the petition and its exhibits, the debtor/petitioner will need to file these as well, which identify:

→ Property, such as land or automobiles (Schedules A and B);
→ **Exempt** property (Schedule C), because federal law might exclude some assets, like a pension, from inclusion in the debtor/petitioner's estate; and

Figure 9.10
National LawForms Bankruptcy Case Software—Pages tab: Petitions link, Schedule C

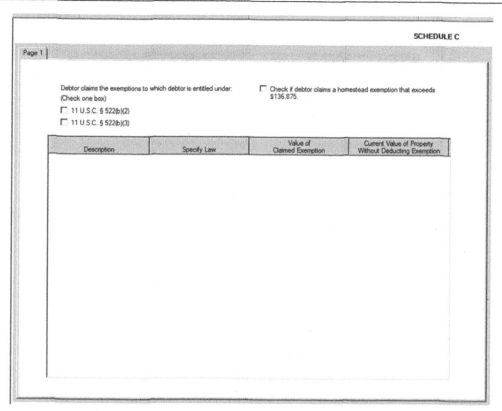

→ Debts, like **unsecured loans** (Schedule E), such as a personal loan, or **secured loans** (Schedule D), such as a car loan, where the lender will have the right to sell the car at auction if the debtor does not make a monthly payment, because secured loans may not be discharged in bankruptcy.

The debtor/petitioner also needs to list such essential information as:

→ Sources of income (Schedule I) and expenditures (Schedule J);
→ Co-debtors (Schedule H), like a spouse; and
→ All uncompleted contracts, like an employment contract (Schedule G).

iii. Statements

Completing these questions helps to get a better sense of the nature of assets, such as if they include income from employment.

Figure 9.11
National LawForms Bankruptcy Case Software—Pages tab: Petitions link, Statements, Questions 1-8 tab

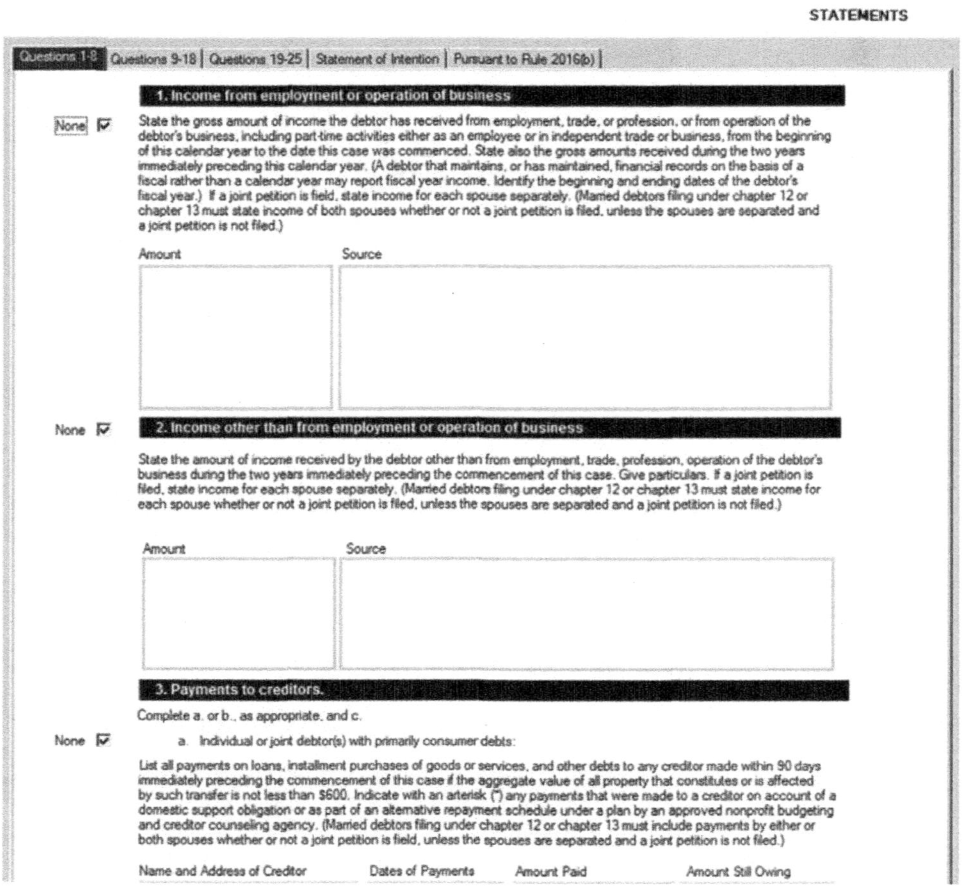
STATEMENTS

Questions 1-8 | Questions 9-18 | Questions 19-25 | Statement of Intention | Pursuant to Rule 2016(b)

1. Income from employment or operation of business

None ☑ State the gross amount of income the debtor has received from employment, trade, or profession, or from operation of the debtor's business, including part-time activities either as an employee or in independent trade or business, from the beginning of this calendar year to the date this case was commenced. State also the gross amounts received during the two years immediately preceding this calendar year. (A debtor that maintains, or has maintained, financial records on the basis of a fiscal rather than a calendar year may report fiscal year income. Identify the beginning and ending dates of the debtor's fiscal year.) If a joint petition is field, state income for each spouse separately. (Married debtors filing under chapter 12 or chapter 13 must state income of both spouses whether or not a joint petition is filed, unless the spouses are separated and a joint petition is not filed.)

Amount Source

None ☑ 2. Income other than from employment or operation of business

State the amount of income received by the debtor other than from employment, trade, profession, operation of the debtor's business during the two years immediately preceding the commencement of this case. Give particulars. If a joint petition is filed, state income for each spouse separately. (Married debtors filing under chapter 12 or chapter 13 must state income for each spouse whether or not a joint petition is filed, unless the spouses are separated and a joint petition is not filed.)

Amount Source

3. Payments to creditors.

Complete a. or b., as appropriate, and c.

None ☑ a. Individual or joint debtor(s) with primarily consumer debts:

List all payments on loans, installment purchases of goods or services, and other debts to any creditor made within 90 days immediately preceding the commencement of this case if the aggregate value of all property that constitutes or is affected by such transfer is not less than $600. Indicate with an asterisk (*) any payments that were made to a creditor on account of a domestic support obligation or as part of an alternative repayment schedule under a plan by an approved nonprofit budgeting and creditor counseling agency. (Married debtors filing under chapter 12 or chapter 13 must include payments by either or both spouses whether or not a joint petition is field, unless the spouses are separated and a joint petition is not filed.)

Name and Address of Creditor Dates of Payments Amount Paid Amount Still Owing

I. Means test

Only those debtor/petitioners with a certain amount of debt qualify for a discharge in bankruptcy. Using the information provided here, the trustee in bankruptcy can determine whether the petitioner has enough debt. This process of evaluation is called a means test. This test varies, depending upon whether the debtor/petitioner seeks:

→ Liquidation (Chapter 7); or

Figure 9.12
National LawForms Bankruptcy Case Software—Means test: Chapter 7 tab

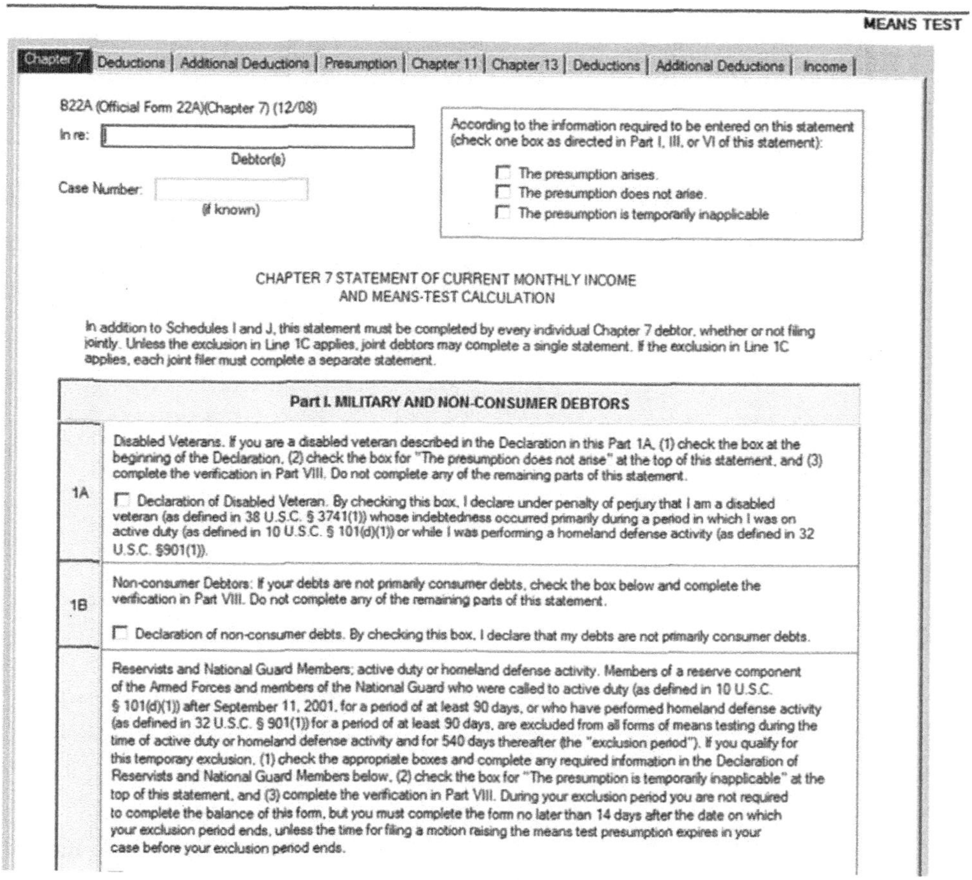

MEANS TEST

Chapter 7 | Deductions | Additional Deductions | Presumption | Chapter 11 | Chapter 13 | Deductions | Additional Deductions | Income |

B22A (Official Form 22A)(Chapter 7) (12/08)

In re: ____________
Debtor(s)

Case Number: ____________
(if known)

According to the information required to be entered on this statement (check one box as directed in Part I, III, or VI of this statement):

☐ The presumption arises.
☐ The presumption does not arise.
☐ The presumption is temporarily inapplicable

CHAPTER 7 STATEMENT OF CURRENT MONTHLY INCOME
AND MEANS-TEST CALCULATION

In addition to Schedules I and J, this statement must be completed by every individual Chapter 7 debtor, whether or not filing jointly. Unless the exclusion in Line 1C applies, joint debtors may complete a single statement. If the exclusion in Line 1C applies, each joint filer must complete a separate statement.

	Part I. MILITARY AND NON-CONSUMER DEBTORS
1A	Disabled Veterans. If you are a disabled veteran described in the Declaration in this Part 1A, (1) check the box at the beginning of the Declaration, (2) check the box for "The presumption does not arise" at the top of this statement, and (3) complete the verification in Part VIII. Do not complete any of the remaining parts of this statement. ☐ Declaration of Disabled Veteran. By checking this box, I declare under penalty of perjury that I am a disabled veteran (as defined in 38 U.S.C. § 3741(1)) whose indebtedness occurred primarily during a period in which I was on active duty (as defined in 10 U.S.C. § 101(d)(1)) or while I was performing a homeland defense activity (as defined in 32 U.S.C. §901(1)).
1B	Non-consumer Debtors: If your debts are not primarily consumer debts, check the box below and complete the verification in Part VIII. Do not complete any of the remaining parts of this statement. ☐ Declaration of non-consumer debts. By checking this box, I declare that my debts are not primarily consumer debts.
	Reservists and National Guard Members; active duty or homeland defense activity. Members of a reserve component of the Armed Forces and members of the National Guard who were called to active duty (as defined in 10 U.S.C. § 101(d)(1)) after September 11, 2001, for a period of at least 90 days, or who have performed homeland defense activity (as defined in 32 U.S.C. § 901(1)) for a period of at least 90 days, are excluded from all forms of means testing during the time of active duty or homeland defense activity and for 540 days thereafter (the "exclusion period"). If you qualify for this temporary exclusion, (1) check the appropriate boxes and complete any required information in the Declaration of Reservists and National Guard Members below, (2) check the box for "The presumption is temporarily inapplicable" at the top of this statement, and (3) complete the verification in Part VIII. During your exclusion period you are not required to complete the balance of this form, but you must complete the form no later than 14 days after the date on which your exclusion period ends, unless the time for filing a motion raising the means test presumption expires in your case before your exclusion period ends.

→ Reorganization, whether for a business (Chapter 11) or an individual (Chapter 13).

iv. Creditor matrix

This listing contains information about creditors, such as:

→ A mailing list of creditors, for example; and

Figure 9.13
National LawForms Bankruptcy Case Software—Creditor Matrix test: Mailing list of creditors tabs

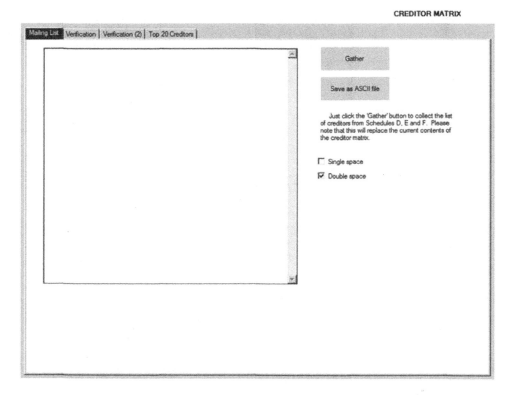

→ A list of the top twenty unsecured creditors (often, those who have made personal loans to the debtor/petitioner).

> *v. Other helpful information*

Other helpful information may include the fees charged for completing and filing the petition and the social security number(s) of all debtor/petitioners, as well as tax identification numbers for businesses.

B. SOFTWARE FOR MANAGING A CORPORATION

1. *What is a Corporation?*

Corporations are business entities created primarily under state law. Unlike with a partnership, the owners of the corporation are not personally liable for corporate debts. This means that if the business files for bankruptcy, individuals involved in the creation and/or management of the corporation will not personally lose their assets, and those people can try again. While they might fail a dozen times to create a thriving business, freeing those people from the debts of those failed businesses makes it possible for them to try again to create a successful business that leads to job creation and tax revenues.

While a corporation will have officers, such as a president and secretary/treasurer to start, it might subsequently sell stock publicly. Stockholders will then be able to elect directors, who then have the primary responsibility for corporate governance. The board of directors will hire the people who manage the corporation daily, such as a chief executive officer.

States require the filing of specific documents for the creation and operation of the corporation. Also, the federal government may require a corporation with publicly traded stock to file financial reports about the corporation's fiscal status.

2. Software

a. Type

The software used to illustrate what corporate compliance software can do is known as BizDoc. A trial version can be downloaded from https://www.businessentitysoftware.com/ BizDoc_setup.exe. A web version will be available in 2014. The publisher's webpage at https://businessentitysoftware.com/ includes tutorial movies. All images taken from this software are copyrighted by Instructional Software, Inc., and inclusion of such images in this text does not constitute any copyright interest or claim in them.

Another program that can perform some of the same functions is from www.nationallawfirms.com. Also, http://www.standardlegal.com/Merchant2/merchant.mvc?Screen=PROD&Product_Code=SLS511 offers forms related to incorporation. All states require documents, like articles of incorporation, resolutions, and meeting minutes. Any quality word processor can generate the documents needed to keep a business entity legally compliant.

b. Features

i. *Tabs*

Upon opening the software, familiar tab headings—File, Edit, Windows, Help, and Edit—appear in the top left corner of the screen.

Figure 9.14
BizDoc Software—Company Profi le: tabs

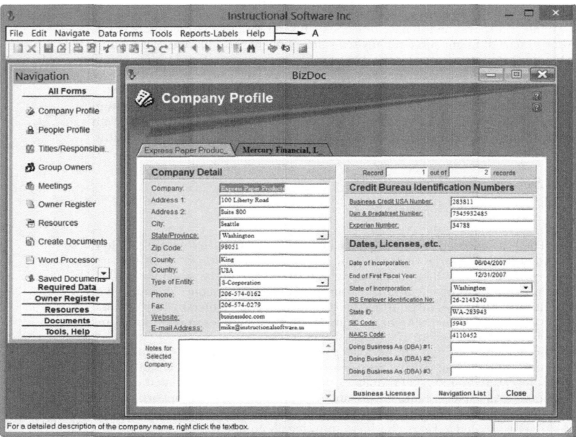

ii.   Toolbar

A toolbar beneath the tabs contains buttons for performing many of the operations common to a Microsoft Office application, from file and save to indent and search.

Figure 9.15
BizDoc Software—Company Profi le: toolbar

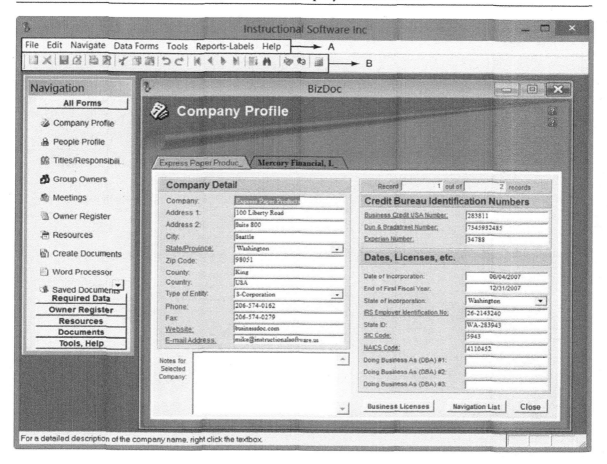

iii.   Sidebar menu

The sidebar menu, entitled Navigation, on the left of the screen provides access to topics related to the operation of a corporation, via tabs and links.

Figure 9.16
BizDoc Software—Company Profi le: Navigation toolbar

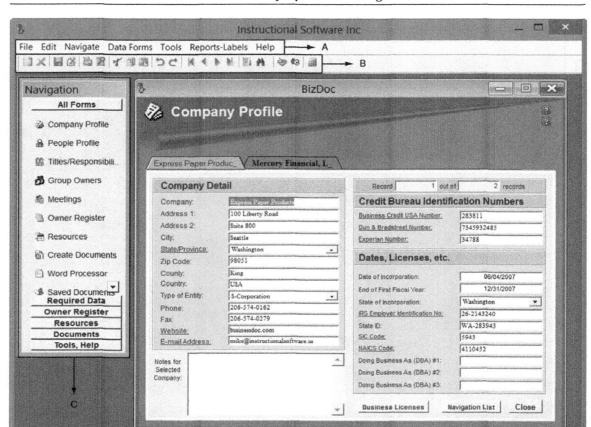

The first link under the Navigation toolbar on the left of the screen, Company Profile, provides the opportunity for recording information related to operating the corporation. For example, the Company Profile link opens to a screen for entering critical information, such as the nature of the corporation and credit bureau identification numbers.

Figure 9.17
BizDoc Software—Company Profile Form

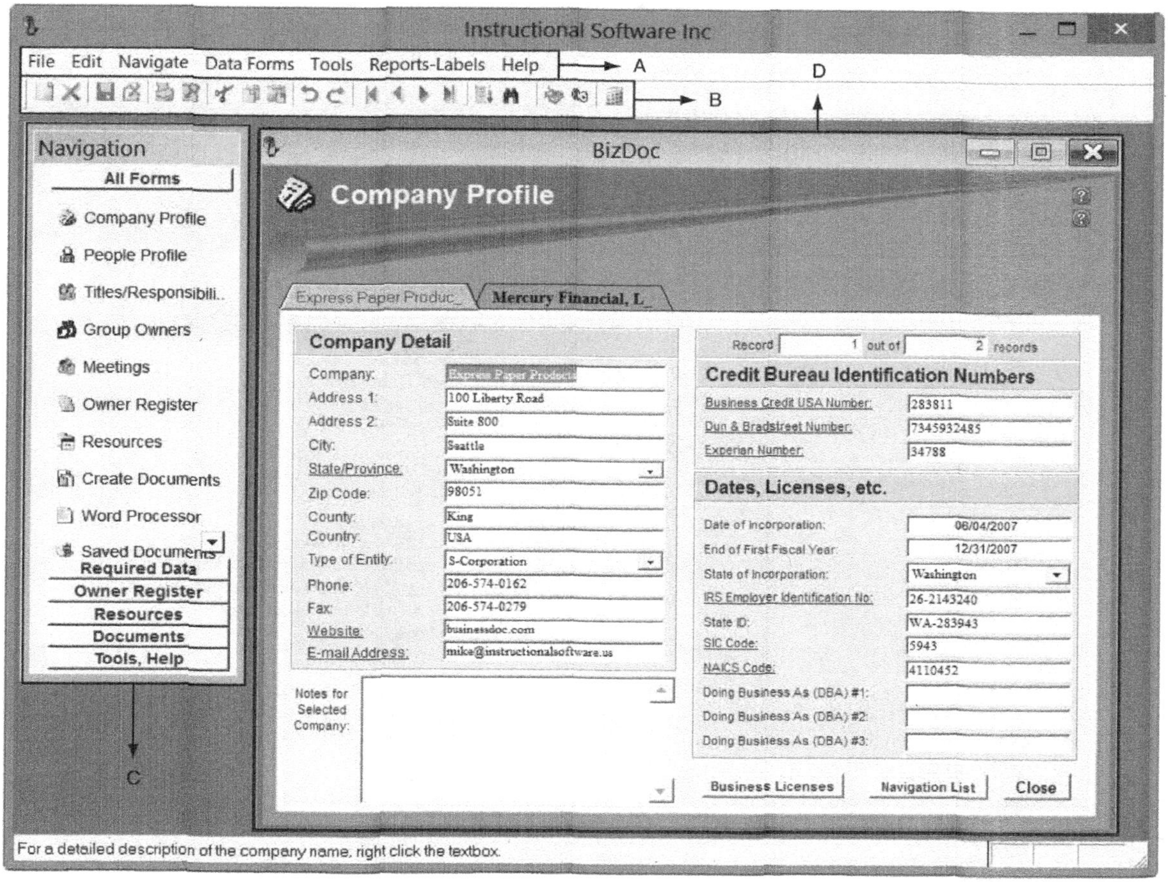

The option exists to include additional information such as:

→ The date and state of incorporation, as part of the Company Profile;
→ The identity and responsibilities of corporate personnel;
→ Who will serve as **Officers**, like president and secretary/treasurer, and as **Directors**; and
→ Who serves as the corporation's attorneys, accountants and resident agent or agents.

Figure 9.18
BizDoc Software—Titles/Responsibilities Form

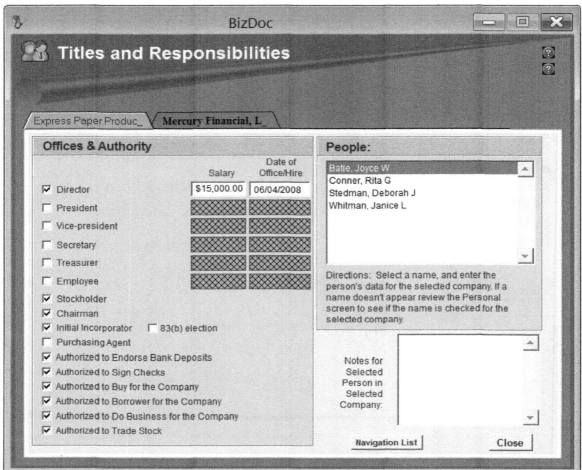

The corporation needs to designate a **resident agent**, who will serve as the corporation's representative to state government when filing reports regarding corporate activity.

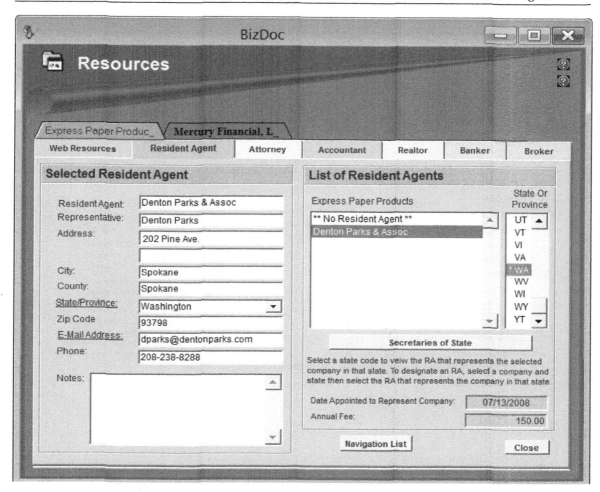

Figure 9.19
BizDoc Software—Company Profi le: Data Forms submenu, Resources link, Resident Agent

3.   *Essential Corporate Documents*

State law will require that a corporation provide a range of documents.

Figure 9.20
BizDoc Software—Create Documents for Corporations

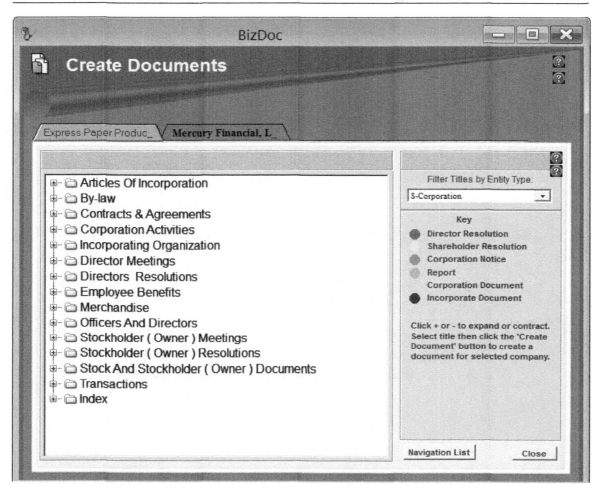

These include **Articles of Incorporation,** to start the corporation, which need to:

→ Describe the purpose of the corporation;
→ Identify the role officers will play;
→ Address issues regarding directors, such as:
    → Their scope of authority for setting corporate policy; and
    → Their appointment or resignation, compensation, and benefits, such as stock options.

→ Issue stock, which represents an ownership interest in the corporation, and stock options, where someone can buy stock at a fixed price by a specific date (often used to reward managers and workers, in addition to employment compensation);

→ Establish what happens at stockholder meetings, such as:

 → Voting for who will serve on the Board of Directors;

 → Passing **resolutions;**

 → Scheduling different types of meetings; and

 → Dealing with procedural concerns, such as issuing notices, waivers, and **proxies,** which contain authorization granted by the stockholder to someone to cast the stockholder's vote.

→ Indicate what happens at director meetings, such as:

 → Hiring personnel, such as a corporate executive officer;

 → Passing resolutions, such as whether the corporation should issue stock for public purchase;

 → Scheduling different types of meetings; and

 → Recording what happens and making those **meeting minutes** available.

→ Enact and modify **bylaws,** which involve the daily operation of the corporation;

→ Change the type of the business from a traditional corporation into a **limited liability** or **Subchapter S** corporation, so as to gain certain tax advantages;

→ Pay out money, or **dividends,** on each share; and

→ Keep track of the certificates representing the shares, via a **stock register,** of the type and number issued and the shares traded.

For example, upon notice of a new stock transaction, the software can generate an updated stock register to reflect the certificate owner, date of transaction, identity of new owner, number of shares, who previously owned the stock, and the amount paid, among other information. This creates an audit trail, from initial offering of stock to who currently owns shares.

Figure 9.21
BizDocs Software—Certificates Form

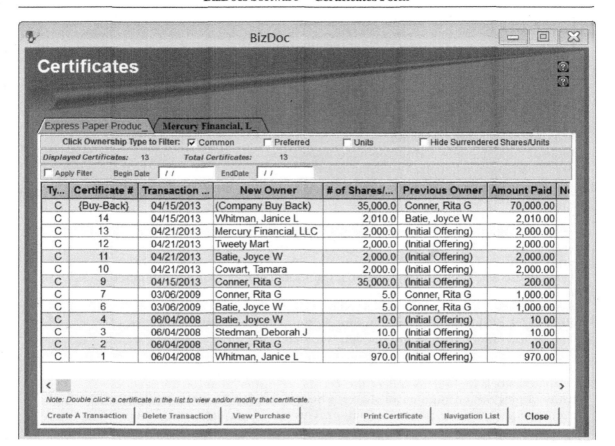

→ Additional important documents that this particular software generates relate to:

→ Assignments, which involve a transfer of rights in something that the corporation owns or possesses;

→ Ownership of real estate and/or **leases;**

→ **Contracts,** which are legally binding agreements, such as for the purchase of land;

→ Inventories, receipts, and bills of sale, when needed;

→ Credit and notes, which relate to a corporation's economic resources;

→ Employee records, regarding hiring, firing, training, compensation and benefits, like pensions; and

→ An index for all documents generated with this software.

For example, a client might prefer to incorporate as a limited liability corporation (LLC), which offers certain tax advantages. The software can generate about 350 documents related to the creation and operation of this type of corporation, such as an easily edited proof copy.

C.   DIVORCE—FINANCIALS

1.   Introduction

A critical issue with the dissolution of a marriage involves the division of assets held by the couple. Beyond a simple division of property, another issue upon dissolution of a marriage involves making regular disbursements, such as **alimony** or **child support.**

2.   Software

a.   Type

The software used here comes from EasySoft, LLC, http://www.easysoft-usa.com/divorce-settlement-software.html, which also makes software for real estate closings, as seen in the next section. All documents generated through the use of this software will end with the suffix .cis.

According to EasySoft, the forms generated here meet the requirements of the law in all states.

All images taken from this software are copyrighted by the creator of such images and inclusion of such images in this text does not constitute any copyright interest or claim in them. Other sources for forms related to a divorce include http://www.familylawsoftware.com/ and http://divorce-forms.com/, among others.

b.   Features

Information recorded here can make up part of an annual income tax filing, since a change in marital status will have an impact on each of the couple's annually filed federal tax returns.

Figure 9.22
Divorce—Financials software: Case Info and Tax Analysis screen

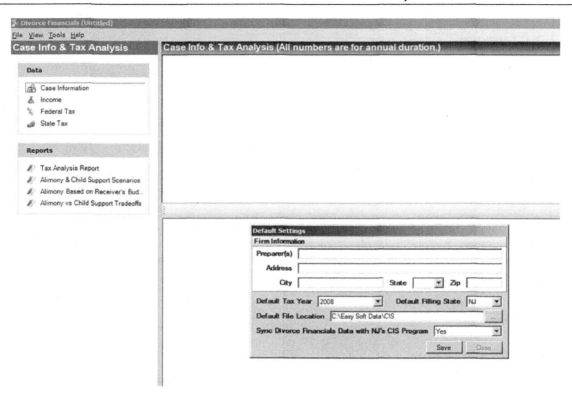

i.   Tabs

Familiar tabs appear across the top: File, View (providing quick access to critical documents, such as Tax Info Case Analysis), Tools, and Help (including a PDF-formatted help manual).

ii. Menu

A sidebar menu allows for the recording of data and the generation of reports.

Figure 9.23
Divorce—Financials software: Sidebar menu

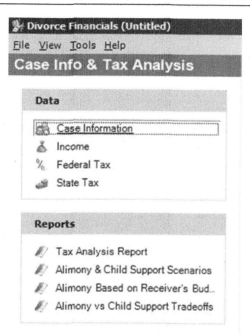

3. Critical Information

a. Case Information

Information about the divorce case, which will appear on documents generated by the software includes the:

Figure 9.24
Divorce—Financials software: Sidebar menu, Data subsection, Case information link

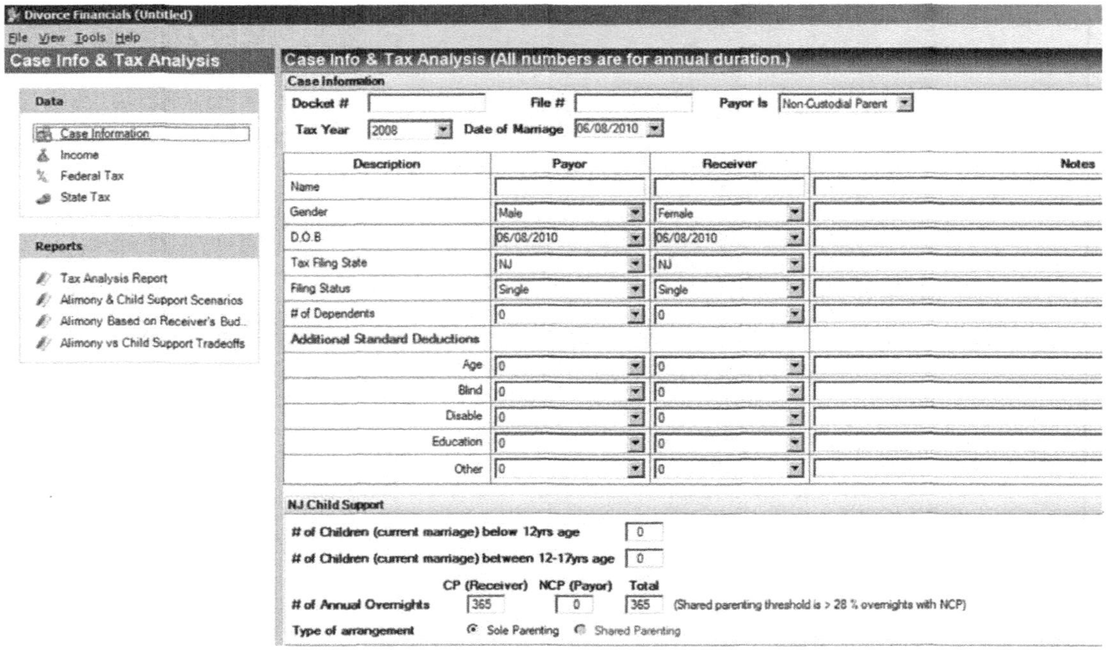

→ **Docket number** for the case; and
→ **Payor** and recipients of funds periodically distributed, like alimony.

Toward the bottom, this software prompts the user for information that a state, which in this example is New Jersey, needs for purpose of identifying relevant custody laws.

b.   Assets and Liabilities

i.   *Income*

Identifying sources of income can make it easier to determine who should pay, and receive, monthly payments such as alimony and child support.

Figure 9.25
Divorce—Financials software: Sidebar menu, Data subsection, Income link

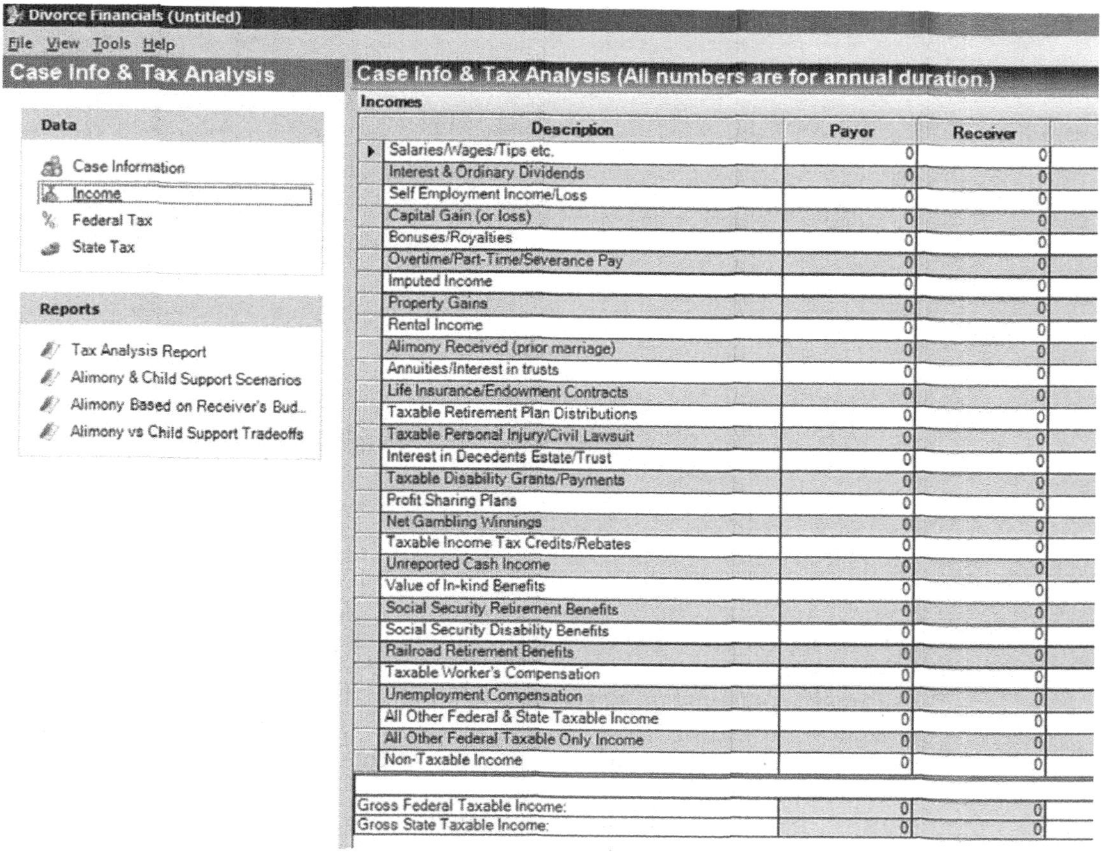

Description	Payor	Receiver
Salaries/Wages/Tips etc.	0	0
Interest & Ordinary Dividends	0	0
Self Employment Income/Loss	0	0
Capital Gain (or loss)	0	0
Bonuses/Royalties	0	0
Overtime/Part-Time/Severance Pay	0	0
Imputed Income	0	0
Property Gains	0	0
Rental Income	0	0
Alimony Received (prior marriage)	0	0
Annuities/Interest in trusts	0	0
Life Insurance/Endowment Contracts	0	0
Taxable Retirement Plan Distributions	0	0
Taxable Personal Injury/Civil Lawsuit	0	0
Interest in Decedents Estate/Trust	0	0
Taxable Disability Grants/Payments	0	0
Profit Sharing Plans	0	0
Net Gambling Winnings	0	0
Taxable Income Tax Credits/Rebates	0	0
Unreported Cash Income	0	0
Value of In-kind Benefits	0	0
Social Security Retirement Benefits	0	0
Social Security Disability Benefits	0	0
Railroad Retirement Benefits	0	0
Taxable Worker's Compensation	0	0
Unemployment Compensation	0	0
All Other Federal & State Taxable Income	0	0
All Other Federal Taxable Only Income	0	0
Non-Taxable Income	0	0
Gross Federal Taxable Income:	0	0
Gross State Taxable Income:	0	0

ii. Additional assets and liabilities

Clicking a button makes it possible to identify and list such assets as:

Figure 9.26
Divorce—Financials software: Sidebar menu, Assets and Liabilities link

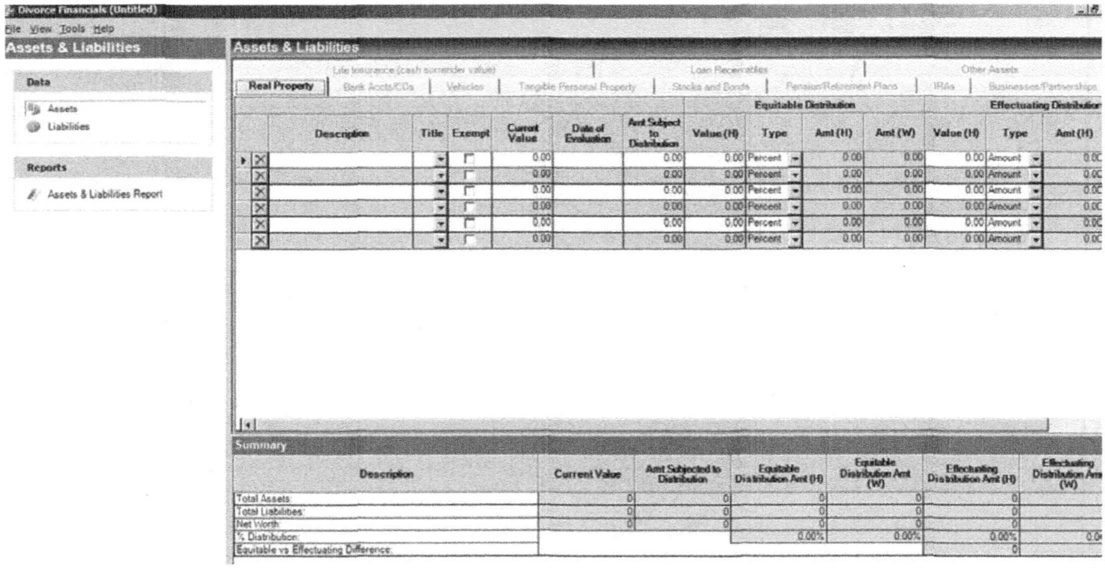

→ Bank accounts and certificates of deposit;
→ Vehicles;
→ Tangible personal property, such as jewelry;
→ Stocks and bonds;
→ Pensions, including the current value of the pension, as well as of expected pension payments;
→ IRAs (individual retirement accounts);
→ An interest in a business, such as a **partnership;**
→ Life insurance policies, at current cash surrender values (the amount that the policyholder would receive upon immediately ending the insurance policy);
→ The present value of any interest in land (like a lease);
→ Loan receivables (payments owed from a loan);
→ An inheritance; and
→ Other assets which were not otherwise identified in the previous tabs.

These documents should also account for:

→ Alimony recapture, where an ex-spouse remarries and would no longer need alimony;

→ The present value of alimony payments, including the amount needed to cover all projected alimony payments; and

→ An alimony buyout amount which, if paid, would discharge all alimony obligations.

The software will also generate a summary regarding liabilities, such as a mortgage on a house, for the total value of all assets.

Figure 9.27
Divorce—Financials software: Sidebar menu, Assets and Liabilities link, Summary box

Description	Current Value	Amt Subjected to Distribution	Equitable Distribution Amt (H)	Equitable Distribution Amt (W)	Effectuating Distribution Amt (H)	Effectuating Distribution Amt (W)
Total Assets:	0	0	0	0	0	
Total Liabilities:	0	0	0	0	0	
Net Worth:	0	0	0	0	0	
% Distribution:			0.00%	0.00%	0.00%	0.00
Equitable vs Effectuating Difference:					0	

c. Tax Information

Having income data may make it easy to determine the taxable income for annual tax filings, especially in light of monthly transfer payments like alimony and child support.

i. *Federal*

In addition to income, the federal government will want tax information about:

→ **Adjustments,** which reflect a transfer of funds, like payments into a pension account;

→ **Personal exemptions,** such as the standard tax deduction, which changes annually;

→ **Itemized deductions,** where listing deductions could produce a number greater than the standardized tax deduction;

→ **Tax credits,** like the earned income tax credit; and

→ The **Alternative Minimum Tax,** a minimum tax owed, regardless of credits and deductions.

Figure 9.28
Divorce—Financials software: Sidebar menu, Data subsection, Federal Tax link

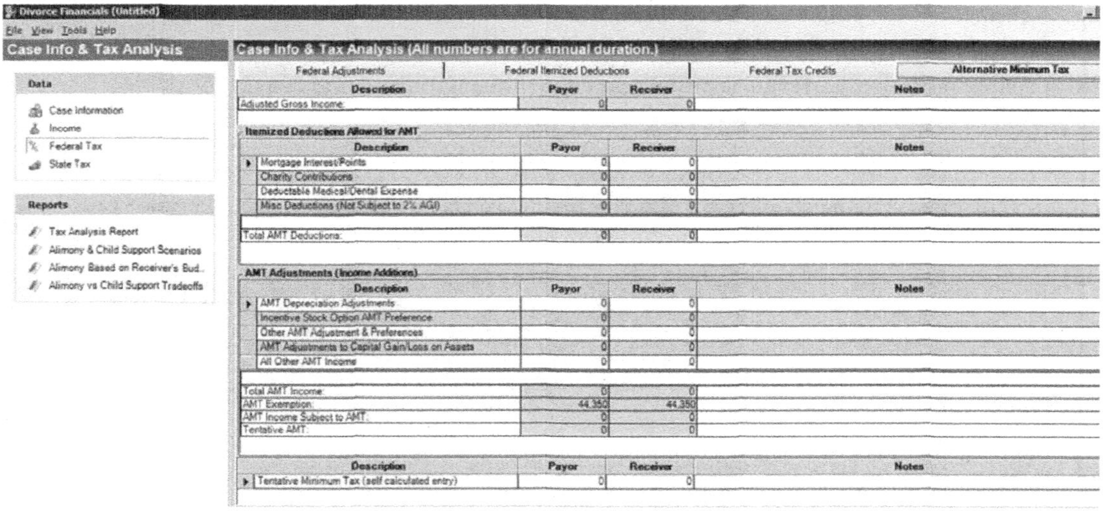

ii.   State

State tax law generally offers different kinds of credits and deductions than those allowed under federal tax law.

Figure 9.29
Divorce—Financials software: Sidebar menu, Data subsection, State Tax link

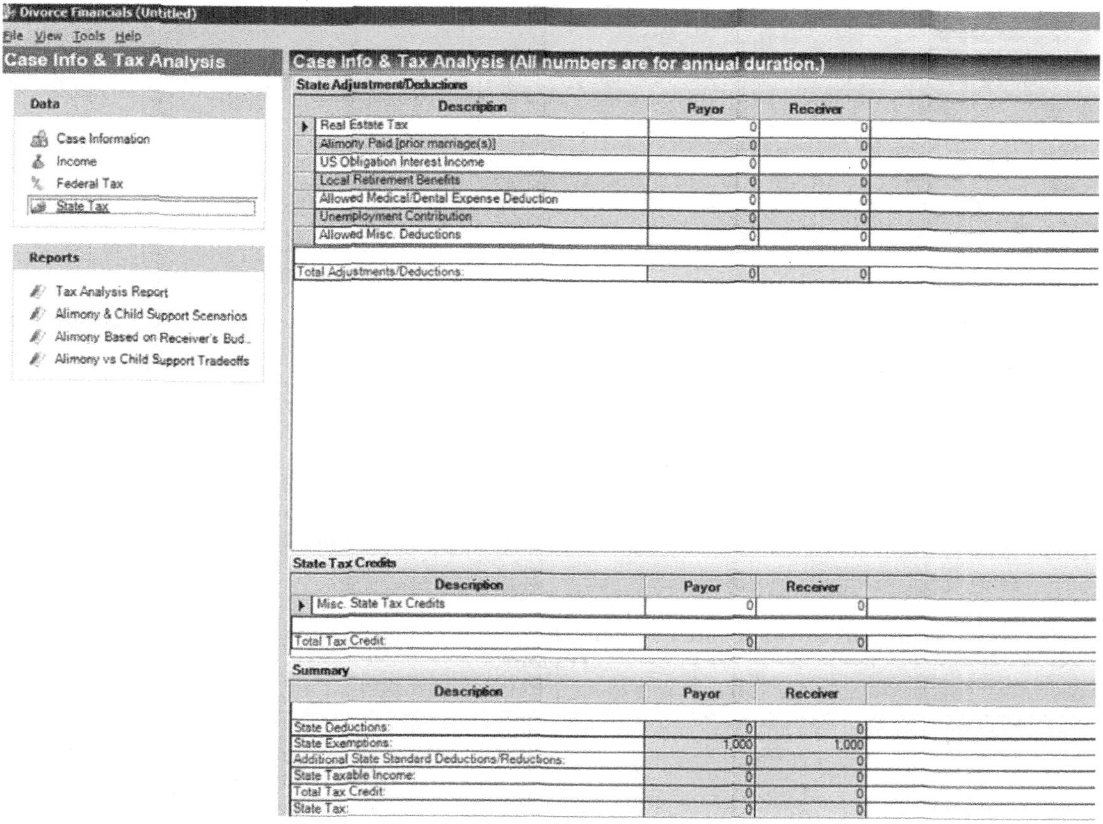

State Adjustment/Deductions		
Description	**Payor**	**Receiver**
Real Estate Tax	0	0
Alimony Paid [prior marriage(s)]	0	0
US Obligation Interest Income	0	0
Local Retirement Benefits	0	0
Allowed Medical/Dental Expense Deduction	0	0
Unemployment Contribution	0	0
Allowed Misc. Deductions	0	0
Total Adjustments/Deductions:	0	0

State Tax Credits		
Description	**Payor**	**Receiver**
Misc. State Tax Credits	0	0
Total Tax Credit:	0	0

Summary		
Description	**Payor**	**Receiver**
State Deductions:	0	0
State Exemptions:	1,000	1,000
Additional State Standard Deductions/Reductions:	0	0
State Taxable Income:	0	0
Total Tax Credit:	0	0
State Tax:	0	0

Sidebar menu:

Case Info & Tax Analysis

Data
- Case Information
- Income
- Federal Tax
- State Tax

Reports
- Tax Analysis Report
- Alimony & Child Support Scenarios
- Alimony Based on Receiver's Bud...
- Alimony vs Child Support Tradeoffs

iii.   Reports

The software can generate reports or charts about the tax consequences for a proposed divorce financial settlement. These can quickly change under different scenarios involving alimony and child support payments, taking into account:

Figure 9.30
Divorce—Financials software: Sidebar menu: Reports subsection, Alimony and ChildSupport Scenarios link

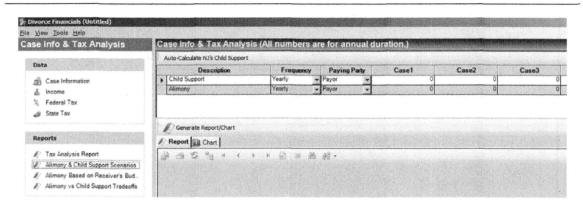

→ Educational expenses for offspring of the marriage;
→ Changes in the expenses of the recipient of any support payments; and
→ Consequences from altering child support or alimony payments.

Figure 9.31
Divorce—Financials software: Sidebar menu: Reports subsection, Alimony versus Child Support Tradeoffs

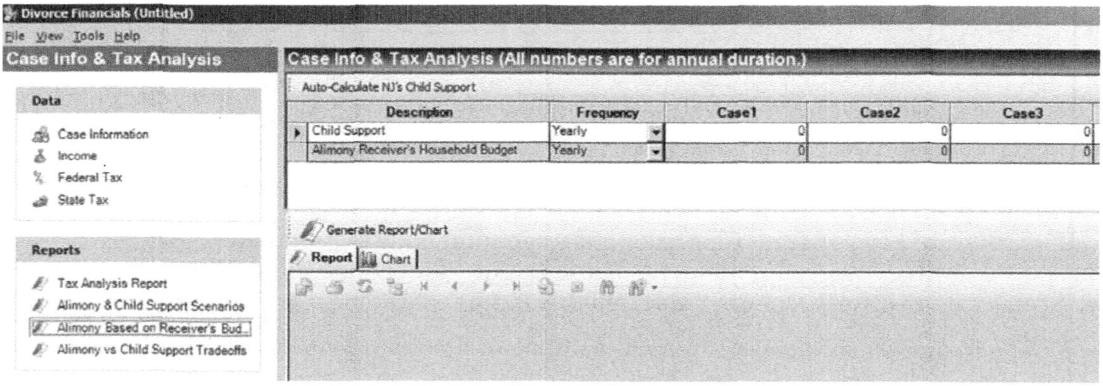

D.   REAL ESTATE

1.   *Real Estate Concepts*

a.   Overview

Because a significant part of the American dream involves home ownership, buying a house can be the most significant legal transaction for a client. After considering some basic real estate concepts, the discussion will shift to the proper completion of that critical financial document, the **HUD-1.**

b.   Property

Real property, commonly called **real estate,** involves land and everything permanently attached to it, like a home. Personal property is everything else.

i.   *Ownership and possession*

An **owner** has an unqualified right to use the land. This includes entering into a lease with a **tenant,** who could then use the land. This renter's rights in the land are limited only by the owner's superior rights.

ii.   *Deeds and title searches*

A **deed** represents ownership in land. It is also called a **title.** It will:

→ Include a detailed description of the property;
→ Identify the previous owner;
→ State when that owner obtained the property; and
→ Describe where to find a copy of the deed at the **registry of deeds,** typically a county building that has copies of all deeds for property in that county.

Checking that the seller actually owns the property involves researching the history of the land's ownership. This process, a **title search,** means reviewing prior deeds for a property to see that when a transfer of the land occurred, on the date of the transfer, the buyer received all of the rights that the seller promised to provide.

iii.   *Mortgages*

I.   Definition

Most people need to borrow money to purchase land. A borrower will pay back the loan over time, with interest, and will provide the lender with a mortgage. The mortgage gives the lender the authority to seize and sell the property at auction if the borrower fails to make the monthly loan payment.

II.   Second mortgage

Another reason for doing a title search arises if the owner needs to take out an additional loan on the property. Anyone lending money will want a mortgage and will want to know whether the borrower has already granted a mortgage. If the owner fails to make a monthly loan payment, forcing the sale of the property at auction, the second lender, who has received a second mortgage, will be repaid only after the first lender has received a full repayment of its loan. Because the price paid at auction to the first lender may not leave much, if any, money to pay off the second loan, second lenders usually charge higher interest rates on their loans to reflect the higher risk of not getting paid.

III.   Liens

A mortgage is a specialized type of **lien.** Someone files a lien on property to collect payment on a debt so that upon a sale of the property, the lienholder will then have the right to collect on the debt out of the moneys transferred during the sale. A carpenter could file a lien on a property to guarantee payment for services rendered, such as making and installing kitchen cabinets. Governments could file liens for nonpayment of taxes.

iv.   *Closing*

I.   Definition

The actual handing over of the deed to the buyer, the **closing,** may take place anywhere. A buyer might want this to happen at the registry of deeds, so that the new owner can immediately record the transfer and reduce the risk that a seller might fraudulently try to sell the land twice.

II.   Closing documents

To make it easier to buy and sell a home, the federal government requires that those borrowing money for such a purchase complete a standardized form, the HUD-1.

2.   *Software*

a.   **Easy HUD Real Estate Software**

Software for completing the HUD-1 can reduce the likelihood of mistakes while speeding up the completion of the form. The HUD-1 form is available at the following website: http://portal.hud.gov/hudportal/documents/huddoc?id=1.pdf.

The copyrighted software used here to show how the software works to generate the HUD-1 and all necessary supporting documents, the Easy HUD v.4.0.02, is available through EasySoft LLC at http://www.easysoft-usa.com/hud-software.html. A partial list of other providers of real estate closing software includes www.nationallawforms.com and http://www.lawfirmsoftware.com/software/closing.htm. Other closing software might ask for information in a different sequence and use different types of graphics, but they all must generate a properly formatted HUD-1.

All images taken from this software are copyrighted by the creator of the software used to generate such images. Inclusion of such images in this text does not constitute any claim of copyright in them.

Figure 9.32
HUD-1 software—File tab and submenu

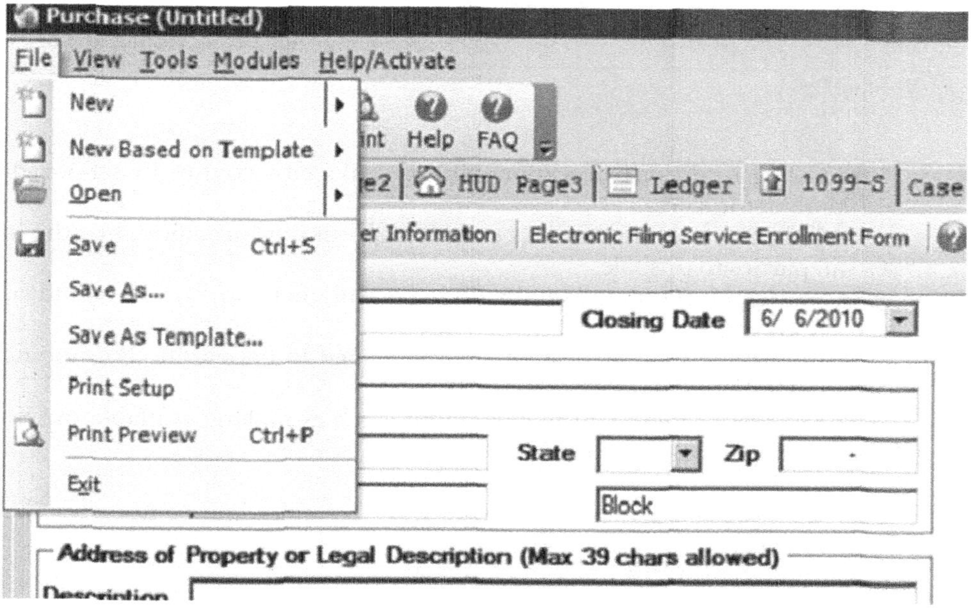

b.   Features

i.   Tabs: top row

I.   Familiar headings

This software uses the system of tabs and toolbars common to many Microsoft products, such as File, for document management, and View, for access to the HUD-1 Form.

II.   Tools tab

This software can:

Figure 9.33
HUD-1 software—Tools tab and submenu

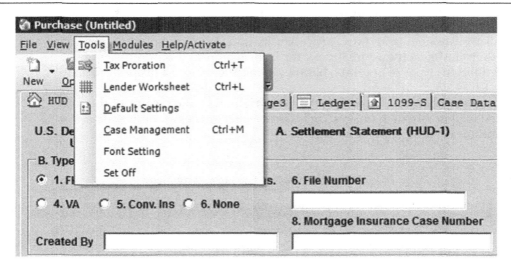

→ Calculate the **tax proration:** all taxes, like city, county, or school, due at the time of the sale;

→ Generate a lender worksheet with important information, like the identity of all parties to this sale;

→ Set default settings, like identifying a **settlement agent,** who would coordinate the closing;

→ Determine set-offs: those expenses related to the closing but not included in the HUD-1; and

→ Engage in document management, such as making available the documents associated with the closing.

ii.   Tabs: bottom row

I.   HUD-1 pages

This software presents screens that correspond to each page of the HUD-1. The HUD-1 uses a double-column approach to present that information about buyer and seller in parallel to one another. For example, payment of the buyer's deposit to create the contract to purchase the home will show up as an expense in the buyer's column and a gain in the seller's column, as seen in Figure 3-34.

II.   HUD page 1 tab

Critical information about the sale includes:

→ Whether the federal government provided the loan via an agency, such as the Fair Housing Administration (FHA);

→ The location of the property;
→ A proposed closing date;

Figure 9.34
HUD-1 software—Toolbar: New Button and submenu, HUD Page 1 tab

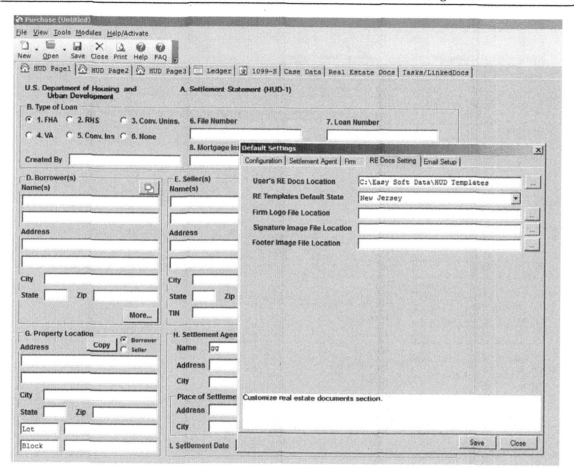

→ A summary of transactions, such as:
   → What the buyer will pay;
   → The price of the property; and
   → Adjustments, like taxes and other assessments, that the seller will pay in
     advance.

Figure 9.35
HUD-1 software—Toolbar: New Button and submenu, HUD Page 1 tab, Summary of Transactions [Lines 100–120 and Lines 400–420]

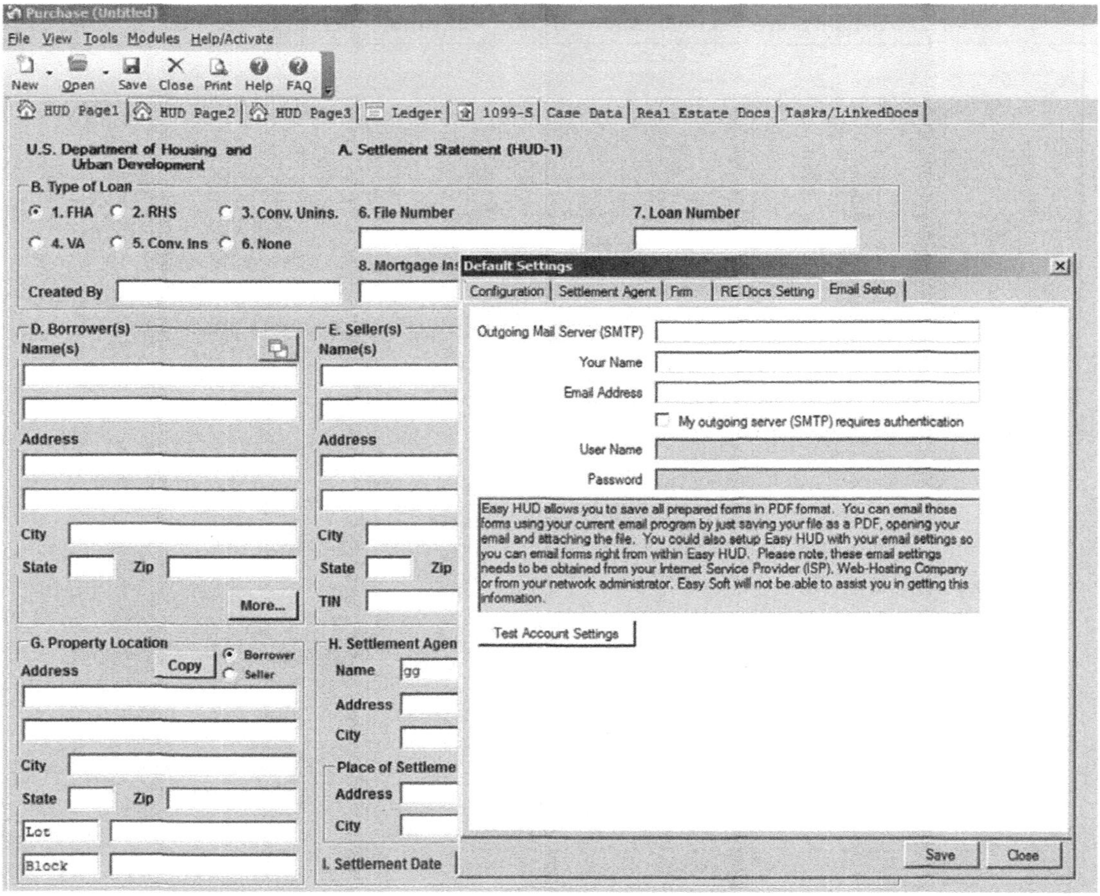

→ Amounts paid by the borrower, including the deposit and the size of the loan;

Figure 9.36
HUD-1 software—Toolbar: New Button and submenu, HUD Page 1 tab, Summary of Transactions [Lines 200–209 and Lines 500–509]

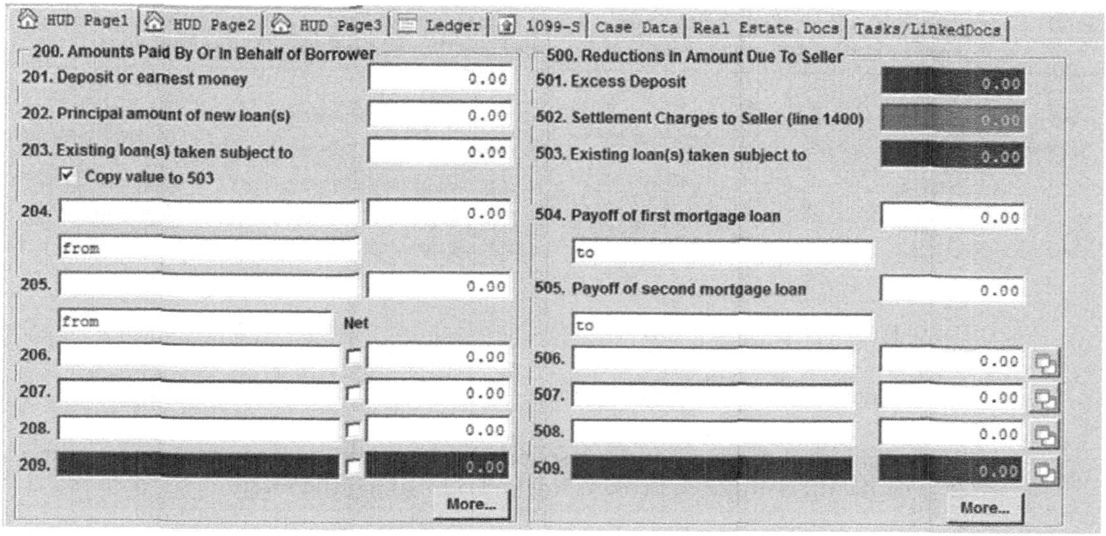

[Note: The More buttons, available at the end of each column, make it possible to add information about existing loans on the property.]

→ Adjustments for items unpaid by the seller, such as outstanding property taxes; and

Figure 9.37
HUD-1 software—Toolbar: New Button and submenu, HUD Page 1 tab, Adjustments for Items Unpaid by Seller [Lines 210–220 and Lines 510–520]

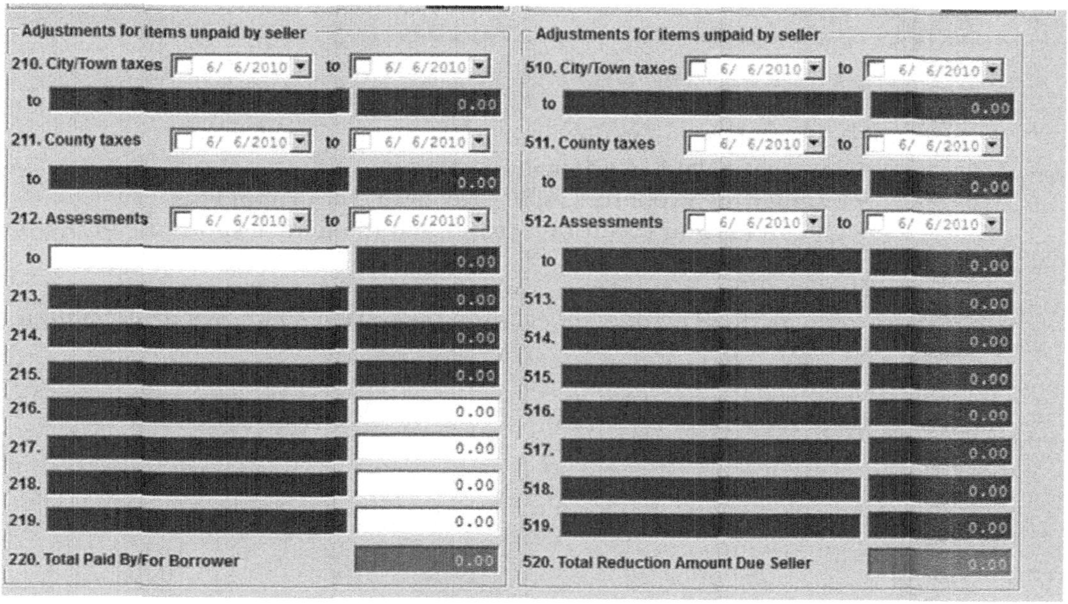

→ Cash settlements, of what the borrower will pay and the seller will receive.

Figure 9.38
HUD-1 software—Toolbar: New Button and submenu, HUD Page 1 tab, Cash at Settlement From/To Borrower [Lines 300–303] and Cash at Settlement To/From Seller [Lines 600–603]

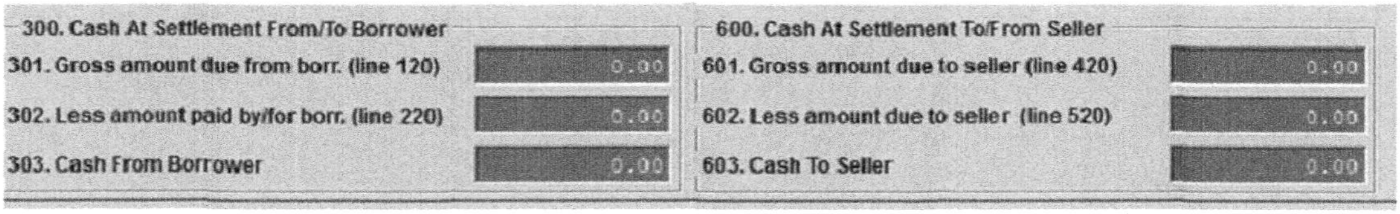

III.   HUD page 2 tab

Critical information includes:

→ Fees paid to buyer and/or seller's **brokers** and how to apportion them, especially when multiple brokers worked on making the sale;

Figure 9.39
HUD-1 software—Toolbar: New Button and submenu, HUD Page 2 tab, Total Real Estate Broker Fees [Lines 700–704]

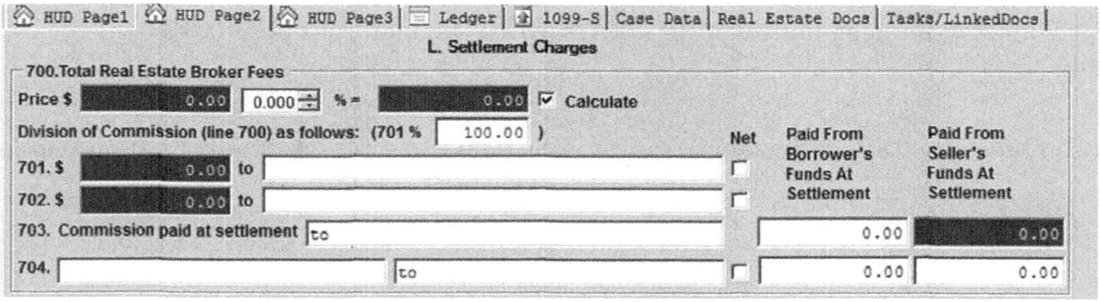

→ Fees related to getting the loan, to:
  → Secure it, called an origination charge;
  → Evaluate the property's value objectively, via an appraisal;
  → Obtain current credit reports, so that the lender knows about the buyer's financial history;
  → Pay for tax service charges; and
  → Obtain flood certification, if the property has a known risk of flooding.

Figure 9.40

HUD-1 software—Toolbar: New Button and submenu, HUD Page 2 tab, Items Payable in Connection with Loan [Lines 800–810]

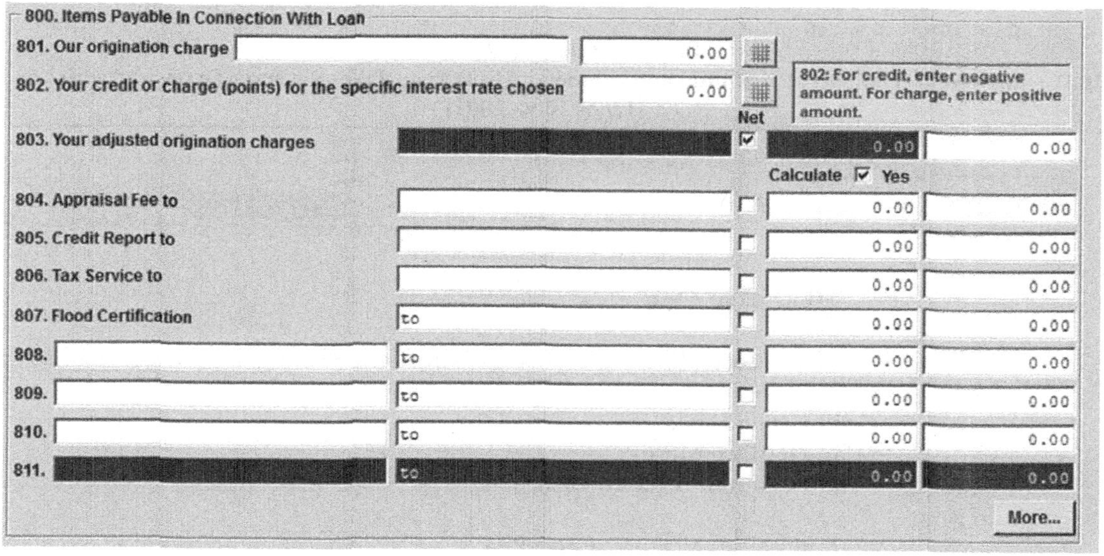

→ Items that the lender wants paid in advance, such as:

   → Interest;

   → A premium for mortgage insurance, which would pay off the loan if a title dispute subsequently arose; and

   → A premium for homeowner's insurance.

Figure 9.41

HUD-1 software—Toolbar: New Button and submenu, HUD Page 2 tab, Items Required by Lender to be Paid in Advance [Lines 900–905]

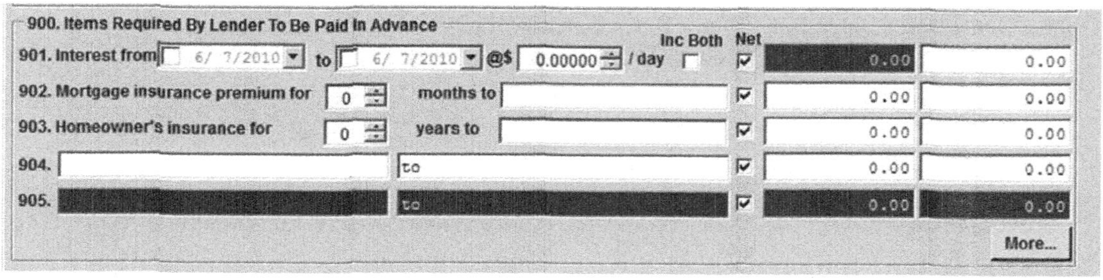

→ Reserves deposited with the lender in an **escrow account.** The lender may require that some of the fees that a new owner will have to pay, like property taxes, be paid ahead of time into this special kind of account so as to be available when those fees become due.

Figure 9.42
HUD-1 software—Toolbar: New Button and submenu, HUD Page 2 tab, Reserves Deposited with Lender [Lines 1000–1001]

1000. Reserves Deposited With Lender				
1001. Initial deposit for your escrow account		Net ☑	0.00	0.00

IV.   HUD page 3 tab

→ Identifying costs that might change before the closing, broken down into categories, of those that:
   → Will not change;
   → Can change; and
   → May rise no more than 10%.

Figure 9.43
HUD-1 software—Toolbar: New Button and submenu, HUD Page 3 tab

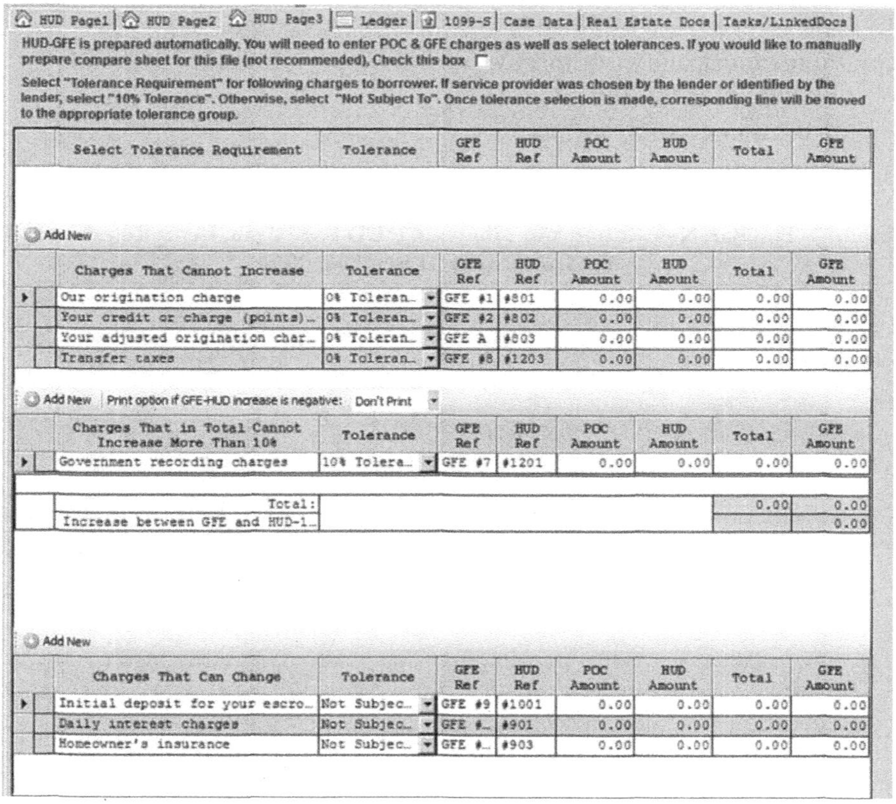

HUD Page1 | HUD Page2 | HUD Page3 | Ledger | 1099-S | Case Data | Real Estate Docs | Tasks/LinkedDocs

HUD-GFE is prepared automatically. You will need to enter POC & GFE charges as well as select tolerances. If you would like to manually prepare compare sheet for this file (not recommended), Check this box ☐

Select "Tolerance Requirement" for following charges to borrower. If service provider was chosen by the lender or identified by the lender, select "10% Tolerance". Otherwise, select "Not Subject To". Once tolerance selection is made, corresponding line will be moved to the appropriate tolerance group.

Select Tolerance Requirement	Tolerance	GFE Ref	HUD Ref	POC Amount	HUD Amount	Total	GFE Amount

Add New

Charges That Cannot Increase	Tolerance	GFE Ref	HUD Ref	POC Amount	HUD Amount	Total	GFE Amount
Our origination charge	0% Toleran..	GFE #1	#801	0.00	0.00	0.00	0.00
Your credit or charge (points)...	0% Toleran..	GFE #2	#802	0.00	0.00	0.00	0.00
Your adjusted origination char..	0% Toleran..	GFE A	#803	0.00	0.00	0.00	0.00
Transfer taxes	0% Toleran..	GFE #8	#1203	0.00	0.00	0.00	0.00

Add New | Print option if GFE+HUD increase is negative: Don't Print

Charges That in Total Cannot Increase More Than 10%	Tolerance	GFE Ref	HUD Ref	POC Amount	HUD Amount	Total	GFE Amount
Government recording charges	10% Tolera..	GFE #7	#1201	0.00	0.00	0.00	0.00
Total:						0.00	0.00
Increase between GFE and HUD-1..							0.00

Add New

Charges That Can Change	Tolerance	GFE Ref	HUD Ref	POC Amount	HUD Amount	Total	GFE Amount
Initial deposit for your escro..	Not Subjec..	GFE #9	#1001	0.00	0.00	0.00	0.00
Daily interest charges	Not Subjec..	GFE #..	#901	0.00	0.00	0.00	0.00
Homeowner's insurance	Not Subjec..	GFE #..	#903	0.00	0.00	0.00	0.00

→ Calculating "the bottom line" about the loan, including:
  → The impact of an increase in the interest rate, when getting an adjustable rate mortgage;
  → Whether and how the loan balance could change;
  → The impact of a change of the mortgage insurance rates;
  → How much of a penalty the borrower may incur by paying off the loan before it is due; and
  → A breakdown of those items that would be paid out of the escrow account, such as insurance.

Figure 9.44

HUD-1 software—Toolbar: New Button and submenu, HUD Page 3 tab, Loan Terms submenu

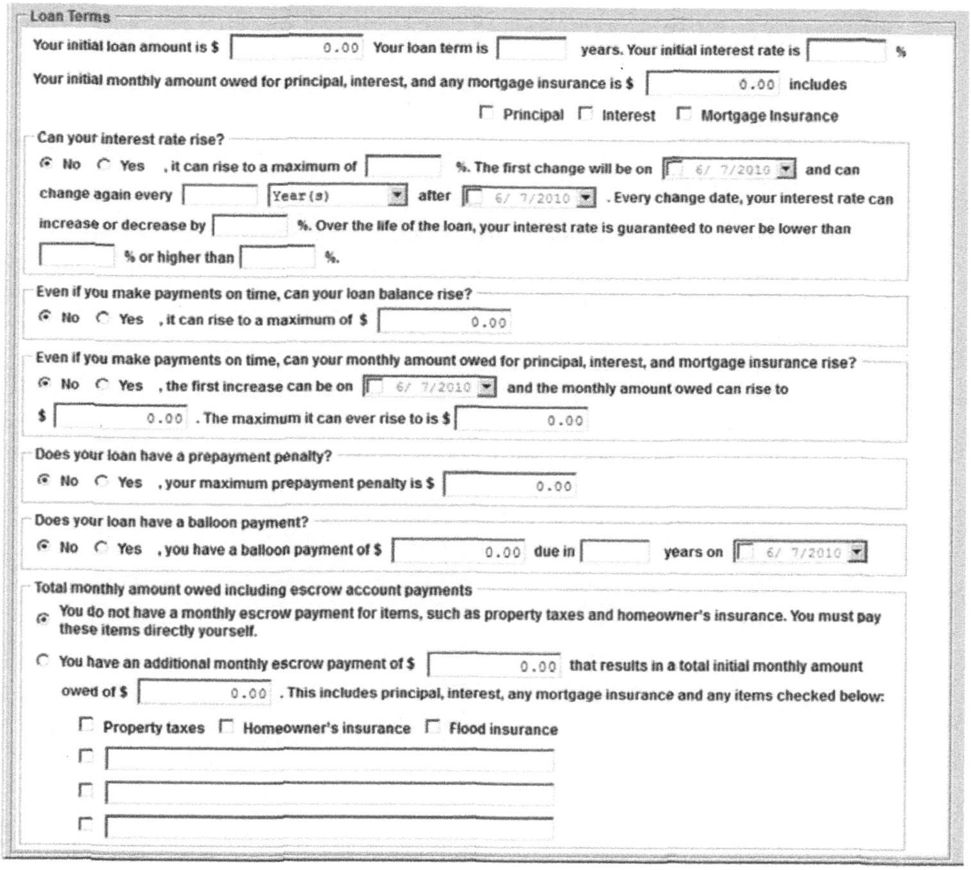
Loan Terms

Your initial loan amount is $ 0.00 Your loan term is years. Your initial interest rate is %

Your initial monthly amount owed for principal, interest, and any mortgage insurance is $ 0.00 includes

Principal Interest Mortgage Insurance

Can your interest rate rise?

No Yes , it can rise to a maximum of %. The first change will be on 6/ 7/2010 and can change again every Year(s) after 6/ 7/2010 . Every change date, your interest rate can increase or decrease by %. Over the life of the loan, your interest rate is guaranteed to never be lower than % or higher than %.

Even if you make payments on time, can your loan balance rise?

No Yes , it can rise to a maximum of $ 0.00

Even if you make payments on time, can your monthly amount owed for principal, interest, and mortgage insurance rise?

No Yes , the first increase can be on 6/ 7/2010 and the monthly amount owed can rise to $ 0.00 . The maximum it can ever rise to is $ 0.00

Does your loan have a prepayment penalty?

No Yes , your maximum prepayment penalty is $ 0.00

Does your loan have a balloon payment?

No Yes , you have a balloon payment of $ 0.00 due in years on 6/ 7/2010

Total monthly amount owed including escrow account payments

You do not have a monthly escrow payment for items, such as property taxes and homeowner's insurance. You must pay these items directly yourself.

You have an additional monthly escrow payment of $ 0.00 that results in a total initial monthly amount owed of $ 0.00 . This includes principal, interest, any mortgage insurance and any items checked below:

Property taxes Homeowner's insurance Flood insurance

V. Ledger tab

Software might provide a ledger, which would describe all financial transactions associated with a closing.

Figure 9.45
HUD-1 software—Toolbar: New Button and submenu, Ledger tab

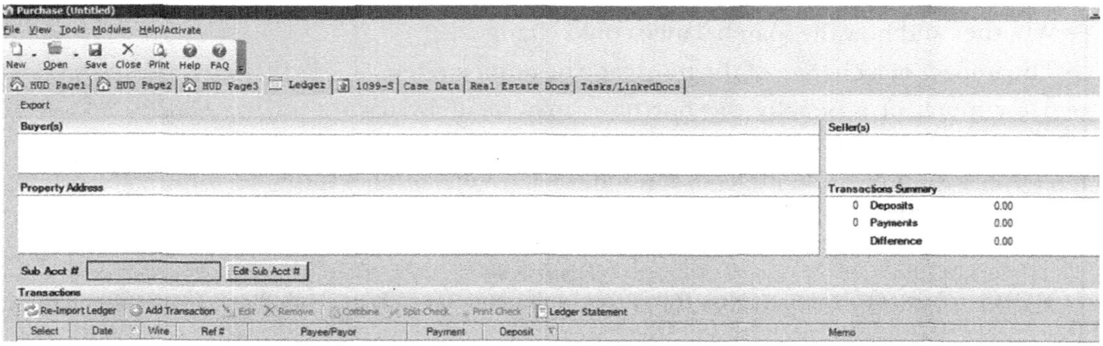

VI.   Form 1099-S tab

Because any transaction that generates income could require the payment of federal taxes, the software can:

→ Generate the appropriate form, called a 1099-S form;
→ Import an existing 1099-S form; and
→ File this document electronically, at least with this software.

Figure 9.46
HUD-1 software—Toolbar: New Button and submenu, 1099-S tab

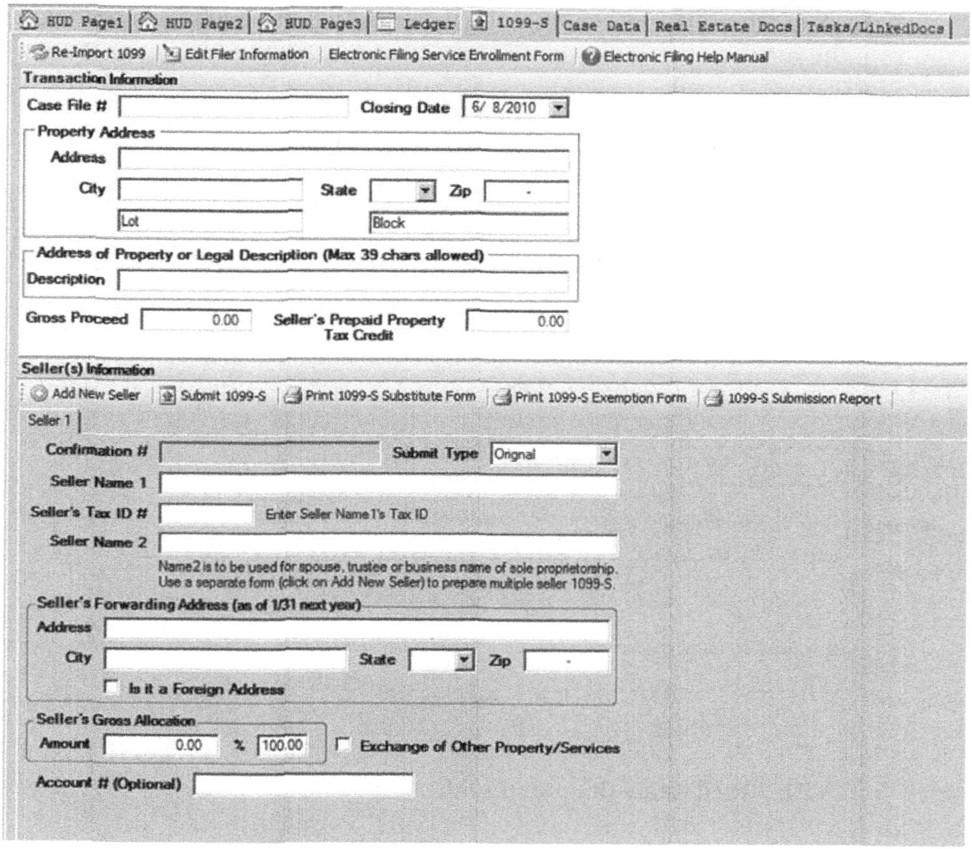

VII.   Case data tab

On the chance that a law firm does business with the client in the future, like arranging for a sale of the newly purchased property, it might want to record information about the closing, such as:

→ Buyer information (when a buyer receives the seller's interest in the property, the buyer is the **grantee**).
→ Seller information, such as the seller's new address upon completion of the sale (when a seller transfers the seller's interest in the property, the seller is the **grantor**);
→ A description of the property, especially its assessed value, which a community would use when calculating the property taxes;
→ The amount needed to pay off the mortgage;
→ Information about all lenders, if this transaction involves more than one lender;

→ Information about the seller's attorney;

→ Information about the real estate broker, including the commission a broker gets; and

→ Any other information that the firm would deem useful, such as who **notarized** the deed.

Figure 9.47
HUD-1 software—Toolbar: New Button and submenu, Case Data tab

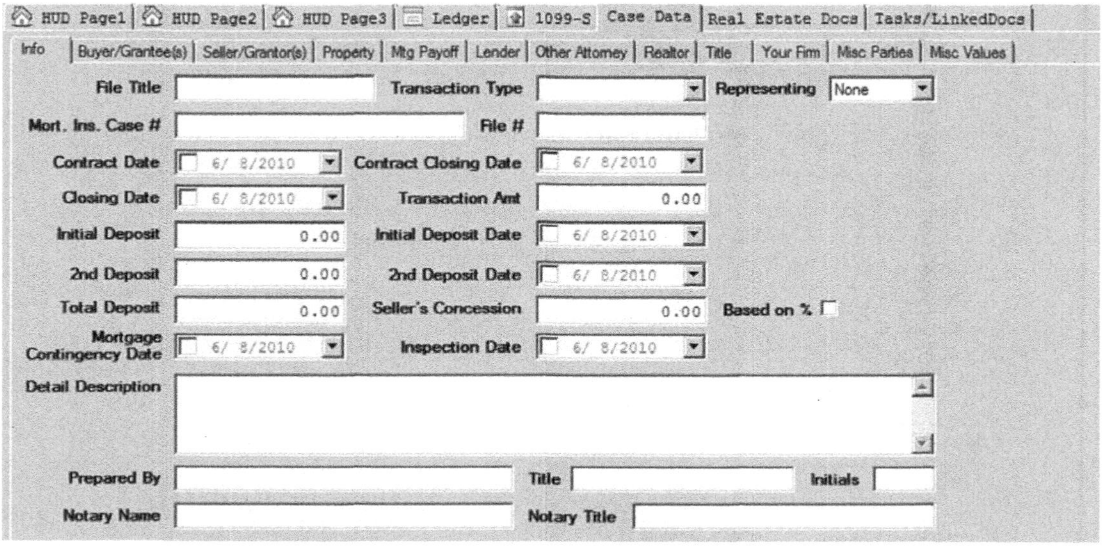

VIII.   Real estate documents tab

This might list useful documents, like correspondence sent to all parties to the transaction.

Figure 9.48
HUD-1 software—Toolbar: New Button and submenu, Real Estate Documents tab

IX.   Tasked/linked documents tab

Among other options, this tab provides access to an expandable checklist that can be prioritized by deadline, of tasks related to the closing, such as:

→ Ordering the title search; and
→ Acknowledging receipt of the **binder** deposit, a sum paid by a prospective buyer to create a binding contract for the purchase of the property.

Figure 9.49
HUD-1 software—Toolbar: New Button and submenu, Tasked/Linked Docs, Tasks tab

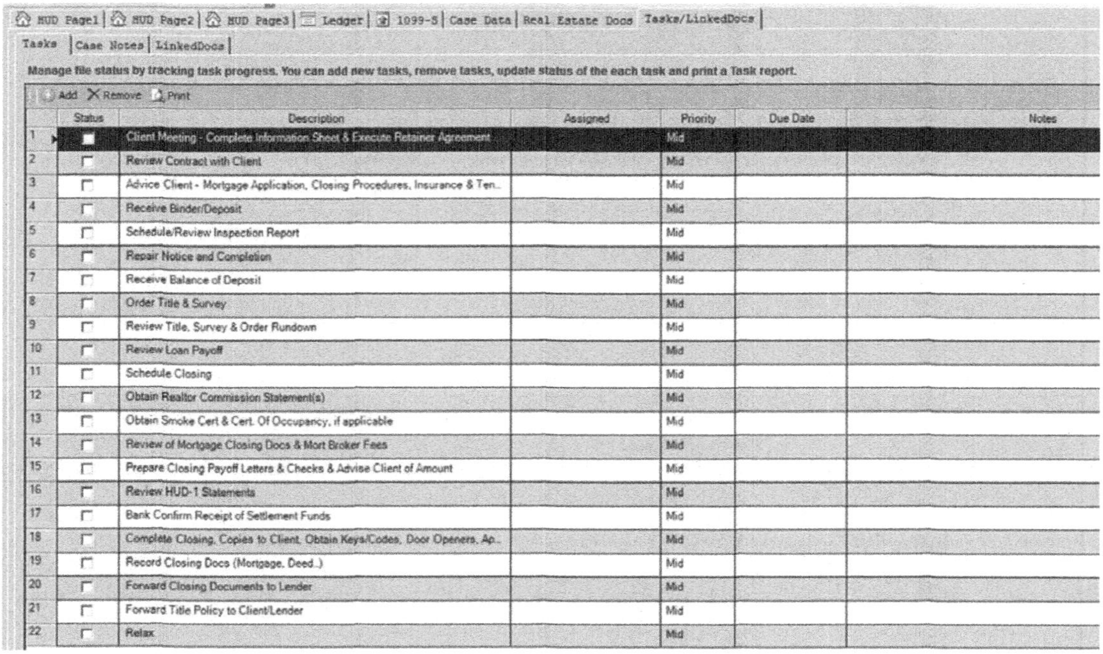

E.   TRUSTS

1.   Introduction

At law, a **trust** involves a separation of the legal and equitable ownership of real and personal property. The trust owns the property, but the **beneficiary** has the use of the property. For example, if the trust contains money for the beneficiary's college education, the beneficiary has the right to claim that money from the trust to pay for college tuition, but does not control the money. The document for creating the trust contains instructions for a **trustee** about how to manage the property in the trust. At a minimum, a trustee has to keep track of the estate's assets, and of the expenses needed to maintain the property held in trust.

2.   Software

EasySoft LLC's EasyTrust-Accounting software provides an example of the kind of software a trustee would use to keep track of income and disbursements. It is available at http://www.easysoft-usa.com/trust-accounting-software.html. All images taken from this software are copyrighted by the creator of such images and inclusion of such images in this text does not constitute any copyright interest or claim in them. Other sources of software to create trusts include http://

legendary willsandtrusts.com/?page_id=247 and Cowles Trust Plus at http://west.thomson.com/products/books-cds/cowles/trust-plus.aspx, among others. This software includes a wizard for setting up basic information that will be used for subsequently generated documents.

3. Features

This software uses buttons, tabs, and pulldown menus, something quite familiar for those who have used Microsoft's office productivity software.

a. Buttons

Buttons at the top of the page provide quick access to commonly used software features for keeping track of:

Figure 9.50
Trust Accounting software—buttons

→ How much time a trustee spent managing the trust, for inclusion in a monthly bill for services;
→ Expenses incurred on behalf of the trust, like filing fees if the trust needs to sue a bank to recover trust funds stolen by a bank employee, or to pay the trustee for services rendered;
→ Receipts, such as for interest paid by a bank on the trust's money held at that bank; and
→ A line of credit available to the trust.

b. Tabs

The top toolbar arranges tabs by function, instead of individually, as with buttons.

Figure 9.51
Trust Accounting software—tabs

i. *File tab*

This pulldown menu makes it easier to manage trust fund data.

Figure 9.52
Trust Accounting software—File tab: Pulldown menu

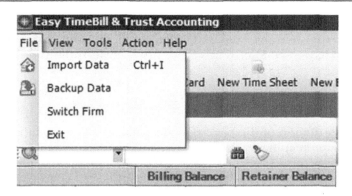

ii. *View tab*

Here, the software provides links for useful information, such as:

Figure 9.53
Trust Accounting software—View tab: Pulldown menu

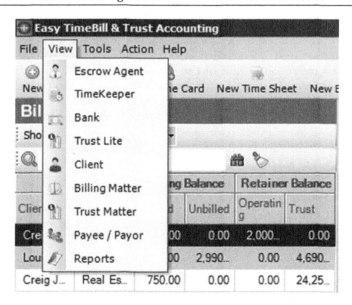

→ Identifying the escrow agent who manages the trust's funds in an escrow account;
→ A breakdown of time spent managing the trust, broken down by:
    → Who worked on behalf of the trust;
    → The nature of the work performed;

→ Time spent on the activity; and

→ The rate of compensation for such work.

→ The bank or banks that have trust fund accounts;

→ "Trust Lite," for a quick overview of the trust's financial transactions, such as holding a buyer's deposit for the purchase of trust fund property;

→ "Client," for keeping track of invoices, including a history of when sent, the number sent, a date for payment, and, if needed, the option to "Print Overdue Invoices with Reminder";

Figure 9.54

Trust Accounting software—View tab: Pulldown menu, Client link, Invoice(s) Overdue submenu

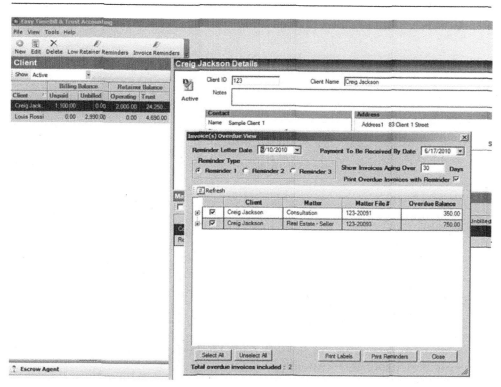

→ Matters related to billing, such as information provided in the buttons described above;

→ "Trust Matter," for a detailed overview of the trust's financial transactions;

→ "Payee/Payor," who received payments from the trust, from a specific account;

→ Reports, with information about trust fund activity including:

Figure 9.55
Trust Accounting software—View tab: Pulldown menu, Reports link

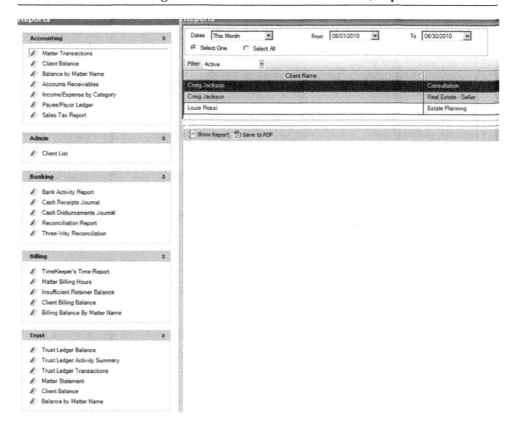

→ Accounting, such as:
   → The subject of a transaction;
   → Balances, broken down by subject matter;
   → Accounts receivable, for invoices issued but not yet paid;
   → Income/expenses by category;
   → The payee/payor ledger; and
   → A tax report for sales involving trust property.
→ Banking, such as a:
   → Record of receipts and disbursements of cash; and
   → Reconciliation report, which tracks all changes to a trust account, by transaction, during a specific time, over multiple accounts.
→ Billing, including:
   → An account of hours billed; and

→ A billing balance, all of which can be broken down by subject matter; and

→ Trust activity as reflected in a ledger, which comprehensively records all financial transactions.

A menu on the left-hand side of the screen also links to these items.

iii.   Tools tab

This tab, via a pulldown menu, provides options regarding other trust-related matters, such as:

Figure 9.56
Trust Accounting software—Tools tab: Dropdown menu

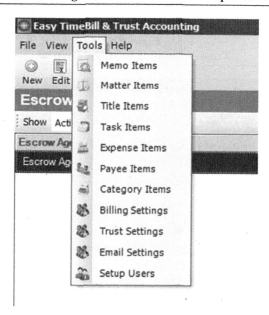

→ Memo items regarding trust-related activities like closings, creating a power of attorney (which empowers another to serve as an agent for the trust), and filing an appeal of a tax assessment;

→ Matter items, regarding leases or litigation, for example;

→ Title items, a breakdown of services rendered to the trust, broken down by a worker's title, including an **accounts payable** clerk and **accounts receivable** clerk and attorney;

→ Task items, breaking down services rendered by activity, such as for the drafting of legal documents like an **affidavit** or a **complaint;**

→ Expense items, regarding non-taxable costs, like:

  → The cost of a **real estate binder;**

  → Court costs, such as in the case of litigation;

→ Copying and printing; and
→ Telecommunication;
→ Payee items, for identifying disbursements of fees for services rendered by:
→ An attorney for the seller in a real estate transaction; or
→ An office rental management company (which might collect rent for occu-
pying trust property).
→ Category items, which list expenses by category, such as for utilities or rent;
→ Billings settings, such as for the generation of invoices; and
→ Trust settings, regarding information like the defaults used on documents
generated from the use of this software.

iv.   Help tab

As with other software offered by EasySoft LLC, this tab provides the user
with access to various kinds of help, including a manual in PDF for using the
software.

Figure 9.57
Trust Accounting software, Help tab

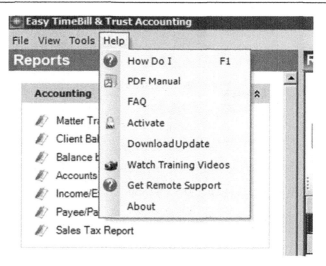

F.   WILLS

1.   *The Nature of a Will*

A **will** is a legally enforceable document that contains the final wishes of a decedent. To make it enforceable, witnesses must have signed the will, indicating that
they had seen the maker of the will sign the document and can subsequently

testify if a question arises whether the maker created the will under duress or coercion.

The maker of the will is called the **testator** (for a man) or the **testatrix** (for a woman). The property that the decedent has left is known as the estate. The person identified in the will and charged with the responsibility of managing and distributing the assets of the estate is called an **executor** (for a man) or **executrix** (for a woman).

A person who has left a will is said to have died testate. Absent a will, state law will provide for the distribution of the estate. In this instance, the decedent died **intestate.** A representative who reports to the court about the distribution of the estate, as per state law, is an **administrator,** if male, and an **administratrix,** if female.

Probating an estate involves distributing the estate according to the instructions in the will. If the decedent died without a will, the process is called administration. Many jurisdictions have created a probate court to deal with such matters, among other things.

2.   *Software*

The following software, offered as an example of what software can do regarding wills, comes from National Lawforms, http://nationallawforms.com/estate/software-last-will-and-testament.asp, copyrighted 2006. Files created by using this software have the suffix .eps.

The software maker has tailored the software to meet the requirements of probate law in each state. For illustrative purposes, the images of the software used here reflect the legal requirements of the Commonwealth of Massachusetts regarding wills. Other sources of this kind of software include http://www.easy-soft-usa.com/, www.lawfirmsoftware.com/software/last_will.htm and http://www.dplprofessionalsolutions.com/will_systems.asp.

All images taken from this software are copyrighted by the creator of such images and inclusion of such images in this text does not constitute any copyright interest or claim in them.

3.   *Estate Planning*

Estate planning means preparing a will that reflects the client's wishes. Critically, this involves identifying a client's assets. Among other functions, the first screen of the software provides an option to launch a client questionnaire to gather necessary information for the drafting of the will.

Figure 9.58
National LawForms Last Will and Testament Software—Getting Started screen

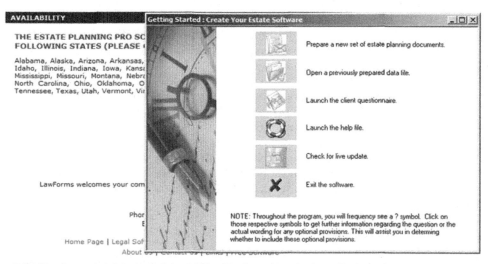

National Law Forms - An Industry Leader in Legal Software Development, targeting the Legal Professional. Streamline the preparation of Legal Documents. Our legal software products include: Bankruptcy Software (Chapters 7, 11, and 13) with Electronic Case Filing, ECF, Estate Planning Software, Trust Software, Wills Software, Incorporation Software, Limited Liability Company Software, LLC Software, LLP Software, Family Limited Partnership Software, Mortgage Loan Software (includes; FNMA 1003 Application, Good Faith Estimate and Truth in Lending Regulation-Z), National Uniform Commercial Code Financing Statement and Real Estate Closing Software (includes; 1099-S, Amortization Software, Escrow Disclosure Software, HUD-1 Software, HUD-1A Software), Living Trust Software. Corporation Record Books, Corporate Seals and Stock Certificates and an extensive list of Legal Forms are also available!

National LawForms, Inc. does not rent, sell, or share any of your personal information with 3rd parties in accordance with our Privacy Policy.

The screen that then appears has tabs and pulldown menus familiar to most users of Microsoft software, including File, Edit, and Help.

a. Gathering Data

To generate a will involves gathering critical information, including:

→ The identity of the maker of the will, as testator or testatrix;
→ A **conservator** (or guardian) of the estate who will preserve the assets pending the probating of the will;
→ A personal representative, to serve as an **agent,** with authority to fulfill the maker's instructions regarding ongoing management of property, pending the probating of the will; and
→ Personal effects, which means any personal property that the decedent had owned.

b. Children

Because children often receive the assets of an estate, identifying these children can have a significant impact. The maker may need to designate in the will a guardian for the care of minor children, and a guardian for management of property in the estate, with instructions about how to distribute it to such minor children once they reach the age of majority.

A child may contest, or challenge, the validity of the will, especially if the maker expressly did not provide for the distribution of the estate's assets to the child, as reflected by the evocative phrase, "I have cut you out of my will." Some states might mandate, however, that any surviving child receive some portion of the estate, regardless of what the will says.

4.   Useful Documents

The software can also generate useful documents, based upon the data gathered, in addition to a will.

Figure 9.59
National LawForms Last Will and Testament Software—Attorney Information submenu: Document assembly

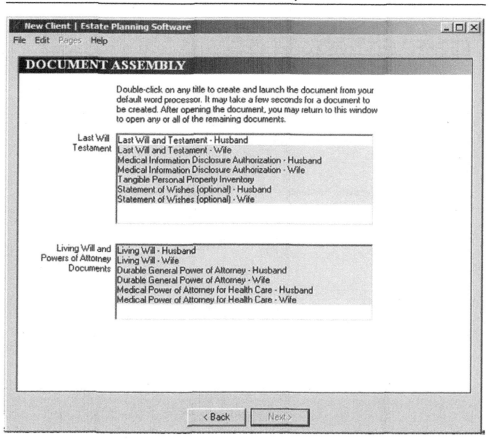

a. Power of Attorney

Under the law, an agent will act on behalf of the interests of a **principal.** This means that the agent has received a grant of authority to accomplish a goal or goals set forth by the principal. Sometimes the document used to create the agency is known as the power of attorney. Creating an agency could mean that an incapacitated person has someone who will look out for that person's interests during the time of such **incapacitation.**

b. Durable Power of Attorney

A durable power of attorney means that the grant of authority in an agent extends beyond the completion of any specific task.

Figure 9.60
**National LawForms Last Will and Testament Software—Attorney Information submenu:
Durable power of attorney**

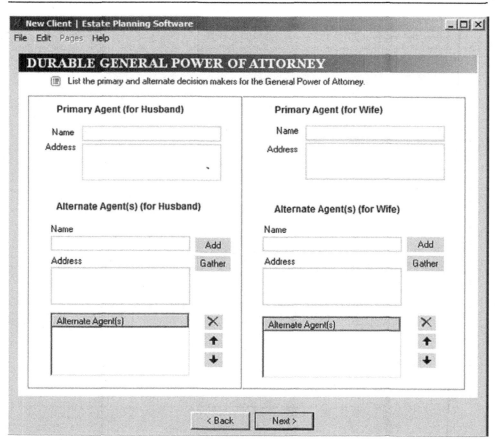

Not surprisingly, the software asks about the scope of the authority that the principal wishes to vest in the agent. This authority might empower the agent to handle:

Figure 9.61
National LawForms Last Will and Testament Software—Attorney Information submenu: Durable power of attorney, continued

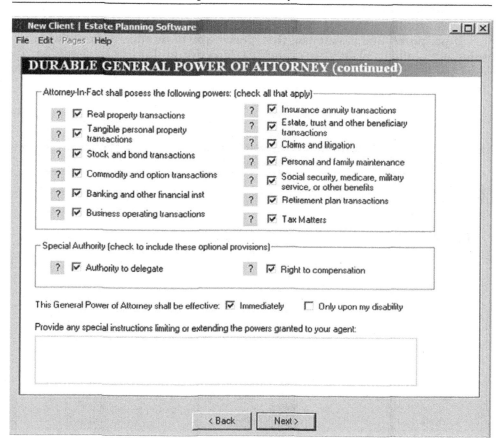

→ Real estate transactions;
→ Personal property transactions;
→ Stocks and bonds transactions;
→ Banking and other such financial matters;
→ Claims and litigation;
→ Personal and family maintenance;
→ Retirement plan transactions; and
→ Tax matters.

Also, the durable power of attorney can empower the agent to:

→ Delegate authority, by having someone else complete the actions required of the agent; and
→ Receive compensation for services rendered.

c.   Medical Power of Attorney

If permitted under state law, this special type of durable power of attorney, sometimes called a healthcare or medical directive, authorizes an agent to make only medical decisions on behalf of an incapacitated principal, during the period of incapacitation.

Figure 9.62
National LawForms Last Will and Testament Software—Attorney Information submenu: Medical power of attorney

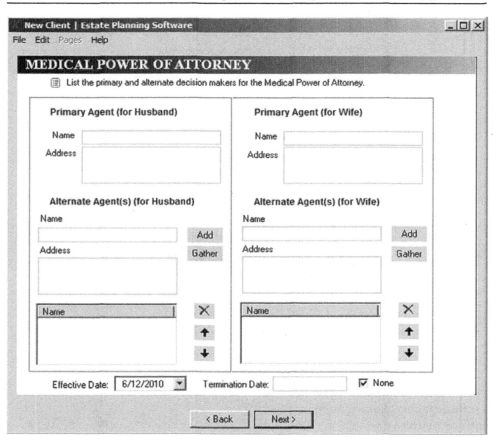

d. Living Will

Depending on a state's laws, a so-called living will can be another way for an agent to act on behalf of an incapacitated principal. Jurisdictions vary on the terms used for this type of power of attorney.

Figure 9.63
National LawForms Last Will and Testament Software—Attorney Information submenu: Living will

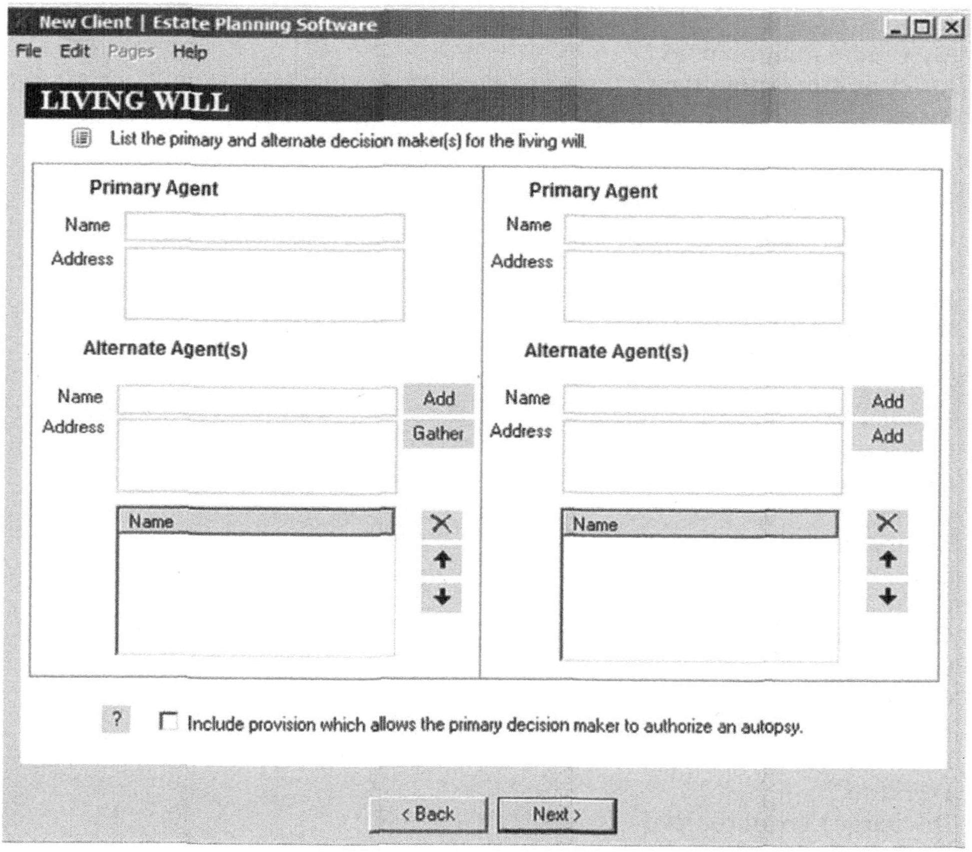

G. CONCLUSION

Lawyers have an obligation to clients to work efficiently and effectively. Given the complexity of many areas of the law, software can streamline the delivery of services to a client, increasing speed and reducing the chance of mistakes. Topic-specific software typically prompts a user for information to generate a form so that, for example, real estate closing software will complete the HUD-1, a document required under federal law, to complete the sale of property.

H.   TERMS

Accounts payable
Accounts receivable
Adjustments
Administrator
Administratrix
Affidavit
Agent
Alimony
Alternative minimum tax
Articles of Incorporation
Assets
Assignments
Attests
Bankruptcy
Bankruptcy code
Beneficiary
Binder
Broker
Bylaws
Chapter 7
Chapter 11
Chapter 13
Child support
Closing
Complaint
Conservator
Contract
Corporation
Creditors
Creditor matrix
Debtor/petitioner
Deed
Directors
Discharge in bankruptcy
Dividends
Docket number
Durable power of attorney
Escrow account
Estate
Executor
Executrix
Exempt
Exhibits
Form 1099-S
Grant
Grantee
Grantor

Guardian
HUD-1
Incapacitation
Intestate
Involuntary petition
Itemized deductions
Lease
Ledger
Liabilities
Lien
Limited liability corporation
Liquidation
Living will
Means test
Medical power of attorney
Meeting minutes
Mortgage
Notarization
Officers
Owner
Pages
Partnership
Payee
Payor
Personal exemptions
Power of attorney
Principal
Probating an estate
Property
Proxy
Real estate
Real estate binder
Registry of deeds
Reorganization
Resident agent
Resolutions
Schedules
Secured loans
Settlement agent
Share
Statements
Stock
Stock options
Stock register
Stockholder
Subchapter S corporation
Tax credits
Tax proration
Tenant
Testator

Testatrix
Title
Title search
Trust
Trustee
Unsecured loans
Voluntary petition
Will

I.   HYPOTHETICALS

1.   Complete the bankruptcy form for a voluntary petition of an individual filing
     under Chapter 7 using the following information.
       Checking account balance $50
          House, valued at $378,000, $298,000 due on mortgage; owned since
       August, 2000
          Rental property, valued at $250,000; mortgage of $197,500; occupied by
       tenant who pays $950/month
          Car, 1997 Mazda Protégé, worth $2300, fair market value
          Computer, tablet, valued at $250
          Computer, desktop, valued at $500
          Computer, laptop, valued at $950
          Computer monitors (2), valued at $50 each
          Laser printer, valued at $45
          TV, valued at $750
          Household goods, approximately $500
          Artwork, Dave Cockrum (2 pieces), $500 each
          SEP-IRA, $19,000
          Roth-IRA, $46,000

       Income
       $500/week from D-U.edu
       $125/week from A-U.edu
       $400/week from B-U.edu
       $85/week from N-U.edu
       $75/week book royalties
       No other sources of income

       Debt
       $12,000/year, tuition
       $24,000/year, credit card debt
       $230,000, gambling debt
       $87,000, personal loan
       $176,000, damages in a lawsuit
       $235,000, student loans
       No other outstanding debt/liabilities

Has never filed for bankruptcy before
No spouse
Social security number XXX-XX-0277

2.   Complete the HUD-1 using the following information.
Buyer:
Cordwainer Smith (M)
Identifies as White; U.S. citizen, not a veteran, not disabled
Age: 54
Highest level of education: Juris Doctor
First-time home buyer
Social security number XXX-XX-0277
Never filed for bankruptcy
$3,000 in savings account
$63,000 in Roth-IRA, SEP-IRA
No other debt or financial obligations
No co-applicant
Monthly living expenses: approx. $2000/month
Current residence: 2154 Cummings Avenue, Unit 3G, Quincy, MA 02171

Two dependents, who reside with buyer: Emil (M), age 13, Jane (F), age 11

Annual income: approx. $80,000, consultant (20+ years); royalties, $200/week
No other source of income
Down payment: $48,000

Property being purchased: 2779 Cummings Avenue, Quincy, MA 02171

Agreed-upon price: $298,000

Able to secure a mortgage of $250,000, at 4%, for 30 years, fixed rate, from
Tesseract Savings and Loan
1958 Aborn Place
Peabody, MA 01960
Telephone: 978-555-5555
Monthly payment: $1350
Monthly escrow: $450

3.   Divorce financials
Use the following information to prepare a financial agreement to accompany a divorce settlement.

Payor:
Cordwainer Smith (M) currently married to payee
D.O.B. 04/01/1958
Residence: 2779 Cummings Avenue, Quincy, MA 02171
Homeowner; approx $2,000 monthly mortgage, escrow payments, total
Annual property tax $3600 (included in escrow)

Two dependents, who reside with payee: Emil (M), age 13, Jane (F), age 11

Annual income: approx. $100,000, licensed psychologist (17 years)
 No other source of income
$43,000 pension
$13,000 Roth-IRA
$7,000 Mutual Fund
Wedding band, $200
Car, 1997 Mazda Protégé, worth $2300, fair market value
Not subject to the Alternative Minimum Tax

Payee:
Jan Harris (F)
D.O.B. 04/01/1960 currently married to payor
Residence: 3124 S. Willard St., Burlington, VT 05401
Homeowner; approx $2,000 monthly mortgage, escrow payments, total
 Annual property tax $3600 (included in escrow)
Two dependents, who reside with payee: Emil (M), age 13, Jane (F), age 11

Annual income: approx. $80,000, consultant (20+years); royalties, $200/week
 No other source of income
$3,000 in savings account
$63,000 in Roth-IRA, SEP-IRA
Car, 2004 Subaru Forester, worth $4000, fair market value
Wedding band and ring: approx. $2000

Not subject to the Alternative Minimum Tax

Proposed

Child support: Payor to Payee, $1800/month

No alimony

Education expenses, both dependents (private school and/or college fund)
 Payor to Payee, $1000/month
Visitation:
Two weeks during summer
   One school vacation/year
   Alternating Christmas, December
   Four weekend visits/year

4. Using the estate planning software, prepare a "single revocable living trust," "wills and powers of attorney documents," using the following data and instructions.
   a. For password, use "Demo"
   b. For estate planning documents, select "single revocable living trust"

    c.   Attorney information
        Attorney:
        Guay Associates, LLP
        Attorney George Guay
        P.O. Box XX1
        Arkham, MA 01066
        Phone: 617-555-0001
        Fax: 617-555-0002

    d.   Grantor: Catullus Family Trust, Arkham, Norfolk County, MA
        Arthur Gordon Pym
        P.O. Box XX2
        Arkham, MA 01066
        Does not have former spouse

    e.   Primary trustee/co-trustee: No
        Attorney George Guay
        P.O. Box XX1
        Arkham, MA 01066
        Co-trustee

    f.   Successor trustee(s)
        Guay Associates, LLP
        Attorney Emile Guay
        P.O. Box XX1
        Arkham, MA 01066
        Will act jointly with co-trustee

    g.   Beneficiaries
        Janine Tym
        P.O. Box XX3
        Arkham, MA 01066
        Relationship: ex-wife
        100%
        Distribution is *per stirpes*
        Beneficiary is not a child of the grantor

    h.   Final distribution to beneficiaries
        Distribute immediately

    i.   Special distributions
        Edwin Jarvis
        P.O. Box XX4
        Arkham, MA 01066
        Property: all my scientific equipment

    j.   Contingent beneficiary: yes
        Edward Jarvis
        P.O. Box XX4
        Arkham, MA 01066

    k.   Durable general power of attorney
        Primary agent:
        Guay Associates, LLP
        Attorney George Guay
        P.O. Box XX1
        Arkham, MA 01066
        Alternate agent:

Guay Associates, LLP
Attorney Emile Guay
P.O. Box XX1
Arkham, MA 01066
Also:
Guay Associates, LLP
P.O. Box XX1
Arkham, MA 01066
Attorney-In -Fact should have all authority, as well as all special
authority, with General Power of Attorney effective immediately.

l. Medical Power of Attorney
Primary Agent:
Guay Associates, LLP
Attorney George Guay
P.O. Box XX1
Arkham, MA 01066
Alternate Agent:
Hamish Blake, MD
P.O. Box XX5
Arkham, MA 01066
Effective immediately, with no termination date

m. Pour over will
Primary Agent:
Guay Associates, LLP
Attorney George Guay
P.O. Box XX1
Arkham, MA 01066
Alternate Agent:
Guay Associates, LLP
Attorney Emile Guay
P.O. Box XX1
Arkham, MA 01066
Guay Associates, LLP
P.O. Box XX1
Arkham, MA 01066
Wishes body to be cremated
No minor children

n. Living will
Primary Agent:
Guay Associates, LLP
Attorney George Guay
P.O. Box XX1
Arkham, MA 01066
Alternate Agent:
Guay Associates, LLP
Attorney Emile Guay
P.O. Box XX1
Arkham, MA 01066
Guay Associates, LLP
P.O. Box XX1

        Arkham, MA 01066

        Check of the option to allow primary decision maker to authorize an autopsy

   o.   Document assembly

        Click "Generate all documents"

        For Living Trust Wizard, designate a folder on a drive, creating all, then close

        Now, close the application

5. Using the estate planning software and the password "Demo," prepare a "last will and testament," with all "wills and powers of attorney documents," using the following data and instructions.

   a.   Attorney information

        Attorney:

        Guay Associates, LLP

        Attorney George Guay

        P.O. Box XX1

        Arkham, MA 01066

        Phone: 617-555-0001

        Fax: 617-555-0002

   b.   Testator

        Norfolk County, MA

        Eric Blair

        P.O. Box XX7

        Arkham, MA 01066

        D.O.B. April 1, 1960

        SSN: 000-00-0000

        Provide for child of testator

        Daniella Blair

        P.O. Box XX8

        Arkham, MA 01066

        Gender: Female

        D.O.B. May 17, 1980

   c.   Conservator of my property

        Attorney George Guay

        P.O. Box XX1

        Arkham, MA 01066

        Alternate:

        Guay Associates, LLP

        Attorney Emile Guay

        P.O. Box XX1

        Arkham, MA 01066

   d.   Guardian of my children

        Desdemona Rathbone

        P.O. Box XX9

        Arkham, MA 01066

        Alternate:

        Attorney George Guay

        P.O. Box XX1

        Arkham, MA 01066

   e.   Personal representative

        Attorney George Guay
        P.O. Box XX1
        Arkham, MA 01066
        Alternate:
        Guay Associates, LLP
        Attorney Emile Guay
        P.O. Box XX1
        Arkham, MA 01066

f.   Trustee of minor children
        Attorney George Guay
        P.O. Box XX1
        Arkham, MA 01066
        Alternate:
        Guay Associates, LLP
        Attorney Emile Guay
        P.O. Box XX1
        Arkham, MA 01066

g.   Personal effects
        Body to be cremated
        Residence to:
        Daniella Blair
        P.O. Box XX8
        Arkham, MA 01066
        Disinherit everyone but:
        Daniella Blair
        P.O. Box XX8
        Arkham, MA 01066
        Special gifts:
        G. Orwell, all intellectual property
        Other directions:
        Provide for the annual reading, in a public forum, of the novel, "1984"
        No surviving beneficiaries, then give to:
        Miskatonic University, English Department
        P.O. Box XX10
        Arkham, MA 01066

h.   Durable power of attorney
        Attorney George Guay
        P.O. Box XX1
        Arkham, MA 01066
        Alternates:
        Guay Associates, LLP
        Attorney Emile Guay
        P.O. Box XX1
        Arkham, MA 01066
        Guay Associates, LLP
        P.O. Box XX1
        Arkham, MA 01066
        Check all items
        Make general power of attorney immediately effective

Special instructions:

Attorney-in-Fact needs to secure services of conservator for all intellectual property

  i. Medical power of attorney

      Primary Agent:

      Guay Associates, LLP

      Attorney George Guay

      P.O. Box XX1

      Arkham, MA 01066

      Alternate Agent:

      Hamish Blake, MD

      P.O. Box XX5

      Arkham, MA 01066

      Effective immediately, with no termination date

  j. Living will

      Primary Agent:

      Guay Associates, LLP

      Attorney George Guay

      P.O. Box XX1

      Arkham, MA 01066

      Alternate Agent:

      Guay Associates, LLP

      Attorney Emile Guay

      P.O. Box XX1

      Arkham, MA 01066

      Guay Associates, LLP

      P.O. Box XX1

      Arkham, MA 01066

Check of the option to allow primary decision maker to authorize an autopsy

  k. Document assembly

      Select "Last Will and Testament"

      Now, close the application

6. Answer

  b. Testator screen: effective date can vary; could also select child of deceased child of testator, using "Add" button.

  g. Personal Effects screen: can change any of these options, especially special gifts and other directions, as opportunity to explore choices.

  h. Durable Power of Attorney screen: can change any of the options checked; could also vary special instructions.

CHAPTER

10

Practice Management and Case Management Software

OBJECTIVES

→ Explore the utility of electronic information management.
→ Study the nature of practice management software.
→ Differentiate between front office and back office applications of practice management software.
→ Contrast the functions of practice management software from case management software.
→ Develop an understanding about case management software and how it differs from practice management software.
→ Investigate how case management software can perform, for example, an analysis of a deposition transcript.
→ Understand how a defensible discovery strategy relates to assessing electronically stored information when preparing a response to a request for discovery.
→ Survey software that does one or the other function, or that integrates them.

INTRODUCTION

Software that can better manage the services offered by a legal practice and simplify routine business practices can enhance a law firm's productivity.

A.   CRITICAL SOFTWARE CONCEPTS

1.   *The Database*

Software for improving the productivity of a law office generally relies upon data, typically kept in a **database.** The database, often stored on a central **server,** organizes data in a series of files, making it accessible to anyone with a connection to the server. A database can contain client-related data, such as:

→ Contact information;
→ Who at the firm did what kind of work and when;
→ Copies of all work done, such as letters, legal memoranda, and briefs; and
→ Bills for the work done.

In a database, data must be recorded in a particular format, such as name first, then date of initial contact, then type of legal problem. Using a standardized format allows different kinds of software, like for billing or generating tax forms, to process data differently, depending upon the need.

2.   *Practice Management Software Versus Case Management Software*

Practice management software would encompass all activity done on behalf of the client, from court appearances to billing. **Case management software** would focus narrowly on the client's legal problem and its status, such as getting ready for trial. Practice management software can integrate neatly with case management software. For example, using case management software, a lawyer could file a complaint on behalf of a client. The practice management software could take note of this to set up a preliminary bill for the lawyer's time spent preparing and filing that complaint. Integrating this software could increase efficiency and decrease the likelihood of error, because the practice management software would automatically keep track of the lawyer's time since the lawyer drafted the complaint on the system.

B.   THE NATURE OF PRACTICE MANAGEMENT SOFTWARE

Practice management software increases the efficiency for performing common business office functions, such as generating correspondence, documents, records of accounting, and data. This can mean harnessing the processing speeds of a CPU through the use of application software, like a spreadsheet.

In addition to automating the process of preparing bills, for example, practice management software could even identify opportunities for increased productivity. By taking note of the types of legal services that a legal practice provides in a month, the firm could launch an Internet marketing campaign, touting the kinds of services that the firm provides.

1.   *Front Office and Back Office*

Most business offices divide their operations into front office or back office activities. **Front office activities** would deal with all aspects of client contact, such as the gathering of client information or the completing of a client transaction. These activities include:

→ Time management, especially focusing on deadlines;

→ Tracking potential conflicts of interest, which can raise ethical issues for a firm;

→ Document management, for keeping track of documents in a client's case;

→ Contract management, relating to legally enforceable agreements;

→ Contact management, critical for remaining connected to client;

→ Communications management, from phone messages to faxes;

→ Report management, especially helpful when deciding how to run a legal practice; and

→ Remote access, for access to a firm's database anywhere outside of the office.

Back office operations involve those business practices common to any business. These include:

→ Accounting and billing, such as accounts payable and accounts receivable; and

→ A ledger, which provides a detailed overview of all income and expenses for a business.

a.   Front Office Functions

Front office activities focus on managing each client's case.

i.   Contact Management

Software can work like the old-style Rolodex, which made contact information quick and easy to find. Now, a lawyer or paralegal can more easily transfer a copy of contact information to a smartphone, for example, and can synchronize changes made to the original information. The software can find contacts faster and make it easier to change contact information. In the example from Time-Matters, buttons on the top toolbar make it easy to find and edit contact information.

Figure 10.1
TimeMatters—Buttons: Example—Contact

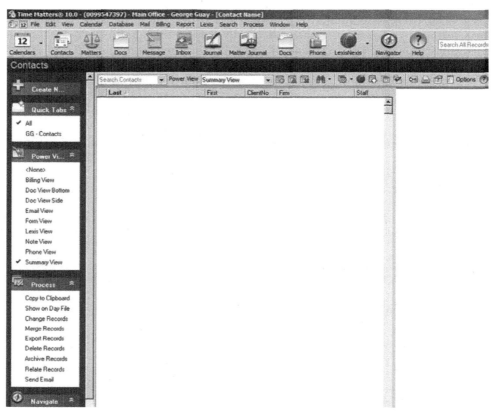

ii. Communications Management

Having software that records text (like e-mail and instant messages), as well as audio messages, can make it easier to search for messages and copy them to a portable device, like a laptop or smartphone, for later reference. The example from TimeMatters depicts the message management screen that the lawyer or paralegal would see upon clicking the Navigator button, seen in the previous figure.

Figure 10.2
TimeMatters—Side toolbar Navigator communications

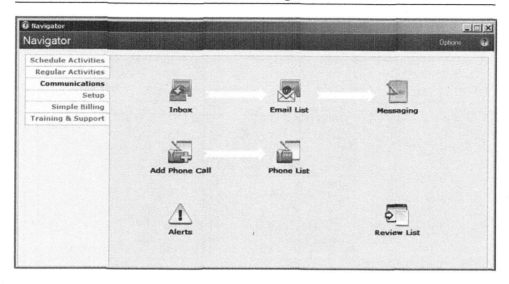

iii. *Time Management*

Time management involves the delivery of services efficiently and effectively. For example, **calendaring software** can keep future appointments organized. A law firm needs good time management software because of several issues typically associated with the practice of law, which are discussed next.

Figure 10.3
AbacusLaw—Daily calendar screen

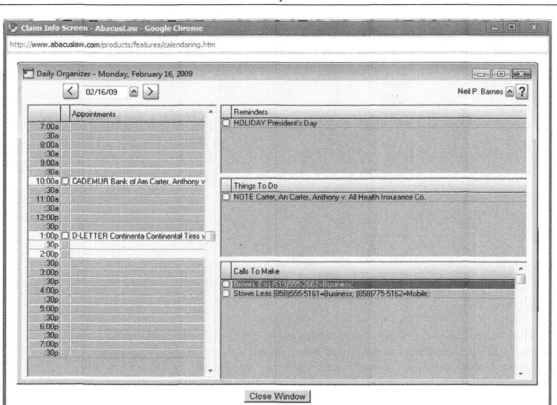

I.   Statutes of Limitation

A lawyer must file a complaint about a client's legal problem by a particular time, usually from the date when the problem arose. Failure to do so means that the complaint is barred because of a **statute of limitation,** which requires the timely filing of a claim. Calendaring software should take note of such deadlines, especially to notify a lawyer when that time is approaching for filing a complaint for a client. By issuing such "**ticklers**" the lawyer has advanced notice of an impending deadline.

II.   Tracking

Courts need to keep track of their cases. To manage a large number of cases, some jurisdictions have created schedules, or **tracks,** which establish a timetable for getting the case to trial. Calendaring software, which records and keeps track of the dates that the court has assigned for a client's case on a particular track, makes it easier for a legal practice to meet tracking deadlines.

III.   Docketing

Courts keep track of deadlines created by the parties. For example, a party might serve on an opponent a request for discovery, which might need to be completed in 30 days. The court records such deadlines in a **docket,** to keep track of activities for a specific case. Software that can synchronize with a court docket serves as another way for a legal practice to keep track of developments in a case.

IV.   Rules

A lawyer could create rules for the calendaring software so that, for example, new deadlines are automatically generated upon a new development in a case. Parties might set up a negotiation deadline that does not correspond to specific deadlines for a case. They might agree to talk about a settlement in a case in two months, but would not necessarily have needed to do this to comply with the track that the court has assigned to the specific case.

V.   Continuing Legal Education

If a jurisdiction requires lawyers to earn continuing education units, calendaring software could keep a running total of time spent keeping up with these obligations, as well as indicate when a lawyer needs to do more.

VI.   Commitments

Calendaring software can generate a timeline to help a lawyer coordinate work commitments at the law firm. For example, it can alert an attorney when a potential scheduling conflict arises.

For a practice, this can produce an overview of the time commitments of every attorney, alerting the firm about a potential need for additional help. The firm would know, for example, when a lawyer plans to take time off for a vacation and would then know how to plan for this.

VII.   Coordinating

Calendaring software can:

→ Allow for the coordination of the schedules of lawyers assigned to a particular case;
→ Facilitate the efficient use of conference rooms and other meeting places;

→ Enhance the usefulness of work collaboration software, like Lotus Notes or Novell Groupwise; and

→ Synchronize a lawyer's calendar across multiple platforms, so that an appointment recorded on a smartphone shows up in the firm's database when the lawyer connects the smartphone to the firm's network.

iv.   Avoiding Conflicts of Interest

Lawyers must take care when considering whether to take on a new client, that a potential client's problems will not involve a previous client of the firm. For example, if a client has sued an insurance carrier to recover under the terms of a policy, the firm might not subsequently represent that insurance carrier to respond to a suit about the validity of a denial of a claim. This example, from Tabs3, shows how software might help a firm to determine whether a conflict exists.

Figure 10.4
Tabs3—Determining whether a potential conflict of interest arises

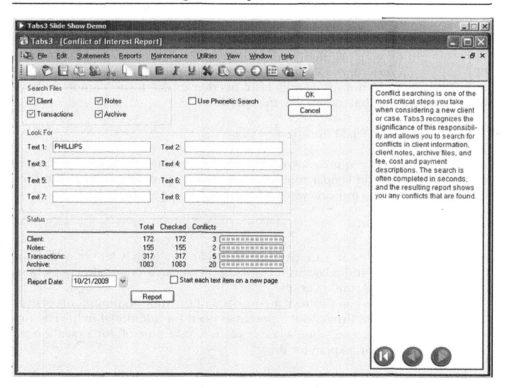

Practice management software could help identify a potential conflict of interest by looking at:

→ The legal services provided, such as making a court appearance or preparing an opinion letter;

→ The nature of a client's problem, such as a divorce or the sale of real estate;
→ Whether lawyers hired from another firm might have done work related to a new client's business; and
→ Identifying characteristics, such as names, case names, or dates.

A firm can still take on the new client's business, even though a conflict exists, if it creates a so-called **ethical wall.** This would effectively isolate those who worked on the first case from working on the new client's case, as though a "wall" had been erected.

v.   Document Management

I.   Index

Software might organize data, via an index, according to client, case type, year, or other sorting-related criteria, making it easier to find documents.

II.   Templates

Documents generated for other cases, such as a complaint or request for discovery, could serve as a **template** for when a lawyer or paralegal needs to create similar documents for a new case. Also, using a template can take advantage of the initial review for accuracy done after creating the template and not have to repeat that review with subsequent uses of the template. In addition to using those documents as the basis for creating a template, the software itself might provide templates. Sites like HotDocs, at www.hotdocs.com, from HotDocs Ltd., has automated the process of generating standardized documents from templates.

vi.   Contract Management

Contracts, which are legally enforceable agreements, can create obligations for a law firm and/or a client. Software that keeps track of these obligations can, for example:

→ Generate a "tickler," a reminder, about an impending deadline;
→ Automate the modification of a contract, such as when the parties want to extend a deadline;
→ Organize priorities, through the coordination of payments as specified within the contract; or
→ Issue bills periodically, per the terms of the contract.

Software might have contract templates which lawyers could use as the starting point for writing up a contract. Using a template can insure that certain standard language, such as the consequences to a party for breaching the contract, will be included.

vii.   Report Management

Reports can help lawyers in a legal practice understand different management concerns regarding the operation of a legal practice. Using an example from TimeMatters, a report could contain:

→ An overview of cases;
→ A history of the installation and upgrading of software used in the legal practice;
→ A description of firm expenses, like rent and insurance, thereby allowing the lawyers to figure out what bills need to be paid first; and
→ A review of services previously provided, like preparing a will or generating a contract for buying real estate, for use in crafting a marketing strategy.

Figure 10.5
TimeMatters—Top toolbar: Pulldown menus, Types of reports

viii.   Remote Access

When out of the office, software can allow an attorney or paralegal to access a firm's database via the World Wide Web, thereby making it easier to work on a client matter. This is known as **remote access.** Because lawyers have an ethical obligation to keep client information confidential, the software needs to have in place safeguards against inadvertent access to or disclosure of such data.

b.   Back Office Operations

Back office operations involve those business practices common to any business. To run efficiently, all businesses need to keep track of bills and generate appropriate tax documents. If "front office" involved working with customers in public, then "back office" historically meant the work that customers typically would not see, such as generating bills or keeping track of payments from clients.

i.   *Accounting and Billing*

Lawyers have an ethical obligation to account for all of a client's property, including funds and personal property.

I.   Client's Funds Accounts

Lawyers may end up holding funds on behalf of a client, such as payments made by an insurance company to settle a client's personal injury suit, but these are the client's funds, not the lawyer's. The lawyer cannot deduct from those funds any fees for services rendered until the lawyer has presented the bill to the client for review and approval. It follows, then, that accounts holding only clients' funds must be kept separate from any of a law firm's accounts, to avoid the risk of commingling funds.

Clients' funds must be kept in an interest-bearing account, known as an **Interest On Lawyer Trust Account (IOLTA).** Whenever a firm receives funds on behalf of a client, it must deposit them in the IOLTA. A failure to do so could result in a lawyer having to face allegations of violation of an ethical obligation. Therefore, back office software needs to record receipt of funds and their deposit into the correct account for clients' funds.

II.   Billing

The lawyer's ethical obligation to provide timely accounting also means that a firm must generate accurate bills. An easy way to generate an accurate monthly bill would involve using software that records time spent on a client's case when any employee works on a case. Software for generating bills needs to take into account the firm's payment arrangement with the client. For example, a client might be billed:

→ By the hour;
→ Under a flat fee;
→ Contingent upon the client receiving a financial recovery;
→ For a minimum, periodically billed, fee;
→ According to a payment plan;
→ Against a retainer; or
→ For recurring work by day, week, or month.

ii.   *Ledger*

The back office functions of a law firm include keeping a **ledger,** which will keep track of income and expenditures. For example, the PCLaw software packages give the firm options to look at monthly or annual financial transactions.

Figure 10.6
PCLaw—Toolbars: General Ledger tab

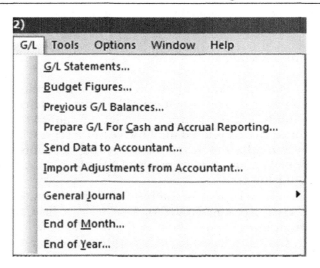

Such software could make it easy to search for transactions by:

→ Ledger entry;
→ Type of transaction;
→ Subject matter; or
→ Client.

A ledger would keep track of:

→ Checks, such as for supplies or for payroll;
→ State and/or federal payroll taxes, and could generate the federal W-2 income tax forms a firm must issue annually for each employee; and
→ The amounts and awarding of bonus pay.

The software could:

→ Keep track of financial transactions for larger firms, for each office, or for the entire legal practice;
→ Generate reports for intervals, such as weekly or monthly, or by type of legal services provided;
→ Integrate with widely used bookkeeping software, such as Quicken; and
→ Facilitate a thorough review of a firm's transactions, when auditing the ledger.

2.   *Types of Practice Management Software*

a.   AbacusLaw

AbacusLaw practice management software, at www.abacuslaw.com, provides these functions, and makes it easy to synchronize computers so that they all contain the same data. For example, a new e-mail sent via a laptop will get copied automatically to a desktop computer, once they are connected for synchronization.

The front office features of AbacusLaw include the option to:

→ Generate the daily calendar of an employee;
→ Produce forms to fill out, like a complaint;
→ Create reports from preselected data;

Figure 10.7
AbacusLaw—Report characteristics screen

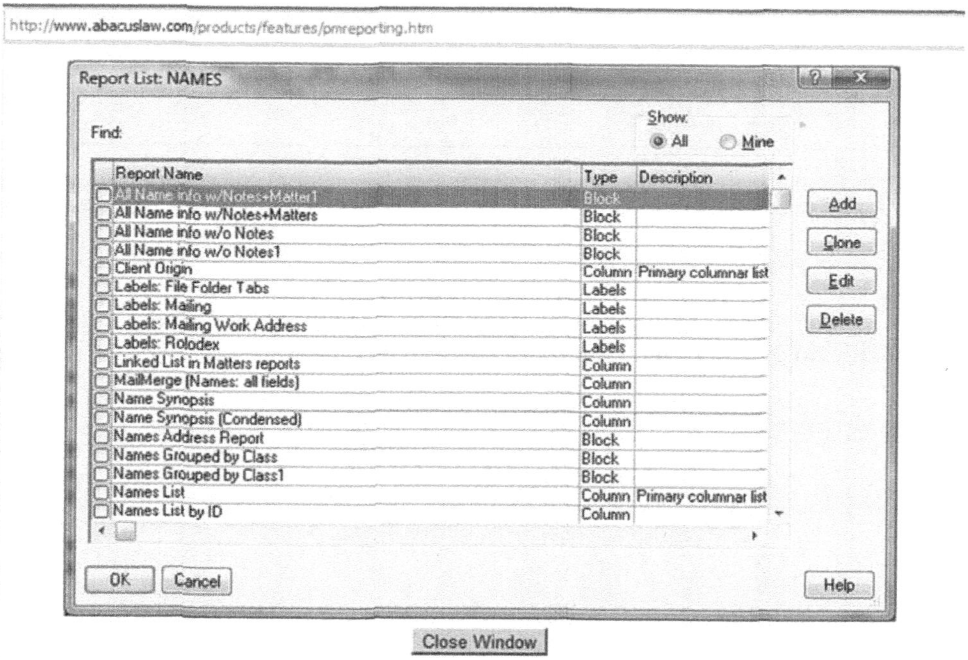

→ Record client information; and

Figure 10.8
AbacusLaw—Client information screen

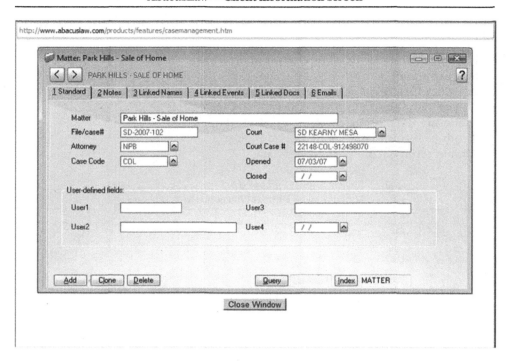

→ Provide an overview of all matters related to a case.

Figure 10.9
AbacusLaw—Client's associated legal matters

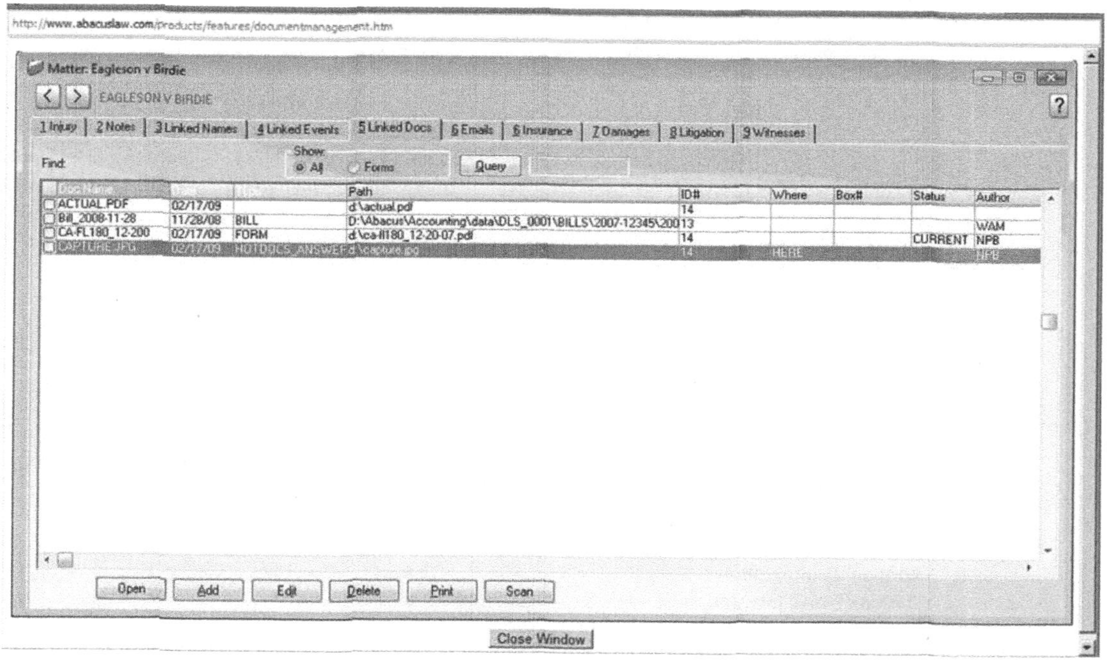

Other front office functions available when using AbacusLaw include:

→ Conflict checking;
→ Automatic creation of legal documents;
→ Contact management;
→ Contract management;
→ Document management;
→ Communications management; and
→ Remote access.

In addition to offering typical back office features, such as keeping track of clients' funds in trust accounts, this software makes it possible for a firm to accept credit card payments and generate 1099 forms, as per federal law, whenever making a payment to a contractor.

b. Amicus Attorney

The robust practice management software offered at www.amicusattorney. com provides a typical array of useful functions. These include front office features, like managing contacts or calendaring, and back office functions, like bill generation and maintaining a ledger. Amicus Attorney comes in different packages, including one designed for a small firm: http://www.amicusattorney.com/products/comparison.html.

Figure 10.10
Amicus—Chart showing features of versions of Amicus software

Product Comparison Chart

This quick reference chart shows some of the key differences between various 2013 Amicus products:

	Premium Edition	Premium Edition with Billing	Small Firm Edition	Amicus Cloud
Maximum Number of Users	Unlimited	Unlimited	10	Unlimited
Complete Matter Management System	x	x	x	x
Contact Management	x	x	x	x
Calendaring & Docketing	x	x	x	x
Time Tracking & Management	x	x	x	x
Communications Management	x	x	x	x
Notes & Stickies Management	x	x	x	
Favorites	x	x	x	
Library For Knowledge Management	x	x	x	
Document Management	x	x	x	x
Document Assembly	x	x	x	coming soon
Microsoft Word Integration	x	x	x	
Corel WordPerfect Integration	x	x	x	
HotDocs Integration	x	x	x	
Adobe PDF Integration	x	x	x	
Outlook E-mail Integration	x	x	x	x
Outlook Calendar & Contacts Synchronization	x	x	x	x
Ability to Synchronize with Mobile Devices	x	x	x	x
Accounting Product Links & Export Templates	x	x	x	x
CompuLaw Integration	x	x	x	
Custom Fields for Files & Contacts	x	x	x	Files only
File Intake Form	x	x	x	
Conflict Checking	x	x	x	x
Precedents	x	x	x	
Group & Firm-Wide Calendars	x	x	x	x
Relate Email & Documents to Events	x	x	x	
Progressive Priority Levels for Tasks	x	x	x	
Show Adjournments	x	x	x	
Customizable Dashboard	x	x	x	
Workgroup Calendars	x	x	x	x
Merge Templates for Email	x	x	x	
Firm Member Availability	x	x	x	x
Work Offline	x	x	x	
End User Reports	x	x	x	x
Scheduled Backups	x	x	x	
Runs on SQL Server 2008/2008R2/2012	x	x		
SQL Report Authoring	x	x		
Receive Daily Agenda Via Email	x	x		
Many-To-Many Relationships	x	x		

Figure 10-10 Continued

	Premium Edition	Premium Edition with Billing	Small Firm Edition	Amicus Cloud
Unlimited Addresses and Phone Numbers	x	x		
Contact Pictures	x	x		
Relate Documents To Contacts	x	x		
Event History Tracking	x	x		
Amicus-Managed Documents (Check-In/Check-Out)	x	x		
Custom Page Designer	x	x		x
Unlimited Custom Fields	x	x		Files only
Custom Records	x	x		
Login From Any Workstation In Your Firm	x	x		x
Connect Over The Internet	x	x		x
Remote Access Capabilities	x	x		x
Citrix / Terminal Services Support	x	x		
Compatible with Amicus Mobile	x	x		
Worldox Integration	x	x		
Dynamic Link With Microsoft Office	x	x		
Sync With Google	x	x		
Firm-Wide Reporting Capabilities	x	x		x
Security Profiles & Record Restrictions	x	x		
Work with Amicus TimeTracker App	x		x	
Work with Amicus Anywhere App	x			
Track Time & Expenses Per Client				x
Easily Generate Bills		x		x
Trust Accounting		x		x
Track Payments		x		x
Manage Trust Accounts		x		x
Track Retainer Balances		x		x
Monitor WIP		x		x
Batch Bill		x		
Send Reminder Statements		x		x
Automatic Backups				x
Pay As You Go				x
Includes Unlimited Support				x
Always Up To Date				x
Billing Alerts		x		

c. Needles

The practice management software provided by Needles, at www.Needles. com, uses toolbars with links, buttons, and drop-down menus in the style of such features used in the Microsoft Office Suite. For front office activities, it also uses tabs for recording critical client information. Lawyers and paralegals have a number of ways to search for data about clients, such as by:

Figure 10.11
Needles—Client information screen

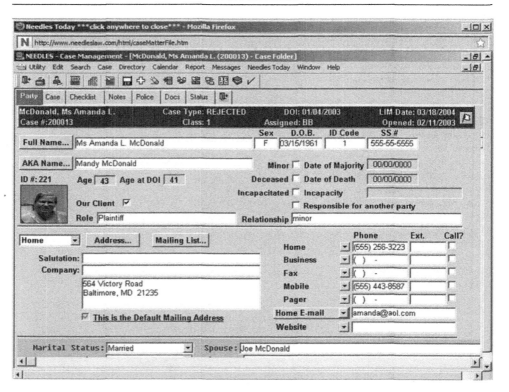

→ The type of case;

Figure 10.12
Needles—Options for search of cases

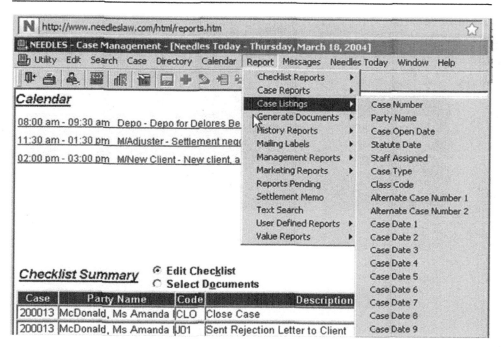

→ Who has worked on a case; and

Figure 10.13
Needles—Screen for searching for documents

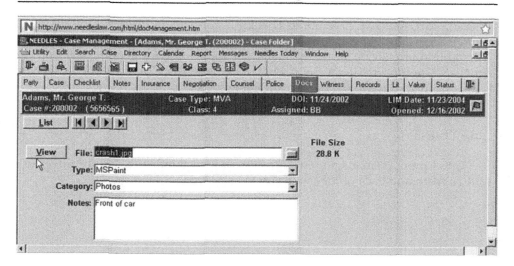

→ Per the particular area of the law, such as personal injury or mass tort cases.

Figure 10.14
Needles—Types of cases that Needles can manage

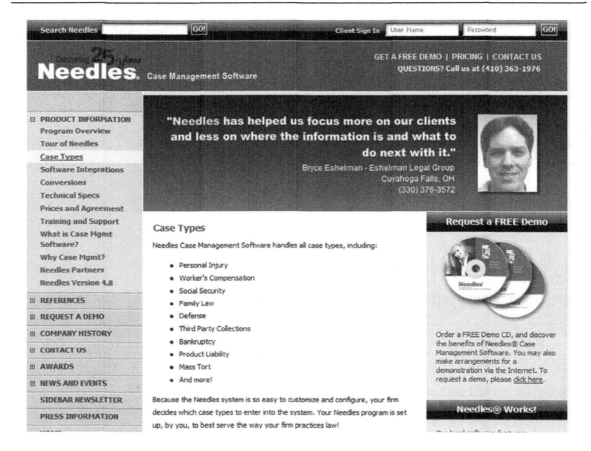

This software makes it possible to check for conflicts of interest and allows for remote access.

In addition to having a case management application for keeping track of case expenses when preparing a client's bill, it can also integrate with the Lexis-Nexis's back office software package, Juris billing software.

d.   Tabs3

Tabs3 practice management software, at www.tabs3.com, has an integrated suite of front and back office functions.

i. Tabs3—Main Task Folder

The default screen for Tabs3, the Main Task Folder, has a toolbar with familiar links, such as View, Window, Help, and File, as well as links to generate reports or statements.

Figure 10.15
Tabs3—Main screen

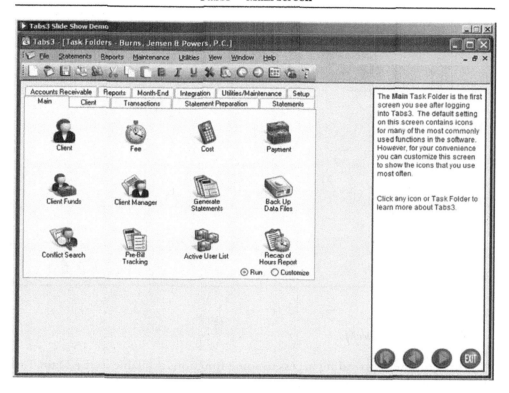

Via tabs, lawyers and paralegals can perform front office functions, like remote access, and back office functions, such as keeping track of bills that clients have not yet paid, known as **accounts receivables.**

Figure 10.16
Tabs3—Links available under the Accounts Receivable tab

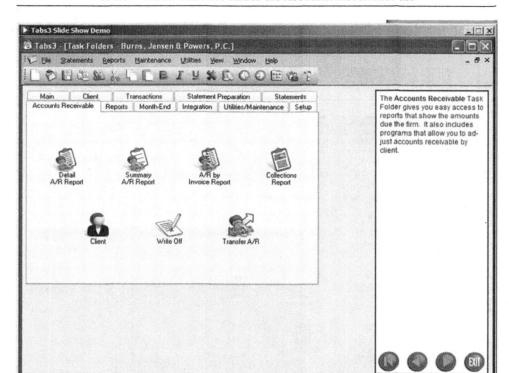

ii.   Tabs3—PracticeMaster

In addition to providing access to some functions available in the Main Task Folder, the Tabs3-PracticeMaster software makes it possible to create e-mail, make eNotes, and browse the web.

Figure 10.17
Tabs3—PracticeMaster: Links available under the Main Screen tab

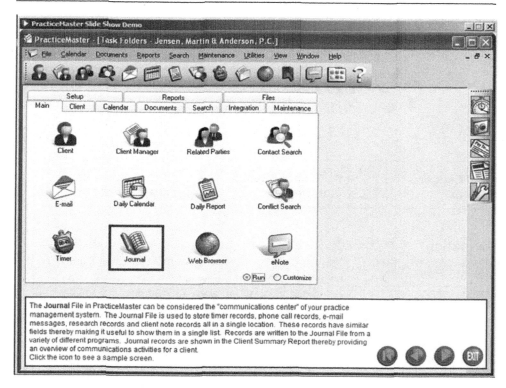

iii. Tabs3—Financial Software

Tabs3 Financial software concentrates on back office activities, including:

→ Obtaining access to a general ledger or accounts payable; and
→ Managing trust accounts, like IOLTA.

Figure 10.18
Tabs3—Financial Software: First screen

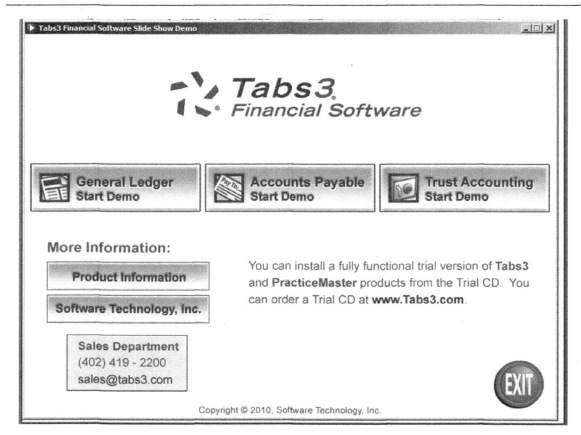

e. Lexis-Nexis Practice Management Software

Lexis-Nexis, famous for its legal research service, also makes practice management software.

i. PCLaw

PCLaw, at http://www.lexisnexis.com/law-firm-practice-management/pclaw/, serves as the umbrella designation for a number of software packages focused on practice management.

The PCLaw package uses a toolbar that has links including:

Figure 10.19
PCLaw—Top toolbar

→ Tools (focusing specifically on balances or, more generally, on lawyer budgeting); and

→ Options (relating to administrative functions for using the software).

Figure 10.20
PCLaw—Top part of toolbar: Tools tab

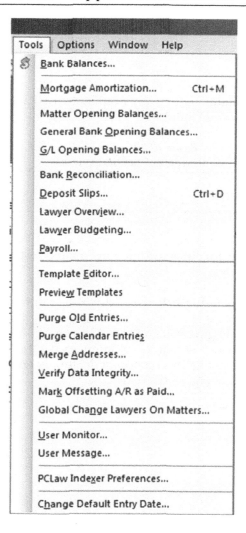

Figure 10.21
PCLaw—Top part of toolbar: Options tab

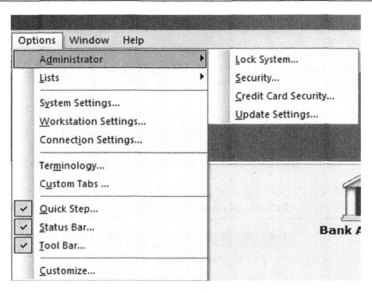

The toolbar also contains buttons for frequently used actions relating to calendaring and contact management.

Figure 10.22
PCLaw—Bottom part of toolbar: buttons

PCLaw uses a sidebar for links to functions related to the operation of a legal practice. These include:

→ Daily tasks, like obtaining balances (with access to bank and general ledger accounts, for example);
→ Accounting (including payroll and trust accounts);
→ End of month/year (a compilation of summary data);
→ General setup (including the creation of document templates); and
→ Training and support (via Lexis-Nexis).

Figure 10.23
PCLaw—Side toolbar: Startup tab

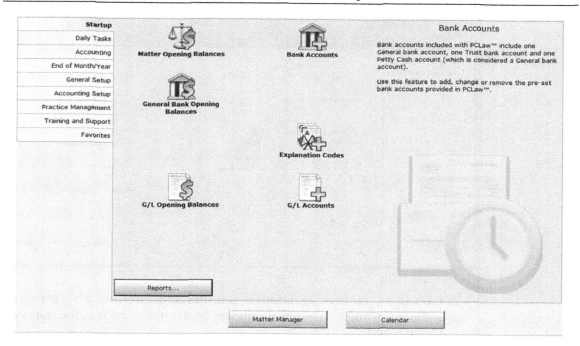

ii. TimeMatters

TimeMatters offers features such as:

→ Navigator, a sidebar menu with tabs that open to a screen with common data management functions, such as tracking activities and managing communications, like the generation of phone lists.

Figure 10.24
TimeMatters—Navigator sidebar options

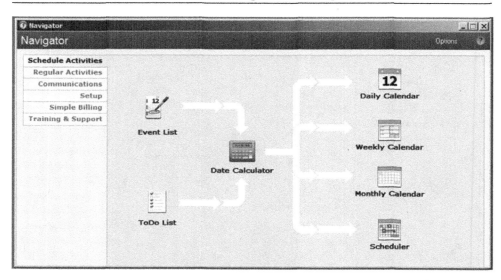

→ A toolbar for monitoring business activities and notifying a legal practice about those activities, via alerts, reminders, and watches, such as the status of a legal matter; and

Figure 10.25
TimeMatters—Top toolbar: Search pulldown menu

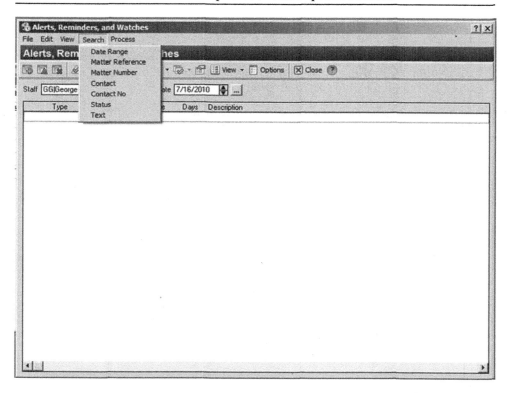

→ A toolbar with links and buttons for access to commonly used functions, such as:

  → Database, including a search of an **SQL** database;

  → Lexis, to obtain access to the Lexis-Nexis database; and

  → Search, includes web searches; and

  → Matter Journal, a record of issue of law for which the legal practice represents the client.

Figure 10.26
TimeMatters—Toolbar: Commonly used links and buttons

iii. Juris

With a focus on the financial management of a firm, Juris helps a law firm understand some of the implications of operating a legal practice. For example, it can identify potential conflicts of interest.

f. Clio

Available at www.goclio.com, this practice management software uses cloud computing, also known as Software as a Service (SaaS) (as discussed in Chapter 1). Accordingly, it has people available who can quickly and accurately diagnose a software problem. Software upgrades happen on Clio's servers, not on the law firm's. Data backups occur daily off-site. Also, a lawyer or paralegal can obtain access to it via any connection to the web.

Clio preserves the confidentiality of a law firm's client data by using 256-bit **SSL** (secure sockets layer) encryption (as discussed in Chapter 6). This version generates passwords made up of 256 bits of information, so large that a hacker would need a great amount of computing power to crack it by trying all possible password combinations.

Clio uses a **dashboard,** a small screen that can reside on a user's screen for quick access, such as for the continuous monitoring of a legal practice's financial health. It provides common front office features, such as:

→ Calendaring;
→ Reporting;
→ Checking conflicts of interest; and
→ Document management.

Clio offers typical back office features, such as generating bills and running a ledger, as well as the means to manage an IOLTA and take electronic payments via a credit card or the web-based PayPal electronic payment service. It offers an interface for use with smartphones, like the iPhone, or those using the Android operating system. Also, it can synchronize with Microsoft's Outlook e-mail program and Google Apps.

g.   ProLaw

ProLaw, the practice management software offered by West Publishing (a Thompson Reuters Company), contains a comprehensive software package at http://www.elite.com/prolaw/front-office/. ProLaw can handle front office or back office functions, as well as integrate general business productivity software like Microsoft Office or Adobe Acrobat.

Figure 10.27
Features of ProLaw

i. Front office

Front office functions available through ProLaw include:

→ Case and matter management, such as creating audit trails, conducting legal research, and providing continuously updated information about practice matters via a dashboard;
→ Client and contact management, including the tracking of vendors and expert witnesses;
→ Document management, such as generating an index of litigation-related documents, including documents in different formats, such as a PDF file or a Word document;
→ Remote access;
→ Report management;
→ Time management, including synchronizing calendars on all computing devices; and
→ Court docketing and calendaring, including synchronizing with groupware, such as IBM Lotus Notes or Novell's GroupWise, and accessing the Westlaw Legal Calendaring Rules.

ii. Back Office

Notable back office features available with ProLaw include:

→ Billing, including handling billing rate overrides and determining the status of accounts receivable;
→ Contingency analysis and disposition, regarding how a legal practice can account for payment to the firm for services only if the legal practice has successfully resolved the client's legal issues;
→ Integrated accounting, involving payroll, bank reconciliation, and the generation of 1099 forms;
→ Time and expense tracking;
→ Budgeting, including how to handle write-offs, which are debts that the firm will no longer seek out for payment;
→ Collections, regarding payment of outstanding bills; and
→ Cost recovery, such as billing to a client's account for conducting research on a proprietary database like Westlaw.

C. CASE MANAGEMENT SOFTWARE

Case management software makes it easier to manage litigating clients' cases because it gives a legal practice an overview of the status of all claims in litigation. Litigation includes several distinct steps, which may include:

→ Interviewing a client about a legal problem;
→ Contacting another party to negotiate a settlement to resolve the legal dispute;

→ Drafting the complaint, to start the litigation process;
→ Doing research about the law and facts of a case; and
→ Preparing motions and jury instructions.

This exploration of the case management software will focus on the pre-trial process of discovery. **Discovery** involves the pre-trial exchange of information related to the dispute, by the parties, that can help to resolve the dispute of law. One reason for such an exchange could result in the parties recognizing the benefits to negotiating a settlement instead of taking their chances to win at a trial. Also, agreeing to a settlement would eliminate costs associated with a trial, such as the time lawyers and paralegals would need to prepare for a trial.

1.   Rules of Discovery

The Federal Rules of Civil Procedure (FRCP) contains the guidelines for litigating a civil claim in federal court. The FRCP describes the goals and scope of discovery and the consequences for failing to comply with a valid request for discovery. Because many states have adopted versions of the FRCP, this material looks at discovery from the perspective of the FRCP. Those that do not will still have rules about the discovery process.

2.   Types of Discovery

Discovery includes an array of different types of information related to the legal dispute. For example, if the plaintiff has been injured, the defendant might ask for the plaintiff to see a physician, to assess the nature of the injury. Obtaining that evaluation can help the parties figure out what would be appropriate damages if the defendant should face liability for the injury.
   In addition to physical examinations, discovery includes:

→ Site visits;
→ Interrogatories, written questions presented to an opposing party; and
→ Production of documents.

3.   Exemptions from Discovery

Two significant **exemptions** exist to a request for discovery, so that the party receiving the request for data does not have to turn over the requested information. The policy behind one exemption, known as the **attorney-client privilege,** reflects the hope that if clients can speak freely to their attorneys, they can get the best legal advice. Frank discussions between a client and a lawyer can provide the attorney with a better understanding of the case and could lead to a quicker, more satisfying resolution of the legal dispute.

The other exemption involves the so-called **work product doctrine.** Communications within the law firm, made in anticipation of litigation, like a discussion about trial strategy, do not have to be disclosed. Because the adversarial process of litigating a problem would reward the party that best presents a claim in court, keeping confidential how a party plans on winning can lead to a more effective resolution of the problem at trial.

4. *Depositions*

a. **Nature of the Process**

Lawyers for the parties can question the parties, their potential witnesses, and anyone who could have useful information about the claim. This form of discovery is called taking a **deposition.** The person being deposed is known as the **deponent.** A record, known as a **transcript,** is generated.

b. **Software**

Software can make it easier to look through the transcripts when they are in electronic form. When only a paper transcript exists, however, a firm can use **optical character reading (OCR)** software to scan the content of the paper transcript to convert it into **electronically stored information (ESI).**

Benefits of having software that can review the ESI of a deposition transcript include:

→ Searchability: as ESI, software can search instantly to find information, like the date when a plaintiff suffered an injury.
→ Annotation: as with some word processing software, software might allow a reader to enter marginal notes on the electronic version of the transcript, which the reader has identified as significant, such as when a deponent talks about weather conditions.
→ Index: some software can generate an index of the transcript's contents and even identify the line on a page where information appears. The illustration, taken from DepoSmart, provides a user with options about features that the index could contain.

Figure 10.28
DepoSmart—Preferences for generating a deposition summary: Transcript, index

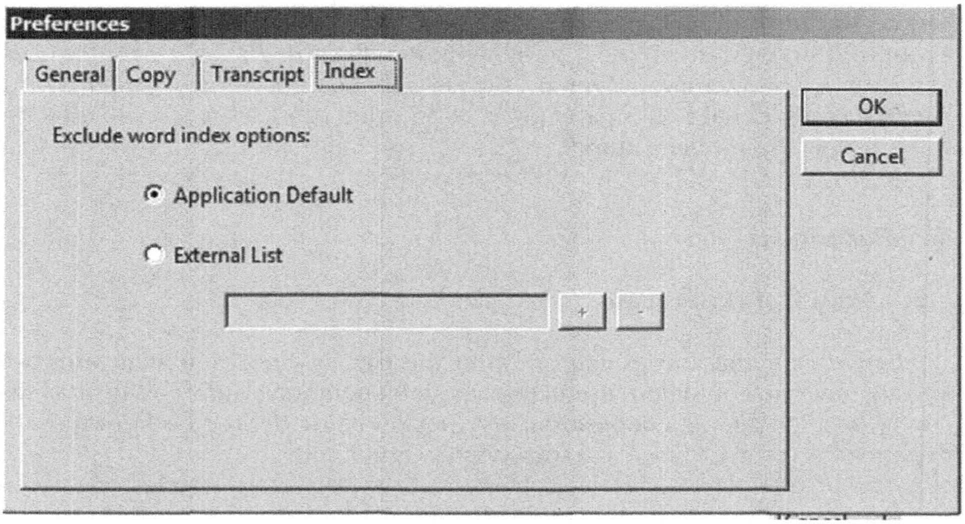

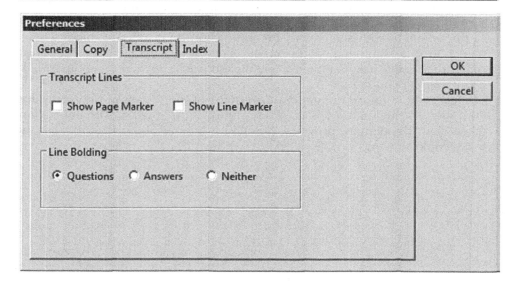

→ Summarizing: deposition transcripts can run to hundreds or thousands of pages. Software that generates a summary of points made during the deposition can make it faster for a reader to understand what happened during the deposition. In the illustration, DepoSmart provides options such as having questions put into boldface.

Figure 10.29
DepoSmart—Preferences for generating a deposition summary: Transcript

c.   Examples of Software

i.   DepoSmart

In addition to the features noted above, DepoSmart, from Clarity Legal Software at www.claritylegalllc, also allows:

→ The reader to change fonts or to magnify text; and
→ Multiple readers to look at the same transcript, when stored in a legal practice's database.

The toolbar provides a selection of tabs familiar to users of Microsoft software. Under the Options link, the reader can tell the software how to prepare the summary.

Figure 10.30
DepoSmart—Toolbar

Figure 10.31
DepoSmart—Preferences for generating a deposition summary: In general

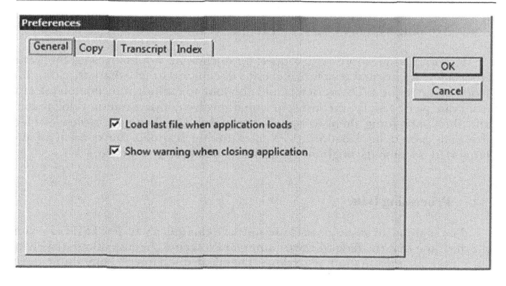

ii.   LiveNote

West Publishing's LiveNote, at http://west.thomson.com/products/services/case-notebook/default.aspx, makes it possible to glean, quickly and efficiently, information from a deposition transcript. Not surprisingly, a user can access this information via other West products, like Westlaw.

Figure 10.32
LiveNote

5.   *Electronically Stored Information*

a.   Avoiding a Manual Review of Requested Information

Historically, a response to a request for documents would involve a time- and labor-intensive manual review of a client's documents to see what was within the scope of the request. This review would also look to exclude information exempt from discovery. Finally, the last step would involve copying relevant documents and then submitting them to opposing counsel. Conducting a review of electronically stored information, even after having scanned the content of the requested documents, might not involve as much time or expense.

b.   Processing Data

The search can go faster because software can quickly review ESI. For example, imagine that the federal Environmental Protection Agency asks that a client turn over all information regarding "chemical discharges," something easily enough and quickly done. But a different issue may arise. To increase the likelihood of fulfilling the request, a paralegal might need to search for more than the phrase "chemical discharge" and search for terms like "waste" or "residue." Software might make this process go faster, but it might not be able to look for those alternative terms or phrases.

c.   E-Mail

An issue with reviewing e-mail, to see whether it falls within the scope of a request for ESI, might involve the format of the content in e-mail, which the software cannot search. Converting e-mail into a searchable format might increase costs and runs the risk of omitting information, perhaps like the addresses of all recipients.

d.   Litigation Holds

An additional complication can arise when trying to comply with a request for discovery because of the way that clients manage their electronic information. Periodically, businesses might destroy ESI because the increased storage costs outweigh the potential benefit of saving the data. A client that is a business might have deleted ten-year-old e-mails since no good reason existed for saving them.

This routine process of purging ESI might present a problem once litigation has started, because some of the ESI might relate to the litigation. Once litigation starts, counsel could ask for a **litigation hold,** which would stop the purging process of a client, at least until the opportunity arose to review the material to determine whether any fell within the scope of the request.

e.   Metadata

i.   *Documents*

Electronically generated material often has information encoded in it, generally known as **metadata,** but also called metacontent, that might not seem obvious. Metadata in a Word document, for example, will identify the number of words, lines, and pages. It might reveal who worked on that document and when.

The request for ESI may emphasize data rather than the process used to produce such information. Good legal practice, then, means making sure that only the data requested gets included in a response. One way to review and strip out some or most of the metadata associated with a client's ESI involves a process that some call **scrubbing.** Failure to take reasonable steps to manage metadata might amount to legal malpractice if a court decides that a competent lawyer should have reviewed and removed information outside of the scope of the discovery request.

ii.   *Deduplication*

Metadata could make it easier to cull out multiple copies of an e-mail. By looking at metadata, like the **MD5 hash,** a firm could reduce the number of multiple, identical copies that would get turned over. **Deduplication** describes the process of comparing metadata, such as MD5 hash, to eliminate such copies. Comparing metadata can also help to establish what differences may exist between a pair of apparently identical data files.

6.   Defensible Discovery Strategy

That metadata can play a role in preparing an effective response to a request for discovery of ESI raises a potential problem for a court: what did the law firm do to comply with an opponent's request for discovery? The court will need to look at the firm's **defensible discovery strategy** — the strategies and techniques used to review ESI — since having a firm turn over all information to comply with a request could be costly and inappropriate. An acceptable strategy could include using statistically valid sampling or some other type of qualitative methodology for evaluating data. Such an approach could show the court that the law firm took reasonable steps when trying to comply with the discovery request.

a.   Preparing a Defensible Discovery Strategy

Such a strategy could include:

→ Figuring out how to preserve appropriate ESI, for the purpose of implementing a litigation hold;
→ Creating and implementing a process to sort through the ESI quickly, efficiently, and accurately, and to know when this review has reached the point of completion;
→ Managing the data produced, such as through the creation of a data map; and
→ Designing and implementing a way to review the effectiveness of this process, such as generating a list of steps taken, known as an **audit trail.**

b.   Inadvertent Disclosure and "Clawback"

If it turns out that a party has inadvertently released privileged or confidential information, the court may review the defensible discovery strategy to determine whether to allow a **clawback,** a recovery of the protected information. The court could allow a clawback without penalty, sparing the law firm that inadvertently released that information from having to pay the costs incurred by opposing counsel to gather and turn back the information. This might critically depend upon whether the inadvertent disclosure happened in spite of the use of a defensible discovery strategy.

c.   The Electronic Data Reference Model

One type of defensible discovery strategy involves the **Electronic Data Reference Model (EDRM).**

Figure 10.33
EDRM — Chart explaining how the Electronic Data Reference Model works

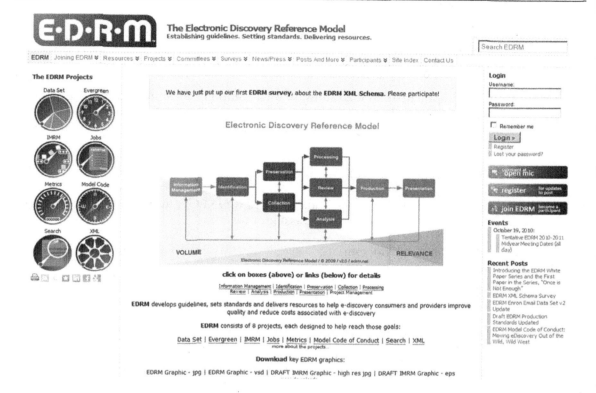

This approach, as seen at www.edrm.net, has a legal practice set out the steps that it would take when reviewing a client's ESI, in the form of a flow chart. The flow chart, a visual depiction of the strategy that the firm uses, could show how an ongoing review process would produce results that most closely meet the scope of the request for discovery. Using the process depicted in the flow chart might mean that the legal practice recognized a need for engaging in an ongoing process of review to select appropriate ESI, instead of waiting until the end of the search for ESI.

EDGE, from ILSTech, at www.ilstech.com, uses the EDRM model to manage the search for relevant ESI. For example, it sorts through e-mail by looking at the unique MD5 hash generated for each e-mail and simultaneously performs deduplication. EDGE keeps track of decisions made by reviewers, so that if a legal practice needs to defend how it searched through a client's ESI, the law firm can show how it reasonably tried to comply with the request for ESI.

7.   Reviewing ESI

To conduct a defensible discovery strategy, a law firm could get software or have the review done by an outside service.

8.   ESI Review Software

A legal practice can load software on a computer for immediate access. The **scalability** of the software could mean that the law firm would be able to use it on different devices, from a desktop to a smartphone.

a.   ICONECT nXT

Among the features available from iCONECT, at http://www.iconect.com, the nXT software package allows a user to:

→ Sort through documents;
→ Store the documents in folders; and
→ Create a log to keep track of what the files contain.

The software can:

→ Show files in their original format;
→ Allow the reviewer to annotate the files;
→ Allow the reviewer to redact files and images, perhaps to protect confidential data; and
→ Generate a detailed report regarding the level of success in using the selected criteria to gather information.

When reviewing ESI in the form of e-mail, the user can select review criteria to identify a chain of e-mails, relating to a topic, and to a single e-mail in that chain. For example, the defendant is alleged to have sold a car without a critical safety feature. Using this software, the plaintiff's lawyer could track the exchange of e-mails between an engineering department's perspective about a critical safety feature and a marketing department's interest in keeping the price low enough to make it competitively priced.

b.   Intella

Intella, from Vound Software, at www.vound-software.com, is ediscovery software that can evaluate ESI. For example, it can provide a visualization of the relationship of data, in the form of a cluster map, such as showing corporate expenses relative to sales.

Figure 10.34
Intella—Visualized search depicting associations of data processed

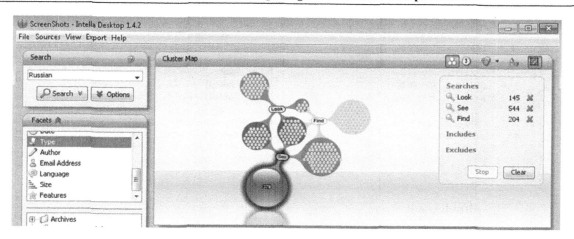

When it detects a relationship among e-mails, like an exchange between the CEO of a corporation and the board of directors about launching an initial public offering of corporate stock, it can depict that visually.

Figure 10.35
Intella—Visual depiction of associations among e-mails in a chain

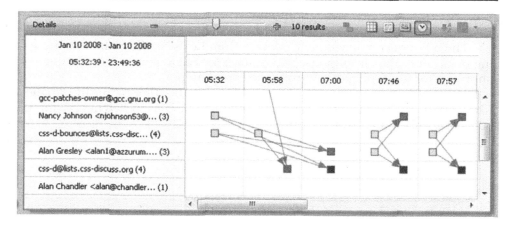

It can also produce results in a more traditional format, such as a list or thumbnail images.

Figure 10.36
Intella—List of e-mails: ranked by priority

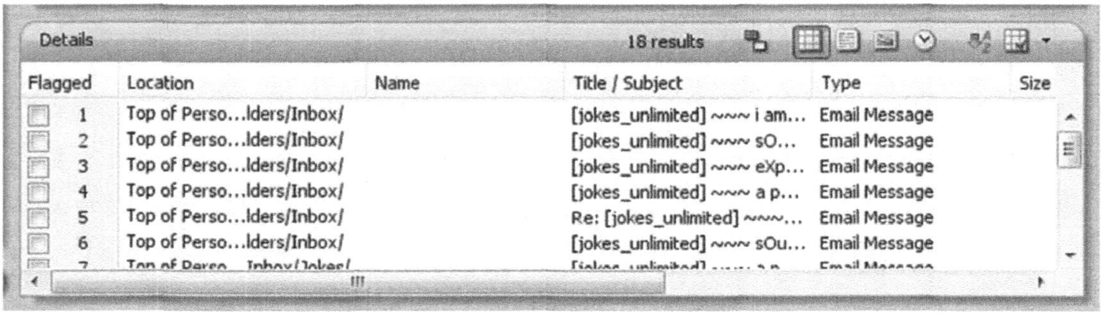

Intella can:

→ Identify all lawyer-client communications, which would be exempt from discovery under the attorney-client privilege;
→ Use MD5 hash values to do deduplication;
→ Generate an index, which can include images embedded in documents;
    → Gain deeper insight into ESI through visualization; and
    → Export results in a choice of formats for later use in other eDiscovery platforms, investigative products, or reporting.

c.   Lexis-Nexis ediscovery Solutions

The ediscovery management software from Lexis-Nexis can handle the sorting of a client's data in response to a request for ESI as part of a comprehensive approach for seeing litigation through to completion.

LAW PreDiscovery software manages ESI by first gathering all information, while preserving metadata. It can then conduct searches in batches, saving the culled information for further review.

Figure 10.37

Lexis-Nexis—LAW PreDiscovery-funnel: Graphic representing the LAW PreDiscovery searching process

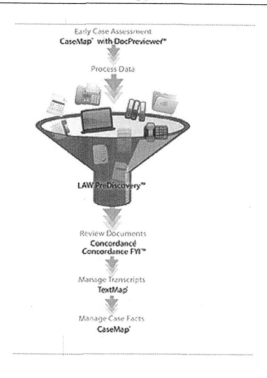

Figure 10.38

Lexis-Nexis—LAW PreDiscovery: Discovery loader

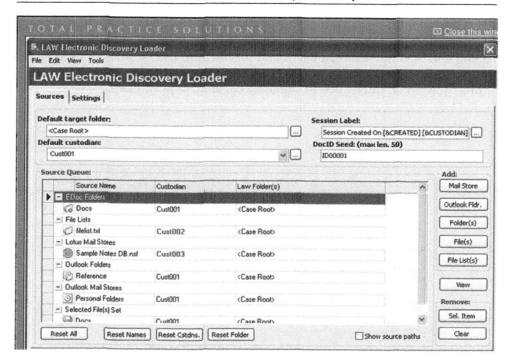

A search of a client's ESI can include documents scanned via optical character reading (OCR) and source material in languages other than English. It can incorporate material drawn from depositions, via TextMap, and from cases, via the CaseMap application.

Figure 10.39
Lexis-Nexis—Concordance

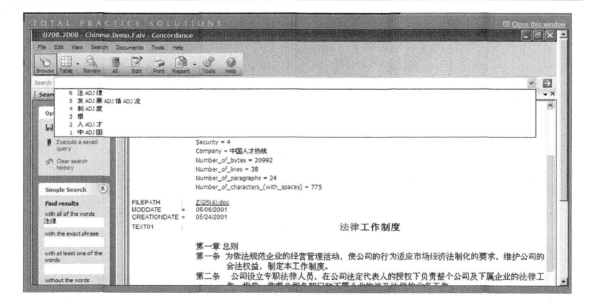

d. Masterfile

MasterFile (www.masterfile.biz) addresses the four core stages of the EDRM model described on page 227 for managing, searching and organizing ESI: processing and loading, review, analysis and production. Its case analysis module can chronologically track facts and sort them, using color coding. Any information within MasterFile can be tied to case issues as analysis progresses.

Figure 10.40
Masterfile—Color coding of facts by relevance

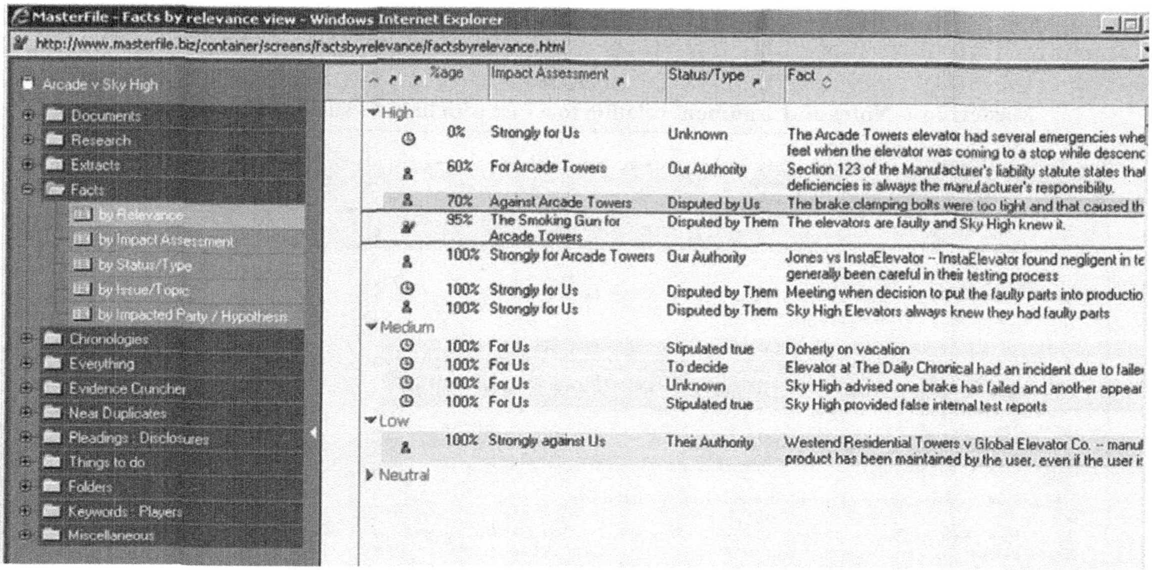

Figure 10.41
Masterfile—Data organized in views tied to case issue

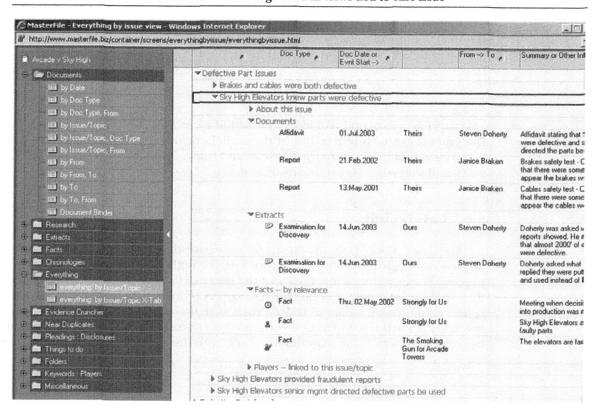

One feature makes it possible to organize case information in terms of how it might support an argument. For example, you could identify and explain accounting reports, prepared according to standard accounting procedures, to show that a business client did have a good understanding of its financial health.

Figure 10.42
Masterfile—Notes and argument relating to a fact with links to substantiating evidence

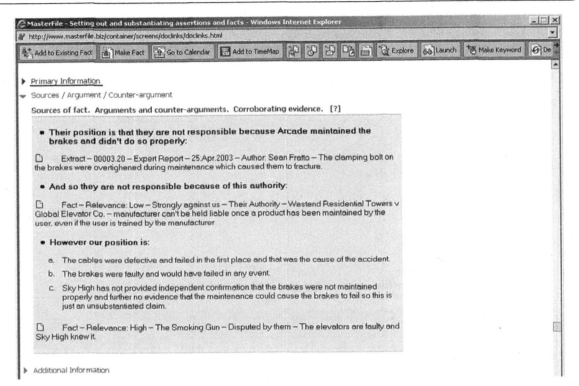

MasterFile's Express Load lets you load ESI including Outlook emails directly. Documents can be found in two or three clicks or searched for. Documents can be produced in PDF and native formats, and tracked with Bates numbers, redactions, and so forth, to meet disclosure requests.

e.   Case Logistix

Westlaw's Case Logistix, at http://store.westlaw.com/products/services/ westlaw-case-logistix/default.aspx, can sort through ESI via a multiple-review process. For example, a first review of the client data might look for information that would substantially comply with a discovery request. A second, more focused review could look for data to redact, such as that covered by the attorney-client privilege. A third review could involve quality control. After that, counsel might be ready to turn over the material to comply with the discovery request.

Figure 10.43
Case Logistix—Review process

An example of **Westlaw CaseLogistix** workflow with review metrics across the process.

The law firm can conduct a native review to understand the context of information that the software has identified. This scalable software can conduct searches based upon synonyms and phonic speech. It includes an option to look for embedded content in a tagged image file format (TIFF) file.

9.   *Examples of ESI Review Services*

A firm might find it easier and cheaper to hire an outside vendor to search through a client's ESI. The vendor would have experience doing such a review and might have better hardware and software to do that review. Of course, the legal practice would need to hire a vendor with impeccable credentials, such as years of experience doing these reviews, a well-earned professional reputation, and evidence of continued training and/or improvement.

a. Categorix

Categorix is a document review litigation service provided by Xerox at http://www.xerox-xls.com/ediscovery/categorix.html. Using statistical measures, the service reviews ESI repeatedly to look at the ratio of relevant data retrieved as a part of the overall amount of data. For example, by calling attention to a particular e-mail, the Categorix service can review ESI for data to determine whether it deserves further attention because of its relationship to the particular e-mail. Using this statistical approach makes it easier for a legal practice to demonstrate that it has used a defensible discovery strategy to satisfy the request for information.

Via a dashboard, the service can show the rate at which it has processed ESI. It can track information, such as when information is transmitted using the FTP (file transfer protocol) method. Also, it can identify who has had custody of the information. This means, for example, that the service can identify the exchange of drafts of a contract for the renovation of a community's downtown and show who has the final draft of the contract.

Figure 10.44
Categorix—Processing and review dashboard

Processing and Review Dashboard (Summary by Custodian · Summary by Media Shipment · Custom Filters)

Show review information for: Primary Review

Loading status	Processing statistics										Review statistics		
	Received GB/docs		Expanded GB/docs		Culled GB/docs		Deduped GB/docs		Loaded GB/docs		Reviewed GB/docs/%		
Complete	797.41	49,058	386.07	2,650,920	18.62	74,419	73.35	254,891	293.55	2,308,259	45.34	255,378	11%
In Progress	16.93	3	22.70	214,684	0	0	0.82	9,482	0	0			

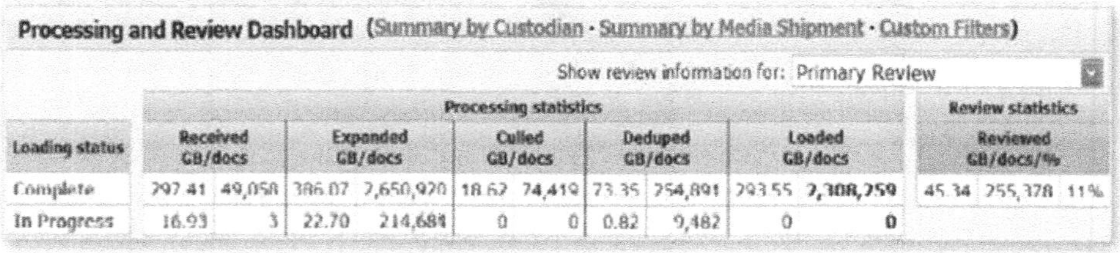

b. Daegis ediscovery

The eDiscovery Analytics Consulting service provided from Daegis at www.daegis.com, uses the electronic data reference model (EDRM; see above) to review ESI.

Figure 10.45
Services that Daegis provides

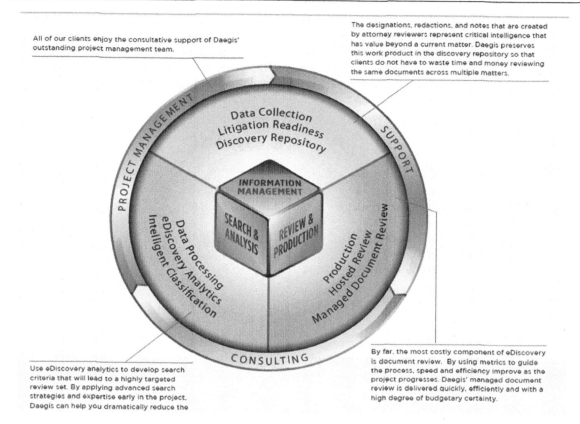

The service:

→ Preserves the integrity of ESI when transferring it from the client;

→ Uses a single interface to streamline the review process;

→ Creates an audit trail if the law firm needs to show that it has engaged in a defensible discovery strategy when preparing a response to a request for information;

→ Can review electronic records from different sources, such as from Lotus Notes, and Microsoft Exchange; and

→ Can identify significant documents. For example, a law firm might need to provide transaction reports sent to the appropriate regulatory agency to show that a publicly traded client filed quarterly reports on time, if the client faces prosecution for a failure to file those on time.

D.   CONCLUSION

Many lawyers have found that better time management works to meet multiple demands for their services. Using software tailored to practice management, with its emphasis on running a business, can help a legal practice do high-quality legal work for its clients. Case management software makes it possible for a legal practice to obtain a quick and accurate understanding of a client's case.

E.   TERMS

Accounts receivables
Attorney-client privilege
Audit trail
Back office operations
Calendaring software
Case management software
Clawback
Cloud computing
Dashboard
Database
Deduplication
Defensible discovery strategy
Deponent
Deposition
Discovery
Docket
Electronic Data Reference Model (EDRM)
ESI
Ethical wall
Exemptions
Federal Rules of Civil Procedure (FRCP)
Firewall protection
Front office activities
Interest On Lawyer Trust Accounts (IOLTA)
Ledger
Litigation hold
MD5 hash
Metadata
Optical character reading (OCR) software
Practice management software
Remote access
Scalability
Scrubbing
Servers
Software as a Service (SaaS)
SQL

SSL
Statute of limitations
Template
Ticklers
Track
Transcript
Work product doctrine

F.   HYPOTHETICALS

1.   Explain what is involved in crafting a defensible discovery strategy.
2.   Based upon the software described in this chapter, evaluate four software packages so that you could recommend to a law firm that it purchase specific software, based upon its ability to handle front office functions. Explain your selection.
3.   Based upon the software described in this chapter, evaluate four software packages so that you could recommend to a law firm that it purchase specific software, based upon its ability to handle back office functions. Explain your selection.
4.   What features would be critical for evaluating data in a deposition transcript ? Why?
5.   a.   When it comes to reviewing a client's ESI when trying to respond to a request for discovery, which is better: having the software or using SaaS? Why?
     b.   Pick one of the types of software packages mentioned in this chapter, for each type, and explain why it would be the best choice in that category. Then, compare any two of the same kind of software, and explain why you think one would be better than the other.

CHAPTER

11

Telecommunications and Data Management

OBJECTIVES

→ **Study** the nature and workings of the types of networks that a legal practice most likely would have.
→ **Differentiate** among Internet-related methods of communication, such as Voice Over Internet Protocol (VOIP), and technology, such as smartphones.
→ **Explore** the security issues associated with any form of telecommunications.
→ **Examine** issues about ethics related to telecommunications.

INTRODUCTION

Telecommunications no longer just involves a telephone, but now includes Internet-based communications, smartphones, and e-mail. Even as law firms rely on networks to transmit data, they need to remain mindful of the ethical obligation to preserve the confidentiality of client information.

A.   TELECOMMUNICATIONS

1.   Networks

Whether in a legal practice, or through the Internet, the creation and use of networks has enhanced the productivity of law firms. The size of a network may present distinct issues for effective data transmission. A way of gauging how much traffic a web-based network can handle is to measure **bandwidth.** This describes the rate for data transfer and usually is expressed in terms of bits per second. It might not take much bandwidth to send a client letter on a network, but would likely take much more when transmitting all case law gathered in support of a brief to the court. A larger batch of data would take more time to arrive at the destination. Networks typically will have a computer that acts as storage that everyone on the network can access, called a **server.**

a. Intranet

An **intranet** is a network accessible to a limited number of users, such as people who work in a law firm. It could also connect those users to the Internet, although security measures could protect it from unauthorized access. Larger computer networks might require the setting up of **hubs,** which will serve as transfer points for information, and the use of repeaters, to offset the loss of quality of data transmitted over long distances.

i.   Local Area Network (LAN)

A **local area network (LAN)** generally describes a small network. Computers in that network may be connected via **coaxial cables,** wiring designed specifically to handle computer-based traffic, and shielded so as to minimize loss of signal strength and to reduce interference from other sources. Most computers have built-in **Ethernet** ports, for connecting coaxial cable to the network.

Figure 11.1
LAN Network Illustration

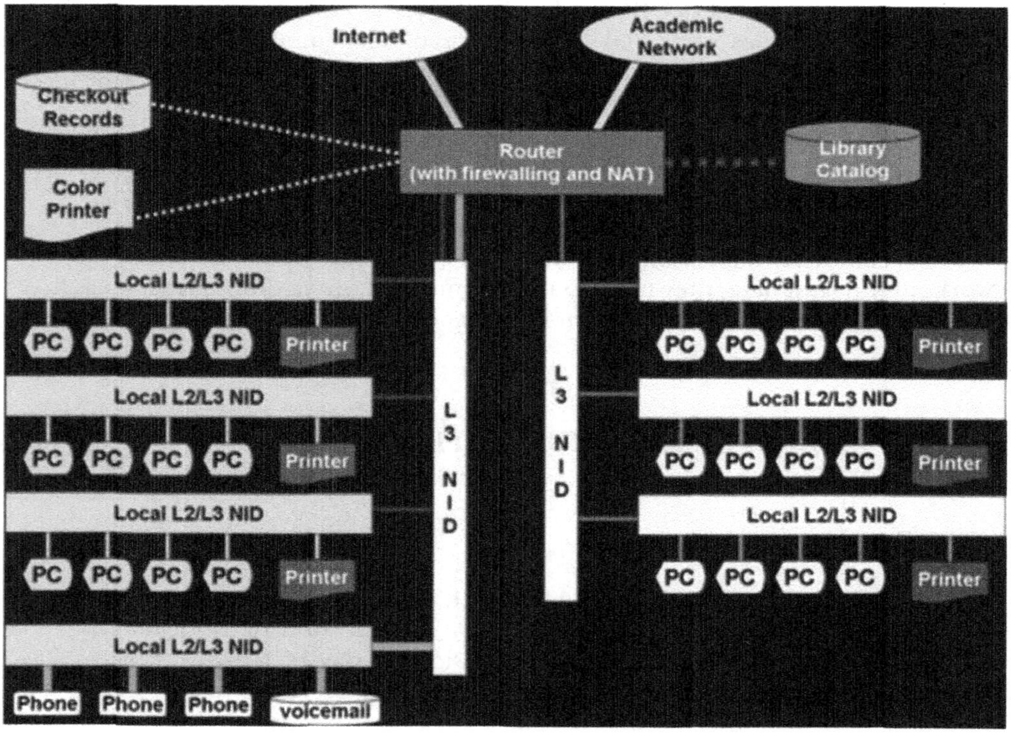

Source: Hcberkowitz

ii. Wireless Local Area Network (WLAN)

A **wireless local area network (WLAN)** can accomplish all that a LAN can without using cables. For example, with a **peer-to-peer network,** computers connect only to one another wirelessly. In this way, lawyers in court could exchange data just between the computers that they are using.

Figure 11.2
WLAN Network Illustration

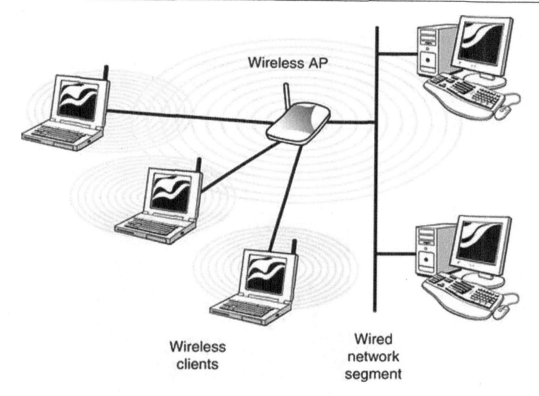

Source: **RedEagle/Wikimedia Commons**

I. Router

Larger networks would rely on a wireless router. A router is a transmitter and receiver that directly connects to the Internet via a cable. The range of access to a router depends upon its capacity to send and receive data wirelessly. For purposes of security, a legal practice should prevent the wireless router from broadcasting the **Service Set Identifier (SSID),** the router's name. This means that a **hacker** will have one less piece of information to use when trying to crack a router's firewall.

II.   Wi-Fi

A common type of WLAN is known as Wi-Fi. Schools, businesses, and libraries have found that offering free Wi-Fi access can serve the public. For example, a coffee shop could offer free Wi-Fi as a way of drawing in customers. Typically, the web page at a business that provides free Wi-Fi access may include a disclaimer regarding the level of security available to users. This would acknowledge the obvious, that using unsecured communication channels can leave users vulnerable to hacking. A law firm that has set up and uses Wi-Fi may have an ethical obligation to secure it against hacking.

iii.   *Wireless Personal Area Network (WPAN)*

A **wireless personal area network (WPAN)** connects devices in a small area, like around a user's body. One way to create a WPAN involves using the **Bluetooth** technology, available on most computers. The convenience of setting up such small networks quickly and easily has meant that a lawyer can engage in hands-free communication via a cordless headset.

Figure 11.3
Bluetooth

Source: **Wikimedia Commons**

iv.   *Virtual Private Network (VPN)*

A variation on this idea, a **virtual private network (VPN),** could make secure data transmissions through the use of a process called **tunneling.** Tunneling establishes a unique connection between a computer and a receiver, often by using layers of security protocols or encryption. Setting up a VPN with a public

Wi-Fi router can make communications between the computer and wireless router less susceptible to hacking.

v. Firewalls

Hardware firewalls, usually a router that allows only those with passwords to connect to a network, typically protect a LAN at the point that it connects to the Internet. Software firewalls might protect a single computer and may not provide the same level of security as a hardware firewall.

Firewalls with more advanced levels of security might also note when applications, like **file transfer protocol (FTP),** are used, since the use of such an application might mask efforts to find unsecure points of entry to a network. Firewalls also can evaluate the sequence of **data packets** transmitted to see whether a message contains the kind of data that could mask an effort to compromise the security of a computer.

b. Internet

The vast network of computers of the World Wide Web, which contains the Internet, uses **websites** as primary "locations" for the point of connection. A piece of software, the browser, makes it possible to connect to websites on the Internet. Examples of browsers include Firefox, Google's Chrome, Microsoft's Internet Explorer, and Apple's Safari.

i. The Home Page

Clicking on a computer's browser software will open a home page, that is, the default destination on a computer that a browser always starts on. Some browsers have an icon of a home, so that clicking on it brings the user back to the home page.

Figure 11.4
Wolters Kluwer Home Page

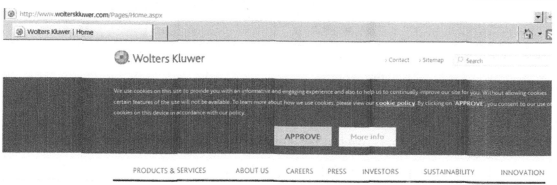

ii.   Web Pages

Websites contain web pages, the documents of the Internet. The uniform resource locator, or **URL,** serves as the address for a website. Web pages may allow users to go to another website or elsewhere on a website with the click of a link. A link contains **hypertext,** the computer code for guiding the browser to the destination associated with the link. The custom has been to identify a link by underlining words, in a color different from that of the text: www.wolter-kulwers.com. By putting the browser's pointer on the link, a small box opens to reveal the URL contained in the link.

Figure 11.5
URL Box

http://www.wolterkulwers.com
Ctrl+Click to follow link
www.wolterkulwers.com.
. contained in the link.

I.   HTTP and HTTPS

A web page whose URL starts with WWW or HTTP runs the risk of not providing a secure connection, which could allow for a kind of electronic eavesdropping. HTTP, which stands for **hypertext transfer protocol,** is the computer code that contains the rules for transferring information over the Internet.

Figure 11.6
HTTP in URL Box

Source: **Salvatore Vouno – freedigitalphotos.net**

That risk diminishes if the URL for the site starts off with HTTPS, which indicates that the site's server has in place certain security protocols. HTTPS means that the website is using **Secure Sockets Layers (SSL),** which decreases the risk of interception because it uses different levels, or layers, of protection.

Figure 11.7
HTTPS in URL Box

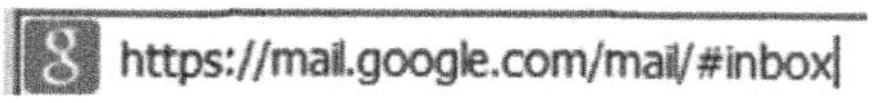

Source: **Vlastni screenshot/Wikimedia Commons**

c.   Security

While the vast network of computers of the Internet makes it easier to communicate, using the Internet can come with a cost: websites might not have an adequate level of security for keeping information confidential. This poses a significant problem for a legal practice, which has an ethical obligation to preserve the confidentiality of client information.

i.   *Security Certificate*

Upon arrival to a website, browsers may automatically look for its security certificate, which describes basic security measures used for that website. The browser could alert the user to the absence of such a certificate, or that the website uses an outdated one, so that a user can decide whether to continue to use that website.

ii.   *Encryption*

Encryption involves the coding of information so that only someone that uses that code, or key, can access the information. A common method for encrypting digital information involves an **algorithm,** a formula for generating numbers for use as keys. One type of encryption uses public and private keys: numbers generated by an algorithm. An algorithm's effectiveness increases as it generates longer numbers because these would be harder to guess. A sender will encrypt data for transmission using a public and a private key, and will then disclose the public key. After having sent the private key to the recipient, the recipient needs to use both keys to decrypt the information.

iii.   *Cookies*

Each time a user directs a browser to a site, the site may automatically load simple software onto the user's computer, called a **cookie.** Allowing a site to store a cookie could, for example, speed up the loading of graphic images used on that site. But cookies could also track a user's web browsing, gathering information that the cookie's owner might use for marketing, perhaps by learning about other sites that a user visits. Most browsers allow for the blocking of cookies, but doing that could mean losing access to a site. One compromise might involve deleting cookies after using a site, while another would mean periodically purging a computer of all cookies.

iv.   *Pop-Up Blockers*

Advertising that automatically appears when visiting a website is called a pop-up. While not necessarily malware, pop-ups distract and annoy. Increasingly, web browsers have a feature to block these from appearing.

d.   Voice Over Internet Protocol (VOIP)

Technology exists to make telephone conversations over the Internet. This involves using **Voice Over Internet Protocol (VOIP).** VOIP translates speech into data packets, to take advantage of the Internet's capacity to send data packets over numerous routes simultaneously. Because a law firm will already have paid for such access to the Internet, it can use VOIP and eliminate the expense for having a traditional telephone hookup.

VOIP service providers usually charge a flat rate for their service. Among others, **Skype** offers a low-cost approach to VOIP communications by not charging for calls made within the Skype network and charging a modest fee for calls to landlines or mobile telecommunication devices.

Phones using VOIP generally will not support the placing of 911 calls because servers that transmit a VOIP signal are scattered throughout the world. E911 can provide a VOIP with emergency services, so long as the caller has associated a phone number with a particular location.

VOIP service providers can offer a Caller ID service, but it works differently than with a traditional telephone system. This leaves VOIP Caller ID vulnerable to **spoofing,** which involves feeding false Caller ID information to trick a person into taking the call and possibly disclosing confidential information.

e.   Videoconferencing

A law firm might want to set up an Internet-based teleconferencing network. For example, a service like **Webex** would set up a special destination on the Internet for the communications to go through, obviating the need for specialized, and potentially costly, video equipment. A business could pay a regular subscription fee for the service or could pay on a per-call basis. Skype users can also engage in video conferencing, although such communications might not match the quality of specialized video-conferencing technology.

Figure 11.8
Videoconferencing over the Internet

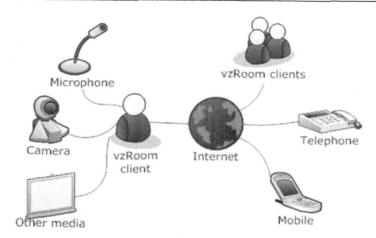

2. E-Mail

E-mail involves the electronic transmission of information via a computer network, akin to the process of using the U.S. Postal Service to convey information, such as in a letter. Software, such as Microsoft's Outlook and Mozilla's Thunderbird, make such transmissions possible. Microsoft's Outlook might integrate with other applications. For example, Lexis-Nexis makes it possible to coordinate the use of Outlook with a search when using Lexis for Microsoft Office, as mentioned in Chapter 5.

a. Risks

Law firms face risks with e-mail that could compromise the security of all of a firm's computers. These can include:

→ Unwanted junk e-mail (called **spam,** after a skit by the comedy troupe Monty Python's Flying Circus that made fun of the many uses of this spiced meat product) may merely take up valuable space on the hard drive of a computer. Many types of e-mail software now have spam filters, designed to automatically remove some e-mail, typically coming from an unknown sender.

→ Fraud, where a type of e-mail may aim to defraud the recipient. For example, an e-mail will supposedly come from a former government official from another country, who needs the help of the recipient to obtain access to funds held in a bank. According to this fraudulent e-mail, known as a "Nigerian 419" letter, all the recipient has to do is to send monies to handle some bureaucratic hurdles. In return, the recipient will receive 10 percent of the funds held at a bank that the sender does not have access to. Even though this may be a new type of fraud, the old adage, "If it's too good to be true, then it's not!" applies.

→ Compromising the computer's security. **Phishing** involves sending unsolicited e-mail, perhaps containing an enticing offer, with an **attachment** bearing a computer **virus,** designed to subvert a computer's security. Viruses and other **malicious software,** also known as **malware,** such as **spyware** and **Trojans,** can make data stored on a computer or network accessible. This could violate an ethical obligation to keep confidential client information or it could co-opt the computer for surreptitious use by the malware creator, perhaps to create a network for launching a **Denial of Service (DoS)** attack on a website. Having **antivirus software,** especially the kind that can receive automatic updates, can cut down on the risks of infection by a virus.

b. Confidentiality

i. *Ethical Obligations*

According to the **American Bar Association (ABA)** Rule 1.6, as adopted by many states, lawyers in that practice have an ethical obligation to keep the client information confidential. Comment 17 to ABA Model Rule 1.6 (a) talks about how a lawyer, when transmitting confidential information, needs to take reasonable precautions to safeguard against accidental disclosure.

ii. *Statutes and Obligations*

A state could impose a duty of care on any business to safeguard confidential client information. A breach of that duty of care could amount to a violation of tort law in negligence. The federal government imposes such a duty on business. The law also requires the keeper of that information to notify the information's owner when a security breach has occurred.

Intercepting electronic communications without authority likely amounts to a violation of the Electronic Communications Privacy Act (18 USC Chapter 119, §§ 2501 *et seq.*). This federal statute provides the national government with the authority to investigate and to prosecute efforts to intercept such communications.

iii. *Encryption*

Encrypting e-mail could also protect against the accidental disclosure of client information if an e-mail is accidentally sent to the wrong recipient. What about unencrypted e-mail? The ABA's Standing Committee On Ethics And Professional Responsibility addressed this issue directly, in Formal Opinion No. 99-413 (Formal Opinion No. 99-413, 1999). The Committee determined that some forms of communication, such as ordinary mail or a fax, also carried a risk of interception, however unlikely. It concluded that e-mail security had to match the level of security used with ordinary mail or a fax.

Advances in technology in the decade since the issuance of this opinion might increase the possibility of illegally intercepting e-mail. Even modest security measures like encrypting the data could reduce the likelihood of the disclosure of client information. Absent special circumstances, such as the sensitive nature of the information, this does not mean that the lawyer has to employ special security measures. Of course, if a client requires greater security measures, then the lawyer needs to implement such measures.

3. Smartphones

If cellphones provided practitioners with greater flexibility for communicating, smartphones exceed them by also offering more resources. Smartphones have more computing power, to the point that they can fairly be characterized as handheld or mobile computers.

a. Operating Systems (OS)

Much like with a personal computer, the CPU of a smartphone requires an operating system tailored to its processing capabilities. Several types of OS exist, such as:

→ Apple iPhone OS: Apple has created an operating system with many of the features of the Macintosh OS X, called iOS. This means that the Apple smartphone, the iPhone, can wirelessly connect with other Apple devices seamlessly. The success of Apple's iOS became obvious because of the explosive development of software applications that took advantage of the iPhone's processing power.
→ Google's Android: Google's Android OS, like Apple's iOS, is built around the Linux OS kernel. Unlike the iOS, Google has made Android open-source, so that developers have an easier time of making applications that will run on Android. This has resulted in the creation of nearly as many applications for Android as for Apple's iOS.

Seen as a competitor to the iOS, Android even has the capacity to use software that the iOS won't run. For example, Adobe's Flash software (often used to create animations) works on Android but not on iOS.

b. Applications (Apps)

A market has developed for software that can fully use the technological features of smartphones. Such software is typically referred to as an **app (application).** Smartphones may come with apps loaded on them or might obtain them via a download.

Legal service/software providers have recognized the potential inherent in apps. Lexis-Nexis offers apps at http://www.lexisnexis.com/mobile/ and West Publishing offers apps at http://legalsolutions.thomsonreuters.com/law-products/law-books/ebooks-apps/mobile-apps. Others, like Fastcase, offer a free smartphone app. Not surprisingly, these and other apps may be part of a practice's subscription to any of these legal content and service providers.

c.   Common Features

Smartphones will typically have the following preloaded features:

→ Maps: the software of a smartphone has to identify its location to figure out where to direct or receive a call. This also can tell a user about his or her position on a map, making it possible to obtain directions via the smartphone. A lawyer who travels to different courts might especially like this feature.

→ Office productivity: a smartphone may have the capacity to use common business office productivity software, yet the size of the handheld device may make it difficult to do data entry, like with a laptop. At worst, a lawyer would at least be able to obtain and use an app to read a downloaded document like a court opinion.

→ Internet connectivity: since smartphones typically have the capacity to connect to the Internet, they could also serve as mobile **hotspots,** a means for a laptop user to connect to the Internet via Wi-Fi. So, a lawyer or paralegal could more easily find data stored on the legal practice's server, such as legal research done on a client's case, by using the cellphone as a mobile hotspot for a laptop, instead of trying to do the legal research via a smartphone's browser.

→ Graphic interface: an appealing feature on some smartphones involves having a **capacitive,** or touch, screen. A user may open and close programs with a stroke of a finger, eliminating the need to maneuver a browser arrow. Some smartphones, however, do have a small, built-in track ball.

→ Bluetooth: as with cellphones, smartphones may have Bluetooth capacity. Like any wireless network, activating the Bluetooth technology on a smartphone can make it vulnerable to hacking. Newer versions provide differing levels of security, but a user should turn off the Bluetooth function on a smartphone when not in use.

→ Keyboard: a smartphone could include a miniature keyboard, thereby making it easier to send a text (**SMS**) message. This process sometimes is identified as instant messaging (IM). Or the user could call up the image of a miniature keyboard, so that with a capacitive screen, a paralegal could type in search terms when using a search engine. It may also have the capacity to connect to a larger scale keyboard, perhaps via a Bluetooth connection.

Figure 11.9
A Smartphone with Full Keyboard

→ Storage: smartphones will have enough space to store documents. Via a cable, they then might work like a Flash drive.

d.   Battery Life

As with laptops, the battery life of a smartphone can pose an issue. But, most will have a setting that automatically shuts off the smartphone at some point. In addition to having the capacity to recharge the batteries of smartphones via wall sockets, some smartphones might also have the capacity to recharge directly from a computer, via a **USB** cable.

e.   Cellular Wireless Standards: 3G and 4G

Many cellphones currently use the 3G (G stands for generation) data transmission standard. This makes it possible to read documents stored on a server, but would not be fast enough to view a video as it loaded into the smartphone. Newer smartphones use 4G, which some consider to be the equivalent of broadband for smartphones because of the speed and the volume of data that can be transmitted.

f.   Firewalls

Smartphones, like laptops and desktop computers, often will have the option for erecting a software firewall. Firewall protection on a smartphone might involve layering types of data, thereby increasing the number and kinds of barriers that someone trying to hack into the device would encounter.

B.   DATA MANAGEMENT

Issues regarding the lawyer's obligation to keep data confidential go beyond telecommunication and into data management.

1.   Passwords

Passwords stand as the first line of defense against unsanctioned access to data.

i.   Complexity

The ideal password should be easy to remember but difficult to guess. Passwords that might be difficult to guess should not use words, names, or commonly used identification information, such as Social Security numbers. One common strategy for generating passwords that a hacker cannot easily guess includes the use of numbers and symbols. A user could substitute a letter with one of the symbols on a keyboard, such as pa$$word, or use a number for a letter, like turnstyle. Doing both can increase the difficulty that a hacker would face when trying to guess a password, such as pa$$worD*1!.

ii.   Updates

To enhance the effectiveness of passwords, the manager of a computer network might require all users to change passwords periodically, destroying the value of old passwords. Frequent changes could also frustrate efforts by former employees to gain unauthorized access to a network.

2.   Retention

A firm might want to craft a policy about how long it will keep copies of data like e-mail, since storing data can quickly demand a lot of storage space. This policy might focus on the retention of certain kinds of e-mail, like modifications to the contract that created the lawyer-client relationship, as opposed to messages that confirm an appointment with a client.

3.   VOIP and Voice Mail

Saving audio conversations made over the Internet, via VOIP, also raises ethical issues regarding proper storage. For example, a firm might use encryption with VOIP communications, which will withstand almost all efforts at cracking the encryption. Where feasible, preserving voice mail messages, at least by using passwords, could also make it easier for a legal practice to fulfill its ethical obligations.

4.   Disposal of Equipment

Given an obligation to preserve client confidentiality, a law firm might have an obligation to dispose of client information, when permitted, in a secure manner. For example, deleted files from a permanent storage media can be recovered. Reformatting a disk drive can make the recovery of data even more difficult, but not impossible. A firm might find it easier to consult with a specialist to achieve safe disposal of a client's confidential information kept on a hard drive.

i.   Remote Access

In 2011, the thief of a laptop encountered some of the risks inherent in stealing a computer. The laptop's owner, who possessed top-notch programming skills, was able to access the laptop remotely, once the thief connected it to the Internet. The owner used the laptop's camera to get a picture of the thief and notified the thief about the laptop's capacity to identify its location. The thief surrendered the laptop, although not before doing an impromptu dance routine, a portion of which accompanied the television news broadcast of the story about the thief.

Owners might install software that allows the user to lockdown the device remotely and/or eliminate data remotely, denying the thief the benefits of the crime. Services might allow the owner to have a laptop disclose its location by activating global positioning software, facilitating the recovery of the stolen device.

C. CONCLUSION

No legal practice could effectively function without telecommunication, involving the use of networks, e-mail, and smartphones. Law firms have an ethical obligation to keep client communication safe, no matter its nature, which could mean using passwords and properly disposing of data, where appropriate.

D. REFERENCES

(n.d.). Massachusetts Rules of Professional Conduct Rule 1.6: Confidentiality of Information, retrieved from http://www.lawlib.state.ma.us/source/mass/rules/sjc/sjc307/rule1-6.html.
(1999). Formal Opinion No. 99-413, from
https://www.lexis.com/research/retrieve?_m=
8a63d3f69b859c0b80f096a45965d1d4&csvc=fo&cform=searchForm&_fmtstr=
FULL&docnum=1&_startdoc=1&wchp=dGLbVtz-zSkAb&_md5=
2adbaa4666661dbea18338aed5d739b1

E. TERMS

Algorithm
American Bar Association (ABA)
Antivirus software
App (application)
Attachment
Bandwidth
Bluetooth
Browser
Capacitive screen
Coaxial cable
Cookie
Data packets

Denial of Service (DoS) attack
E-mail
Encrypts
Ethernet
File transfer protocol (FTP)
Firewall
FireWire
Hacker
Home page
Hotspot
HTTPS
Hubs
Hypertext
Hypertext transfer protocol (HTTP)
Instant messaging
Intranet
Local area network (LAN)
Malicious software (malware)
Network
Operating system (OS)
Peer-to-peer network
Phishing
Pop-up blockers
Router
Secure sockets layers (SSL)
Security certificate
Servers
Service set identifier (SSID)
Skype
Smartphones
SMS (short message service)
Spam
Spyware
Telecommunications
Trojans
Tunneling
USB (universal serial bus)
Uniform resource locator (URL)
Virtual private network (VPN)
Virus
Voice Over Internet Protocol (VOIP)
Webex
Web pages
Websites
Wi-Fi
Wireless local area network (WLAN)
Wireless personal area network (WPAN)

Hypotheticals

1. Describe the apps available through Lexis-Nexis and WestLaw. Then identify three features of each that you would find to be most useful. Presume that you have access to all platforms, such as an iPhone or a smartphone that uses the Android OS.

2. Describe the ethical concerns that a legal practice needs to keep in mind when engaging in electronic communication.

3. Describe at least three levels of security mentioned in this chapter. Identify, from that trio, the one that provides the greatest level of security, then explain why.

4. If asked why a law firm would need to purchase software to protect against malware and attacks on the integrity of a network's computer, what points should be raised?

5. Identify different characteristics of at least five types of networks mentioned in this chapter.

CHAPTER

12

Technology and the Law Firm of the Future

CHAPTER OUTCOMES

By the end of this chapter, a student will be able to:

- Demonstrate how technological advances have affected the legal industry
- Assess the advantages of virtual law practice
- Use social networking platforms for promotional purposes
- Identify opportunities to change the way the legal industry functions and to make it more efficient
- Evaluate the impact of technological advances on professional ethics
- Understand economic pressures on the legal industry
- Discuss typical technology used by law firms

Words such as *cables, lithographs, telex,* and *dictaphone* aren't exactly common vocabulary in a law office anymore—but they once were. Similarly, words like *webinar, podcast, voice mail,* and *smartphone* may be obsolete 10, 15, or 25 years from now. Think of technology in your own world that you might already use less than you once did or not at all: answering machines, fax machines, film, floppy discs, even a landline telephone! Technology is really a tool to help lawyers and others work better, smarter, and faster.

Law office managers must anticipate and plan for emerging technology, and lawyers and staff must use current technologies responsibly. Law firms that spend lavishly on the latest technology tools that lawyers or staff find too time-consuming or challenging to learn how to use are not budgeting wisely. Law firms that choose not to upgrade technologically may actually find that they're losing clients. Some prospective clients even specify that information technology capability be addressed when they issue requests for proposals from prospective law firms.[1] Training is necessary for new technology, and managerial support for lawyers and others to attend training sessions is also vital—without it, expensive gadgetry may lie fallow until it, too, becomes obsolete.

---

1. Douglas Caddell, *Selling Your Law Firm's Tech*, Law.com Legal Technology, June 4, 2007.

A.   HOW TECHNOLOGY HAS CHANGED THE PRACTICE OF LAW AND LAW OFFICE MANAGEMENT

Fifty or 60 years ago, lawyers largely relied on secretaries for help completing tasks. Secretaries in the days before printers and copiers had to take dictation and then type numerous versions of a document, sometimes making multiple carbon copies as they typed. In the days before answering machines and voice mail, switchboard operators answered telephones and took messages.

Technological advances have changed how lawyers do their jobs. Lawyers and their support staffs need different skill sets today. Lawyers should know how to type, how to conduct legal research electronically, how to communicate with clients and others via the Internet, and how to use different types of software—for word processing, creating documents, tracking time, measuring performance, and handling other tasks and assignments that might arise. Likewise, secretaries must be comfortable using many different computer programs, not just word processing software. Law office managers today might find that much of their work is automated. Spread sheets tabulate income and outgo when data are entered into a computer program, client invoices are generated electronically and may well be transmitted via the Internet, supplies and postage might be ordered online, calendars are maintained on computers, and conflict of interest checks are conducted electronically.

The development of notebook and tablet computers, smartphones, easy and constant Internet access, small and affordable scanners, and lightweight copiers means that workplaces now have more flexibility. Lawyers can work well remotely—whether they're on the road and working from a hotel room near a client or working from a home office or from their car. Legal research need not be conducted in a library with reference books; it can be done using online databases such as Lexis and Westlaw. Secretaries aren't necessarily needed to work on the first drafts of documents; lawyers might be able to pull up templates and forms right on their own computers. Workspaces aren't limited to the confines of a traditional office. According to the 2013 ABA Legal Technology Survey Report, 5 percent of lawyers surveyed have a **virtual law office**,[2] meaning one for which there is no centralized office. Instead, lawyers and staff work from different locations (often their home offices) and generally communicate electronically rather than face to face. Seventy-three percent of lawyers work remotely at least some of the time.[3]

virtual law office: A law office for which there is no formal, centralized office; instead, lawyers and staff work at remote locations (often their home offices) and generally communicate electronically rather than face-to-face.

In some ways, although advances in technology mean that lawyers are free to roam, they're actually more chained to their work than in the past. The ease of communication via e-mail, texting, and smartphone means that clients may expect their lawyer to be available and working around the clock.

Today, a large law firm may have an information technology (IT) staff or department. A small firm might outsource this function to a contractor. A large firm with an IT staff may well customize software that it purchases or actually have the IT staff develop its own software.

---

2. Robert Ambrogi, *Number of "Virtual" Law Practices Shows Decline in 2013 ABA Technology Survey,* Robert Ambrogi's LawSites blog (Aug. 13, 2013), http://www.lawsitesblog.com/2013/08/number-of-virtual-law-practices-shows-decline-in-aba-tech-survey.html.

3. *Id.*

1.   Consolidation

Technology has also made the administration of law firms easier. Lawyers in large law firms, with multiple offices in the United States and around the world, are able to communicate easily and efficiently thanks to e-mail; wikis; Google Drive (Google Docs) and SharePoint sites; software such as Skype, which allows voice and video calls to be placed via the Internet; and other communication platforms. A **wiki** is a Web site that can be modified and added to by visitors to the site. The word *wiki* means "quick" in Hawaiian.[4] For instance, visitors might post messages, write lists, post helpful materials, and create Web casts that other visitors can access. Wikis are sometimes described as virtual white boards or notebooks, where thoughts and other ideas can be jotted down and then elaborated on.

wiki: A Web site that can be modified and added to by visitors to the site.

The convenience of wikis is that rather than trying to track e-mail messages back and forth among multiple addressees, users can alter documents and other materials directly online. Users need not be online all at the same time; they can arrange to be notified via e-mail when a change to a document on the wiki is made. Wikis can be especially useful to large law firms that have lawyers in different offices working on a client matter.

An example of a large wiki is Wikipedia.com, an online encyclopedia where visitors can modify entries to the site. Wikis need not be accessible to the public at large; wiki sites can be limited to only certain visitors. Documents can also be managed and shared via SharePoint sites, which are Web sites that use Microsoft SharePoint's Server Platform. Access to SharePoint sites, too, can be restricted to specified persons. Google Drive allows documents to be shared with specified users and to be accessed remotely.

2.   Outsourcing and Offshoring

Technological advances allow law firms to hire others to do portions of their work. **Outsourcing** is the practice of retaining a third party to perform a portion of a business's activities. At a basic level, some firms outsource mail-room activities rather than hiring their own employees to work there. Law firms are not in the business of disseminating received materials in the most efficient fashion; expert consultants can do that better and more cheaply, especially for a small law firm. In addition, certain services that are outsourced are probably done by people who have skills superior to those of the staff the firm itself might hire. For instance, a mail delivery clerk who works for a large organization that firms outsource to has the potential to be promoted. That outsourced clerk will likely be more motivated to do a good job and to make improvements in the service provided. At a small law firm, that person would probably not move beyond the top job in the mail room.

outsource: The practice of retaining a third party to perform a portion of a business's activities.

Firms might outsource back-office functions such as accounting or technical support. Again, a hired consultant may well have more up-to-date expertise than an employee at a law firm. Moreover, thanks to the ease of electronic communications, those accountants and technical support consultants need not

---

4. Peter Buck, *Wikis Put Lawyers on a Collaborative Path,* Law Technology News, May 8, 2008, *available at* http://www.law.com.

necessarily be located near the law firm's office. They might be halfway around the world in countries where labor is significantly less expensive than it is in the United States and other Western countries.[5]

offshoring: Relocating a business's activities to an area in another country where the jobs may be done more efficiently.

Offshoring is the relocation of a business's activities to an area in another country where the jobs may be done more efficiently (typically, lower employment costs). Not only accounting and other back-office functions are outsourced; legal services are outsourced and offshored as well. "Outsourcing relationships are typically governed by an outsourcing agreement that must address and specify things such as: the scope of services to be provided, service levels (i.e., benchmarks), the length of the contract (typically long), choice of laws, and privacy and data protection."[6] A law firm might hire lawyers in another country, such as India, to handle routine legal matters for a client. A large law firm might hire an inexpensive, small law firm located in the United States to handle discovery to appease a client who is trying to keep down costs. A firm or even a client might use temporary lawyers, temporary paralegals, e-discovery services, and other low-cost alternatives to performing functions internally.[7]

Some corporate in-house legal departments are opening offices in remote locations. For example, General Electric uses lawyers and paralegals in Gurgaon, India, for basic contracts work, which is then reviewed by its U.S.-based counsel.[8]

Whether legal work is outsourced or offshored, or both, some concerns arise about the ethics of using cheaper workers, maintaining confidentiality as material is transmitted back and forth between various offices or shared via Google Drive and SharePoint sites or in other ways, and ensuring quality. The American Bar Association, in an ethics opinion, approved the outsourcing of legal work to both lawyers and nonlawyers provided that ethics rules on competence, supervision, and protection of confidential information are met, along with rules barring the unauthorized practice of law and reasonableness of fees.[9] Clients typically must be informed that a lawyer is outsourcing work, especially since a client's confidential information cannot be revealed to another without the client's consent.[10] A lawyer may charge a client only the actual cost of the outsourced work along with a portion of the costs for overhead and for supervising the outsourced services—unless a client agrees to pay a higher rate.

A somewhat elevated inquiry into the abilities of lawyers located in remote jurisdictions may be necessary before a firm outsources legal work. For instance, are those lawyers trained sufficiently in legal matters? Was their education adequate? Are they sufficiently familiar with the requirements of confidentiality and other duties owed to clients?

---

5. *See, e.g.,* Julie Creswell, *Law Firms Are Starting to Adopt Outsourcing,* N.Y. Times (Oct. 27, 2006), *available at* http://www.nytimes.com.

6. Alexandra Hanson, *Comment: Legal Process Outsourcing to India: So Hot Right Now!,* 62 SMU L. Rev. 1889, 1891 (Fall 2009).

7. *See, e.g.,* Nina Cunningham, *Is Outsourcing an Opportunity for Law Firms?,* LJN's Legal Tech Newsletter (May 2013), *available at* http://www.altmanweil.com /Outsourcing0613.

8. *See, e.g.,* Ellen L. Rosen, *Corporate America Sending More Legal Work to Bombay,* N.Y. Times (Mar. 14, 2004), *available at* http://www.nytimes.com.

9. ABA Standing Comm. on Ethics and Prof'l Responsibility, Lawyer's Obligations When Outsourcing Legal and Non-Legal Support Services, Formal Op. 08-451 (Aug. 5, 2008).

10. Peter H. Geraghty, *Recent Ethics Opinion: Outsourcing,* Your ABA, *available at* http://www.abanet.org/media/youraba/200809/article11.html (last visited Dec. 5, 2010).

3.   Virtual Law Practices

Thanks to the growth of online databases, the development of ebooks and other resources, and the ease with which technology can be used to access documents, to conduct conferences, and to communicate in other ways, some lawyers find that they can provide more cost-efficient legal services to clients by working from a home office rather than commuting to an office building every day. Clients can be drawn to virtual law practices because their legal fees might be lower than those they would pay to a lawyer with a lot of overhead costs. Lawyers and support staff might be drawn to virtual law practices because they can work more comfortably from home. Some states have expressly allowed virtual law practices to be developed.[11] Other states require that lawyers have a physical address, which can limit the development of virtual law practices. Monitoring the unauthorized practice of law can become more challenging for states when law firms are operating in virtual law offices and clients can be geographically dispersed.

When operating as a virtual office, law firms must take care to protect private client data and must still observe applicable ethics rules in the states in which they are operating.[12]

4.   Social Networking

Lawyers should market themselves on various social networking sites such as LinkedIn, Twitter, and Facebook. One survey found that almost 85 percent of law firms are using social media.[13] Such sites allow lawyers to set up accounts and to post information about their experience. Lawyers can post messages and demonstrate their expertise in a particular area of the law. Law firms might also establish a presence on these sites, which can be used for multiple reasons to attract prospective employees, and to keep in touch with firm alumni—who might one day funnel business to the firm or actually become a client. Moreover, lawyers and others in the field can use these sites to gather competitive intelligence about competitors. By assessing the information rival lawyers and law firms are posting, a lawyer might be able to differentiate herself from her competitors or highlight capabilities that distinguish her from the competition.

Even when a lawyer opts not to use social networking sites, other lawyers and prospective, current, or former clients still use these sites for professional reasons. Prospective clients doing online research to locate prospective lawyers are less likely to find a lawyer who does not have a social media presence.

Social networking sites can pose hazards for lawyers, though, even if the lawyers themselves do not have accounts on these sites. For instance, audience members listening to a lawyer's presentation might be tweeting, or posting updates via Twitter, in which they assess the lawyer's remarks. This can happen

---

11. *See, e.g.,* State Bar of Cal. Standing Comm. on Prof'l Responsibility & Conduct, Formal Op. 2012-184 (2012); N.C. State Bar, Formal Ethics Op. 10 (2005).

12. A.B.A. Law Practice Management Section eLawyering Task Force, *Suggested Minimum Requirements for Law Firms Delivering Legal Services Online* (Oct. 15, 2009), http://meetings.american-bar.org/webupload/commupload/EP024500/relatedresources /Minimum_Requirements_for_Lawyers_2009_10_24.pdf-5k-2009-11-19.

13. John G. Browning, *Facebook, Twitter, and LinkedIn—Oh My! The ABA Ethics 20/20/ Commission and Evolving Ethical Issues in the Use of Social Media,* 40 N. Ky L. Rev. 255, 256 (2013).

in real time, thereby limiting the lawyer's ability to respond right away. Similar updates might be posted via cell phone on Facebook, LinkedIn, and other sites. Someone might also be sending text messages via cell phone during a presentation. Even if a lawyer chooses not to participate on these sites, the sites should be periodically checked for mentions of the lawyer or the lawyer's law firm. The lawyer can then decide whether, or how, to respond. Some search engines, such as Google, allow users to set up alerts so that they will be notified when new material with their selected search term (which can be their name) is posted on the Internet.

Lawyers can also make use of the Internet and social media sites to gather information and evidence about parties to a lawsuit:

> Whether you're a family lawyer looking for evidence that will affect a custody or property settlement, an employment lawyer discovering that a sexual harassment plaintiff isn't as innocent as he or she purports to be, or a personal injury litigator seeking evidence that a plaintiff isn't as physically limited as he or she claims to be, social networking sites are a virtual treasure trove of information for both sides. Prosecutors have used Facebook ... photos to impeach murder and drunk driving defendants, and criminal defense attorneys are using everything from YouTube video footage to Facebook status updates to clear their clients.[14]

Lawyers must take precautions not to act inappropriately on social networking sites, such as by adding judges before whom they appear as friends or by engaging jurors on a case. This is an evolving area of the law. A Florida Advisory Opinion warned judges not to "friend" lawyers who appear before them, because it might give the appearance that the lawyer has undue influence before the judge:

> The Committee believes that listing lawyers who may appear before the judge as "friends" on a judge's social networking page reasonably conveys to others the impression that these lawyer "friends" are in a special position to influence the judge. This is not to say, of course, that simply because a lawyer is listed as a "friend" on a social networking site or because a lawyer is a friend of the judge, as the term friend is used in its traditional sense, means that this lawyer is, in fact, in a special position to influence the judge. The issue, however, is not whether the lawyer actually is in a position to influence the judge, but instead whether the proposed conduct, the identification of the lawyer as a "friend" on the social networking site, conveys the impression that the lawyer is in a position to influence the judge. The Committee concludes that such identification in a public forum of a lawyer who may appear before the judge does convey this impression and therefore is not permitted.[15]

In comparison, the California Judges Association found that judges can be active on social networks and be friends with lawyers who may appear before them,

---

14. Judge Gena Slaughter & John G. Browning, *The Attorney and Social Media: Social Networking Dos and Don'ts for Lawyers and Judges*, 73 Tex. B.J. 192, 192 (Mar. 2010).

15. Florida Supreme Court Judicial Ethics Advisory Committee, Opinion No. 2009-20 (Nov. 27, 2009), *available at* http://www.jud6.org/legalcommunity/legalpractice /opinions/jeacopinions/ 2009/2009-20.html. *See also* Florida Supreme Court Judicial Ethics Advisory Committee, Opinion No. 2012-12 (May 9, 2012), *available at* http://www.jud6.org/legalcommunity/legalpractice/opinions/jeacopinions/2012/2012-12 .html.

although judges should take certain precautions to avoid any appearance of impropriety.[16]

Lawyers must also consider potential ethical repercussions if they establish blogs, Web sites that are, in some measure, a personal journal (even one that addresses professional matters) that typically allows comments on the material to be made by visitors to the blog. A number of lawyers have blogs that focus on their particular practice area. A lawyer's blog is sometimes called a "blawg" because it is a blog involving a legal subject.

Lawyers, when writing on blogs, must remember client confidentiality and other ethical constraints. One lawyer in Illinois faced disciplinary action for allegedly publishing confidential information about a client on the Internet via the lawyer's blog.[17] In a separate matter, a judge was disciplined for having ex parte communications with a lawyer via Facebook.[18]

In certain circumstances, a presence on Facebook or a blog might be considered to be lawyer advertising and thus subject to ethical rules on advertising. For example, the Kentucky Attorneys' Advertising Commission proposed a new amendment on social media:

> "'Advertise' means to furnish any information or communication containing a lawyer's name or other identifying information, and an 'advertisement' is any information containing a lawyer's name or other identifying information, except the following. . . . Information and communication by a lawyer to members of the public in the format of web log journals on the internet that permit real time communication and exchanges on topics of general interest in legal issues provided there is no reference to an offer by the lawyer to render legal services."
>
> Communications made by a lawyer using a social media website such as MySpace and Facebook that are of a non-legal nature are not considered advertisements; however, those that are of a legal nature are governed by SCR 3.130-7.02(1(j).[19]

This stance was somewhat controversial, and the regulation had not been adopted as of Sept. 18, 2013. In New York, blogs, newsletters, and client alerts are sometimes considered advertising. General information about developments in the law is not considered advertising, but information disseminated by a lawyer or law firm about that specific lawyer or firm is.[20]

Lawyers who use social media sites should be certain to check state ethics rules regarding interactions on and use of these sites. In particular, they should take care not to give legal advice via their blog or form an attorney-client relationship—and they should include disclaimers so that visitors to the blog site are aware that posts do not constitute legal advice or establish a lawyer-client relationship.

---

16. California Judges Association Judicial Ethics Committee, Opinion No. 66 (2010), *available at* http://www.caljudges.org/ethics_opinions.vp.html.

17. *In re Peshek*, No. 09CH89 (Hearing B. Ill. Att'y. Registration & Disciplinary Commn. *filed* Aug. 25, 2009), *available at* http://www.iardc.org/09CH0089CM.html. Peshek was suspended from practicing for a couple of months in 2010. Att'y Registration & Disciplinary Commn. of the Sup. Ct. of Ill., https://www.iardc.org/ldetail .asp?id=388941527 (last visited June 20, 2011).

18. *In re Terry*, No. 08-234, at 1 (N.C. Jud. Standards Commn. Apr. 1, 2009), *available at* http://www.aoc.state.nc.us/www/public/coa/jsc/publicreprimands/jsc08-234.pdf.

19. AAC Regulation No. 17: (proposed new regulation) SOCIAL MEDIA SCR 3.130-7.020(1)(j), *available at* http://www.kybar.org/30 (approved by Kentucky Board of Governors on July 30, 2010, subject to review and comment).

20. *See, e.g.*, N.Y. State Rules of Prof'l Conduct R. 7.1 Comment (as amended through Dec. 20, 2012), *available at* http://www.nysba.org/AM/Template.cfm?Section=For_Attorneys&ContentID=152184&template=/CM/ContentDisplay.cfm.

5. *Unbundling Legal Services*

Effective legal representation is unavailable to many people who could not possibly pay the associated legal fees for any counsel they seek. Technological developments, however, have made information about the legal system and pertinent documents far more available to those in need of legal advice than they once were. Some people who need legal help are willing to take a "do it yourself" approach and to buy less expensive materials that can help them. A person might set up her own business and prepare and file appropriate legal paperwork for doing so. Another might represent himself in his own divorce action but get a little help from a lawyer in preparing the underlying paperwork. In-house counsel, in an effort to cut legal costs, may hire a legal services outsourcing vendor to handle some matters rather than going to its high-priced law firms for everything. Computer software can guide users to prospective solutions to their legal problems:

> Technology promises to change the nature of the legal information product niche. Document assembly software that presents different documents based on answers to questions can go beyond the "one size fits all" forms and present tailored documents. Despite a temporarily successful effort to ban it in Texas, Intuit's WillMaker Plus software is now sold throughout the U.S. Online, companies such as LegalZoom offer a wide variety of documents. LegalZoom claims to have created more than one million legal documents, [and] has attracted funding from A-list venture capitalists that clearly see a substantial business opportunity . . . [21]

These do-it-yourself vendors are making a significant impact on the legal industry. More than one million wills have been prepared by users of Legal Zoom.[22] Another do-it-yourself service, Rocket Lawyer, had 70,000 daily visitors as far back as 2011.[23]

Whether and to what extent legal outsourcing services owned by nonlawyers and electronic aids for do-it-yourselfers are violating proscriptions on the unauthorized practice of law is a matter that is still being debated. Some bars have explicitly allowed this unbundling of legal services provided that the client is fully informed.[24] Those involved in these unbundled legal services must also take care not to violate ethics rules prohibiting fee-splitting with nonlawyers.

B.   MARKET AND GENERATIONAL SHIFTS

Market pressures and law firm inefficiencies, combined with technological advances, have changed the legal industry significantly in recent years. Thanks

---

21. Ray Worthy Campbell, *Rethinking Regulation and Innovation in the U.S. Legal Services Market,* 9 N.Y.U. J. L. & Bus. 1, 39 (Fall 2012).

22. AbacusLaw, Don't Let These 5 Big Changes in the Legal Profession Be Catastrophic to Your Law Firm, *available at* http://www.abacuslaw.com/form-five-changes/ (last visited Sept. 18, 2013).

23. Daniel Fisher, *Google Jumps Into Online-Law Business With Rocket Lawyer,* Forbes.com (Aug. 11, 2011), http://www.forbes.com/sites/danielfisher/2011/08/11/google-jumps-into-online-law-business-with-rocket-lawyer.

24. *See, e.g.,* D.C. Bar, Opin. No. 330 (July 2005), *available at* http://www.dcbar.org /for_lawyers/ethics/legal_ethics/opinions/opinion330.cfm.

to economic recession, clients remain disinclined to spend excessively for legal assistance. Some became disinclined to pay high hourly fees for the work of inexperienced junior associates who have not received much practical training in law school.

Due to technological advances, reasonable alternatives can be had for reasonable prices. Corporate clients are more likely to funnel routine work to less expensive law firms or to use legal services providers at a reduced cost. A client might offshore some legal work or use legal software to generate documents associated with less complex matters. Individuals at modest income levels might choose to represent themselves in court, perhaps with a little assistance from a lawyer who has helped them prepare papers to file.

1. Price and Performance

Large law firms, especially, have been challenged both by the economy and by their own structures. The trend toward consolidation by merger has meant that law firms are able to offer more services to a broader pool of clients around the world, but the marriage of firms has not always been compatible. Firms might find their resources stretched when they have agreed to compensate highly certain high-visibility, big-name partners. They might also become bloated with expensive nonequity partners whom they have hired because clients did not want to pay less experienced associates. A firm's compensation scheme and pressure to meet billable hour requirements might mean that lawyers do not delegate tasks that could be performed less expensively by others but instead keep them to themselves. Lawyers sensing trouble are disinclined to stay and might jump to another firm.[25]

These developments are bringing about significant changes in the legal field:

> The new law firm model will have a much smaller ownership base. Firms will hire fewer lawyers but keep more as permanent employees, although most will not become equity partners. The size of support staff will also diminish as legal process and knowledge management become automated. Many functions, including basic legal tasks, will be outsourced to individuals and organizations that can provide these functions at lower cost than the firm could if it handled them itself. The physical footprint of the law office will be dramatically smaller as fewer people will actually work at a desk in a traditional office building. A handful of global megafirms will dominate the international legal business, and specialized boutiques will replace regional generalist firms in most metropolitan legal markets.[26]

These changes have created opportunities for those in the legal field with an entrepreneurial bent. Increasingly, legal services are being provided by entities other than lawyers or with less direct involvement by lawyers. Legal document preparers, legal software Web sites, and do-it-yourself law books have made the law more accessible to people who are disinclined to pay high prices for legal advice.

---

25. *See generally* Noam Scheiber, *The Last Days of Big Law*, New Republic, Aug. 5, 2013, at 25.
26. Gary Munneke, *When Brahmins Bumble: Dewey Really Care?*, 84-SEP N.Y. St. B.J. 28, 33 (Sept. 2012).

Although restrictions on the unauthorized practice of law and professional responsibility rules still pertain, they are evolving in some areas. For instance, Texas explicitly allows the sale of legal forms and other materials via the Internet:

> the "practice of law" does not include the design, creation, publication, distribution, display, or sale, including publication, distribution, display, or sale by means of an Internet web site, of written materials, books, forms, computer software, or similar products if the products clearly and conspicuously state that the products are not a substitute for the advice of an attorney.[27]

2.   *Working with Millennials*

Changes in the legal industry and the high price of attending law school mean that some new lawyers are looking for more satisfying alternatives than working for a large law firm. Although the pay at such firms is certainly good, the hours can be grueling. Associates might be disinclined to put in so much time at the office and prefer quality of life to being on the partnership path—especially because so few people allegedly on that path actually ascend to partnership. Cultural differences among generations—with law firm elders insisting that younger lawyers "pay their dues" and more junior associates preferring different work atmospheres where collegiality, plenty of feedback, and a pleasant day-to-day work experience may be more paramount—can create conflicts.

Younger members of the workforce, such as those born between 1992 and 1995, referred to as millennials, grew up in a digital world and have approaches to work that differ from older generations. Millennials have been described as "lazy, entitled, and selfish,"[28] and some older people have been challenged to work with them. Because millennials grew up using computers and cell phones, they are technologically adept and realize that they need not be seated in an office, at a desk, for 15 hours a day to work effectively.[29] They work well collaboratively and are interested in feedback. Many[30] realize they will never make partner, and so refuse to work lengthy hours to meet high billable hour requirements to entertain the fiction that they might. They also realize that they are unlikely to stay more than a few years at any given employer. Law firms have had to adapt as this new generation enters the legal field by focusing more on quality-of-the-workplace issues.[31]

---

27. Tex. Gov't Code Ann. § 81.101(c) (2013).

28. Jeanne Meister, *The Boomer-Millennial Workplace Clash: Is It Real?*, Forbes.com (June 4, 2013), http://www.forbes.com/sites/jeannemeister/2013/06/04/the-boomer-millennial-workplace-clash-is-it-real/.

29. *See, e.g.,* Lawrence J. Centola III, *Bridging the Divide Between Baby Boomers and Millennials,* 61 La. B.J. 18 (June/July 2013).

30. *See generally* Rodney G. Snow, *Baby Boomers Meet Millennials in the Legal Workplace: From Face-Lift to Facebook,* 4-DEC Utah B.J. 8 (Nov./Dec. 2011).

31. *See generally An Anniversary Roundtable: Transformations in Law Firm Management,* 30-SUM Del. Law. 8 (Spring/Summer 2012).

C.   TYPICAL TECHNOLOGY USED BY LAW FIRMS

Hardware and software are expensive. A law firm should develop a technology plan to assess its hardware and software needs, anticipate future growth, and provide for maintenance and purchases of warranties. Depending on the law firm's needs and budget, the plan may even prioritize purchases.

Hardware is the physical electronic equipment a firm needs (as distinguished from **software,** the computer programs needed to run much of the hardware). A firm's hardware needs are likely to include the following items:

hardware: The machines, wiring, and other physical components of a computer or other electronic system.

- desktop computers
- laptop computers
- computer server for a networked computer system
- webcam for use in online video conferencing and for the creation of podcasts and Web casts
- USB sticks on which to store documents
- interface controllers (such as USB cords) to connect devices to the computer
- smartphones
- landline telephones
- telephone and voice mail system (for forwarding calls and to allow callers to leave voice messages for recipients)
- digital cameras
- digital video recorders
- digital voice recorders
- printer
- copier
- scanner
- fax machine

software: The programs and other operating information used by a computer.

A firm's software needs are likely to include these items:

- an operating system, such as Microsoft Windows 8 or Mac OS
- calendaring and docket management program
- time, billing, and accounting program
- case management program
- file management program
- document management program
- electronic spreadsheet program, such as Excel
- word processing program, such as WordPerfect or Microsoft Word
- slide presentation preparation program, such as PowerPoint
- software for handling digital images, such as PhotoShop
- software for creating PDFs, such as Adobe Acrobat
- trial preparation software
- e-mail program
- antivirus program
- firewall and anti-spyware programs to defend against computer intruders
- videoconferencing program such as Adobe Connect
- cloud computing software for document storage and sharing

- Skype or other software enabling voice and video calls to be made via the Internet
- encryption software
- voice recognition software, which automatically transcribes a user's dictation
- text messaging software
- graphics presentation program

Performance, in addition to cost, should be considered when selecting software. Try to find out how often software tends to crash. Think about how much time and effort will be devoted to addressing and fixing problems. Will the original software vendor be able to handle problems? If not, is there off-site and helpful technical support? Will technical problems be handled in-house by the law firm's IT personnel? Whether the software can be easily customized should be taken into account, as should the frequency of upgrades in the software. Training requirements and ease of use should also be considered. How likely are lawyers and others to use the software if extensive training is necessary? Is training free? How committed is the firm to providing training sessions and requiring staff and others to attend?

Given the demands of the modern office and the 24/7 accessibility clients tend to expect of their lawyers, remote access to information must also be provided to attorneys and appropriate staff members. Legal uses of conventional consumer electronics should be considered. For instance, the Apple iPad tablet computer and the Kindle reader are potentially very useful to lawyers as more applications are available for the iPad and more materials, such as continuing legal education documents, are available for the Kindle. Lawyers meeting with clients need not bring boxes of documents with them; they need only upload them to electronic devices such as the iPad and then pull them up as needed. A law firm's IT personnel should stay abreast of developments in the field so they can alert lawyers to useful software that may help them do their jobs better. New programs are often debuting, especially applications for smartphones and the iPad. For instance, Jury Tracker, an application for the iPad, allows lawyers to track jury members and record their observations about juror responses.

What much contemporary technology actually does is allow a lawyer to work in a virtual law office. The lawyer need not be tethered to a desk at firm headquarters. As a practical matter, a virtual law office is really the ability to work from home, to work off-site, such as at a client's office or, if traveling, in a hotel room or airport. Some law firms, recognizing the attraction of low overhead and convenience that a virtual law office provides, are setting up shop as a virtual business, meaning that there is no central office building where the law firm is sited. Virtual law practices are likely to make use of Web-based word processing and document management applications and to invoice electronically. As with brick-and-mortar law firms, however, client communications must be protected and secure.

Lawyers and staff involved in litigation must pay particular attention to changing court requirements and adapt their own technology to that required for litigation. Some courts allow electronic filing of documents; for example, Federal Rules of Civil Procedure Rule 5(d)(3) allows federal courts, in their local rules, to establish electronic filing requirements:

(3) Electronic Filing, Signing, or Verification.

A court may, by local rule, allow papers to be filed, signed, or verified by electronic means that are consistent with any technical standards established by the Judicial Conference of the United States. A local rule may require electronic filing only if reasonable exceptions are allowed. A paper filed electronically in compliance with a local rule is a written paper for purposes of these rules.

A number of courts use videoconferencing.

Graphics may need to be created electronically for use in the courtroom, and compatibility of the firm's technology with the equipment available for trial must be determined beforehand.

D.   SAFEGUARDING INFORMATION

Confidential client information as well as confidential information about the law firm's business itself that is stored electronically must be protected against hacking by outsiders and against unauthorized intrusion by a user. Computers in networks pose a special hazard, because if someone manages to access one portal, it's possible that all of the information in the network might be in jeopardy. Access to networks must be limited, in terms of both who has access and what information can be accessed by a given individual. For instance, a firm's financial records and human resources files should not be accessible by everyone who works at the firm. Access must be limited to authorized users only. Access to a law firm's network should be password-protected.

The Computer Fraud and Abuse Act, 18 U.S.C. § 1030, outlaws certain acts related to the unauthorized access to computers. Lawyers who access computerized data inappropriately may be subject to professional disciplinary action. Consider the following case.

LAWYER DISCIPLINARY BOARD V. MARKINS
663 S.E.2d 614 (W. Va. 2008)

OPINION

LAWYER DISCIPLINARY PROCEEDING
TWO-YEAR SUSPENSION, WITH ADDITIONAL SANCTIONS
Per curiam.

In this lawyer disciplinary proceeding, Respondent Michael P. Markins ("Respondent") objects to the sanctions recommended by a Hearing Panel

Subcommittee of the Lawyer Disciplinary Board ("Board") for violations of the West Virginia Rules of Professional Conduct ("Rules"). Following a disciplinary hearing conducted on July 20, 2007, the Board determined that Respondent violated Rules 8.4(b) and (c) by repeatedly accessing the email accounts of other attorneys, without their knowledge or permission, for over a two-year period. The Board recommends, *inter alia,* that Respondent be suspended from the practice of law for a period of two (2) years. Though Respondent does not dispute the facts giving rise to the disciplinary charges filed against him, he contends the recommended sanctions are too harsh.

For the reasons discussed below, we adopt the Board's recommendations.

I. Factual and Procedural Background

The facts of this case are not in dispute. Respondent has been a practicing attorney since October, 2001. At all times relevant, Respondent was employed as an associate attorney at the law firm of Huddleston Bolen, LLP ("Huddleston").[1] His wife, also an attorney, was similarly employed at the law firm of Offutt, Fisher & Nord ("OFN"). In late October or early November of 2003, Respondent began accessing his wife's OFN e-mail account without her permission or knowledge.[2] Respondent testified that the purpose of reading his wife's e-mails was to secretly monitor her activities because he believed she had become involved in an extramarital affair with an OFN client. Respondent further testified that, initially, he improperly accessed only his wife's account and later, that of another attorney, an OFN partner.[3] Eventually, however, Respondent's curiosity got the better of him, and he began accessing the e-mail accounts of seven other OFN attorneys. Obviously, Respondent did so without either the knowledge or permission of the account holders.

When an OFN attorney began to suspect that her e-mail account had been improperly accessed, OFN retained Paul Law, a computer systems engineer, and launched an investigation. From Mr. Law's investigation, it was learned that on numerous occasions from sometime prior to November 7, 2003, until March 16, 2006, Respondent gained unauthorized access to OFN e-mail accounts from three IP accounts:[4] Respondent's Huddleston IP account; Respondent's residential IP account; and the IP account at the Hampton Inn in Beckley, West Virginia, where Respondent had been monitoring a trial in which both Huddleston and OFN clients were being represented.

According to D.C. Offutt, Jr., the managing partner of OFN, although they were not able to view the actual e-mail messages read by Respondent, they were able to determine which e-mail accounts were accessed, the date and time they were accessed, and from what IP account. Furthermore, Mr. Offutt testified that if there was an attachment to an e-mail, they could determine whether the attachment had been opened. More specifically, they were able to determine that on one occasion certain confidential OFN financial information sent by the firm's chief accountant to the firm's partners by e-mail attachment was opened by Respondent.

It is undisputed that Respondent improperly accessed the e-mail accounts of OFN attorneys on more than 150 occasions. In so doing, Respondent learned personal information about certain attorneys which had been relayed

---

1.   It is undisputed that while in law school Respondent was an outstanding student, graduating near the top of his class. While at Huddleston, Respondent was well thought of in the legal community and was on the firm's "Partnership Track."

2.   The password to his wife's e-mail account was her last name. Similarly, the passwords to the e-mail accounts of all OFN attorneys was the individual account holder's last name.

3.   During his testimony before the Board, Respondent described an e-mail between his wife and an OFN partner in which the partner encouraged Respondent's wife to join her and a particular client in an evening out. (It is unclear from Respondent's testimony if this is the same client with whom he suspected his wife of having an affair.) According to Respondent, the partner's e-mail suggested that they would keep the evening a secret from Respondent.

4.   Mr. Law explained that, "[i]n layman's terms, an IP address is basically a phone number for a computer. . . . It's basically Caller ID for computer systems."

confidentially via e-mail. With regard to confidential client information that had been accessed by Respondent, Mr. Offutt was particularly concerned with the fact that OFN and Huddleston, Respondent's employer, represented co-defendants in a large mass tort case that was in litigation during the time period at issue. In March, 2006, Respondent, along with other lawyers whose firms were involved in the mass litigation, was monitoring the trial from the Hampton Inn in Beckley, West Virginia. While monitoring the proceedings, Respondent gained unauthorized access into various OFN email accounts from the Hampton Inn's IP account. According to Mr. Offutt, Huddleston's mass tort client had a contractual relationship with and a claim for indemnity against OFN's client. Though the claim was not then being litigated, Mr. Offutt testified that information included in the firm's e-mail system would have been "helpful" to Huddleston's client. However, neither Huddleston nor OFN found evidence that any information between OFN attorneys and its client in that case had been compromised.[5]

Following the disciplinary hearing in this case, Mr. Offutt indicated in an affidavit that, since Respondent's misconduct was reported by the Charleston Gazette newspaper and the Associated Press, OFN "has suffered further damage to its image and reputation." Mr. Offutt further indicated that one of the firm's clients expressed "serious concerns" about the security breach and about whether Respondent improperly accessed important information concerning that client. According to Mr. Offutt, this client has put the firm on notice of a potential claim for damages against it. Mr. Offutt indicated that he anticipates that similar concerns will be expressed by other clients in the future and that the negative ramifications and stigma of Respondent's misconduct will be felt for many years. Finally, Mr. Offutt indicated that his firm suffered direct economic losses as a result of Respondent's actions: Mr. Offutt, along with other firm lawyers and staff, spent considerable time and resources investigating and attending internal meetings on the matter and were distracted by the events and their aftermath.

In March 2006, Respondent's wife, who had been completely unaware of Respondent's misconduct, told Respondent that someone had been breaking into OFN e-mail accounts and that the firm was getting close to finding out who it was. Shortly thereafter, Respondent revealed to his wife that it was he who had been improperly accessing the OFN e-mail accounts. The following day, Mr. Offutt, who had learned from the computer expert's investigation that Respondent was responsible for the unauthorized access of the e-mail accounts, inquired of Respondent's wife if she was aware of Respondent's actions. Though she had just learned of Respondent's misconduct, she denied any knowledge of it to Mr. Offutt. Immediately thereafter, Respondent's counsel contacted Mr. Offutt and others at the firm to disclose his actions. Both Respondent and his wife were eventually terminated from employment by their respective law firms as a result.[7]

---

5. When contacted by Mr. Offutt about the breach in OFN's e-mail system by one of its employees, Huddleston conducted its own investigation to determine if Respondent had ever saved OFN e-mails or other OFN computer files in Huddleston's computer system. From its investigation, Huddleston found no information improperly accessed from the OFN e-mails on its computer system.

7. Respondent's wife was initially placed on administrative leave, with pay. When Mr. Offutt learned that Respondent's wife did not answer truthfully when she denied knowledge of Respondent's misconduct, her employment was terminated. As indicated above, Respondent's wife did not know about Respondent's misconduct until he disclosed it to her the evening before she met with Mr. Offutt.

Respondent has consistently maintained that he has never disclosed to anyone any information he obtained from improperly accessing the various OFN e-mail accounts. He testified that he has never used any of the information in an improper manner; did not save any of the accessed emails onto his computer; and did not forward any of the emails to another person.

On December 18, 2006, the Board filed a Statement of Charges against Respondent, alleging violations of Rule 8.4(b) and (c) of the West Virginia Rules of Professional Conduct. The Board alleged violations of Rule 8.4(c) "[b]ecause Respondent engaged in the repetitive unauthorized access of [OFN] e-mail accounts by improperly using various e-mail account passwords assigned to various [OFN] attorneys." Under Rule 8.4(c), "[i]t is professional misconduct for a lawyer to: . . . (c) engage in conduct involving dishonesty, fraud, deceit or misrepresentation."

The Board also alleged violations of Rule 8.4(b) "[b]ecause Respondent's repetitive unauthorized access of [OFN] e-mail accounts was criminal in nature, violated West Virginia Code 61-3C-12,[10] and adversely reflected on his honesty, trustworthiness or fitness as a lawyer[.]" (Footnote added). Under Rule 8.4(b), "[i]t is professional misconduct for a lawyer to: . . . (b) commit a criminal act that reflects adversely on the lawyer's honesty, trustworthiness or fitness as a lawyer in other respects[.]" The Board further alleged there to be "aggravating factors," stating that "Respondent's conduct involved multiple offenses and a pattern of misconduct, was for a selfish motive, and constituted illegal acts."

No criminal charges arising out of Respondent's unauthorized access of OFN e-mail accounts have ever been filed against Respondent.

Following the disciplinary hearing before the Board, the Board found Respondent had violated Rules 8.4(b) and (c), as charged, and recommended the following sanctions:

1. That Respondent be suspended from the practice of law for a period of two (2) years;
2. That, upon reinstatement, Respondent's private practice be supervised for a period of one (1) year;
3. That Respondent complete twelve (12) hours of CLE in ethics in addition to such ethics hours he is otherwise required to complete to maintain his active license to practice, said additional twelve (12) hours to be completed before he is reinstated; and
4. That Respondent pay the costs of these proceedings.

In the instant matter, we are mindful of the mitigating factors presented by Respondent, including the unique circumstances which motivated his misconduct in the first place. However, there are also several aggravating factors which

---

10. W. Va. Code § 61-3C-12 (1989) (Repl. Vol. 2005) states:

Any person who knowingly, willfully and without authorization accesses a computer or computer network and examines any employment, salary, credit or any other financial or personal information relating to any other person, after the time at which the offender knows or reasonably should know that he is without authorization to view the information displayed, shall be guilty of a misdemeanor, and, upon conviction thereof, shall be fined not more than five hundred dollars or confined in the county jail for not more than six months, or both.

this Court cannot ignore or minimize. Though Respondent initially accessed his wife's OFN e-mail account with motives very personal to his marriage, his misconduct eventually became more rampant. Out of simple curiosity, he broke into the e-mail accounts of eight of his wife's unsuspecting co-workers on almost a daily basis for over a two-year period. He did not cease or disclose his actions until he learned OFN's computer experts were on the verge of discovering who was behind the unauthorized intrusions. Moreover, in addition to confidential personal information, Respondent viewed confidential financial information intended to be read exclusively by OFN partners. With regard to confidential client information, in one instance, his firm and OFN represented separate co-defendants which had interests adverse to each other because Respondent's client had an indemnity claim against OFN's client.

Finally, we recognize that with the widespread use of computer e-mail as an important method of communication between and among attorneys and their clients comes the potentiality that the communication might be improperly infiltrated. This Court does not take lightly the fact that, in this case, it was an attorney who repeatedly accessed the confidential e-mails of other attorneys without their knowledge or permission. Thus, the imposition of a suitable sanction in a case such as this is not exclusively dictated by what sanction would appropriately punish the offending attorney, but, just as importantly, this Court must ensure that the discipline imposed adequately serve as an effective deterrent to other attorneys, "to protect the public, to reassure it as to the reliability and integrity of attorneys and to safeguard its interest in the administration of justice." *Battistelli,* 206 W.Va. at 201, 523 S.E.2d at 261, quoting *Lawyer Disciplinary Board v. Taylor,* 192 W.Va. at 144, 451 S.E.2d at 445. Accordingly, based upon the foregoing, we are compelled to adopt the recommendation of discipline tendered by the Board.

IV. CONCLUSION

For the reasons stated above, we adopt the Board's recommendations and hereby impose the following sanctions upon Respondent: (1) Respondent is suspended from the practice of law in West Virginia for a period of two years; (2) upon reinstatement, Respondent's private practice shall be supervised for a period of one year; (3) Respondent is ordered to complete twelve hours of CLE in ethics in addition to such ethics hours he is otherwise required to complete to maintain his active license to practice, said additional twelve hours to be completed before he is reinstated; and (4) Respondent is ordered to pay the costs of these proceedings.

License suspended, with additional sanctions.

In addition to protecting themselves against unauthorized intrusion, law firms must arm their computers against **viruses,** computer scripts and programs that interfere with the use of one's computer. A virus might slow a computer down, disable it entirely, disseminate information inappropriately, or destroy files or entire programs. Viruses are disseminated via the Internet. They are often attached to documents that are downloaded to someone's computer. Before downloading, a document should be scanned for viruses. New viruses are constantly being disseminated, so a firm must have antivirus software that is frequently updated. Other precautions must also be taken. A firm should have a

virus: Computer code that has a detrimental effect on one's computer by slowing it down, disabling it entirely, disseminating information inappropriately, or destroying files and programs.

firewall: A computer program that blocks unauthorized access to a computer from outside intruders.

spyware: Malicious tracking software that disseminates information over the Internet.

metadata: Information embedded in an electronic file about the creation and modification of that file.

firewall program installed in its computers. A **firewall** limits access to a computer from outside intruders. An anti-spyware program is also vital for computers that have access to the Internet. Malicious **spyware** is tracking software that disseminates information over the Internet. Spyware is typically unknowingly downloaded by an Internet user. An anti-spyware program will block the transmission of unauthorized data that the spyware is trying to disseminate.

A firm should also establish a policy regarding metadata, information about other data that a computer software program might automatically tabulate. **Metadata** is embedded in documents and tracks information about the creation of and modifications to the document. It is technically defined as "data about data." If metadata is not removed from a document, it may provide information about the changes to a document that were made, how many people reviewed the document, how much time each person spent on it, and specific editorial revisions that were made.

In some jurisdictions, there may even be an ethical obligation to remove metadata before a document is disseminated.[32]

Information should be backed up frequently so that, should a catastrophic destruction occur, data can still be retrieved. In addition, a law firm should have a policy for disposing of computer equipment. It is vitally important that confidential information be removed from the computer's hard drive before the hardware is discarded.

1. The Internet and the Cloud

Lawyers and appropriate staff members must have Internet access to send e-mail messages, to transmit data to clients, to conduct legal research, and possibly to make telephone calls. A firm must plan and budget for its Internet accessibility. Will access to the Internet be via cable and then by wireless connection? Will access be via high-speed telephone lines? A firm may need to be wired with additional cable or phone lines. Wireless routers, which allow wireless access to the Internet within the firm, may also be needed. If a firm does have wireless access, such access must be password-protected. In addition, material transmitted over the Internet should be encrypted. Encryption software scrambles data to protect it as it travels over the Internet. It is then unscrambled, or decrypted, when the appropriate recipient of the data gains access to it, typically by entering a password.

In addition to having a firm Web site for promotional purposes, a firm may need to use document sharing sites (such as SharePoint or Google Drive, home to Google Docs) so that lawyers and clients can collaborate easily on very large files that cannot easily be transmitted via e-mail. In the past, this was done by printing a long document out and shipping it to a client by, for instance, FedEx. Today, documents can be transferred much more easily. Access to document-sharing sites is limited to specified users with a user name and a password.

Increasingly, lawyers and other users are turning to cloud computing, which allows for the storage of documents on a remote server rather than on an

---

32. See, e.g., Maryland State Bar Association, Inc. Committee on Ethics, Ethics of Viewing and/or Using Metadata, No. 2007-09 (2007).

individual computer.[33] "The obvious advantage to 'cloud computing' is the law-yer's increased access to client data. As long as there is an internet connection available, the lawyer would have the capability of accessing client data whether he was out of the office, out of the state, or even out of the country."[34] Security of files in the "cloud" is a concern, but some state bars have approved the storage of files in the cloud so long as protective measures are taken to preserve confidentiality.[35]

2.   Intranets and Extranets

A firm should have an **intranet,** its own computer network that allows users within the firm to access information and to communicate with one another internally. Via a firm's intranet, lawyers and others can access forms, standar-dized language for documents, and other documents stored in the intranet. An intranet is also likely to have a message board for announcements and may fea-ture internal e-mail. An **extranet** allows controlled access to information from outside the firm. An extranet might be used to allow both clients and their law-yers to work on documents.[36]

3.   Disaster Recovery Plan

A disaster recovery plan should be in place to provide instructions in the event the firm experiences a catastrophic loss of its own hardware or software. If a law firm's computer servers are destroyed in a fire or in an earthquake, how will backed-up files be located, when, and by whom? How will clients be notified that the firm has experienced a setback? If clients must be contacted because the firm needs their help to reconstruct its databases, how will that scenario be handled? Who will make sure that any necessary insurance claims are filed? If legal action must be instituted against someone because of the disaster, who will oversee and coordinate that effort? A disaster recovery plan should also specify the procedure to be followed if a laptop, smartphone, tablet computer, or other hardware is lost or stolen.

Some states now have statutes requiring certain procedures to be followed if a breach of computer security occurs. Often, notice must be provided to the peo-ple whose personal information may have been inadvertently disclosed.[37]

Lawyers and staff members should be apprised of extra precautions they should take when using hardware, such as laptops, outside the office. Computers and smartphones should be password protected. A disaster recovery plan should identify precise steps someone within the firm should take if a laptop is lost or stolen or if some other breach of confidentiality occurs. Who should be alerted first if a laptop is stolen? At what point should the police be notified? At what point should clients be notified, and by whom?

intranet: A computer net-work that allows users within a firm to access informa-tion and to communicate with one another internally.

extranet: A computer net-work that allows con-trolled access to information from outside the firm.

---

33. Richard Acello, *Get Your Head in the Cloud,* A.B.A. J., April 2010, at 28-29.

34. Alabama State Bar Ethics Opinions 2010-02, Retention, Storage, Ownership, Production and Destruction of Client Files, at 14, *available at* http://www.alabar.org /ogc/PDF/2010-02.pdf (last visited Dec. 16, 2010).

35. *See id.*

36. *See, e.g.,* Douglas Caddell, *Selling Your Law Firm's Tech,* Law Tech. News, June 4, 2007, *available at* www.law.com/tech.

37. *See, e.g.,* N.Y. Gen. Bus. Law § 899-aa (2013).

E. THE FUTURE OF THE LEGAL INDUSTRY

This is an exciting time to be working in the legal profession, especially in the realm of law office management. As clients try new means to hire lawyers, by, for instance, using online bidding; as lawyers work more collaboratively with their clients and with other lawyers; as solid law office management principles can help control budgets; and as legal advice and legal products become accessible to a broader audience that needs legal help, one can't help but be enthused about the possibilities for entrepreneurship and innovation. Sure, the industry is changing. Those working the legal field can change with it and find new ways to run the business side of their operations.

CHECKLIST

- Law office managers must anticipate and plan for emerging technology, and lawyers and staff must use current technologies responsibly.
- Some prospective clients specify that information technology capability be addressed when they issue requests for proposals from prospective law firms.
- Lawyers should know how to type, conduct legal research electronically, communicate and collaborate with clients and others via the Internet, and use different types of software—for word processing, creating documents, tracking time, and handling other tasks and assignments that might arise.
- Outsourcing and offshoring legal work has become viable for both law firms and clients.
- Rules allowing the unbundling of legal services allow more do-it-yourself activities and supporting businesses in the legal marketplace.
- The development of lightweight laptops, smartphones, easy and constant Internet access, affordable scanners, and copiers means that workplaces now have more flexibility.
- Social networking sites such as LinkedIn, Twitter, and Facebook allow lawyers to set up accounts and post information about their experience. In certain circumstances, a presence on Facebook or a blog might be considered to be lawyer advertising and thus subject to ethical rules on advertising.
- Lawyers can also make use of the Internet and social media sites to gather information and evidence about parties to a lawsuit.
- Lawyers must take precautions not to act inappropriately on social networking sites, such as by adding as "friends" judges before whom they appear or by engaging jurors on a case.
- A law firm should develop a technology plan to assess its hardware and software needs, anticipate future growth, and provide for maintenance and purchases of warranties. Depending on the law firm's needs and budget, the plan may even prioritize purchases.
- Performance, in addition to cost, should be considered when selecting software.

- Lawyers and staff involved in litigation must pay particular attention to changing court requirements and adapt their own technology to that required for litigation. Some courts allow electronic filing of documents.
- Confidential client information as well as confidential information about the law firm's business itself that is stored electronically must be protected against hacking by outsiders and against unauthorized intrusion by a user.
- The Computer Fraud and Abuse Act, 18 U.S.C. § 1030, outlaws certain acts related to unauthorized access to computers. Lawyers who access computerized data inappropriately may be subject to professional disciplinary action.
- A firm should establish a policy regarding metadata and its removal from documents prior to their dissemination.
- Information should be backed up frequently so that, should catastrophic destruction occur, data can still be retrieved. In addition, a law firm should have a policy for the disposal of computer equipment.
- It is vitally important that confidential information be removed from the computer's hard drive before the hardware is discarded.
- A disaster recovery plan should be in place to provide instructions in the event the firm experiences a catastrophic loss of its own hardware or software. A disaster recovery plan should also specify the procedure to be followed if a laptop, smartphone, tablet or notebook computer, or other hardware is lost or stolen. Some states now have statutes requiring certain procedures to be followed if a breach of computer security occurs. Often, notice must be provided to the people whose personal information may have been inadvertently disclosed.
- Economic and technological changes have also contributed to changes in the legal industry and how it operates. Lawyers and others in the field may find more entrepreneurial opportunities open to them.

VOCABULARY

extranet (434)
firewall (433)
hardware (427)
intranet (434)
metadata (433)
offshoring (419)
outsource (418)
software (427)
spyware (433)
virtual law office (417)
virus (433)
wiki (418)

CAREER PREPARATION TIPS

Elders of the legal industry recognize that the market is changing and that startup technology businesses might well post the biggest challenge to the traditional law firm in the future. Embrace your own entrepreneurial spirit. As you review the chapters in this book, think of opportunities to change the way the legal industry has done business in the past. Undertake a bit of competitive intelligence data gathering: Is anyone currently doing this? Could you do this in a better, more efficient way? Would your proposal work within the parameters of your state's professional responsibility rules and unauthorized practice of law statutes? Try pitching your ideas to prospective investors or to prospective employers.

IF YOU WANT TO LEARN MORE

Above the Law blog. http://abovethelaw.com

Google Analytics. http://www.google.com/analytics

Greedy Associates blog. http://blogs.findlaw.com/greedy_associates/

International Legal Technology Association. http://www.iltanet.org

Jury Tracker. http://www.jurytracker.com/JuryTracker/JuryTracker.html

Microsoft SharePoint. http://office.microsoft.com/en-us/microsoft-sharepoint-collaboration-software-FX103479517.aspx

Virtual Law Practice. http://virtuallawpractice.org/about/

World Legal Information Institute. http://www.worldlii.org

Clio is a client-collaboration, time and billing, and practice management platform. http://www.goclio.com

Rocket Matter offers online law practice management software and document storage. http://www.rocketlawyer.com

Another practice management and client-collaboration platform is Total Attorneys. http://www.totalattorneys.com

Adobe Connect is software that enables online meetings to occur. http://www.adobe.com/products/adobeconnect/web-meetings.html

Axiom Law is a legal services outsourcing vendor that provides legal services to in-house counsel. http://www.axiomlaw.com/index.php /overview

Riverviewlaw also provides unbundled legal services. http://www.riverviewlaw.com

An online legal document service is Legal Zoom. http://www.legalzoom.com/

READING COMPREHENSION

1. How has automation changed the practice of law?
2. Under what circumstances is the outsourcing of legal work ethically acceptable to the American Bar Association?
3. Why would a law firm be interested in offshoring certain work?
4. How can lawyers use social networking sites to build their business?
5. How can social networking sites be harmful to lawyers?
6. What is the difference between an advertisement and a blog?
7. What factors should a law firm consider when purchasing software?
8. How might an iPad be useful to a lawyer?
9. What is the difference between a computer virus and spyware?
10. How can lawyers transmit very large files efficiently?
11. Why is cloud computing convenient for lawyers?
12. How should confidential business information be protected?
13. What economic pressures do law firms face?
14. Why are rules allowing legal services to be unbundled important for the field?

DISCUSSION STARTERS

1. Look up and compare *Shurgard Storage Centers Inc. v. Safeguard Self Storage Inc.*, 119 F. Supp. 2d 1121 (W.D. Wash. 2000) to *International Association of Machinists and Aerospace Workers v. Werner-Matsuda*, 390 F. Supp. 2d 479 (D. Md. 2005). In what ways are the decisions similar? How are they different? How can law firms prevent unauthorized access to confidential materials in their own computer systems?
2. Google "Everyone's a Winner at Nixon Peabody," a promotional song released by a law firm. What was the controversy concerning the song released by the law firm Nixon Peabody? Did the firm receive positive or negative attention because of the song? What does the retrievability of information about this matter even though it took place a number of years ago tell you about a law firm's history on the Internet?
3. Find three law firms that have accounts on Facebook, Twitter, and LinkedIn. What information is posted on each site? Is any negative information posted? How does the type of information posted vary? Why do you suppose the law firm is posting in each of these venues? Do you think the firm's postings are effective?
4. Look up ethical rules on social networking sites in your jurisdiction. Are judges allowed to use the sites? Are lawyers allowed to use them? Do any restrictions apply? Look up the ethical rules in a neighboring jurisdiction and compare them with your jurisdiction's rules. Which set of rules to you think is preferable? Why?
5. Try to find some information accessible on the Internet that focuses on the negative aspects of a firm. How might this affect the firm's

business? Do you think the information might alter a client's opinion of the firm? What action, if any, might the firm take to prevent this information from being posted?

6. Find two blog postings by lawyers at a large law firm. Why do you suppose the lawyers selected the topic they did to write about? What was their ulterior purpose in writing about the topic? Is the posting specific, or do you find the information to be somewhat vague? Did anyone comment in response to the blog postings?

7. Using an online legal database such as Lexis or Westlaw, locate a recent court decision involving a blog, Twitter, or Facebook. What was the issue regarding the blog, Twitter, or Facebook? How was the issue resolved? What might future bloggers or users of Twitter or Facebook learn from this decision?

CASE STUDIES

1. You are the law office manager for a five-lawyer firm that focuses on family law. What hardware and software should you purchase? If the firm's budget does not allow for all of the purchases you recommend, which items would you forgo?

2. You are the law office manager for a 700-lawyer, full-service firm with five offices in the United States, one in Asia, and one in Europe. What software might such a firm need that a five-lawyer firm based in Missouri does not?

3. Look up help-wanted ads for IT staff people at a local law firm. What qualifications are required? What job responsibilities are involved? Are salaries mentioned?

4. Suppose you work for an intellectual property boutique based in Washington, D.C., that has 25 lawyers. Draft a disaster preparedness plan for the firm. Are any special considerations necessary given the firm's focus?

5. Suppose you work for a ten-lawyer litigation firm. The firm is thinking of switching from Dell computers to Apple computers. What would be the reason for such a change? Would the switch make the law firm more efficient in some way?

6. Suppose you work for the environmental group of a major national law firm. Your firm is competing for the business of a major client that manufactures pesticides. Find three competing law firms that might be interested in the business, and conduct some competitive intelligence research. What sorts of clients do these firms represent? What kinds of cases have these firms been successful in winning? Might these firms have any conflicts of interest regarding the prospective new client? Do these firms have any weaknesses your firm might capitalize on? How can your law firm distinguish itself from the competition?

7. Research several virtual law firms. In what jurisdictions do they operate? What sorts of services do they provide? Do you notice any special measures being taken to comply with pertinent ethical rules?

8. Research several legal support services providers. What services do they offer? What do they charge? Do they make any claims about the quality of their work or provide notice explaining whether they are providing legal advice?

INDEX

"Back office" activity, 153
"Front office" activity, 153

A Call to Action, 50
AbacusLaw (www.abacuslaw.com), 315, 320-321
Accept credit card payments, 322, 330
Accessibility of office space, 72
Access, 231
Accounting, 98, 319, 328
Accounts payable, 293
Accounts receivable, 293, 326
Adjustments, 277
Administrator, 295
Administratrix, 295
Affidavit, 293
Age Discrimination in Employment Act of 1967
        (ADEA), 37, 41
Agent, 297
Alcohol abuse, 53
Algorithm, 352
Alignment, 219
Alimony, 273
Alphabetic filing systems, 116
Alphanumeric filing systems, 116
Alternative Minimum Tax, 278
Alternative work schedule, 49
Amazon Kindle, 371
Amenities of law offices, 74
American Bar Association (ABA), 354
Americans with Disabilities Act of 1990
        (ADA), 33, 37
Amicus Attorney (www.amicusattorney.com), 323
Android, 355
Animations, 243
Antivirus software, 161, 354
Apple, 65, 372
App, 355
Arrange, 196
Articles of incorporation, 271
Assets, 259
Assignments, 273
Associations, 4
Attachment, 354
Attests, 263
Attorney-client privilege, 333
Attorney-client relationship, 2-3
Attrition, 49
Audit trail, 338, 344
Audits, 99
Automated calendar, 137, 141
Automated docketing programs, 136
Avoiding conflicts of interest, 317

Back office operations, 313, 318, 321, 332

Background checks of job candidates, 43
Bandwidth, 347
Bankruptcy Code, 262
Bankruptcy, 259-267
    electronic filing, 260
    software
        www.bankruptcysoftware.com, 260
        www.bestcase.com, 261
        www.ezfiling.com, 261
        www.nationallawforms.com, 260
    tabs
        a and b, property, 265
        a, assets, 264
        attestation as to accuracy of statements, 263
        c, exempt property, 265
        c, real estate, 264
        chapter 11, 262
        chapter 13, 262
        creditor matrix, 267
        d, education requirements, 264
        d, secured loans, 265
        e, unsecured loans, 265
        h, co-debtors, 265
        i, sources of income, 265
        identity of creditors, 262
        j, expenditures, 265
        liabilities, 262
        liquidation—chapter 7, 262
        means test, 266
        notification of the securities and exchange
                commission, 263
        other bankruptcy cases, 263
        page 3, 263
        property that could pose an imminent
                public safety threat, 263
        reorganization, 262
Bar coding, 118
Base, 250
Beneficiary, 290
Benefits, 47, 49
Bibliography, 198
Billable hours
    alternatives to, 49
    calculation of, 82
    requirements for, 85
    tracking, 84, 86
Billing systems, 87-88
Billing, 319, 328, 332
Binder, 290, 293
Blacklining, 211
Blended rates, 88-89
Bluetooth, 349, 356
Bookmark, 187
Bread-and-butter client, 3
Brokers, 285
Budgets, 82, 84

income, 83
operating, 83
sample, 84
Business continuity plans, 63
Buttons, 175
Bylaws, 273

Calculation, 228
Calc, 250
Calendaring errors, 141
Calendaring software, 315
Calendaring, 129, 136, 139
Capacitive, 356
Captions, 201
Carpal tunnel syndrome, 69
Case management software, 312, 332-333, 335-341, 343-344
    defensible discovery strategy, 337
        audit trail, 338
        claw back, 338
        edge, from ilstech (www.ilstech.com), 338
        electronic data reference model (www.edrm.net), 338
        inadvertent disclosure, 338
    depositions, 333
        deponent, 333
        deposition, 333
        deposmart (claritylegalsoftware.co/eposmart.html), 335
        electronically stored information (esi), 333
        livenote (west.thomson.co/roduct/ervice/ase-noteboo/efault.aspx), 335
        optical character reading (ocr), 333
        transcript, 333
    discovery, 332
    electronically stored information (esi), 333, 336
        avoiding a manual review of requested information, 336
        deduplication, 337
        e-mail, 337
        litigation hold, 337
        md5 hash, 337
        metadata, 337
        processing data, 336
        scrubbing, 337
    esi review services, 343
        audit trail, 344
        categorix (www.xerox-xls.co/discover/ategorix.html), 343
        daegis ediscovery (www.daegis.com), 343
        dashboard, 343
        reliance on statistical measures, 343
        single interface, 344
    esi review software, 339
        casemap, 341
        e-mail exchanges, 339
        iconect (www.iconect.com), 339
        intella (www.vound-software.com), 339
        lexis-nexis ediscovery solutions: law prediscovery software, 340
        list of e-mails, ranked by priority, 340
        redacting files and images, 339
        scalability, 339
        sorting, 339
        textmap, 341

visualized search depicting associations of data processed, 339
    exemptions from discovery, 333
        attorney-client privilege, 333
        work product doctrine, 333
    nature of case management, 332
    reviewing esi, 339
    rules of discovery, 333
        federal rules of civil procedure (frcp), 333
    types of discovery, 333
Case management systems, 145
Case management, 145
CaseMap, 341
Cellular wireless standards: 3G and 4G, 357
Cell, 217, 223
    combining, 222
    conditional formatting, 222
    formatting, 219
    positioning material in a, 219
Centralized file systems, 118
Chapter 7, 262
Chapter 11, 262
Chapter 13, 262
Charts, 223
Child support, 273
Churning, 3
Citations, 198
Civil Rights Act of 1964, 29
Clawback, 338
Client activity reports, 87
Client billing, 86, 96
    billing systems, 87-88
    contingent fees, 89, 94
    court-awarded fees, 95
    flat fees, 94
    hourly rates, 88-89
    incentive billing, 89
    prepaid legal services, 94
    referral fees, 96
    retainers, 94
    statutory fees, 95
    task-based billing, 89
Client confidentiality, 19-20, 373
Client files
    contents of, 114-115
    disposal of, 120, 122, 156-157
    file ownership, 120
    filing conventions, 116, 118
    management of, 105, 127
    opening new files, 107, 114
    paperless files, 119-120
    standard types of, 115
    storage and tracking, 118-119
Client intake form, 106
Client intelligence, 6
Client matters, 105
Client relationship management software, 10-11
Client satisfaction surveys, 19
Client teams, 10
Client trust funds, 97
Client's funds accounts, 319
Clients, 1, 25
    additional resources, 22-23
    associations, 4
    attorney-client relationship, 2-3
    bread-and-butter, 3

career preparation tips, 22
checklist, 21
choosing, 5, 10
corporate, 3
external, 3
fee agreements with, 88, 96
government, 5
individual, 4-5
internal, 3
managing relationships with, 10-11
retaining, 11
satisfaction of, 19
solicitation of, 5, 10
terminating representation, 19-20, 96
types of, 3, 5
Clio (www.goclio.com), 330
Clip art, 187
Clipboard, 178
Closing, 280
Cloud computing, 154, 252, 378
Coaxial cables, 348
Combine, 209
Comments, 209
Commitments, 316
Communications management, 315, 321, 323
Communications
  between lawyers and clients, 2-3
Compare, 209
Compensation
  in offer letters, 46-47
Complaint, 293
Computer Fraud and Abuse Act of 1986, 373
Computer viruses, 377
Computers, safeguarding information
  on, 372, 378
Conference rooms, 74
Confidentiality, 19-20, 352, 367, 373
Conflict checking, 321, 323, 326, 330
Conflict of interest search form, 107
Conflicts of interest, 108, 114
Connections, 231
Connectivity, 355
Conservator, 297
Consolidated Omnibus Budget Reconciliation Act
  of 1985, 39
Consolidation of firms, 363
Contact management, 312, 321, 323, 331
Contingent fees, 89, 93
Continuing legal education, 315
Contract employees, 29
Contract management, 317, 321
Contracts, 273
Convergence, 4
Cookies, 352
Coordinating, 316
Corporate clients, 4
Corporations, 3, 268-273, 293
  essential corporate
    accounts payable, 293
    accounts receivable, 293
    articles of incorporation, 271
    assignments, 273
    bylaws, 273
    contracts, 273
    directors, 271
    documents, 272

information, 271
    leases, 273
    meeting minutes, 272
    officers, 271
    proxies, 272
    resolutions, 272
    stock options, 271
    stock register, 273
    stock, 272
  features
    sidebar menu, 270
    tabs, 269
    toolbar, 270
  software
    www.corporateforms.net, 268
    www.nationallawfirms.com, 269
    www.standardlegal.com, 268
Cost of relocating law offices, 71
Court-awarded fees, 95
Create mailings, 204
Creditor matrix, 267
Creditors, 259
Cross-reference, 187
Cross-selling, 10

Dashboard, 330, 343
Data management, 357
  disposal of equipment, 357
  passwords, 357
    complexity, 357
    updates, 357
  remote access, 358
  retention, 357
  voip and voice mail, 358
Data packets, 352
Data tools, 231
Database, 311, 330
Data, 228
Deadlines, 136, 140
Debto/etitioner, 260
Decentralized file systems, 118
Deduplication, 337
Deed, 279
Deep pockets, 3
Default date, 137
Defensible discovery strategy, 337
Defined names, 226
Delinquent bills, 96
Denial of Service (DoS), 354
Deponent, 333
Deposition, 333
Depression, 53
Design, 243
Destruction of records, 156-157
Directors, 271
Disaster preparedness plans, 63, 161
Disaster preparedness, 63
Disaster recovery plans, 378
Discharge in bankruptcy, 260
Disciplinary action, 48
Discovery, 332
Disengagement letters, 20
Disposal of files, 120, 122
Diversity in law firms, 50, 52
Dividends, 273

Divorce, financials, 273, 275-278
  assets and liabilities
    additional assets, 276
    income, 275
  case information, 275
    docket number, 275
    payor, 275
  software
    www.divorcesoftware.co/porde/ivinf/
      roduct_financial_advisor.htm, 273
    www.easysoft-usa.co/ivorce-settlement-
      software.html, 273
    www.familylawsoftware.com, 273
  tax information
    federal, 277
    state, 278
Docket control, 136, 145
Docket management, 129, 150
  additional resources, 147
  calendaring, 129, 136
  career preparation tips, 146
  case management, 145
  checklist, 145-146
  deadlines, 136, 140
  docket control, 136, 145
  reminders to meet deadlines, 140, 145
Docket number, 275
Docket, docketing, 315, 332
Dockets, 137
Document management, 317, 321, 323, 330, 332
Document views, 215
Drawing, 239
Draw, 252
Durable power of attorney, 298

E-billing, 87
E-mail, 64, 167-168, 337, 339-340, 353
Early retirement, 33
Editing
  excel, 223
  word, 184
Efficiency of law offices, 69
Electronic alert systems, 63
Electronic data reference model, 338
Electronic filing of documents, 372-373
Electronic filing, 260
Electronically stored information (ESI), 333
Emergency preparedness, 62-63
Employee handbooks, 44, 46
Employee relations, 47
Employees
  compensation and benefits for, 47
  contract, 29
  disciplinary action for, 48
  impact of disasters on, 62, 64
  morale of, 52-53
  orientation and training of, 46
  performance evaluation of, 46
  recruiting and hiring process, 42-43
  retention of, 49, 52
  termination of, 48
Employment at will, 29
Employment law, 29, 41
  age discrimination in employment act of 1967
    (adea), 37, 41

americans with disabilities act of 1990
    (ada), 33, 37
consolidated omnibus budget reconciliation act
    of 1985 (cobra), 39
equal employment opportunity act of
    1964, 29-30
equal pay act of 1963, 39
fair labor standards act of 1938 (flsa), 33
family and medical leave act of 1993 (fmla), 36
federal, 29, 41
patient protection and affordable care act of
    2010 (ppaca), 39, 41
state laws, 41
Employment, types of, 29
Encryption software, 378
Encryption, 352, 354
Energy efficiency in law offices, 76
Engagement letters, 115
Equal Employment Opportunity Act of
    1964, 29-30
Equal Employment Opportunity Commission
    (EEOC), 30, 41
Equal Pay Act of 1963, 39
Equipment and supplies, 64-65
Ergonomics in law offices, 69
Escrow account, 287
Escrow funds, 97-98
Estate, 260
Ethernet, 348
Ethical obligations, 354
Ethical wall, 317
Ethics
  client trust funds, 97
  of records management, 160, 167
Excel, 217, 219, 222-223, 225-226, 228, 231-232
  function box, 217
  grids, 217
  sheets, 217
  tabs, 219
    alignment, 219
    calculation, 228
    cell styles, 223
    cells, 223
    charts, 223
    combining cells, 222
    conditional formatting, 222
    connections, 231
    content, 223
    data tools, 231
    data, 228
    defined names, 226
    editing, 223
    filter, 231
    format as table, 223
    formatting of a cell, 219
    formula auditing, 228
    formulas, 225
    function library, 225
    get external data, 231
    home, 219
    insert, 223
    outline, 232
    page layout, 225
    positioning material in a cell, 219
    review, 232
    sort, 231

styles, 222
Excusable neglect, 141
Executor, 295
Executrix, 295
Exemptions, 333
Exempt, 265
Exhibits, 261, 264-265
External clients, 3
Extranets, 378

Facebook, 365, 380-381
Facility management, 60-61
Fair Labor Standards Act of 1938 (FLSA), 33
Family and Medical Leave Act of 1993 (FMLA), 36
Federal employment laws, 29, 41
Federal Rules of Appellate Procedure, 138-139
Federal Rules of Civil Procedure (FRCP), 333
Federal Rules of Civil Procedure, 137
Fee agreements, 88, 96
  contingent fees, 89, 94
  court-awarded fees, 95
  flat fees, 94
  hourly rates, 88-89
  incentive billing, 89
  prepaid legal services, 94
  referral fees, 96
  retainers, 94
  statutory fees, 95
  task-based billing, 89
Fee collection, 96-97
Feedback from clients, 19
Feng shui, 70
File management, 105, 127
  additional resources, 123
  career preparation tips, 123
  checklist, 122-123
  conflicts of interest and, 108, 114
  contents of client files, 114-115
  disposal of files, 120, 122
  file ownership, 120
  filing conventions, 116, 118
  opening new files, 107, 114
  paperless files, 119-120
  standard types of files, 115
  storage and tracking, 118-119
  systems, 115, 122
File ownership, 120
File transfer protocol (FTP), 350
Filing conventions, 116, 118
Filter, 231
Firewalls, 350, 357, 377
Firm culture, 59-60
Firm histories, 28
Firm image, 59-60, 68, 75
Flat fees, 94
Font, 181
Footer, 187
Footnotes, 198
Form 1099-S, 288
Format, 223
Formula auditing, 228
Formulas, 225
Front office activities, 312, 320, 331
Function
  box, 217

library, 225
Future trends, 379

Gender diversity, 51-52
Generate 1099 forms, 322
Generational shifts, 368, 370
Google Docs, 252
  access, 253
  link, 254
  search, 254
  toolbar and tabs, 254
Google Drive, 363
Government clients, 5
Government lawyers, 5
Grantee, 288
Grantor, 289
Graphic interface, 354
Graphic user interface, 175
Green buildings, 76
Grids, 217
Growth projection and law offices, 71-72

Hacker, 349
Handbooks, employee, 44, 46
Hardware, 370
Header, 187
Headhunters, 42
Hiring process, 42-43
Home page, 349
Home
  excel, 217
  powerpoint, 233
  word, 178
Hotspot, 354
Hourly rates, 87-89
HUD-1, 293
Human resources, 27, 58
  additional resources, 55
  career preparation tips, 55
  checklist, 54
  compensation and benefits, 47
  disciplinary action, 48
  diversity issues, 49, 52
  employee handbooks, 44, 46
  employee relations, 47
  employee retention, 49, 52
  employment law and, 29, 41
  mission statements and, 28
  performance evaluation, 46
  recruiting and hiring process, 42-43
  supervisory techniques, 48
  termination of employees, 48
  workplace morale, 52-53
  workplace policies and procedures, 44
Hyperlink, 187
Hypertext transfer protocol, 351
Hypertext, 348

ICONECt (www.iconect.com), 339
Illustrations, 186
Impress, 251
Inadvertent disclosure, 338
Incentive billing, 89

Income budgets, 83
Income, calculating, 82-83
Indexing, 155-156
Index, 201, 317
Individual clients, 4-5
Information technology (IT)
        departments, 64, 362
Information technology, 64, 66
Information, safeguarding, 372, 378
Insert
    charts, 223
    excel, 223
    powerpoint, 235
    table of authorities, 201
    word, 183
Intella (www.vound-software.com), 339
Interest On Lawyer Trust Account (IOLTA), 319,
        323, 327, 330
Interest on lawyers' trust accounts (IOLTA), 97
Interior designers for law offices, 69
Internal clients, 3
Internet
    access, 377
Interviews of job candidates, 42
Intestate, 295
Intranets, 10, 378
Intranet, 348
Involuntary termination, 48
IPad, 372
IPhone OS, 355
Itemized deductions, 278

Job candidates
    interviewing, 42
    reference and background checks, 43
Job satisfaction, 52
Job-related injuries, 69
Juris, 330
Justice Department, 5

Keyboard, 356
Kindle, 372
Knowledge management, 159-160

Labor Department, 33
Law firms
    consolidation of, 362
    diversity in, 50, 52
    financing of, 82
    histories of, 28
    mission statement of, 27
    offshoring, 363-364
    outsourcing, 363
    stresses in, 53
    technological changes and, 362, 368
    virtual law offices, 362, 371
Law office (physical), 59, 80
    accessibility, 72
    additional resources, 77-78
    amenities, 74
    career preparation tips, 77
    checklist, 76
    disaster preparedness, 63

    efficiency, 69
    equipment and supplies, 64, 66
    ergonomics, 69
    facility management, 60-61
    growth projections, 71-72
    image presented by, 59-60, 68, 75
    lease options, 71
    mechanical systems, 75
    office design and decor, 67, 69
    office size and firm politics, 68
    office space planning, 70, 76
    parking spaces, 66, 75
    professional designers for, 69
    public areas, 72, 74
    relocating, 70, 75
    security, 74
    telecommunication systems, 65
    work areas, 72, 74
    worker efficiency and, 69
    workplace safety, 61-62
Lawyers
    government, 5
    minority, 50
    moving to other firms, 161, 167
    social networking by, 365, 367
    turnover rate of, 49
    women, 50, 52
Lease options for law offices, 71
Leases, 273
Ledger, 287, 320
Legal project management, 6
Legal research, 362
Lexis-Nexis ediscovery solutions: LAW
        PreDiscovery software, 340
Lexis-Nexis practice management software, 327
Liabilities, 263
Lien, 280
Limited liability corporation, 273
LinkedIn, 365, 380-381
Links, 187, 253
Liquidation, 260
Litigation hold, 337
Living will, 299
Local Area Network (LAN), 348
Location of law offices, 70-71

Macro, 216
Mail merge, 206
Mailing date, 137
Mailings, 205
Malicious software, 354
Malpractice, 141
Malware, 354
Maps, 355
Mark Citation, 202
Market shifts, 368, 370
Master calendar, 129-130, 135
Masterfile (www.masterfile.biz), 341
Math, 251
MD5 hash, 337
Means test, 266
Mechanical systems of law offices, 75
Medical power of attorney, 299
Metadata, 119, 337, 377
Microsoft, 65, 98, 363

Millennials, 370
Minimum wage, 33
Minorities, 50
Mission statements, 28
Money management, 81, 103
   accounting, 98
   additional resources, 101
   budgets, 82, 84
   career preparation tips, 100
   checklist, 99
   client billing and, 86, 88
   client trust funds, 97
   escrow funds, 97-98
   fee agreements, 88, 96
   fee collection, 96-97
   financing of law practice, 82
   safeguards, 98-99
   timekeeping and, 84, 86
Morale, 52-53
Mortgage, 263, 280

Naming conventions for documents, 156
Needles (www.Needles.com), 323
Net profit, 83
New York
   civil practice law and rules, 140
Nonlegal staff
   relations between lawyers and, 47
   teamwork building with, 47
Notarized, 289
Numerical filing systems, 116

Offer letters, 46-47
Office button, 178
Office politics, 68
Office productivity software
   google docs, 252
   microsoft office, 176
   openoffice.org, 247
Office productivity, 353
Office size, 68
Officers, 271
Offshoring, 363-364
OpenOffice.org, 247
   base, 250
   calc, 250
   draw, 252
   impress, 251
   math, 251
   writer, 248
Operating budgets, 83
Operating system (OS), 355
Optical character reading (OCR), 333
Oregon Rules of Civil Procedure, 139
Orientation of new hires, 46
Outline, 232
Outlook, Microsoft, 250
Outsource, 362-363
Overtime pay, 33

Pages, 186, 261
Page, 190, 225
   background, 195

layout
   excel, 225
   word, 190
  setup, 195
Panic button, 62
Paperless files, 119-120
Paragraph, 181, 196
Paralegals
   file management by, 117, 119
Parking spaces, 66, 75
Part-time work, 53
Partnership, 276
Passwords, 357
Patient Protection and Affordable Care Act of
   2010, 39, 41
Payor, 275
PCLaw (www.lexisnexis.co/aw-firm-practice-
   managemen/claw/), 327
Peer-to-peer network, 348
Performance evaluation, 46
Perquisites (perks), 48
Personal calendar, 136
Personal exemptions, 277
Phishing, 354
Pivot Table, 223
Pop-up blockers, 352
Popular Name Table, 349
Power of attorney, 297
PowerPoint, 234-235, 237, 239-240, 243, 245, 247
  tabs
     animations, 243
     design, 243
     drawing, 239
     home, 234
     insert, 240
     review, 247
     slide show, 245
     slides, 237
     view, 247
Practice management software, 312-332
  back office, 312, 318
     accept credit card payments, 322, 330
     accounting, 319, 328
     accounts receivables, 326
     billing, 319, 328, 332
     client's funds accounts, 319
     generate 1099 forms, 322
     interest on lawyer trust account (iolta), 319,
       327, 330
     ledger, 320, 327, 329
  front office, 312
     avoiding conflicts of interest, 317
     calendaring, 315, 323, 330, 332
     commitments, 316
     communications management, 315,
       321, 323
     conflict checking, 321, 323, 326, 330
     contact management, 312, 321, 323, 331
     continuing legal education, 315
     contract management, 317, 321
     coordinating, 316
     docketing, 315, 332
     document management, 317, 321, 323,
       330, 332
     ethical wall, 317
     index, 317

remote access, 318, 321, 325, 332
report management, 318, 332
rules, 315
statute of limitations, 314
tabs 3, 317
templates, 317
ticklers, 315
time management, 315
tracking, 315
www.hotdocs.com, 317, 323
types of practice management software, 320
    abacuslaw (www.abacuslaw.com), 315,
        320-321
    amicus attorney
        (www.amicusattorney.com), 323
    back office, 321, 332
    client information, 325
    clio (www.goclio.com), 330
    dashboard, 330
    features, 322, 326
    financial software, 326
    front office, 320, 331
    juris, 330
    lexis-nexis practice management
        software, 327
    pclaw (www.lexisnexis.co/aw-firm-practice-
        managemen/claw/), 327
    practicemaster, 326
    prolaw [westlaw] (www.elite.co/rola/ront-
        office/), 331
    searching for cases, 324
    searching for documents, 324
    security socket layer (ssl), 330
    software as a service (saas), 330
    sql, 330
    tabs3 (www.tabs3.com), 317
    timematters, 313, 315, 318, 329
    toolbar, 327, 330
    types of cases, 325
    web searches, 330
Practice-specific software, 260-261, 268-269, 273,
    280-281, 291, 293, 295
    bankruptcy, 259
        bankruptcysoftware.com, 260
        bestcase.com, 260
        ezfiling.com, 261
        nationallawforms.com, 260
    corporations, 267
        corporateforms.net, 269
        nationallawfirms.com, 269
        standardlegal.com, 268
    divorce, financials, 273
        divorcesoftware.co/porde/ivinf/
            roduct_financial_advisor.htm, 273
        easysoft-usa.co/ivorce-settlement-
            software.html, 273
        familylawsoftware.com, 273
    real estate, 279
        easysoft-usa.co/ud-software.html, 293
        hud.go/ffice/d/udclip/orm/iles/
            1.pdf, 280
        lawfirmsoftware.co/oftwar/losing.htm, 281
        nationallawforms.com, 281
    trusts, 290
        easysoft-usa.co/rust-accounting-
            software.html, 291
        legendarywillsandtrusts.com/
            ?page_id=247, 291
        west.thomson.co/roduct/ooks-cd/owle/
            rust-plus.aspx, 291
    wills, 294
        dplprofessionalsolutions.co/
            ill_systems.asp, 295
        easysoft-usa.com, 295
        lawfirmsoftware.co/oftwar/
            ast_will.htm, 295
        nationallawforms.co/stat/oftware-last-will-
            and-testament.asp, 295
PracticeMaster, 326
Prepaid legal services, 94
Principal, 298
Private clients, 4
Probating an estate, 295
Probationary period for new hires, 47
ProLaw [Westlaw] (www.elite.co/rola/ront-
    office/), 331
Proofing, 206
Property, 259
Protect document, 211
Proxies, 272
Public areas of law offices, 72, 74

Racial diversity, 51
Real estate binder, 289, 293
Real estate, 280, 282-290, 293
    software
        www.easysoft-usa.co/ud-software.html, 280
        www.hud.go/ffice/d/udclip/orm/iles/
            1.pdf, 280
        www.lawfirmsoftware.co/oftwar/
            losing.htm, 282
        www.nationallawforms.com, 293
    tabs
        adjustments for items unpaid by seller, 285
        broker's reserves deposited with lender in
            an escrow account, 287
        calculating "the bottom line" about the
            loan, 287
        case data, 288
        cash settlements, 285
        costs that might change before the
            closing, 287
        form 1099-s, 288
        hud-1 pages, 284
        items that the lender wants paid in
            advance, 287
        ledger, 287
        page 1, 282
        page 2, 285
        page 3, 287
        paid to brokers, 285
        real estate, 289
        related to getting the loan, 286
        settlement agent, 283
        summary of transactions, 284
        taske/inked, 290
        tax proration, 284
Realization rate, 83
Reception areas, 73
Records management, 151, 173
    additional resources, 170

career preparation tips, 169-170
checklist, 168-169
destruction, 156-157
e-mail and, 168
ethical issues, 160, 167
importance of, 151-152
indexing, 155-156
knowledge management, 159-160
lawyer and staff training in, 157-158
lawyers leaving law firms, 161, 167
overview of, 152, 158
retention, 153, 155
retrieval, 155-156
security, 160-161
systems, 158-159
Records retention, 153, 155
Records retrieval, 155-156
Recruitment process, 41, 43
Redacting files and images, 339
Redlining, 211
Reference checks of job candidates, 43
Referral fees, 96
Registry of deeds, 279
Reminders to meet deadlines, 140, 145
Remote access, 318, 321, 325, 332, 358
Remote work, 362, 372
Reorganization, 260
Repetitive stress injuries, 69
Report management, 318, 332
Reports about trust fund activity, 293
Representation, termination of, 19-20, 97
Resident agent, 271
Resolutions, 272
Retainers, 94
Retaining clients, 11
Retention, 355
    of employees, 49, 52
    of records, 153-154
Review
    excel, 232
    powerpoint, 235
    word, 206
Ribbon, 175
Router, 348
Rules of discovery, 333
Runners, 6

Safeguards
    financial, 98-99
    information, 372, 378
Safety in workplace, 61-62
Salaries
    in offer letters, 46, 48
Scalability, 339
Schedules, 261, 265
Scrubbing, 337
Secondment, 4
Secure socket layering (SSL), 351
Secured Loans, 265
Security certificate, 352
Security
    breaches, 378
    in law offices, 62, 74
    of records, 161
Server, 213, 311, 347

Service Set Identifier (SSID), 349
Settlement agent, 283
Sexual harassment, 30
Sheets, 217
Sho/ide (Word), 215
Skype, 352
Slides, 237
Smartphones, 355
SMS, 356
Software as a Service (SaaS), 252, 330
Software, 176, 247, 252
    accounting, 98
    antivirus, 161
    billing systems, 88
    case management, 145
    client relationship management, 10-11
    docketing programs, 136
    encryption, 378
    for timekeeping, 86
    office productivity
        google docs, 252
        microsoft office, 176
        openoffice.org, 247
    selection of, 371
    training in use of, 65
    types of, 371
Solicitation of clients, 5, 10
Sorting, 339
Sort, 231
Spam, 354
Spoofing, 353
Spreadsheet, 176
Spyware, 354, 377
SQL, 231, 329-330
Staff areas, 73-74
State employment laws, 41
Statute of limitations, 315
Statutes of limitation, 140-141
Statutory fees, 95
Stock options, 271
Stock register, 299
Stockholder, 272
Stock, 263, 272
Stress, 53
Styles
    excel, 222-223
    word, 184
Subchapter S corporation, 273
Substance abuse, 52-53
Suites, 176
Supervisory techniques, 48
Supplies, 64-65
Surveys of clients, 19
Sustainability, 60
Sustainable design of law offices, 69
Symbols, 190

Tables, 186
Table
    authorities, 201
    contents, 198
    format, 223
Tabs3 (www.tabs3.com), 316, 326
Tabs, 178, 219, 232, 255
    excel, 219

google docs, 255
powerpoint, 235
word, 178
Task-based billing, 89
Tax credits, 278
Tax proration, 284
Technology, 361, 384
    additional resources, 382
    career preparation tips, 381
    changes brought by, 362, 369
    checklist, 379, 381
    cloud computing, 154, 377-378
    consolidation of firms and, 363
    disaster recovery plans, 377-378
    extranets, 378
    future trends, 380
    generational shifts, 368, 370
    in physical law office, 65
    intranets, 10, 378
    market shifts, 368, 370
    millennials and, 370
    offshoring and, 363-364
    outsourcing and, 363-364
    performance, effect on, 368, 370
    price, effect on, 369-370
    safeguarding information and, 372, 378
    social networking and, 365, 367
    typically used, 370, 373
    unbundling legal services, 367-368
    virtual law practices, 364-365
Telecommunication systems, 65
Telecommunications, 347-357
    e-mail, 353
        confidentiality, 354
        encryption, 354
        ethical obligations, 354
        risks, 353
        statutes and obligations, 354
    internet
        home page, 350
        web pages, 351
    networks, 347
        firewalls, 350
        intranet, 348
        local area network (lan), 348
        router, 349
        virtual private network (vpn), 350
        wi-fi, 349
        wireless local area network (wlan), 347
        wireless personal area network (wpan), 349
    security
        cookies, 352
        encryption, 352
        pop-up blockers, 352
        security certificate, 352
    smartphones, 355
        android, 355
        applications (apps), 355
        battery life, 357
        bluetooth, 356
        cellular wireless standards: 3g and 4g, 357
        common features, 356
        firewalls, 357
        graphic interface, 356
        internet connectivity, 356
        iphone os, 355

keyboard, 356
        maps, 356
        office productivity, 356
        operating systems, 355
        storage, 356
    videoconferencing, 353
    voice over internet protocol (voip), 352
Telecommuting, 53
Templates, 154
Template
    www.hotdocs.com, 317, 323
Tenant, 279
Termination
    of employees, 48
    of representation, 19-20, 96
Testator, 294
Testatrix, 294
TextMap, 341
Text, 190
Themes, 195
Thumbnails, 215
Ticklers, 140, 315
Time commitment, 53
Time management, 315
Time sheets, 85
Time-to-billing percentage, 83
Timekeeper, 292
Timekeeping, 84, 86
TimeMatters, 313, 318, 329
Title search, 280
Title, 279
Toolbar, 175, 255
Tracking changes, 209
Tracks, 315
Training
    in records management, 157
    of new hires, 45-46
Transcript, 333
Trigger date, 137
Trojans, 354
Trust funds, 97
Trustee, 260, 290
Trusts, 290-293
    software
        easysoft-usa.co/rust-accounting-
            software.html, 291
        legendarywillsandtrusts.com/
            ?page_id=247, 291
        west.thomson.co/roduct/ooks-cd/owle/
            rust-plus.aspx, 291
    tabs
        bank, 292
        billing, 293
        client, 293
        escrow agent, 292
        expenses, 293
        file, 291
        memo, 293
        paye/ayor, 293
        reports about trust fund activity, 293
        timekeeper, 292
        tools, 293
        view, 292
Tunneling, 350
Twitter, 365, 380-381

Unbundling legal services, 367-368
Universal Serial Bus (USB), 357
Unsecured loans, 265
URL, 351

Variance reporting, 83
Videoconferencing, 353, 372
View
   powerpoint, 247
   word, 215
Violence in workplace, 61-62
Virtual law offices, 362, 372
Virtual law practices, 364-365
Virtual Private Network (VPN), 350
Viruses, 377
Virus, 354
Visualization of data, 340
Voice over Internet Protocol (VoIP), 66, 352, 358
Voluntary termination, 48

Web pages, 351
Webex, 353
Websites, 350
Wellness programs, 52-53
West's CaseLogistix (store.westlaw.co/roduct/
     ervice/estlaw-case-logisti/efault.aspx), 342
Wi-Fi, 349
Wikipedia.com, 363
Wikis, 363
Wills, 294-295
   durable power of attorney, 298
   living will, 299
   medical power of attorney, 299
   software
      dplprofessionalsolutions.co/
        ill_systems.asp, 295
      easysoft-usa.com, 295
      lawfirmsoftware.co/oftwar/
        ast_will.htm, 295
      nationallawforms.co/stat/oftware-last-will-
        and-testament.asp, 295
Window (Word), 215
Wireless Local Area Network (WLAN), 348
Wireless Personal Area Network (WPAN), 349
Wizard, 202
Women, 50, 52
Word 2007, 178, 181-182, 184, 186-187, 190, 195-
    196, 198, 201-202, 205-207, 209, 211, 215
   office button, 178
   page layout, 190
      arrange, 196
      page background, 195
      page setup, 195
      paragraph, 196
      themes, 195
   references, 196

authorities, 201
bibliography, 198
captions, 201
changes, 207
citations, 198
comments, 209
compare and combine, 209
compare, 209
contents, 198
footnotes, 198
index, 201
insert table of authorities, 202
mark citation, 202
proofing, 198
protect document, 211
review, 206
tracking changes, 209
using compare, 211
tabs, 178
   clipboard, 178
   create, 206
   editing, 182
   font, 181
   footer, 187
   header, 187
   home, 178
   illustrations, 186
   insert, 186
   links, 187
   mail merge, 206
   mailings, 205
   pages, 186
   paragraph, 181
   styles, 184
   symbols, 190
   tables, 186
   text, 190
view, 214
   document views, 215
   macros, 215
   sho/ide, 215
   window, 215
   zoom, 215
Work areas of law offices, 72, 74
Work product doctrine, 333
Work-life balance, 53
Workbook, 217
Workplace morale, 52-53
Workplace policies and procedures, 44
Workplace safety, 61-62
Workplace stress, 53
Writer, 248

YouTube, 366

Zoom, 215

ISBN 978-1-4548-8055-4

9 781454 880554